Carson-Newman University

CARSON-NEWMAN UNIVERSITY

From Appalachian Dream to Thriving Educational Community

MELODY MARION AND AMANDA FORD

THE UNIVERSITY OF TENNESSEE PRESS | KNOXVILLE

First Edition.

Frontis: Porch of Sarah Swann Hall. Photo courtesy Ricke Hester.

Financial support for publication of this book was made by
Linda Natiello Friedland (C-N class of 1972) in memory of her parents,
Dante Natiello (1903–1994), Chief Warrant Officer, US Navy,
and Isabella Hislop Tait Hunter Natiello (1911–1971).

Library of Congress Cataloging-in-Publication Data
Names: Marion, Melody, 1954– author. | Ford, Amanda, 1984– author.
Title: Carson-Newman University : from Appalachian dream to thriving educational community / Melody Marion and Amanda Ford.
Description: First edition. | Knoxville : The University of Tennessee Press, [2023] | Includes bibliographical references and index. | Summary: "Melody Marion and Amanda Ford trace the formation of this Jefferson City, Tennessee, institution from its founding as Mossy Creek Missionary Baptist Seminary in 1850 to the one-hundred-and-twenty acre university campus that is Carson-Newman today. Along the way, Marion and Ford discuss the school's Baptist foundations, its coeducational merger in the late nineteenth century, a string of presidents both exceptional and misguided, and its expansion from college to university in the twenty-first century"
—Provided by publisher.
Identifiers: LCCN 2023004670 (print) | LCCN 2023004671 (ebook) | ISBN 9781621908166 (hardcover) | ISBN 9781621908173 (pdf)
Subjects: LCSH: Carson-Newman University—History. | Christian universities and colleges—United States—History.
Classification: LCC LD801.C252 M37 2023 (print) | LCC LD801.C252 (ebook) | DDC 378.768/924—dc23/eng/20230301
LC record available at https://lccn.loc.gov/2023004670
LC ebook record available at https://lccn.loc.gov/2023004671

To the memory of
Frieda C. and Robert M. Burts,
historians, researchers, and writers par excellence
with deep appreciation for their
contributions to this book

Contents

Illustrations

Preface

If only a contemporary video camera could have been trained on Carson-Newman University's campus since 1851, available for playback now! Even without that anachronistic aid, though, all kinds of persons have contributed to the written records that inform our understanding of Carson-Newman's early history. Many of these sources are not considered "real" historians—informal letter and postcard writers, alumni who wrote about commencement ceremonies, census takers, and student newspaper reporters, for example. Yet each presented unique facts and recollections that add flavor and spice to our knowledge of Carson-Newman's early years. Their notations along with those of trained historians reveal the many ways a Carson-Newman education has improved lives all over the world.

Carson-Newman's last comprehensive history was published in 1959. Retired dean and history professor Isaac Newton Carr's *The History of Carson-Newman College* is full of valuable information and follows a topical outline. Although history books must conclude at some definite point, a new chapter is usually waiting to be written. When the college began planning for its 150th birthday celebration in 2001, a new linear history book was part of the agenda, as was a beautiful coffee-table book featuring hundreds of striking photos from Carson-Newman's long history. Happily, the coffee-table book was published: *Carson-Newman College: 150 Years of Faith and Excellence 1851–2001.*

Retired history professor Robert M. Burts and his wife, Frieda C. Burts, had accepted the immense task of writing the updated history book. They conducted significant original research and produced hundreds of pages of information. But in the end, both fell victim to serious health concerns and were unable to complete the book.

Readers may wonder why this book has been published between Carson-Newman anniversaries, but the phrase "better late than never" definitely applies in this situation. In 2017, a committee began new work to get the book back on track. Melody Gill Marion (Class of 1975) and Amanda Ford (Class of 2006 and current Carson-Newman history professor) were chosen as writers. Melody used the Burtses' information as the backbone of chapters one through eleven on the nineteenth to twentieth centuries, also adding new research. Amanda compiled important historical material from the twenty-first century and broke new ground writing chapter twelve. For all practical purposes, the book covers Carson-Newman through the end of 2018.

Now a new chapter in Carson-Newman's history is being shaped day by day. May the university's years ahead continue to uphold the tradition of a solid education and lifelong learning within a meaningful Christian setting!

Acknowledgments

We are indebted to many individuals who assisted in contributing material for this book, especially the invaluable Albert L. Lang, Carson-Newman archivist, and Linda T. Gass, archives assistant. Bruce Kocour and Danny Niceley of the Stephens-Burnett Library staff were also most helpful. Ricke Hester of Hester Photography generously provided most of the excellent cover photographs, and Carson-Newman president Dr. Charles A. Fowler and his staff were most gracious with their assistance.

All the committee members who planned this book gave their time, energy, and creative thinking skills to the project for years without reservation—and we had fun, too. To Carolyn Blevins (chair), Patsy Boyce, Albert Lang, Suzanne Matheny, and Kara Stooksbury—you were the greatest co-workers!

Other significant contributors who helped us greatly include Dr. Sheridan Barker, Dr. Vicki Vivrett Barker, Dr. William Blevins, Ms. Vickie Butler, Dr. R. Barry Clark, Dr. Jim Coppock, Mrs. Imogene Baker Brewer, Mr. Mark Brown, Mrs. Mary Darby, Ms. Rose Christa Denor, Dr. Mark Heinrich, Dr. Carey Herring, Professor Emeritus William C. Houston, Dr. Peggy Hypes, Mr. Jeff Daniel Marion, Ms. Kay O'Brien, Dr. Randall O'Brien, Dr. Larry Osborne, Mrs. Alice Pryor, Dr. Jennifer Sauceman, and Professor Joe Bill Sloan.

Many, many thanks to you all!

CHAPTER ONE

Before the Beginning

1832–1851

> "We are all part of a larger stream of events, past, present, and future. We are all the beneficiaries of those who went before us—who built the cathedrals, who braved the unknown, who gave of their time and service, and who kept faith in the possibilities of the mind and the human spirit."
>
> —David McCullough[1]

Situated on a small hill off Highway 11-E in Jefferson City, Tennessee, sandwiched between the local elementary and middle schools, is a startling reminder of the nineteenth century with a particular tie to Carson-Newman University. It is a replica of the one-room log schoolhouse that was built for the education of young students by one of Carson-Newman's founders and presidents. Only a few miles from present-day Carson-Newman, Robert Reedy Bryan's log schoolhouse represents a real world of the past that we have trouble visualizing today, perhaps because so few buildings of its vintage are left. Yet a bright ribbon of Bryan's dedication to education, commitment to students, and faith in the future stretches figuratively from the log structure to the varied, spacious buildings of Carson-Newman's twenty-first-century campus and its leaders today.

A look back at the sweeping changes and growth that have occurred since 1851 reveals Carson-Newman's storied history. Not only has the very name of the institution changed multiple times; but between 1851 and 1889, the school would be headquartered on three different campuses in Mossy Creek, Tennessee, the town in which it was chartered. And even the town, Mossy Creek, would be renamed Jefferson City in 1901. Carson-Newman's story harkens back to the early growth of East Tennessee in the eighteenth century.

THE NAMES OF CARSON-NEWMAN

1851	Mossy Creek Missionary Baptist Seminary, for men
1855	Mossy Creek Baptist College, for men
1879	Carson College, for men
1882	Mossy Creek Female Seminary/Newman College, for women
1889	Carson and Newman College, for men and women
1930	Carson-Newman College
2013	Carson-Newman University

Native Americans and Early Settlers

Carson-Newman University could not even be imagined in the 1770s, when a few white pioneers first ventured into mountainous terrain seeking a safe haven in which to establish a new life. The territory of present-day East Tennessee had been part of the homeland of Native Americans, especially Cherokees, for about three thousand years. The European descendants wanted to settle within sight of the beautiful Smoky Mountains and near the plentiful sources of water that had been the Native Americans' domain. Farmers and hunters, the Cherokee people lived in small villages and believed that persons were part of nature, placed on the earth to be its stewards. They did not accept the idea that land itself could be bought, sold, or owned; it was to be used to benefit everyone.[2]

As more and more white settlers arrived and expanded their living areas, they cut down acres of trees to make homes and forts, "scalping" the wooded land sacred to the Cherokees. Both groups hunted and competed to kill the same animals for food. Because the settlers killed some animals simply to sell their pelts as a source of income, the Native Americans were appalled.[3] The chasm between the two groups' priorities and ways of life deepened; conflicts and acts of violence between the two groups caused great loss of life on both sides.

Treaties came and went, including the Treaty of Dumplin Creek, signed in 1785 in the vicinity of present-day Jefferson County, where Carson-Newman is now located. Some white settlers had opted for self-rule, rebelling against North Carolina, the territory that governed them at the time, and the federal government. Their government of choice, the short-lived State of Franklin, was formed in 1784 and dissolved in 1790.[4] The Treaty of Dumplin Creek, actually a violation of federal law, proclaimed peace between the inhabitants of Franklin and the Overhill Cherokees and promised the latter group restitution for lands claimed by the white people. The Cherokees did not receive the money promised to them, however, and attacks against white settlers continued.

The more successful Treaty of Holston (1791) established a boundary line between the white settlers and the Cherokee Nation and protection for white travelers and settlers in certain areas.[5] However, the boundary lines did not satisfy the white pioneers for long. So many Americans wanted to move westward and settle on lands belonging to the Indians that the United States government became increasingly aggressive in seeking ways to eliminate the Indian population.

In the 1830s, Congress passed the Indian Removal Act and promised the Cherokees a large sum of money and a new homeland west of the Mississippi River, leading to the 1838 forced march of about thirteen thousand Cherokees from their ancient homeland to Oklahoma. This journey of several thousand miles in extremely inhumane conditions became known as the infamous Trail of Tears.[6]

About one-quarter of the Cherokees died on the westward march. Roughly one thousand managed to escape and return to the mountains they loved. Most resettled on the North Carolina side of the Smoky Mountains.[7] For those who survived the long march, their new home in Oklahoma later became known as the Qualla Boundary, now an area of some 56,500 acres.[8]

On the Tennessee side of the mountains, the land was populated mostly by descendants of Scots and Irish families. To a lesser degree, people of other nationalities were part of the settling of the area. But the dominance of the Scots-Irish settlers was the key to the cultural foundation of Appalachia, as the broad region became known.[9] Their way of life continues to be an important part of the legend and the reality of the people of East Tennessee.

The Importance of Religion to the White Settlers

By the 1830s, many East Tennessee white settlers had acquired enough farmland to spread out and form family homesteads, but they lived in primitive dwellings in poverty. Families depended on their neighbors for help and support. Most youngsters growing up in this new land of promise attended school sporadically, and their "formal" education tended to end in primary (elementary) school.

In such homes, the Bible was often a family's most treasured possession. Familiar Scriptures gave them comfort and peace, as they were far from their extended family members and threatened by Indian attacks. Many adults were illiterate and relied on long-ago memorization to quote the Scriptures that guided their lives.

When a settlement became large enough to support a church, most area families eagerly attended services as often as they were available. The majority of churches founded in the area in these early years were Presbyterian, Methodist, and Baptist. The Baptists were the first to establish churches in the state, and Baptist churches were the most numerous.[10]

The people of all three denominations appreciated their pioneer preachers, who were generally faithful. But most such ministers lacked the ability to do much more than string pertinent Scriptures together in a sincere but inconsistent effort to reveal God's will to them. The people began to yearn for trained ministers, who were scarce in the mountain regions of East Tennessee. They wanted preachers who could better reveal the Scriptures to them and give them hope to counterbalance the dailiness of their hard and uncertain lives. And they dreamed of reading the Bible themselves and understanding God's Word more clearly. However, for the most part, schools were not established easily or swiftly in the region.

The Fruitful Efforts of Presbyterians and Methodists

Before the public school system was established in Tennessee, "the task of education was performed by private academies. The difficulty of financing these institutions, however, limited their number and usefulness. They had their origin and served in a period which was stormy and financially uncertain."[11] Yet a few lasted long enough to educate a number of persons whose influence would linger and spread across East Tennessee.

The ensuing pairing of education with religious groups was not at all unusual. "Churches . . . were from the earliest colonial times in charge of the education of the young. The earliest schools were controlled by the church and dominated by the religious motive. The church set up the courses of study, and the state looked to the church to establish institutions necessary to carry on a proper program of education."[12]

In East Tennessee, the Presbyterians were the first to realize the dream of establishing a school. A prominent Presbyterian minister, Samuel Doak, founded Martin Academy, the first school west of the Appalachian Mountains, in 1783 in Washington County. Over time, some academies grew into institutions of higher education. In 1794, Doak and his son founded Tusculum Academy in Greene County—the forerunner of Tusculum College (now University) in Greeneville, the first school of higher education in Tennessee.[13]

Blount County's Maryville College was founded in 1819; its name unchanged over the years, this academic institution still takes pride in its Presbyterian roots.[14] By means of these schools, Presbyterians grew in number and influence across Tennessee and the adjoining states.[15]

SEMINARY, COLLEGE, OR ACADEMY?

In the early to mid-1800s the terms *seminary, academy,* and *college* were used somewhat interchangeably. All could have degree-granting powers. Often, *academy* meant a preparatory school, roughly equivalent to a high school. *College* could refer to a high school or to a higher level of education. *Seminary* was used often to denote a school for women and was only later applied to theological education. (However, Mossy Creek Missionary Baptist Seminary, the first incarnation of Carson-Newman, was chartered exclusively for men.)

The Methodists' growth originated in the Great Awakening that swept across the country in the nineteenth century and was perpetuated by camp meetings, revivals, and emotional fervor.[16] In East Tennessee, they planted their schools in Jefferson County—Holston College in New Market in 1830 and Strawberry Plains College in 1848. Both educated a number of prominent persons in the county until the Civil War, when studies were abandoned and their main buildings were damaged beyond repair. Strawberry Plains College never reopened, but Holston College was reconstituted in 1874 as Holston Seminary. Functioning as an academy, the Seminary gave up its struggle to survive in 1885.[17]

But there were no early Baptist schools to report. What was delaying Baptists from accomplishing the same strides forward in education as their Presbyterian and Methodist counterparts?

The Temporary Preoccupations and Distractions of Baptists

The advantages of education for everyone, and especially ministers, were beginning to dawn on some Baptists as well. And they observed that the Presbyterians and Methodists were ahead of them in founding educational institutions. "An educated ministry was necessary if Baptist views were to be taught, and a general education for the people was necessary if the denomination was to be rightly indoctrinated. Other denominations were utilizing the institutions of learning in promoting their own growth, and Baptists realized that, in order to keep step, they must likewise establish such institutions."[18]

But even though Baptists were more numerous than Presbyterians and Methodists, they were not yet ready to match the other denominations' educational efforts. Baptists were busy organizing and reorganizing themselves into groups of regional cooperating churches called associations. (Baptist associations still operate today.) As more and more Baptist churches were planted, leaders' oversight of ever-larger numbers of churches became hopelessly unwieldy.

The earliest associations were divided several times to enable efficient supervision in these days, as travel was limited to horseback. Within an association, representatives from member churches met annually for inspiration and preaching, fellowship, the election of officers, and examinations of priorities affecting the churches. Although Baptists held that all churches were equal and the denomination had no formal overall hierarchy of leadership, there was still an increasing number of major issues to discuss and settle among themselves in order to establish Baptist standards common to their churches.

In 1828, the Nolachucky Association was formed of various Baptist churches from six East Tennessee counties through which the Nolachucky River flowed: Cocke, Grainger, Greene, Hamblen, Hawkins, and Jefferson. The new association had grown out of the Sandy Creek,

Holston, and Tennessee associations.[19] Education was not a high priority for the group at first, even for ministerial training.

The first mention of a desire for ministerial education at a Nolachucky Association meeting occurred in 1832. A representative from the Warrensburg Baptist Church in rural Greene County rose to ask the association to "devise some plan to assist young men of piety and promising gifts" to obtain a useful ministerial education.[20] The group's leaders would consider the request until the next annual meeting.

The following year, the Association reported its disappointment that no clear path toward religious education could be discerned. However, its members "recommended to the friends of religion to fall upon some plan" that would accomplish the purpose.[21] The matter would lie dormant for sixteen years while major controversies were debated and ultimately resolved.

CONTEXT: 1832 EVENTS IN WORLD HISTORY

Greece became an independent nation. Thousands of people in Scotland, England, and Canada were killed by a cholera epidemic. American geographer Henry Schoolcraft discovered the source of the Mississippi River: Lake Itasca in Minnesota. The first wagon train crossed the Rocky Mountains via Wyoming's South Pass. The first streetcar (horse-drawn) debuted in New York City, with passengers paying a fare of twelve cents. Andrew Jackson was re-elected as president of the United States after defeating opponent Henry Clay.

HINDRANCES TO ESTABLISHING BAPTIST SCHOOLS

Discussions at annual associational meetings grew heated over many issues, and agreement among church representatives was difficult to reach. The Baptists were mired in various controversies, not just in East Tennessee but across the state. Should the laying on of hands (a ritual practiced on baptized believers to produce a deeper level of indwelling of the Holy Spirit) be considered a church ordinance like baptism and the Lord's Supper?[22] Should only a church's own members be allowed to participate in the Lord's Supper? On what grounds would a member be disfellowshipped?

But the biggest and most bitter disagreements among Baptists arose from a group opposed to so many established Baptist programs and policies that they were called the "anti-group." They were against "missions, education, conventions, Sunday Schools, and all benevolent enterprises."[23] Should a given church declare itself Missionary Baptist (in favor of sending missionaries to evangelize the world and teaching the values of missions work to members) or Primitive Baptist (anti-missionary) because its members believe all people are predestined to be either saved or hell-bound?

Feelings ran high on both sides, and both felt justified by scriptural interpretation in their preferred practices. Although numerous attempts toward reconciliation were made, the two groups eventually split. Churches once simply designated as Baptist now declared themselves either Missionary Baptist or Primitive Baptist. Newly planted churches were founded as one or the other. By about 1840, the split was complete all across the state.[24]

An Unfolding Path for Baptist Education

During the 1840s, then, with their most intense controversy resolved, Baptists finally felt able to concentrate on positive matters. Active sentiment began to grow among East Tennessee Baptists for beginning a school, which would be a solid investment for many reasons. Young men in general could be educated, providing an informed citizenry for voting and governing; ministers in particular could be trained in the Scriptures and impart God's will and ways to all who attended church; and Baptist church members would grow more numerous, starting new churches and finally spreading their religious influence just as the Presbyterians and Methodists had already done.[25]

Indeed, the progress of the other two denominations "convinced East Tennessee Baptists that they must build a Baptist school to educate their preachers and to give a general education to Baptist youth. Otherwise, they would be unable to defend adequately Baptist principles; and many of their young people, educated at rival church schools, would be drawn away from the Baptist faith."[26]

Between 1783, when Samuel Doak established Martin Academy, and 1851, when Carson-Newman was founded, "there were chartered in East Tennessee forty-two academies, one institute, and two seminaries. Of these, however, not one was a Baptist school. Union Academy (later University), a Baptist school, had been established in West Tennessee, but was much too far removed from East Tennessee to serve the need most prevalent at this time. There seemed to have arisen in the minds of Baptists the fear that their people were being educated away from them" because of the Presbyterians' and Methodists' successful educational efforts.[27]

By 1836, Baptists in West and Middle Tennessee had established separate educational societies in order to form and launch successful Baptist institutions of higher learning.[28] 1849 was the pivotal year for Baptists in East Tennessee to make the same choice. Finally, they were ready to take active steps toward forming their own educational institution—the first such school in East Tennessee. "Considerable research . . . has failed to reveal any record of a Baptist school in East Tennessee prior to the founding of Mossy Creek Missionary Baptist Seminary."[29]

But before a Baptist school could become a reality in East Tennessee, any number of practical decisions had to be considered. What county and what town would be best for the new venture? What amenities did any particular site have to offer? Who would teach? Who would administer?

Few details are known of the formative deliberations among Baptists that eventually led to the founding of the Baptist school in Mossy Creek. But one name in the scant information stands out like a beacon: "Considerable interest in education had been aroused in Mossy Creek, Tennessee, by Professor Robert R. Bryan." [30]

The Founders and the Legend of the Oak Tree Five

Appropriately for a school in southern Appalachia, Carson-Newman's origins are usually recounted in story form. According to a well-established oral tradition, five men met in the spring of 1849 to discuss the dream of a Baptist institution of higher learning in impoverished East Tennessee. The "Oak Tree Five" were so named because legend says these men, neighbors, and family members met under the shady canopy of an oak tree after a day of haying in their fields. They were all landowners in Carsonville, a farming community south of the village of Mossy Creek named for the extended Carson family. [31] Certainly, they were among the Baptists who saw the need for a school where the classics and the Bible would be taught:

R. R. (Robert Reedy) Bryan (1822–1878) was a teacher and passionate educator. He was also a trained surveyor and licensed to preach, a graduate of both Strawberry Plains College and Holston College.[32] Bryan had a decided gift for teaching and leading; he was considered "a born teacher."[33] He had established the first school for young children in Jefferson County—the aforementioned one-room log schoolhouse—and later twice served the Mossy Creek institution of higher learning he co-founded as president.

William Cate Newman (1809–1890) was a farmer, builder, and brick mason widely known in the community and nicknamed "Uncle Billy."[34] He was a first cousin of R. R. Bryan. On his tombstone in Westview Cemetery in Jefferson City, the following words are engraved: "A true friend of Christian education and one of the founders of Carson-Newman College."

Isaac McLin Newman (1804–1880), William's older brother, was also a farmer, builder, brick mason, and R. R. Bryan's first cousin. As a layman active in the Mossy Creek Baptist Church, he helped to construct the original church building and many of the brick homes in the area. He contributed his influence and assets to the fledgling institution in various ways.[35]

Samuel Irwin Newman (1809–1887) was a first cousin of William and Isaac, a builder and brick mason, and related by marriage to R. R. Bryan.[36] He participated in constructing, among other buildings, Mossy Creek Baptist Church, the first three college buildings, the Presbyterian church, and the A. J. Mountcastle home, which would figure prominently in Carson-Newman's history. His gravestone in Westview Cemetery is inscribed, "One of the principal founders and a constant friend of Carson-Newman College." In about 2005, his family home, "Five Chimneys," constructed of handmade bricks, would be offered free to the college but was deemed too expensive to maintain. It was later razed.

Nelson Bowen (1821–1882) was a Sevier County native who moved to Jefferson County in 1844. He was an influential member of Mossy Creek Baptist Church and was licensed to preach; thus he had a deep interest in ministerial education. In 1854, he

> moved to Hendersonville, North Carolina, where he planted his life thereafter. He became a pastor of that city's First Baptist Church and published several Baptist newspapers. Interestingly, he also became the first president of Western North Carolina Female College, later called Judson Female College, and gave of himself sacrificially to maintain its growth. Records acknowledge that while he lived in East Tennessee, he helped organize Carson-Newman.[37]

In a very real way, these five men represented the three elements that would come together to create Carson-Newman: passion for teaching (Bryan), interest in ministerial education (Bowen), and laypersons (the Newmans) who were doers and perceived the benefits of higher education.

Unfortunately, no documentation exists today that directly confirms the legend of the Oak Tree Five as fact—meeting on Newman land under an oak tree to discuss the dream of a Baptist school. Some sources indicate that the group met more than once.[38] At any rate, it is a matter of record that the five men comprising this legend are the visionaries who founded Carson-Newman. And the appealing mental image of the men's gathering under an oak tree is shared to this day among students and faculty who enjoy this story of Carson-Newman's beginnings.

Significantly, the informal meeting(s) of this group of Jefferson County Baptists led to the formal organization of the deliberative body that would launch the first Baptist school in East Tennessee within two years.[39] They were all members of Baptist churches within the Nolachucky Baptist Association; quite possibly some or all also became members of the deliberative body, the East Tennessee Baptist Education Society.[40]

Vital Advocate: The East Tennessee Baptist Education Society

In 1849, the East Tennessee Baptist Education Society was formed from interested members of the Nolachucky Baptist Association.[41] Their purpose was "to promote education in general and among the ministry in particular."[42] Pro-education Baptists of the time believed that intelligent discussions in matters of religion called for an educated ministry, that education was essential to democracy, and that education was an important element of the freedom that individuals seek in a fuller, richer life for themselves

John Roper Branner, a local railroad executive who donated land for the Mossy Creek Missionary Baptist Seminary and later facilitated the return of Mossy Creek Baptist College's campus after the Civil War. (Courtesy of the Tennessee State Library and Archives, Colonial Dames of America Portraits Painted Before 1866 Photograph Collection.)

and their associates. This would be the official group to "fall upon a plan" for religious education in East Tennessee in the coming years.

The East Tennessee Baptist Education Society met in 1849 to plan for the development of a Baptist high school somewhere in Jefferson County. The next surviving documented action by the group occurred in August 1850, after they had acquired two acres of land beside Mossy Creek, for the express purpose of erecting suitable buildings for educational purposes.

Earlier in 1850, John Roper Branner, a leading citizen of Mossy Creek, had deeded two acres of land for the fledgling school at no cost. In doing so, he specified certain caveats, including the proviso that if the school failed, the land would revert to his ownership. Branner was president of the East Tennessee and Virginia Railroad, which was then under construction; he specified that each passenger train would make a stop in Mossy Creek.[43]

This important development meant that in the past year, the town of Mossy Creek had been chosen for the educational venture over other possible locations in Jefferson County, notably Dandridge. Likely reasons for choosing Mossy Creek included the fact that the railroad was coming there and land for a school had been donated by its president, John Roper Branner; a master teacher, Robert R. Bryan, resided there; a reliable source of water was available in Mossy Creek; and the town needed a good preparatory school (high school), as it had none. Although a Tennessee state law had been passed in 1806 to provide endowment for one public educational academy per county, several factors (prejudice, mismanagement of funds, and other pressures) had delayed the development of such an academy in Jefferson County.[44]

Initial legal documents referred to the school as "Mossy Creek Baptist Academy," but it was chartered in 1851 as Mossy Creek Missionary Baptist Seminary.[45]

A Concise History of Mossy Creek, Tennessee

The first settlers in the area that became Mossy Creek, Tennessee, were Adam and Elizabeth Peck. They had made the arduous journey from Virginia by handmade boat, floating down the Holston River, and arrived in 1788.[46] Other such settlers came from North Carolina via the French Broad River. Both waterways proved challenging routes because of the water's varying depths and the difficulty of finding a place to ford safely to shore. Most pioneers came overland by covered wagons through gaps in the mountains, following the old Indian trails to develop and inhabit settlements.

Even before Tennessee achieved statehood in 1796, Jefferson County had been formed in 1792.[47] Local history does not reveal exactly when the village of Mossy Creek was named, but the timing was probably also in the late eighteenth century.

MOSSY CREEK, TENNESSEE, IN THE EARLY DAYS

Mossy Creek was an unincorporated town in Jefferson County, named for the stream that rises out of the ground there. Its source is an underground aquifer that flows about five miles to join the Holston River. In its early days, long, graceful fronds of green moss grew on the banks and floor of the creek and floated in the water. These fronds have long since disappeared due to the harmful effects of nearby zinc mining.

Early white settlers established businesses beside Mossy Creek: an ironworks that served the wagon trains by repairing broken axles, three gristmills, a wool-carding business, a woolen mill, an ax handle factory, two cotton mills, and livery stables.[48]

Later, the rutted wagon roads were paved, leading to their use as stagecoach routes. Later still, the same roads ran parallel to the railroad tracks. To a large extent, the original Highway 11 East covers the same ground as the Indian trails and other early transportation routes.

By 1851, the town of Mossy Creek had one of the four post offices in the county. The other such towns were Dandridge (the county seat), New Market, and Oak Grove.[49] From Mossy Creek and Dandridge, both the Smoky Mountains and Clinch Mountains were (and are) visible.

Although Jefferson County settlers lived in a rural area, they were interested in events occurring in the larger world, to the extent that news was available. Most were churchgoers and followed local religious developments. Many welcomed the prospect of a good school in their area.

The Baptist Education Society's Next Steps

With the prospective school's location secured in Mossy Creek, on February 11, 1851, the East Tennessee Baptist Education Society appointed C. C. (Caswell Cobb) Tipton and William P. Rogers, both local pastors, as financial agents. They were "to raise money to complete the building, purchase library [books] and apparatus and also for endowment."[50] Right away, both began to travel and to appeal to residents of the region for funding of the newly proposed school.

In August 1851, Rogers presented a financial report to members of the society. It is not clear whether this report was his alone or a joint report for himself and Tipton. Already several thousand dollars had been garnered in bonds, notes, books, and cash in hand for the college, representing sacrificial gifts from individuals and families.[51] From his travels, he also reported the favor and goodwill of many friends, a spirit of anticipation among Baptists, and a sentiment voiced in favor of educating local ministers.[52]

Society members moved quickly to discuss and answer crucial questions. First, what should the school be called? The name Mossy Creek Missionary Baptist Seminary was chosen: Mossy Creek for the place; Baptist because the school was to be a Baptist institution; Missionary to distinguish it from the anti-missionary or Primitive Baptist movement; and Seminary because it was to be an institution of higher learning. Although the school had first been visualized as an academy or high school, a decision had been made to accept preparatory students and to educate them as quickly as possible so they could achieve the study skills necessary to enter higher education.

Second, who would compose the faculty for the new school? The members of the Education Society chose William Rogers to serve dual responsibilities as president and teacher. At once, Rogers submitted his resignation to the Dandridge Baptist Church as their pastor in order to lead the new school.[53] Robert Reedy Bryan would be the other teacher.

Third, should they wait until the school's own building was completed to open the school? The charter would presumably be approved in the fall 1851 session of the state legislature, but construction of a classroom building could not be completed until fall 1852. The decision was made to open the school the first Monday in September 1851.[54] With the energy and motivation of young men, Rogers and Bryan were eager to get started. Between them, they had already decided how they would divide the classroom responsibilities.

The Mossy Creek Baptist Church across the creek was the logical place to hold classes in 1851 and the first half of 1852. Apparently, the church's trustees (one of whom was Isaac Newman), acting in their capacity of legal agents for the building, gave permission.

The biggest problem was going to be raising the money needed to run the school. C. C. Tipton would continue to serve as a financial agent.[55]

Robert Reedy Bryan, a founder and consummate teacher, president 1851–1853, 1868–1869, and tireless advocate of the fledgling school that became Carson-Newman.

The Planting of a College

Plans called for the new classroom building to be a standard two-story structure with chimneys at either end and a small bell tower. The Newmans, brick masons by profession, would build it. Newman family descendants believe that Samuel, with the support and financial assistance of his cousins Isaac and William, contributed much of the material used in the building.

Large trees on the two acres were cut and the lumber planed. According to Newman family tradition, one hundred cords of wood were needed to burn the bricks, with Samuel ensuring the quality of each newly made

(*Left*) William Cate Newman, a founder and strong supporter of the college.

(*Right*) Isaac McLin Newman, William C. Newman's brother and also a founder and contributor.

brick. His young sons helped cut the wood from the knobs on Bays Mountain and hauled it on mule-drawn sleds to the site. Shingles were rived on Newman land. For the Newmans, this activity was a labor of love.

With the major questions about the school answered and verifiable progress being made on a new building, the East Tennessee Baptist Education Society members felt that their organization was no longer needed. They named twenty-one trustees composed of qualified and willing local Baptists to sign the charter and oversee the new school.[56] No extant sources reveal the names of the men involved in the East Tennessee Baptist Education Society, but it seems likely that some of them also served as the school's first trustees.

The twenty-one names included that of Dandridge lawyer James Harvey Carson—a member of the family after whom Carsonville was named—who would later make many significant contributions to the new educational institution.[57] From that point on, ever-changing teams of trustees would assume the responsibility of helping college administrators make decisions crucial to the school's growth and health.

Meaningful and enduring institutions such as Carson-Newman University are born of both farsighted visionaries and resolute doers. The five original founders of Carson-Newman were such men. They were "not misled, emotional, ignorant men following blindly after a belief without knowing why they followed. They were men of vision, and they planned for the future of the denomination." [58]

Four of the five stayed in place and watched their dream take shape in reality, with one leading the school through years of immense challenges. Fortunate indeed is the school that can trace its history and growth through a succession of aspirations, setbacks, changes, heartaches, and expansions but that stays focused on its main goal: the education and training of young adult minds and hearts. With a promising future, the first Baptist school in East Tennessee was finally underway.

CHAPTER TWO

Birth and Rebirth

1851–1869

"O brave new world, / That has such people in't!"
—William Shakespeare[59]

"These studies are a spur to the young, a delight to the old; an ornament in prosperity, a consoling refuge in adversity; they are pleasure for us at home, and no burden abroad; they stay up with us at night, they accompany us when we travel."
—Marcus Tullius Cicero[60]

Most of Mossy Creek Seminary's first students were on the preparatory level—not yet up to the rigorous college curriculum. These young men were from farming backgrounds and rural communities and had had only limited acquaintance with learning. Some were local, arriving by walking or on horseback each day. Others came from longer distances by wagon or on horseback, needing to board with local families while school was in session. Some were already older than the average student.

Construction work continued on the two-acre campus for the school's first classroom building of its own. Across the creek, inside the Mossy Creek Baptist Church, the preparatory students labored to learn quickly so they could achieve the best education possible in their area.

1851, the Landmark Year of Carson-Newman's Birth

In September 1851, one student at Mossy Creek Missionary Baptist Seminary was fully ready to begin college work—Richard Scruggs, the son of a Baptist preacher who was a local authority in Greek.[61] Thanks to his father's influence, he was a keen student.

William Rogers, the president, and R. R. Bryan worked together well as the school's two teachers. Both educators could teach any course—an evidence of their keenly developed intellects and excellent educations. Thus Mossy Creek Missionary Baptist Seminary was launched with two acres owned, two teachers, a borrowed building, and great faith and hope.

A GOOD BEGINNING AND A SAD ENDING: WILLIAM P. ROGERS, FIRST PRESIDENT (1851)

William Rogers was considered one of East Tennessee's most forward-thinking men of his day. A literary education at Maryville College had prepared him for a teaching career, but he had chosen to go into the ministry. As the pastor of a local church, he organized a Sunday School for religious instruction before most other churches had done so (including a Sunday School for African American families), set up a library for the use of the church, and held a monthly emphasis on prayer for the extension of the gospel across the world.[62] Known as an effective pastor by the churches he led, including Dandridge Baptist Church, he changed careers again when he agreed to become the first president of Mossy Creek Seminary in 1851.

Sadly, after only a few months as president, William Rogers contracted typhoid fever and died in November 1851.[63] His tombstone in the Branner Cemetery in Jefferson City bears witness to his character: "An exemplary member of the Baptist church, a useful minister of the gospel, humble and persevering in the cause of Christ. He sacrificed property, health, and life for truth's sake."

From the beginning, the college's leaders were committed to truth as a life standard. This dedication to truth symbolically planted a seed toward the later establishment of the Carson-Newman motto: "Truth, Beauty, and Goodness."

Highlights of Carson-Newman's First Eight Years

SEAMLESS CONTINUITY OF LEADERSHIP: ROBERT R. BRYAN, SECOND PRESIDENT (1851–1853)

With Rogers's death, Robert Reedy Bryan was left to carry on alone with the fledgling school and to assume the title of president as well as professor.

Records do not indicate that a new teacher was hired at this time, but Bryan may have used some of the more advanced students to tutor those less advanced. At any rate, he continued to do what he loved—teaching—along with his administrative duties. Over the years, he likely taught every course offered by the school during his time on the faculty, although his preference was in the natural sciences.

CONTEXT: 1851 EVENTS IN WORLD HISTORY

American inventor Cyrus McCormick exhibited his reaper at the London World's Fair, while Isaac Singer patented his sewing machine. Millard Fillmore was president of the United States. The Yosemite Valley in California was discovered. *Moby Dick* by Herman Melville was published, and Northwestern University was founded in Chicago. San Francisco experienced two major fires, which together destroyed a quarter of the city.

In September 1852 Bryan opened the school in its own building. There was space for a chapel, classrooms, a library, and meeting areas for the two literary societies that had been newly formed for the young men—Columbian and Philomathean. The Columbians had adopted the motto "Wisdom, Truth, and Eloquence."[64] The Philomatheans upheld an emphasis on "Love of Honor, Learning, and Power" (*The Orange and Blue*, September 14, 1948). Now the school could accommodate its students in serious study, fellowship, spiritual growth, and Friday night entertainment.

No enrollment records have survived for the second year, but likely six freshmen enrolled, those who would form the graduating Class of 1856. They would be the first to have their entire college experience in the new building.

Understandably, R. R. Bryan could not serve as both president and professor forever. Still preferring to teach, in 1853 he relinquished the role of president of Mossy Creek Missionary Baptist Seminary to another well-qualified educator. Having been led by two ministers up to this point, now the school would be in the hands of a layman.

The first classroom building of Mossy Creek Missionary Baptist Seminary and Mossy Creek Baptist College.

A GIFT FOR ORGANIZATION: SAMUEL ANDERSON, THIRD PRESIDENT (1853–1857)

Born in a corner of Jefferson County, Tennessee, Samuel Anderson (1821–1885) had received BA and MA degrees from nearby Tusculum College. He then served Tusculum as both president and professor of mathematics before accepting the trustees' invitation to become president of Mossy Creek Seminary.[65]

Anderson brought beneficial administrative skills to the Seminary along with his teaching abilities. He likely published the school's first catalogue for 1855–1856.[66] That issue is lost, but the next one is a major source of information about the early years of the school. He would have a "back and forth" relationship with both Tusculum and Mossy Creek in the 1850s–1860s, leaving one for the other only to return in a few years.

Later in life, by 1873, Samuel Anderson was again living in Mossy Creek in an educational capacity, but not with the college. He became the superintendent of Public Instruction for Jefferson County and served in this role at least until 1878; no doubt he had some connections with the Masonic school formed about that time.[67]

EARLY CURRICULUM AT MOSSY CREEK BAPTIST COLLEGE

The 1856–1857 catalogue course list reveals the classical education Mossy Creek students received and also the amazing nature of some early presidents' abilities to teach every course! At this time, the sole curriculum choice offered to students was whether to take Hebrew. Only upon completion of all listed courses and the corresponding examinations would a student earn his Baccalaureate degree.

FRESHMAN YEAR: Latin Reader; Caesar's Commentaries (5 books); Algebra; Greek Reader; Geometry (6 books); Isocrates; Ovid; Xenophon's Cyropedia; Composition and Declamation

SOPHOMORE YEAR: Virgil; Xenophon's Anabasia; Geometry (completed); Trigonometry (plain and spherical); Surveying (with field practice); Heights and Distances; Herodotus; Demosthenes' de Corona; Practical Mathematics; Cicero's Orations; Elocution; Composition and Declamation

JUNIOR YEAR: Horace's Odes and Satires; Thucydides; Longinus' De Sublimitate; Homer's Iliad; Natural Philosophy; Anatomy, Physiology, and Hygiene; Plato; Aristotle; Logic and Rhetoric; Political Economy; Moral Philosophy; Book-keeping; Composition and Declamation

SENIOR YEAR: Horace's Ars Poetica; Tacitus and Syntax; Astronomy; Chemistry; Mineralogy and Geology; General Review of Mathematics; Natural Theology; Mental Philosophy; Upham on the Will; Law of Nations; Constitution of the United States; Evidences of Christianity; Composition and Declamation[68]

THE START OF THE RUSSELL FAMILY'S ASSOCIATION WITH CARSON-NEWMAN

In the fall of 1852, a young man named William Thomas Russell enrolled in Mossy Creek Baptist Seminary as a junior. He was a transfer student from Clinton Seminary in Clinton, Tennessee. While at Mossy Creek

Seminary, Russell "devoted himself to earnest study . . . including Hebrew and French" and was considered brilliant in debate. He completed his studies in 1855, but the exact date is unclear.[69] He was either the Seminary's first graduate (a few months earlier than Richard Scruggs) or the second. (Apparently he did not wait to graduate formally before leaving Mossy Creek.) The important distinction is that Richard Scruggs was Mossy Creek Seminary's first four-year graduate and is officially recognized as the first graduate.

THE FIRST GRADUATION (1855)

Mossy Creek Missionary Baptist Seminary held its first graduation exercise in 1855 for Richard Scruggs, literary orator. He received the AB degree (from the Latin *artium baccalaureus),* the Bachelor of Arts. Scruggs later became a physician and a businessman, returning to live in his hometown of Sweetwater, Tennessee.[70]

After William Thomas Russell graduated from Mossy Creek Seminary, he spent about a year as a financial agent for the college.[71] Afterward he led several Baptist congregations in Tennessee and other Southern states as a distinguished and learned pastor. His alma mater granted him an honorary Doctor of Divinity degree (DD) in 1872.[72]

CAMPUS NEWS AND EXPANSIONS

In June 1855, the trustees purchased an additional eight acres of land adjoining the original two acres. John Roper Branner, who had donated the first two acres, transferred ownership of the additional land for $700. This time, he gave the trustees a warranty deed, wrapping the entire ten acres together, without the caveat he had previously specified for the land to revert to him if the Seminary failed.[73] Apparently, by now, he had more confidence in the Seminary's success. These ten acres would later become known as Campus #1 as the school moved physically to other nearby campuses.

Also in 1855, as ratified by the state legislature in 1856, the school's name was changed to Mossy Creek Baptist College in order to reflect a broader emphasis and curriculum than ministerial studies alone.[74] The college was growing swiftly; in 1856 there were seventy-two college students from five states and forty-nine preparatory students![75]

Heavily increasing attendance led the trustees to authorize a building program for two dormitories, the first to be ready by the fall of 1857. It was the larger of the two, with a kitchen and dining-room wing at the rear. The bricks were burned locally by the ever-faithful Newmans, who supervised the construction. William Cate Newman advanced most of the funds for the buildings, which became known as Newman Dormitories #1 and #2. About this time, John Roper Branner loaned the school $300, possibly for the building project. Also, financial agent C. C. Tipton raised $4,000. The total cost of both buildings was reportedly $10,840.[76]

The two-story dormitory buildings had no internal stairways; instead, students climbed stairs between the two porches. Every room had a fireplace; wood was the only source of fuel.

REVELATIONS OF THE FIRST SURVIVING SCHOOL CATALOGUE

For the school year 1856–1857, the cost of board per week, with the student furnishing his bed, fuel, and lights, was $1.25. Each room was furnished with a bedstead, table, and a pair of andirons. Tuition for the twenty-week term was $12 for college students and $10 for preparatory students with a contingent (required) fee of fifty cents.[77]

An entire college semester then would be $37.50, "but it will be less in a plentiful year," according to the catalogue—apparently meaning that board would cost less if harvests were plentiful and food prices were lower or if the college received above-average donations of food. Students preparing for the gospel ministry who came recommended by their churches were to receive their tuition free, provided they passed the examination of the Committee on Beneficiaries.[78]

R. R. Bryan, Esq., was listed as vice-president as well as professor of natural philosophy, astronomy, and chemistry. Rev. N. B. Goforth (a future president) was professor of Latin, Greek, and Hebrew. J. A. Russell tutored students in mathematics, and E. E. McCroskey tutored Latin and Greek students in the preparatory Department; both instructors were juniors at Mossy Creek Baptist College.[79]

MOSSY CREEK'S IDYLLIC NATURE

"The College Edifice is situated on a commanding eminence, overlooking the beautiful and healthy stream Mossy Creek, within four hundred yards of Mossy Creek Depot, on the East Tennessee and Virginia Railroad, in the midst of a neighborhood noted for the purity of its atmosphere, the general health, sociability, and sobriety of its inhabitants, and for the absence of all the temptations to vice and idleness.

"Young men of immoral habits seldom resort here—and when they do, a speedy reform or departure is inevitable."[80]

At the end of the 1856–1857 school year, Samuel Anderson left Mossy Creek in order to return to his alma mater, Tusculum College, in an academic position.[81] He was succeeded by the third minister-president in the young Mossy Creek College's history.

MAINTAINING THE STATUS QUO: MATTHEW HILLSMAN, FOURTH PRESIDENT (1857–1859)

With deep roots in Knoxville, Tennessee, where he was born, Matthew Hillsman (1814–1892) was the pastor of that city's First Baptist Church and also served as a professor of logic, rhetoric, and moral science at Mossy Creek Baptist College at the time he was invited to become the new president.[82] Largely self-taught in the classics, he was apparently much admired for his unusual beard.

Hillsman's term in office was brief, one year as acting president and one year as president, while he continued to teach at the college. During the 1858–1859 school year, he preached every Sunday in Knoxville, Morristown, or New Market.[83] In the two commencements during his tenure there were eleven graduates with AB degrees, five in the Class of 1858 and six in 1859. Notably, one of the 1859 graduates was Jesse Baker, a revered future president of Mossy Creek Baptist College.

The 1858–1859 catalogue lists three other professors besides Hillsman: R. H. Keeling, professor of mathematics and modern languages; N. B. Goforth, professor of ancient languages; and R. R. Bryan, who taught natural philosophy, chemistry, "& etc." The total school enrollment was

149, with seventy-five students in the Preparatory Department.[84] At the collegiate level there were five seniors, fifty-six undergraduates, and thirteen "irregular" students (those who were taking classes above or below their designated level).[85]

There was now a two-track curriculum: "Those who do not wish to study the Ancient Languages may pursue an exclusively English course, which will be prescribed by the faculty, and on completing it, will be entitled to a certificate" (as compared to an AB degree).[86] Extant sources do not reveal how many students took advantage of the English curriculum choice.

Board was now $1.35 per week including room with bedstead, table, and andirons, and tuition was $18 for seniors for a five-month session. Classes in Hebrew, French, Spanish, and engineering were each $5 extra.[87]

Because Matthew Hillsman continued to be much in demand as a preacher, he concluded that he should preach full-time in the gospel ministry and resigned as president of the college at the end of the 1858–1859 school year. He later became an outstanding pastor in West Tennessee, and Union University conferred an honorary DD on him in 1870.[88]

The Larger World Intrudes on Mossy Creek

A PERIOD OF TRANSITION: N. B. GOFORTH, FIFTH PRESIDENT (1859–1862)

The trustees had no trouble choosing Hillsman's successor, Napoleon Bonaparte Goforth (1828–1907), who had been teaching classical languages at Mossy Creek Baptist College since 1855. He had grown up on a farm in Sevier County and was ordained to preach by his home church. He graduated from Maryville College in 1854.[89]

On being named president, Goforth dedicated himself to the growth and development of the college. He believed in teaching by example and by training and discussion. Characterized as possessing "mental energy and rugged strength rather than polish," he was loyal and a hard worker.[90]

A PERILOUS TIME FOR MOSSY CREEK BAPTIST COLLEGE

The school was meeting a great need in the area, training leaders for Baptist churches as well as providing an excellent liberal arts education for all students. In 1860, former president Samuel Anderson was warmly welcomed back to Mossy Creek College as a mathematics professor; he would teach there until 1862.[91] But in the early 1860s in East Tennessee, as in all areas of the nation, war clouds were gathering; and they portended calamity for the young college.

The school itself reflected the divided loyalties of the region, and debates about slavery and states' rights must have been lively in the dormitories and literary society halls. Because many Jefferson County landowners made their living in agriculture, some were slaveholders. Others were passionately anti-slavery.[92]

When Abraham Lincoln was elected president, the Southern states began to withdraw from the Union, and Tennessee had to choose sides. Governor Isham Harris and the General Assembly scheduled a referendum for February 9, 1861, when citizens could vote whether Tennessee should secede from or remain in the Union. Three of every four votes cast in East Tennessee were against secession. But the voters of West and Middle Tennessee overwhelmed those of East Tennessee in favoring secession.[93]

The state formally seceded from the Union on June 8, 1861. But the Civil War had begun in April when shots were fired at Fort Sumter, South Carolina.[94] Some Mossy Creek students had enlisted as soldiers before the 1861 commencement. More were Confederate sympathizers than those pro-Union, although this was not the general pattern in East Tennessee.[95] Students wishing to join the Confederate Army or cavalry could do so easily. For example, Confederate Colonel Benjamin Branner, younger brother of John Roper Branner, recruited thirty-one Mossy Creek Baptist College students for a cavalry unit; the students were required to furnish their own mounts.[96]

After May 1862, when the Confederate Conscription Law was passed, all males in Tennessee between the ages of eighteen and thirty-five were subject to be drafted for the Confederate cause.[97] That severely limited the options of students wishing to join the Union Army; they had to flee the state in order to do so. Many such young men attempted to reach the Union Army in Kentucky to enlist; some were captured in Tennessee and jailed or imprisoned.[98] As a young man, Samuel Watson Tindell, a future Mossy Creek Baptist College president, was successful in making the dangerous trip to Kentucky on his second attempt to enlist in the Union Army.[99]

Whether as Union or Confederate soldiers, college men tended to receive commissions as officers or specialty assignments such as quartermaster clerks, teachers in the training of draftees, or medical support. At the very least, college students had the capacity to read and understand more complex duties than did less educated men.

The college was in the midst of the war's desolation, but there was little that its remaining personnel could do to alleviate the situation. They did assist in relieving individual cases of distress whenever possible. But by June 1862, the usual time for commencement, there were likely no students left at Mossy Creek Baptist College. The trustees officially closed the school, and President Goforth left to serve as a chaplain to Confederate forces.[100]

The Desolate War Years (1862–1865)

Everyone associated with Mossy Creek Baptist College, many of whom had made heroic efforts to begin and maintain the school, must have been crushed at its closure a mere eleven years after its founding—just as it was expanding and meeting many educational needs for area residents. Dark days ensued over the course of the war, and there seemed to be little hope of the school's ever reopening, even though it still existed on paper; its charter had not been withdrawn.

After the college closed, Union soldiers occupied Newman Dormitories #1 and #2 as their quarters and barracks.[101] Nearby Mossy Creek Baptist Church, temporary home to the college for its first year, was used to stable horses. The Battle of Mossy Creek occurred on December 29, 1863, with the Union forces victorious.[102] Four times during the long years of the war, both Union and Confederate soldiers traversed the length and breadth of East Tennessee, each time confiscating whatever food supplies could be found, further impoverishing local inhabitants, and widening the path of destruction.[103]

By the war's end in 1865, the Union soldiers inhabiting the college's two dormitories had left the brick structures dismantled beyond recognition—the doors, window casings, joists, and flooring were completely destroyed. During the cold winters, troops had burned anything flammable within reach, including doors and window frames, for heating.[104]

The college had been in debt before the war began, owing John Roper Branner $1,000 and William "Uncle Billy" Newman $1,500, advanced to construct the two dormitories.[105] Now with the countryside largely destroyed and bankruptcies, business failures, and unpaid financial obligations common, repayment of the college's debt seemed impossible.

Local Baptist church members in Mossy Creek, Morristown, Dandridge, and New Market prayed fervently for the reopening of the college. But at the war's end in 1865, the college property was scheduled to be sold at auction through the chancery court, with Branner and Newman to receive the proceeds of its sale.

When the hour of the sale arrived, crowds gathered but only one bidder was present—John Roper Branner himself, who paid $50 down and gave a note of $950 for the balance. The chancellor decreed that the title for the ten acres should be vested solely in John R. Branner's name, without anyone else having the right of redemption.[106]

The saddest day in the life of the young college had arrived. Mossy Creek Baptist College had lost its students, its faculty, its campus, and all equipment and other assets. The first Baptist school in East Tennessee appeared to be dead without any possibility of being revived.

Reconstruction at Mossy Creek (1865–1868)

But all hope was not lost, thanks to the prayers of church members and the faith and determination of Robert Reedy Bryan, founder, past president, and longtime professor. With the school's trustees, he led a two-year campaign to raise funds to purchase the property back from Branner on behalf of the college. Also, in 1866, the trustees made a claim against the government for damages inflicted by Union soldiers. (Three decades later, this claim finally bore fruit in the amount of $6,000 in reparations.[107])

John Roper Branner had held the ten acres without selling them to anyone else. Late in 1866, he resold the campus, consisting of ten acres and three ruined buildings, to Mossy Creek Baptist College's Board of Trustees for $1,272 cash—the impressive amount Bryan and the trustees raised from area residents. East Tennessee Baptists knew the school was needed for young men who had survived the war or who were now eligible to attend.[108]

With the return of the campus property to Mossy Creek Baptist College and the original vision for the school still intact, R. R. Bryan and the trustees could begin to revive the shattered property for future students.

FUTURE AUTHOR FRANCES HODGSON BURNETT IN 1865

About the time she turned sixteen in 1865, Frances Hodgson and her family emigrated from Manchester, England, to New Market, Tennessee, where her mother's brother lived close to Mossy Creek Baptist College. The family spent at least one bitterly cold winter without a source of income. Hodgson later commented that they would not have survived the winter without the kindness of their neighbors. During this time, Hodgson became friends with a neighbor, Swan M. Burnett, whom she later married. (He was part of the extended Burnett family of East Tennessee prominent in Carson-Newman's history.[109])

In New Market, Hodgson lived in a two-story log cabin that still exists under a newer façade; a historical plaque marks the site. She later said, "During those years spent among the woods and mountains of East Tennessee, I had been accumulating material out of which I could build and from which I should draw as long as I lived" (*Orange and Blue,* October 31, 1991).

The family later moved to Knoxville, and Hodgson began writing short stories—some reminiscent of her life in East Tennessee—that became the steppingstones to her books beloved all over the world: *The Secret Garden, A Little Princess,* and *Little Lord Fauntleroy.* Later in life, she and Swan Burnett divorced, and she divided her time between England and Long Island, New York. She passed away in 1924.

In 2015, Carson-Newman University would formally celebrate the 150th anniversary of well-known author Frances Hodgson Burnett's arrival in East Tennessee and her longtime literary career.

For the next two years, the faithful R. R. Bryan was the leading spirit and motivator behind the restoration of Mossy Creek Baptist College. He functioned as financial agent, student recruiter, dean, professor, and ultimately as president again, to the detriment of his health. As money became available, the classroom building was evidently renovated sufficiently to hold classes. Bringing the dormitories back to usable condition would have to wait. Once again students had to board with local families until Newman Dormitories #1 and #2 could be reconstructed.

The East Tennessee Baptist Education Society no longer existed. But in 1868, Robert Reedy Bryan, Samuel I. Newman, and pastor W. A. Montgomery (another future president) joined together to make a stirring and convincing presentation before the members of the local Nolachucky Baptist Association. The result was that East Tennessee Baptists officially put their strong support behind the rebuilding of Mossy Creek Baptist College. Determinedly Bryan and the school's trustees moved ahead with plans to reopen the school that fall.

Rebirth: Rising from the Ashes of War

REGAINING LOST GROUND: R. R. BRYAN'S REPEAT PRESIDENCY (1868–1869)

By 1868, the school had been closed for six years. However, it is possible that R. R. Bryan had been teaching young students in his log schoolhouse while Mossy Creek Baptist College was not operating. At any rate, in 1868, Bryan resumed his former role as both president and professor for the college. But this time he did not do all the teaching alone. Jesse Baker from the Class of 1859, who had been serving Mossy Creek Baptist Church as pastor, joined him as a teacher.

BRYAN'S LOG SCHOOLHOUSE

The original site of Bryan's log schoolhouse was on what is now East Ellis Avenue in Jefferson City, close to the present-day Maple Crest Apartments. R. R. Bryan had owned eight acres in the area, not far from the original ten acres of Campus #1. In the 1990s, Helen Gray, a Jefferson City resident with an interest in local history and a can-do spirit, had the vision to try to preserve this important relic of the past. However, the crumbling logs proved too fragile to be saved. Thankfully, the local Historical Society supported Helen Gray's efforts, and a replica of the schoolhouse was built close to Highway 11 East. True to the nineteenth century, the post beside the structure holds a school bell.

Robert Reedy Bryan's rebuilt log schoolhouse.

With its academic momentum lost, the college reopened with both preparatory and college freshman students—with two exceptions. Brothers W. T. and T. R. Russell from Monroe County enrolled as seniors. They were the nephews of William Thomas Russell, the transfer student who may have been Mossy Creek's first graduate. W. T. Russell was named for his uncle.

The Russell brothers had likely received their preparatory education from the Riceville Literary and Classical Institute between Athens and Cleveland, Tennessee. After the Civil War ended, N. B. Goforth had gone there to lead the school.[110] The Russells may also have had at least one tutor or mentor at home, perhaps their uncle.

In June 1869, R. R. Bryan presided over the first postwar college commencement, with special exercises for the lower classmen and preparatory students and the awarding of AB degrees to the two Russell brothers. (There would be no other degrees awarded until the 1868 entering freshmen had completed four years of study.) By now, many young students had been motivated to learn by Bryan, the master teacher, and were making solid contributions to their communities in East Tennessee and beyond.

R. R. Bryan's health was endangered by all he had undertaken since he consistently did the work of two or three persons. His health was failing, and the college's trustees did not want him to continue risking his health in his dual role of president and professor. They turned to Jesse Baker, alumnus, pastor, and professor to assume the presidency of Mossy Creek Baptist College for the 1869–1870 school year.

Bryan lived several more years and served the school as a trustee, but his physical condition declined with each passing year. In all likelihood, Mossy Creek Baptist College would not have been revived after the Civil War without his spirited and dedicated leadership.

R. R. BRYAN IN THE WORDS OF OTHERS

"He was a live wire and shot electric currents through thick skins and drowsy brains, waking up the dormant powers of the mind."
—J. J. Burnett[111]

"He had a sharp, incisive mind and strong will power . . . and soon won the hearts of all the young men in the institution."
—Jesse Baker[112]

"Professor R. R. Bryan has many and lasting monuments, not of marble or brass, but more enduring—monuments of immortal minds, molded by personal contact of teacher and pupils in the schoolroom."
—N. B. Goforth[113]

In the remaining years of the nineteenth century, most Mossy Creek Baptist College presidents would have short tenures, but some would be dedicated to maintaining and growing the college with a commitment akin to that of its founders. The progressive spirit behind their ensuring educational opportunities for young men would soon extend to equal opportunities for young women as well.

CHAPTER THREE

Progress and Pain, Hand in Hand

1869–1882

"Need and struggle are what excite and inspire us. Not a victory is gained, nor a deed of faithfulness or courage is done, except upon a maybe. . . . Refuse to believe in your need, and you shall [fail]. . . . It is only by risking our persons from one hour to another that we live at all. And often enough our faith beforehand in an uncertified result is the only thing that makes the result come true."
—William James[114]

Solar eclipses are always remarkable sights, and the one that occurred on August 7, 1869, in East Tennessee was also symbolic. It was a dark day, "the day of the total eclipse of the sun," recalled W. T. Russell over thirty years later.[115] The date stood out in his memory over the years because of an event only partially related to the eclipse, however. W. T. Russell and his brother, T. R., had just graduated from Mossy Creek Baptist College in June under the tutelage of Robert R. Bryan and Jesse Baker, their professors.[116] After the June commencement, the school's trustees had asked Jesse Baker to assume the presidency of the college, relieving the legendary Bryan of his responsibilities. The Russell brothers had accepted Baker's invitation to stay on and teach at Mossy Creek for the 1869–1870 school year.[117]

In 1869, the campus still bore the obvious marks of the Civil War devastation. Both Newman Dormitories were still in terrible shape from the Union soldiers' grave misuse of them, and the classroom building's condition was barely functional at best.

Sometime between the early June commencement and August 7, 1869, a dire, unexpected situation arose that again threatened Mossy Creek Baptist College's very existence. The college had not done a good job of paying its bills. Creditors, including those who had made basic repairs on the campus, demanded payment and threatened foreclosure. They sued in chancery court in the amount of $6,000. (The exact amount varies among sources, but $6,000 is the most commonly cited amount.[118])

Beyond the much-needed renovation of the classroom building, surviving college records do not give specifics of what factors comprised such a large debt. Perhaps a new mortgage was drawn on the campus. At any rate, "the trustees were allowed one year to pay off the debts, and in consequence of failure, the property was to be sold in bar of redemption."[119]

The Long, Courageous Journey to Save the College

"Let Us Undertake It": Jesse Baker, Sixth President (1869–1870)

Jesse Baker (1836–1902), a native of Sneedville in Hancock County, would be considered a bivocational pastor in today's parlance.[120] Preaching at Mossy Creek Baptist Church (which met in the college's classroom building at this time), he performed ongoing pastoral duties as well as teaching at the college.[121]

CIRCUIT-RIDING PREACHERS

In these early days when churches were few in Tennessee, a minister could and often did hold multiple pastorates in a general area—preaching a different Sunday or two Sundays for each. Such pastors rode horseback on various Sundays to preach at the more distant churches. Thus they "rode the circuit of their churches" on Sundays each month. Most East Tennessee churches could not financially support a full-time pastor, so a pastor earned his living by preaching at several churches at a time. At this time Jesse Baker served Mossy Creek Baptist Church as pastor, possibly along with other churches in the general area.

Baker took on a huge responsibility when the college trustees elected him as president during the June 1869 commencement. He felt deeply his call from the Lord to preach the gospel, but he also felt a strong calling to serve his alma mater.

Jesse Baker was now in charge of a college that East Tennessee needed more than ever, but that would die within one year if $6,000—a mind-boggling amount of money at the time—were not raised promptly. (For perspective, $6,000 in 1869 is currently equivalent to well over $100,000.)

On August 7, as the sky darkened with the approaching solar eclipse, Jesse Baker invited W. T. Russell to walk across the campus with him. Russell later recalled, "As we looked over the wrecked buildings and grounds, it seemed fitting to have the light of the sun shut out. Dr. Baker was distressed because the property was in ruins and the people discouraged, the college about to be sold under debt, and its history about to end in dishonor."[122]

It was Baker's next statement to Russell that evidenced the new president's courage and proved him a worthy successor to Robert Reedy Bryan. Russell recounted, "As we turned to leave the cheerless spot he said, 'Let us undertake it.' That was heroic faith."[123]

Baker determined that he would do his best to raise the $6,000 himself, acting primarily as financial agent. But that role necessitated his leaving the just-reborn Baptist college in the hands of the young Russell brothers as Baker rode horseback all over East Tennessee, pleading for money for the college. Between them, the Russell brothers would teach all the classes, and W. T. would also assume the daily administrative duties of the absent president. Russell recognized his youth and inexperience in the face of such a huge task, calling himself "a mere boy," but rose to the challenge and proved faithful as well as gaining invaluable experience as the leader of a faith-based college.[124]

Baker returned to Mossy Creek occasionally during the 1869–1870 school year, fulfilling his preaching duties at the church, spending all-too-brief time with his family, and counseling the Russell brothers regarding their roles at the college. Most of his time, however, was spent in service to Mossy Creek Baptist College among the people of East Tennessee, asking for donations from each person—whatever he or she could spare—and traveling over 3,500 miles with only the Lord and his horse as constant companions.[125] No doubt he preached and prayed along the way, using his power and eloquence as a speaker to make friends for the college.

AN APOCRYPHAL JESSE BAKER STORY

"Legend has it that some highwaymen waylaid Baker in a gap in the mountains. They demanded the contents of the saddlebags he was carrying. 'I've not got any money of my own in there,' he was said to have replied. 'All there belongs to the Baptist College at Mossy Creek.' The bushwhackers huddled for a moment, discussing what they would do. Finally, they told Baker: 'Be on your way and keep your money—we're Baptists, too.'"[126]

JESSE BAKER'S AMAZING ACCOMPLISHMENT

Miraculously, by May 1870, Baker had achieved the goal of raising the money needed to pay off the school's debt. He returned to Mossy Creek in triumph, enabling the trustees to pay the school's creditors.[127] For the first time in its history, Mossy Creek Baptist College was free of debt! Great rejoicing ensued among the college community and beyond. Surely this was a time when Goodness reigned on campus—a significant element of Carson-Newman's later motto, "Truth, Beauty, and Goodness."

For the rest of 1870, Jesse Baker was able to assume the role of president and professor along with that of church pastor and family man. In his less than two years as president, about one hundred young men matriculated into the college. He held revivals at the church to great success, and many persons were converted. In one particular service about one hundred souls were saved, including some Mossy Creek College students, a cause for great rejoicing.[128]

Mossy Creek Baptist Church asked him to renew his yearly contract as their pastor, and Baker delayed doing so for several months. But at the end of 1870, he made the difficult decision to devote most of his time to preaching and resigned as president of the college. Of no other president can it be said so literally, "Jesse Baker's presidency was a wild ride!"

However, Jesse Baker's active association with Mossy Creek Baptist College did not end until his death in 1902. (W. T. Russell's remembrances of Baker, quoted in this chapter, were in fact part of Russell's eulogy for Baker in 1902.)[129] Beginning in 1871, Baker served as an officer

Jesse Baker, known as "the savior of Carson-Newman," president 1869–1870.

and an influential trustee for the rest of his life, continuing to use creative means to raise money for the school over the years. He taught as needed at the college on an adjunct basis. In 1882, Baker's alma mater granted him an honorary doctorate.[130]

As the pastor of nearby Mossy Creek Baptist Church, he had at least weekly contact with the college students, many of whom greatly admired him. John T. Henderson, a student in the early 1880s and future president of the college, later said he was a nominal Christian when he came to the school. He gave credit to Baker's sermons and testimonies for deepening his faith. By the time he graduated, he said, he strove to follow Jesus every day.[131]

To this day, Jesse Baker is called "the savior of Carson-Newman." His saddlebags, aged and worn in unparalleled service to his alma mater, are a prized possession of the university. The archives area of the library displays the beautiful Mossy Creek Baptist Church stained-glass window dedicated to Jesse Baker; but likely, comparatively few students see it. (The Baker Building on campus was not named for Jesse Baker, but for a later trustee chairman.) Only one visible reminder of him is close by; his tombstone stands behind Sarah Swann Hall in the old church cemetery.

MOSSY CREEK BAPTIST CHURCH IN THE EARLY 1870S

Giving up on restoring their war-ravaged building across Mossy Creek from the college campus, the church sold that property to a zinc-mining developer. Church representatives then purchased lots where Sarah Swann Hall now stands, intending to build their sanctuary and educational area there. However, the brick-making kiln installed there failed, as did repeated attempts to make good use of the land. Eventually this property too was sold, except for the church cemetery that was already in use. Today, the cemetery still spans the area behind Sarah Swann and Bertie Maples Butler Halls on the Carson-Newman campus.

But in 2020, a long-forgotten relic of Jesse Baker's past was discovered. When a dilapidated old house was slated to be torn down on Hillview Lane in Jefferson City, research led to indications that Jesse Baker had once lived on the property in a log cabin. Isaac M. Newman, one of Carson-Newman's founders, had given Baker the home in appreciation of his pastoral gifts.

Carson-Newman's archives assistant, Linda T. Gass, participated in the verification process and was present when a probe confirmed that the log cabin was still present under the home's façade. Property owner Nick Lakins generously donated the cabin to Carson-Newman; it was disassembled and transported to university-owned land off campus. Carson-Newman's leaders will make an announcement with more details about the log cabin's future when the time is right.[132]

Debt-Free Mossy Creek College Begins to Bloom

A LONG-OVERDUE PERIOD OF STABILITY: N. B. GOFORTH'S REPEAT PRESIDENCY (1870–1882)

After Baker's resignation, the trustees turned once again to Napoleon Bonaparte Goforth (1828–1907) to assume the presidency of Mossy Creek Baptist College. Goforth had been the president when the Civil War closed the school. After the war ended, he and his brother-in-law, William Albert Gallatin (W. A. G.) Brown, had led the Riceville Literary and Classical Institute near Cleveland, Tennessee.[133] (Goforth's and Brown's wives were sisters and Newman descendants.)[134] Goforth was still teaching at Riceville when Mossy Creek's trustees summoned him back. This time his presidency would be the longest in the history of the school thus far, over eleven years of steadfastness and growth. As an older man, he wanted to be a father figure to the young men of the college.

"Hundreds of young men, from all parts of East Tennessee and elsewhere, received mental and moral quickening from Dr. Goforth at Mossy Creek, and had their lives shaped by his molding touch. Under his influence, the mind of many a dull boy waked up and felt the thrill of a new life. He was not only a successful teacher but a great moral force in the school. As a disciplinarian, he had few equals. The observance of a few reasonable rules and a moral purpose to study and to get an education was emphasized as the law of the school and the 'whole duty' of the student. If the moral purpose was found wanting, the student was not wanted in the school, and was sent home, or elsewhere, till he came to a better mind."[135]

HOW THE CARSON-NEWMAN ALUMNI ASSOCIATION WAS FORMED

In the early 1870s, for colleges to have alumni organizations was a new idea. The alumni association of Mossy Creek Baptist College was initiated in 1871, thanks to the thoughtful influence of Professor W. T. Russell. Russell's suggestion was approved by Jesse Baker in the latter's new capacity as secretary of the trustees.

Russell later wrote, "During the year 1871, I had just visited several schools and colleges, and from an alumnus of one of the old eastern colleges, learned something of their alumni association. It then occurred to me that it would be wise and feasible to organize the graduates of the

College. I came back and laid the matter before Dr. Baker. After thinking the matter over for a day, he said, 'I like the suggestion.' He wrote letters all during that year and got together as many of the old graduates as possible and the association was formed."[136]

The first alumni association meeting was probably held the following June at commencement. For years, the meeting became a regular feature of the commencement program, with an alumni address presented by a prominent graduate.

ALUMNI THEN AND NOW

In the 1877–1878 Mossy Creek Baptist College catalogue—the first to publish the names of alumni—the total number of Mossy Creek College graduates since 1855 was sixty-eight. Today, Carson-Newman's Alumni Relations Office corresponds with over twenty thousand graduates.

A GLIMPSE INTO COLLEGE LIFE IN THE MID-1870S

Few records of Mossy Creek Baptist College in the early 1870s have survived. Gradually, as funds became available, the campus was improved and Newman Dormitories #1 and #2 were restored.

An anonymous alumnus and observer at the 1874 commencement praised the quality of education evident in the June exercises. "Professor Goforth's ability as a linguist, and the facility and thoroughness with which he imparts of knowledge of the Latin and Greek tongues, are well known. . . . Professor Russell is a young man, yet very far in advance of many of riper years, in scholarship and method of teaching." The commencement speaker, a pastor in Knoxville, "awakened in the memory of the student of Grecian history, panoramic visions of Academic Groves, with the magisterial figure of Plato in the foreground." And a stimulating debate took place between members of the Columbian and Philomathean Literary Societies on the subject "Ought Education to Be Compulsory?"[137]

The Mossy Creek Baptist College catalogue of 1875–1876 reveals that semesters were still twenty weeks long. Tuition per five-month term was $15-$20 for the college and $10-$13 for the primary and preparatory schools.[138]

The college curriculum was still similar to that of 1858–1859, the last previous extant catalogue.

College students in 1875–1876 were encouraged to live in the dormitories on campus, where they could furnish and prepare their own meals for about $1.50 per week. Room rent was $2 per year. By comparison, meals furnished by a steward cost about $6.50 per month. Boarding with families would cost $9-$10 per month.[139]

Ministerial students who came highly recommended by their churches would receive a deduction of one-third of their tuition, a gift from the faculty.[140] Churches and associations were urged to assist them further. Previously such young men had received their tuition free.

Interestingly, by this time, the college offered both Bachelor of Arts (AB) and Master of Arts (AM) degrees. The AB candidates were required to pass an examination over their college curriculum to the satisfaction of the faculty and to prepare and deliver an original oration or essay. The AM degree was conferred on students who had achieved the AB and who could supply evidence that they had maintained a good moral character and pursued literary studies for at least two years.[141]

The faculty expected the students to be serious about learning, with the young men evidencing their determination to make study their business. Further, faculty members required each student to be consistent in displaying "the manhood necessary" to obey all rules relating to his conduct.[142]

The professors consisted of President Goforth, teaching ancient languages and moral science; W. T. Russell, teaching mathematics and mechanical philosophy; and J. J. (John Jefferson) Huff, Class of 1873, teaching English language and natural sciences. D. H. Cooper, a recent graduate, was the principal of the Preparatory Department, where college students were also used as tutors.[143] There were forty college students and 124 in the Preparatory-Primary Department, including forty-eight in the first and second classes.[144] All of the younger students were from the immediate area, not boarding students.

At this time, commencement was a five-day event in early June, starting on Sunday and ending on Thursday. On Sunday, the baccalaureate sermon was delivered, and apparently examinations were conducted on Monday. The all-alumni reunion was held on Tuesday. On Wednesday, the annual alumni address was given, and the meeting of the trustees took place.

Faculty for the 1881–1882 school year. *Seated left*, N. B. Goforth, president 1859–1862, 1870–1882; *right*, W. T. Russell, math professor. *Standing*, Shelby E. Jones, Latin and Greek professor, and J. J. Huff, English professor.

A popular event of Wednesday evening was the public debate held by the two literary societies. Formal commencement activities took place on Thursday, including the annual literary address by the valedictorian.[145]

THE BIG NEWS: A DIFFERENT CAMPUS

The most significant announcement in the 1875–1876 catalogue was the purchase of a new campus, which would officially transfer to the college's ownership in 1876. Wealthy real-estate agent A. J. Mountcastle had offered to sell his estate to the college.[146] It consisted of thirty-five acres with a beautiful Italianate brick mansion suitable for a classroom and administration building and was within easy walking distance of the creekside campus. Also on the grounds were a large barn, said to have a seating capacity of seven hundred, and four two-room houses.[147]

COMMENCEMENT DAYS IN MOSSY CREEK

Commencement was an exciting time for the town as well as the college, with many guests pouring into town for the big event. The local hotels enjoyed an economic resurgence. Most out-of-towners would have arrived by train at the Mossy Creek depot, and the livery stable had hacks for hire. Many area residents would be waiting to greet relatives or friends returning for the event. Just about everyone in town celebrated the success of another year at the college.[148]

About a year before, at the 1874 commencement, the gathered alumni had asked the trustees to take active steps toward erecting a new college building. These alumni, united in purpose, pledged to support a financial agent to raise $30,000 toward such an endeavor. Apparently they were not satisfied with the status quo and "dreamed big" for their school. I. B. (Isaac Barton) Kimbrough was employed as the financial agent to secure the money.[149]

When Kimbrough had raised $16,000 or more (detailed records were lost in a 1916 fire), plans changed because of a fortuitous circumstance.[150] Now the college had the opportunity to buy the Mountcastle estate for $13,462 instead of constructing a new building.[151]

President Goforth commented in the 1876–1877 catalogue: "We now occupy a building of which we are truly proud—a building that will not suffer when compared with the best in the State. It is situated rather more than one-fourth of a mile south of the village of Mossy Creek, close enough to be of easy access from the depot, and sufficiently retired to be free from the noise and other disturbances of the town. Standing on the summit of a gently sloping eminence, it commands a magnificent view of the surrounding country."[152]

The "old College," the original classroom building, would be used for the preparatory students, and the dormitories would accommodate those who needed inexpensive housing.[153] Now the original ten-acre campus would be termed Campus #1. The new Mountcastle property became Campus #2.

The trustees planned to sell fifty lots from the thirty-five acres of Campus #2.[154] A. J. Mountcastle had already promised to sell lots to President Goforth and I. B. Kimbrough, and he specified in the deed that he wanted the college to honor those promises. Lots were also sold immediately to J. J. Huff and the Mossy Creek Baptist Church.

THE LOCATION AND ADVANTAGES OF CAMPUS #2

The exact boundaries of the Mountcastle thirty-five-acre campus are hard to discern now. "This property extended from Russell Avenue eastward as far as Odell Avenue and was three or more blocks deep. In front of the college building the property extended northward to Ellis Street."[155] The mansion was situated where present-day Burger King and Taco Bell lie between Highway 11 East and East Jefferson Street. Its front entrance faced toward the current campus, away from 11-E.

The acreage encompassed the opposite side of present-day Highway 11 East; Mossy Creek Baptist Church built and occupied the current George Street Methodist Church until 1907. For years, the new church would be used for college commencements and other special occasions—"college in the church" again, as in the first year of the college's life, instead of "church in the college" as in the years just past.

The 1876–1877 catalogue contained a plea for money or donations of suitable books for the library as well as classroom and laboratory supplies.[156] Yet the present state of the college was a great achievement. From a campus that was in the hands of a receiver in 1866 and threatened with loss again in 1869, in 1876 there were two campuses—one of ten acres, one of thirty-five, almost but not quite adjoining. A boardwalk (planks laid side by side) connected them.

And Dr. Goforth stated the goals of the college with faith and hope: "This institution looks to the highest possible grade of intellectual and Christian culture of all its pupils. It hopes to contribute much to the welfare of this beautiful country, and especially to assist in lifting up the hosts of Baptists of Tennessee and the surrounding States to that degree of intelligence so preeminently worthy [of] a great people. The struggle has been long and hard, but the morning light has broken in and the present betokens that the hopes of the most sanguine friends of the College will be fully realized."[157]

THE 1879 MOSSY CREEK COMMENCEMENT

To the Editor of the *Morristown Gazette:*
"The commencement exercises were unusually interesting. . . . On Monday several essays were read, which reflected credit on their authors. Tuesday night came the junior orations, and Wednesday the Alumni address by Rev. J. J. Burnett of Winchester. The address was well prepared and the delivery earnest and forcible. At night was the public debate . . . and the next morning being Thursday and the closing day, the crowd had reached its maximum. The whole of the college hill seemed to be alive."[158]

MOSSY CREEK BAPTIST COLLEGE BECOMES CARSON COLLEGE

As the 1879–1880 school year began, a big change took place. Mossy Creek Baptist College was renamed Carson College in honor of James Harvey Carson, one of its most faithful benefactors and a long-standing trustee. The college mansion then became known as Carson Hall.

Harvey Carson, as he was known to distinguish himself from his first cousin, James Carson, was a lawyer in Dandridge who was one of the original twenty-one trustees of Mossy Creek Baptist Seminary in 1851. Very active in the Dandridge Baptist Church, he was the only lawyer connected with the East Tennessee Baptist Education Society and doubtless wrote all of their legal documents. He also served in the Tennessee House of Representatives and in the state Senate.[159]

Harvey Carson seemed to take to heart the cause of ministerial education. Over the years, he continued to serve the college as a trustee and

Carson Hall, formerly the Mountcastle mansion.

as one of its primary promoters and benefactors. The 1879 name change recognized Carson's longtime service and valuable aid. In 1880 when he died, Carson College received $17,000 from his estate—an utterly amazing gift.[160] Soon afterward a few other faithful friends willed their estates to Carson College, raising the endowment to an astounding $20,000.

CONTEXT: 1880 EVENTS IN WORLD HISTORY

Rutherford B. Hayes was the nineteenth president of the United States, with James A. Garfield elected as the next president. The United States population was 50,155,783. The Salvation Army was formed in London, and work began on building the Panama Canal. Auguste Rodin was commissioned to sculpt the doorway "The Gates of Hell." Meanwhile, John Philip Sousa was named the director of the US Marine Corps Band, and Dr. Emily Stowe became the first woman licensed to practice medicine in Canada.

James Harvey Carson, for whom Carson College was named.

Trends Toward Educating Women Take Hold

As Carson College was gaining stability, even little Mossy Creek, Tennessee, was aware that the world of education was changing in a major way. Opportunities were opening up for young women to be educated, a trend that was slowly but steadily growing across the United States. Some did not see why women needed an education. But many others came to understand how American society would benefit from the intelligent involvement of women—among them the faculty and trustees of Carson College.

A LOOK BACK: THE FIRST SCHOOL FOR FEMALES IN MOSSY CREEK

About the time Dr. Goforth left Riceville to return to Mossy Creek in late 1870, W. A. G. Brown left Riceville as well. He had accepted a position as a mathematics teacher at Mary Sharp College in Winchester,

Tennessee. It was the premier regional Baptist college for young women of its day, famed for its rigorous standards and nicknamed "the Vassar of the South."[161] Soon, Brown would bring his experience and influence back to Mossy Creek.

W. A. G. BROWN, MOSSY CREEK COLLEGE CLASS OF 1857

The background of W. A. G. Brown provides the only known later association with Oak Tree Five member Nelson Bowen, who moved to Hendersonville, North Carolina, in 1854. The two men must have been friends. For a number of years, Brown moved back and forth between East Tennessee and North Carolina. In Hendersonville, he and Bowen worked together to publish Baptist newspapers and were both on the staff of Judson Female College.[162] Brown was also acknowledged as the first president of Mars Hill Baptist College in North Carolina.[163] He moved back to Mossy Creek in 1873 to teach, the first of several educational posts he would hold in the area, before returning permanently to North Carolina.[164]

After the Civil War's devastation had lifted somewhat, Mossy Creek residents began to consider the needs of their town. The Masons of Chapter No. 353 decided to build a lodge hall and school on four town lots John Roper Branner donated to them for educational purposes in 1868.[165] (The two-story building still stands at the corner of Branner Street and the Old Andrew Johnson Highway, the latter the former stagecoach road. Popularly called "The Old Town Hall," the building has been used for many purposes over the years.)

Many Tennessee residents were waking up to the advantages of educating girls and young women as well as men. In general, as with the long process to launch Mossy Creek Baptist College in 1851, acceptance of this idea was slower to develop in East Tennessee. Area Baptists were not yet interested in women's education. But secular groups such as the Masons led the way in adopting education for both girls and boys as their primary project, and their success proved that the time was right.

In all likelihood, considering his career in construction, William Cate

Newman was a Mason. Tradition holds that when the Mossy Creek Masons decided to house a school for females in their lodge building, "Uncle Billy" Newman and his extended family helped pave the way for its establishment. As one of Mossy Creek College's founders, he was gratified that the men's college was achieving its purpose of graduating a more educated citizenry and brotherhood of ministers. Now he was ready to support a different venture in area education.

By 1871, this first of the two forerunners of Newman College (the subsequent women's college that provided the "Newman" part of Carson-Newman's name) was underway. Classes were held in three departments: primary, intermediate, and high school. Little is known about their curriculum.

By the fall of 1873, the principal of the Masonic Female Institute was W. A. G. Brown; Dr. Goforth had probably recommended him for the position. Brown, who had a staff of three female teachers, was engaged for an indefinite period of years to lead the Masonic Female Institute. He elevated the quality of the education the young ladies received, cultivating their minds beyond the usual standard of rote memorization.[166] He taught them several levels of mathematics—arithmetic, algebra, and geometry—in addition to the previous, more domestic curriculum. Even the musical class offerings were of a higher quality.

WONDERS WILL NEVER CEASE: NOT JUST ONE SCHOOL FOR WOMEN, BUT TWO

In the fall of 1876, a new school for young women was introduced in Mossy Creek.[167] Called the Branner Institute, it was a boarding and finishing school that operated in the large Victorian mansion built by John Roper Branner a short distance from the Masonic lodge. (A later owner, Milton Preston Jarnagin, renamed the Branner house the Glenmore Mansion; it still stands.)[168] The Branner Institute, the second of the two forerunners of Newman College, was more exclusive and expensive than its competitor, the Masonic school.

Although the wealthier area residents held the Branner Institute in high esteem for their daughters, it lasted only until 1879. Joseph Branner, its leader, moved to Asheville and was unable to find anyone to continue the school.[169] At some point, apparently the Masonic school merged with the Branner Institute. (No related public documents have survived.)

W. A. G. Brown briefly became the head of the combined school, which retained the Branner Institute name for the following year. But no one seemed quite sure how the merged women's school should proceed.

EDUCATION FOR WOMEN "ORNAMENTAL NO LONGER"

By 1881, East Tennessee Baptists were fully engaged in providing quality, rigorous higher education to women as well as to men. That year, the women's college awarded its first three degrees. The recipients were Rhoda Long, who moved to Russellville, Texas, afterward; Tennessee "Tennie" Williams, who later married Carson College student Dudley F. Brown and lived in Kingsport; and her sister, Ella Williams (later the wife of Jesse Taylor Pope, also a Carson College student; they eventually moved to Butler, Tennessee). Ella taught French, German, and English literature at Newman College.[170] The three received MA degrees—Mistress of Arts—as women could not be considered bachelors! The issuing school name that appeared on those three diplomas might have been Carson College, although that is not certain.[171]

By this time, many area Baptists were ready to see the advantages of educating women as well as men. Naturally, the uncertain future of the combined women's school presented an opportunity for them to offer education to all. The 1877–1878 Mossy Creek Baptist College catalogue carried an advertisement for the final year of the Branner Institute, with "charges greatly reduced."[172] Perhaps the women's school was already under the management of the Baptists, albeit still located at the Branner Mansion.

In 1879, W. A. G. Brown moved back to North Carolina to become the president of Judson Female College.[173] Probably his indefinite contract in Mossy Creek had run its course. President Goforth and his faculty then solidified their plans to run the female school as well as the men's school, accommodating parents who wished to educate their sons and daughters in close proximity. The faculty would also upgrade the curriculum offerings for young women, who would now have access to college-level courses and much more rigorous classes.

The 1879–1880 Carson College catalogue carried an ad for "The School for Females" under the management of the college faculty. Technically, it was not a part of Carson College, although the ad was attributed to Dr. Goforth. Professor S. N. (Samuel) Newman, an 1874 graduate of Mossy Creek Baptist College, led the female school with a "competent corps of teachers" for primary and preparatory students. (Later he would teach at the women's college named for his family.)[174]

For female college students, the rate of tuition was the same as Carson College students. Music lessons were optional at a higher rate of tuition, with a piano furnished. The female school was now held at the Masonic Hall and probably operated under the Masonic school charter.[175]

The Times, They Were A-Changin'

Once the women's college had successfully graduated three studious young women of merit, there was no stopping the educational potential of either gender in Mossy Creek. Plans to launch an official, yet-to-be-named East Tennessee Baptist women's college in the town were underway by the time the ink dried on the three women's diplomas.

TRUTH, BEAUTY, AND GOODNESS

Sadly, today the specific origin of Carson-Newman's longtime motto is unknown. Mid-twentieth-century college president Harley Fite stated: "Since before 1900 the College motto has been TRUTH, BEAUTY, AND GOODNESS; but no explanation or elaboration had been printed."[176] But the 1881–1882 Carson College catalogue provides an intriguing clue about when the seed for the motto may have been planted.

A senior English course taught in the spring of 1882, probably by J. J. Huff, explored a French philosophy of life developed by Victor Cousin. A revised edition of his work was published in France in 1854 and later translated into English.[177] It was entitled "The True, the Beautiful, and the Good."

The thrust of Cousin's philosophy is that an individual's life has the greatest meaning and makes the highest contributions to the world when one is self-governed by the principles of Truth, Beauty, and Goodness. Countless Carson-Newman students over the generations have been inspired by the school's motto.

At the same time, a transition of leadership was about to occur at the well-established Carson College for men. Spring 1882 proved to be Dr. Goforth's last semester there. He returned to Riceville and lived there the rest of his life, preaching and spending another twenty years teaching at the Riceville Literary and Classical Institute.[178] Like Jesse Baker, however, he served the college on the Board of trustees for years to come.

Decisions, Decisions—and All of Them Major

By 1882, Carson College faculty and trustees were ready to formalize the women's college they had been supervising. For several reasons, the time seemed ripe for such a venture. But where could it be located with adequate facilities and safe lodgings for the young ladies? This question was deemed so important that the trustees invited a visiting panel of twenty regional Baptist pastors and laymen to Mossy Creek to help them make the best decisions. Future president W. A. Montgomery from Chattanooga was among those invited.[179]

The trustees and visitors toured Campus #1, which housed the college's Primary and Preparatory Departments, as well as the Masonic Lodge and the Branner Mansion. Two of the possible sites soon became unavailable. Mossy Creek citizens were pushing for a truly public school for their children; a public school had not existed there before. The only suitable place in town for such a school was the Masonic Lodge, which reopened in the fall for this purpose. And the Branner Institute mansion was sold as a private residence. Apparently there were no other sites to consider.

With the opening of the public school, the children of Carson College's Primary Department were transferred there. That solved half of the problem in locating the women's college at Campus #1. Now no student would be received at Carson College who could not enter either the preparatory or collegiate course. The preparatory students were moved from the creekside location, too; perhaps the large barn on the Carson Hall campus became their new classroom "home." Now without any impediments, the final decision was made to use the original Campus #1 for educating women. The Newman Dormitories would house women instead of men.

Trustees were also named for the women's college that would later be called Newman College. For the 1882–1883 school year, the trustees had other important choices to make: they needed new presidents for both the women's school and for Carson College.

The Newman Dormitories in 1882, home to young women. The building at left is probably a storage facility. The middle building is Dormitory #1, and on the right is Dormitory #2.

CARSON COLLEGE LEADER:
B. G. MANARD, SEVENTH PRESIDENT (1882)

B. G. (Birdwell Gibson) Manard (1837–1899) was the trustees' choice as the next president of Carson College. "Bird," as his friends called him, a Jefferson County native, had attended Mossy Creek Baptist College in the early 1860s before the school closed in 1862.[180] After the Civil War, he graduated from the University of Virginia and chose to become a minister and educator.[181]

Moving to Bristol in 1871, Manard (pronounced Maynard) became the pastor of Goodson Baptist Church and also headed the school associated with the church. "Bird" upgraded the school to a college for women, which was eventually incorporated as the Bristol Female College. (The Bristol college lasted until 1904 and did quality work.[182]) In 1873, Mossy Creek Baptist College awarded Manard an honorary DD in recognition of his excellent work in the educational field.[183]

Having successfully launched the college for women in Bristol, B. G. accepted pastorates elsewhere. He was in Tazewell when the trustees tapped him to lead Carson College. Doubtless his previous familiarity with a women's college was one factor in the trustees' choice. He moved to Mossy Creek in August but his wife did not, remaining in her hometown of Tazewell. Perhaps this was because Manard was to be gone much of the fall term; he had decided to serve as his own financial agent. Both he and his wife did, however, move their letters to Mossy Creek Baptist Church.[184]

Not committing to purchase a home in Mossy Creek, B. G. boarded with a local relative, Gideon Cate.[185] Manard taught literature and metaphysics (philosophy) while serving as president and financial agent. S. W. (Samuel Watson) Tindell, a new and well-qualified faculty member, was charged with teaching ancient and modern languages. The young men were delighted with him.[186] Another new professor, S. E. (Shelby Elliott) Jones from the Mossy Creek College Class of 1877, was to teach mathematics, and J. J. Huff would continue his role as the English and science professor.[187]

MOSSY CREEK FEMALE SEMINARY/NEWMAN COLLEGE LEADER: W. T. RUSSELL, EIGHTH PRESIDENT (1882–1889)

Professor William Thomas Russell, the namesake of his uncle who was one of Carson-Newman's first graduates, was placed in charge of the new women's school, becoming the first and only president of Newman College. He immediately oversaw improvements to the campus suitable for young ladies and contracted with a local homeowner to run a boarding house for them, or they could have rooms to themselves in the Newman Dormitories. W. T. Russell (1848–1919) was a known and respected quantity as a trustee, one of five supervisors of the ministerial fund, a mathematics professor, a church layman, and a born administrator.

By 1882, Professor Russell's interest in women's education was evident. He had assumed leadership positions in the last years of the Masonic and Branner Institutes. After Newman College merged with Carson College in 1889, he served as vice-president of the coed school for several years, continuing thereafter as a college trustee and business manager in various capacities. He also took in his orphaned niece, Tennessee Hoskins, and oversaw her education; she graduated from Carson and Newman in 1905. Later, Russell's own daughter and son graduated from the college.

Pursuing second and third careers as the director of the Mossy Creek Bank and as a civic leader, W. T. Russell became the first mayor of Jefferson City in 1901 when it was formed from Mossy Creek, Carsonville, and Frame Addition.[188] He and his wife and children lived in a lovely home on the property where Bertie Maples Butler Hall is now located. This house later became the first official president's home for Carson and Newman College.

Long after Russell's death in 1919, an unfortunate shadow fell on his legacy. Presumably because his presidency was of a women's institution, Newman College—one-half of today's Carson-Newman University—he was deemed unworthy of being pictured and described in the gallery of presidents in today's university's library.[189] Even interim presidents who never became fulltime presidents were pictured there until very recently.

Yet Russell had overseen the management of Mossy Creek Baptist College as a young man while Jesse Baker was away fundraising and had served the college in other important capacities for many years. The main street on which the campus is located is named for him. This outstanding educator's lifetime achievements, character, and devotion would compare favorably with those of any Carson-Newman president.

Newman College by Any Other Name

Rather like an infant who goes unnamed for a long time and is called simply "Baby," the women's college proceeded for years without an official name except "the Seminary." In the summer of 1882, W. T. Russell and S. N. Newman published a one-page leaflet to announce the opening of a "Seminary for Young Ladies" in Mossy Creek, Tennessee: "Feeling the necessity of increased facilities for female education, the trustees of Carson College have set apart the old college property to be used exclusively for a female school."[190]

Carson College trustees took the significant step of officially deeding Campus #1 to the Seminary. Curriculum standards for the young ladies were to match those at Mary Sharp College in Winchester, a high-quality Baptist female college, as much as possible. Tuition was about the same as that for Carson College.

Beginning in 1882, among the students and local residents, the two Mossy Creek schools were called "the College" and "the Seminary." It would be 1885 before the women's college was chartered as the Mossy Creek Female Seminary and Academy (the latter because the Seminary continued to offer primary and secondary education for girls).[191] In the meantime, local residents knew that the primary financial supporters and promoters of the women's school were the Newman family members.

William Cate Newman and Samuel Irwin Newman of the Oak Tree

Five were still living. They had constructed the original three buildings on Campus #1 and later helped to renovate them for the women's college. J. N. (Jonathan Nelson) Newman (1813–1898), the younger brother of William and Isaac Newman and a well-to-do farmer, gave strong financial support for the Seminary.[192] Rachel Murrin Newman and her husband, John C. Newman, also supported the new women's school, likely in memory of their young daughter, Ida.[193]

The name Newman College was probably in casual, local use before the Seminary's official name was changed to Newman Female College. Soon "Female" would be dropped, and by 1886 the young ladies were glad to tell family and friends that they attended Newman College.

Side-by-Side Colleges

Both colleges opened on Thursday, August 24, 1882, one established thirty-one years before and the other brand-new. Their curricula were to be almost identical. For the young ladies of the Seminary, a course in calisthenics was required. For language study, they had their choice of learning Greek, French, or German. They had optional courses in art, drawing, music, and "wax work, hair work, zephyr, and embroidery."[194]

The young men of Carson College were delighted with their sister students. The Philomathean and Columbian Literary Societies began publishing a monthly school newsletter, *The Carson Index*, from which a few charming issues survive (September 1882–April 1884). They offer a revealing student perspective for the time period on both campuses. The contents are by turns enthralling, hilarious, heartbreaking, academic, and personal. The student editors were John T. Henderson, a senior and a future president of the college, and Edmund Cody Burnett, future professor and librarian, who promised their inaugural readers a "chaste, dignified, educational journal."[195]

According to the first issue of *The Carson Index* (September 15, 1882), Manard's presidency began well. The young men liked him and appreciated the improvements he made to the campus.[196] However, they were less impressed with his recommended restrictions: "Prof. B. G. Manard advises us to observe the laws of hygiene in the species and amount of food we consume, as our ability to study depends very much upon the state of our physical constitution. We fear this will require more self-denial than many of us profess."[197]

The student editors and others wrote lofty academic editorials and articles in *The Carson Index* but obviously kept a close watch on the new inhabitants of Campus #1: "All the buildings have been repaired and newly repainted. Indeed the spade, the joiner's planes, and the brush have converted this into a place of charming beauty. It is also a place of interest, filling up, as it is, with intelligent young ladies."[198] The young men lost no time in making the acquaintance of the female students.

The joy of the new school year's opening was soon blighted. J. J. Huff, the beloved and effective English and science professor, was sick, staying at his father's home in Big Creek (later Del Rio). A week later he died of "fever," possibly typhoid fever. Huff's colleague S. E. Jones wrote a moving eulogy for his fellow professor in *The Carson Index.* Student J. H. Bloom, recording secretary of the Philomatheans, wrote the thoughtful resolutions of sympathy for all mourning Professor Huff.[199]

PESTILENCES IN THE 1880S

Close to the turn of the nineteenth century, infectious diseases were the most serious threat to an individual's health and well-being. With no vaccines and few effective medical remedies available, when disease struck, everyone in the patient's circle of acquaintance had cause for concern. The most common life-threatening diseases at this time were typhoid fever, pneumonia, influenza, whooping cough, diphtheria, measles, chicken pox, malaria, cholera, tuberculosis, and smallpox.

Despite their sorrow, the young men were irresistibly drawn to their sister students. Given that the collegiate women were required to wear clothing of navy blue flannel every day except Sunday, the Carson College students observed in the October 15 issue of *The Carson Index:* "When the young ladies of the Seminary collect into one company upon Sabbath morning, robed in various and splendid colors, and begin their line of march to the church, they form a very attractive procession. The young men of Carson declare that Switzerland, with its delightful and picturesque scenery, could not so charm the eye."[200]

Within *The Carson Index,* such lighthearted topics kept company with more somber articles. J. H. Bloom wrote an essay on "The Ruins of Time," ending with: "Though death will terminate our earthly existence, and our bodies will fall victim to the destroying road of time, let us endeavor to so live that we may have a happy home after death among the redeemed and blessed on the bright eternal shore."[201] No doubt these spiritual sentiments were applauded by the faculty.

Shockingly, the November 15 issue of *The Carson Index* carried the news that J. H. Bloom had died. He had gone home, feeling unwell but expecting to return in a few days. Carson College students unexpectedly came face to face with the fragility of life for one of their own: "But a few mornings before, he had occupied a seat, as one of our number, vigorous in both mind and body, and having bright anticipations for a life of happiness and usefulness. To-day he is in the great eternity of God—all his and his friends' fond hopes are blasted."[202]

Shortly thereafter, the students received word of the death of another friend in Sevier County. We do not know what specific maladies caused the death of these two young men, but their loss was felt deeply and contributed to a sense of unease about the various illnesses spreading through East Tennessee at the time.

CHAPEL

Surprisingly, there is no mention of chapel in any college catalogue until the 1882–1883 issue. In the same time frame, *The Carson Index* indicates that during chapel President Manard received word of J. H. Bloom's death and announced the sad news to the students. On happier occasions, Carson College scholars liked having joint chapel with the Seminary, as they did on Saturday, November 18, when President Manard spoke entertainingly on "Success in Life."[203]

THE AREA EXPERIENCES A POPULATION BOOM

Carsonville, where Campus #2 was located, was growing, as was the more established town of Mossy Creek. New and interesting faces were seen every week as students and families took advantage of the educational opportunities provided by the College and the Seminary: "G. W. Lee has made definite arrangements to move his family to Mossy Creek for the purpose of educating his children. The facilities afforded by Carson College and the Seminary are bound to attract patronage."[204] Perhaps Mr. Lee bought one of the fifty lots the college was selling from the Mountcastle estate.

Many families in town boarded young out-of-town relatives or friends due to a housing and boarding shortage. For example, both W. T. Russell and S. W. Tindell had students living in their homes.[205] According to *The Carson Index:* "Mr. Ellis is erecting a handsome and substantial residence, with which he can accommodate quite a number of boarders. Others have purchased lots, and talk of building soon. Hope the good work may continue, as facilities for board are very much needed."[206]

Another *Carson Index* item on this topic provides a smile along with a wince. "Rev. W. D. McPhetridge has moved his family into our town and will patronize the schools, not only by sending his sons and daughters, but will become a student himself. He is studying for the ministry. Never too old to learn."[207]

Established businesses were growing and new ones were opening. Some in the area catered to the interest of the young men and women in each other, with packs of "courting cards" advertised for twenty-five cents.[208] Naturally, however, any encounters between men and women students were overseen by the watchful eyes of matrons and faculty members and limited to the standards of what was strictly proper.

By the time the December 15 issue of *The Carson Index* was published, hyperbole and high spirits were once again in evidence in Mossy Creek. The editors bemoaned a snow on November 24 that had reached "six feet and two inches deep" and was "a great inconvenience to the young ladies."[209] But yet another tragedy was looming.

Danger! Smallpox Infiltrates Mossy Creek

A case of smallpox was diagnosed in Mossy Creek about the third week of December, shortly before the students were to depart for the Christmas holidays. By early January, there were sixteen cases and two deaths in and around Mossy Creek. Two more cases were diagnosed later in the month. Residents of Mossy Creek sprang into action to take all possible precautions; as a result, the outbreak was limited. Yet, of course, the human toll was keenly felt and the outbreak was judged a terrible plague.[210]

Fortunately, no deaths from smallpox or even cases of smallpox in either the Seminary or the College were reported. However, Carson College did suffer great losses. Both President Manard and Professor Jones resigned in late December. Jones returned the following year, but Manard was gone for good. Apparently a number of students went home for the holidays but did not return; others who were about to register canceled their plans. Student enrollment plunged for the spring semester.

The reasons for Manard's abrupt departure are unclear. His leaving has been attributed solely to fear of smallpox and cowardice by at least one college historian.[211] In any case, fear of a deadly infectious disease is not an unreasonable response. Manard's wife may already have been unwilling to move to Mossy Creek for some reason, and the fact that he did not purchase a home there may indicate that he never intended to stay long. Perhaps he longed to return to the ministry.

Manard and his wife moved to Plattsburg, Missouri, in January 1883, where he became pastor of the local Baptist church.[212] Afterward he served a number of churches as pastor and became a trustee of other Baptist schools. He wrote prolifically for various Baptist newspapers and was generally well regarded.[213] However, his reputation suffered in his native East Tennessee because Carson College and the community felt he had betrayed their trust and confidence in him.

In the final issue of the school year, *The Carson Index* staff recounted the losses they had suffered in recent months. They wrote poignantly:

> The year just closed has been a trying ordeal in the history of Carson College. It has been one fruitful of misfortunes, which, at one time, seemed to threaten complete destruction. A dreadful pestilence with impartial and destructive hand entered into our vicinity. . . . The institution suffered an irreparable loss in the death of Prof. J. J. Huff. His untiring energy, unlimited popularity, and effective labor rendered him one of the main pillars in the framework of the college. . . . Two of the Professors, including the President, tendered their resignations and retired to other and more promising fields.[214]

At the end of 1883, Carson College students were deeply disheartened over experiencing so many significant losses. Thankfully, a strong and capable leader would rise and redeem the broken spirits of the young men, bringing positive changes and giving them renewed optimism. At the same time, Newman College was growing and reaping the benefits provided by a sound, progressive leader who was a man of character and influence. Within a few years, new considerations would propel both Carson and Newman to commit to a form of education heretofore untried in Mossy Creek. For both schools, the best way forward would be together.

CHAPTER FOUR

Coexistence, Then Confluence

1883–1892

"The two streams meet precisely as two roads. . . . The one flow does not end in the other, but continues in it, one with it, two clarities merged without a shadow. . . . Here is the work of the world going on. The creation is felt, alive and intent on its materials, in such places."
—Wendell Berry[215]

To everyone's relief, the dark cloud of fear and anxiety over Mossy Creek began to disperse in early 1883 with the end of the smallpox threat. The Seminary was largely untouched. But the crisis had left Carson College in a weakened state. With a considerably smaller student population than expected and no president, the school's stability was in question.

Although B. G. Manard had abruptly resigned in December, the trustees chose not to name a new president right away. They did select Professor S. W. Tindell as chairman of the faculty, a title akin to interim president. Although Tindell had been teaching ancient languages (Latin and Greek) at Carson for only one semester, his impressive credentials included having taught in two Tennessee schools and served three Tennessee Baptist churches as pastor.[216] In addition, he was well regarded by faculty and students alike. Now he also assumed the role of metaphysics professor that "Bird" Manard had filled.

For this semester, two outstanding Carson students filled the other faculty vacancies. Busy senior John T. Henderson served as the mathematics professor for the position vacated by Professor S. E. Jones and as the principal of the Preparatory Department. (Jones would return in the fall as professor of natural sciences and secretary/registrar.) Junior student S. H. Fletcher became the interim English instructor, replacing J. J. Huff, as well as the campus librarian.[217]

Carson College faculty and students in 1887, in front of Carson Hall. Samuel W. Tindell, president 1883–1888, is on the back row wearing a top hat. Pictured to his right is the young John T. Henderson, math professor, with mustache.

Professor Tindell's wisdom, purposeful energy, and goodwill proved to be the perfect antidote for Carson College's malaise. He was neither overly concerned by the smallpox scare nor hesitant to use his considerable organizational skills to shore up the flagging men's school. With the help of John Henderson, he began rounding up students and getting them back in school. Later in the semester, the trustees made Tindell's presidency official.

Broadening the Scope and Outcome of Education

A FRUITFUL PERIOD OF INNOVATIONS: SAMUEL WATSON TINDELL, NINTH PRESIDENT (1883–1888)

Although S. W. Tindell (1844–1939) had been born and raised in nearby Knox County, he had seen more of the outside world than had most Carson College faculty members. He apparently liked what he saw in the North while serving as an officer in the Union Army during the Civil

War. He was the first Carson president to receive degrees from above the Mason-Dixon line—Amherst College in Massachusetts, where he was president of the Class of 1871, receiving the AB that year and the AM in 1874. He was also the first Carson president with a theological degree, an earned MA from Newton Theological Seminary in Andover, Massachusetts.[218] In 1887, Carson College would confer an honorary DD on him.

One's character and interior life were as important to Professor Tindell as setting a high academic standard for studies. Under his influence, the aim of Carson College was "to fit young men for a higher sphere of usefulness by giving them information, well trained minds, polished manners, refined feelings and tastes, pure morals, and an exalted Christian character."[219]

S. W. TINDELL'S QUICK WIT

Professor Tindell did not lack a sense of humor, which no doubt partly accounted for the students' having liked him from the beginning. Apparently he took an understanding view of the Carson students' interest in the young ladies from the Seminary: "When Prof. T. asked J. H. S. to read his Latin sentence, he replied: 'Prof., I got a letter from—a friend this morning and didn't translate all the lesson.' 'A very good excuse indeed,' said Prof., 'but we hope she will write less often and not so much at a time hereafter.'"[220]

As chairman of the faculty, Dr. Tindell cast an evaluating eye over the resources and curriculum of Carson College and resolved to extend the school's offerings. He provided several "first-class journals from the leading colleges of the country" to the library, giving the students an intriguing glimpse of the outside educational world's standards and advantages."[221] According to the Carson College catalogue published in 1883: "There is a small but select Library for the use of students in addition to the libraries belonging to the two Literary Societies. During the present year a Reading Room has been fitted up and furnished with leading papers and magazines."[222]

One of Tindell's greatest long-term contributions to Carson College students lay in encouraging them to attend strong graduate schools, both within and outside the South. For the first time, Carson graduates began attending such notable schools as George Washington University, Southern Baptist Theological Seminary, the University of Louisville Medical College, Eastman Business College, Brown University, Newton Theological Seminary, and Yale University.

Tindell was not afraid to try new things at the college. Thankfully, he also was not reluctant to admit when his experiments failed. One year, he put Carson College and the preparatory school on the quarter system with three terms and allowed only two days for Christmas recess. This experiment lasted only one year before the semester system was reinstated and the Christmas break lasted a full week.

WELCOME ENRICHMENT OF THE CURRICULUM

The surviving catalogues of Dr. Tindell's years as president reveal the major organizational and academic changes he brought to the college. Under his leadership the first break from the strictly classical AB degree was made. Carson College began to offer a second degree, the BS, bachelor of science, for which German could be substituted for Latin. All AB candidates were still expected to study Greek and Latin, but French could be substituted for Latin in the second term of the junior year.[223]

The time frame required for granting an AM degree was lengthened. The Master of Arts would be conferred on graduates of *three* years' standing who had spent at least two years in professional studies.[224]

The new president instituted departments of learning, such as English literature, history, psychology, and moral philosophy, under which were noted the specific classes offered. Also, systematic theology was established as a department. Church history, homiletics, and biblical interpretation were new courses. President Tindell knew that not all young men called to the ministry would be able to attend a seminary, so he undertook to better equip such students for their future careers while they were undergraduates.[225]

Emphasizing the advantages of polishing the public speaking skills of Carson students, Tindell introduced rhetoric, elocution, and parliamentary practice as required courses.[226] He "preached" the necessity of being perceived as well spoken by others and how that perception could enhance the students' chances for success and good relationships in the future.

T. C. KARNS

A new name on the Carson College faculty list for 1883–1884 was that of T. C. (Thomas Conner) Karns—professor of modern languages and English literature, principal of the Normal Department, and treasurer.[227] In future years, he became the first Superintendent of Public Instruction for Knox County. He also wrote or contributed to several books about Tennessee and taught at the University of Tennessee, his alma mater.[228] The Karns area of Knox County and its high school were named for him.[229]

T. C. Karns continued to support Carson and Newman after his move back to Knoxville. In 1893–1894, he gave a gold medal for the best essay on debate prepared and read by a young woman student, doing so until medals were abolished.[230]

The term "physical culture," meaning health and wellness, appeared in the catalogue for the first time. A need for a gymnasium was expressed along with a hope that courses in regular and systematic exercise might someday lead to a distinct department in physical culture.[231]

Vocational courses were added for a two-year "Normal and Business Department." Teacher training (the Normal School) consisted of only two courses, normal methods and the science of education. But it was a start. Certificates rather than diplomas were given for this course work.[232]

Snapshots: How the Two Colleges Worked Together

1883 COMMENCEMENT PROGRAMS

The June 15, 1883, issue of *The Carson Index* was full of news about the events of Commencement Week, including rousing debates between the men's literary societies. The three Carson College graduates included brothers John T. and Robert A. Henderson, both of whom gave well-received orations. Of the former's address on "True Culture," the *Index* reported: "Mr. Henderson made a profound impression. His style was very lucid, simple, forcible, and unpretending, free from all 'sky-scraping'"(grandstanding).[233] John Henderson was asked to stay on at Carson as the mathematics professor. Within ten years he would be president.

Of perhaps even more interest in the *Index* is the glimpse into end-of-year "exercises" at the Seminary. No young ladies graduated at the end of this first year of the Seminary's "separate but equal" relationship with Carson College. But a presentation from the Seminary occupied the first hour of Carson's commencement celebration, with its leaders W. T. Russell and S. N. Newman speaking of the successes of its first year and a demonstration of the young ladies' prowess in their calisthenics class.[234] The young men of Carson College were awed by the young women's limber movements and healthful vigor.

On a separate occasion during Commencement Week, Mossy Creek Baptist Church was crowded with supporters who had come to witness the Seminarians' display of academics and learning. Nine young ladies and one female teacher were on the program. Three delivered orations or themes; four gave recitations; and two quoted literary soliloquies. Musical interludes were provided between these events, showcasing the talents of other Seminary students. The evening was a crowd-pleaser, and those present observed that the young ladies were receiving a strong education.[235]

THE NATIVE AMERICAN EXPERIMENT

By passing the misguided General Appropriations Act of 1870, the United States government provided funds for the education of Indian children in white schools. "The main objective of these schools was to remove children from family and tribal influences and to instill values and perspectives of white Americans. Parents were often coerced into sending their young children to boarding schools on the grounds that they would become better equipped to survive in the white man's world."[236]

Before the government began this educational interference, Cherokee children were taught by their families and their tribe, using a variety of teaching techniques that included storytelling and relating life experiences. But according to white America, Cherokees needed to be saved from their culture and civilization, learning to read and write in

English. Boarding schools were established to accomplish this purpose and other standard educational practices. Some religious-based boarding schools were also zealous about converting the Cherokee children to Christianity.[237]

For 1884 and 1885, both Carson College and the Seminary planned to conduct an experiment regarding group education of young Indian children from the Eastern Band of the Cherokee in North Carolina. The children chosen lived in remote areas where there was no way for them to get to a school. The names of the towns where they lived were Robbinsville, Ducktown, Murphy, Ogreeta, and Valley Town.[238] Representatives of both colleges signed a contract with the United States government for this trial program.

The contract specified that up to twenty boys and fifteen girls would participate in the program. There was a financial incentive for the colleges to educate Native Americans; the government was to pay $167 per child per year plus traveling expenses.[239] This amounted to an income of $3,340 for Carson College and $2,505 for the Seminary—a substantial amount when regular tuition for a year ranged from $18.75 for preparatory students to $30 for Carson College seniors.

In April 1884, twenty Cherokee boys and eight Cherokee girls came to live in Mossy Creek. Each child had a Native American name and an English name; a physician had certified that each one was physically and mentally sound. Ranging in age from eight to eighteen, they were placed in local homes, including President Tindell's and President Russell's, and expected to learn to speak English quickly.[240] They must have felt completely displaced, removed as they were from their families, villages, proud culture, and historic relationship with the land that sustained them.

The 1883–1884 Carson College catalogue stated, "The Commissioner of Indian Affairs has placed a number of Indian boys in the College at the expense of the Government. These are taught under the direction of the faculty, but they occupy a separate department. During the past year the Indians have done well, and the faculty have great hope of doing much for them."[241]

But in hindsight, to expect these students to adapt overnight to a strict regimen and discipline that could be difficult for regular students was an insurmountable challenge. Most of the Cherokee youth did not even understand, much less read or write, the English language at first. Some

Indian students evidently chose to go home, perhaps all the females; the 1884–1885 catalogue lists only eight male Cherokee students.[242]

One Sunday morning, faculty members went to collect the boys for church. None could be found, but someone had seen them heading in the direction of Mossy Creek. Indeed, the boys were discovered enjoying a carefree swim. Swiftly, they were sent back to their Mossy Creek homes in shame.[243]

Mandatory haircuts proved to be a point of contention for the boys too. The professors could have long beards on their chins; the Cherokee males wanted their long hair on their heads. When permission to grow their hair long was refused, all but one male Native American returned home. Before long, the remaining Cherokee student apparently departed for home.[244]

How long any of the students lived at Carson College and the Seminary is unclear, but likely none stayed even one year. Dr. Tindell stated without elaboration in the 1884–1885 Carson College catalogue, "The Indian Department has been suspended."[245] But the officials of both colleges learned a lot from the experiment. And midway through the twentieth century, other Native American students would voluntarily come to study at Carson-Newman. They had the qualifications for success in college, and most graduated and went on to have professional careers.

A Fascinating Look at Newman College's Culture

By the dawn of 1886, the Seminary was known to all as Newman College. Of the seven years of its independent existence, two catalogues have survived: 1886–1887 and 1887–1888. Excerpts from the latter catalogue reveal how Newman's academics and environment shaped the young ladies' experiences during their college years.

President W. T. Russell stated, "The purpose of this Institution is to fit young ladies for the higher spheres of usefulness, by developing in them symmetrical character and independent thought. No pains are spared to inculcate polished manners, refined feelings and tastes, pure morals and the highest type of Christian characters. . . . Elegance and correctness of expression are required as far as possible, even in conversation."[246]

An announcement was made that a new campus had been purchased for Newman College; the old buildings of Campus #1 would not suffice for the women students much longer. In the summer of 1887, President

Newman College faculty and students in the 1880s. W. T. Russell, president 1882–1889, is on the back row in front of the middle window.

Russell had bought thirteen acres for a new campus on a beautiful elevation, bounded by Russell, Branner, North College, and South College Streets. "The new property was ideal for the location of a college plant."[247] (These thirteen acres would form the nucleus of the current Carson-Newman campus—Campus #3.)

A WIDE-AWAKE FACULTY AND A RIGOROUS CURRICULUM

President Russell noted in the 1887–1888 Newman College catalogue: "Every department is supplied with wide-awake teachers. Each one makes a specialty of what he teaches. Students are taught to grasp underlying principles and to discover the reason of things."[248] He taught metaphysics and pure/applied mathematics. S. N. Newman, the secretary/registrar, taught Latin and Greek. Miss Ella Williams taught French, German, and natural science that year. Miss Ida Kimbrough taught English literature and mathematics. The principal of the preparatory school, Mrs. W. N. Brown, had her hands full with over one hundred students from first grade through high school.[249]

Professor J. I. Simpson was the principal of instrumental music. The catalogue extols his background: "Late of England, Prof. Simpson is a sound and accomplished musician. He was a pupil of one of the most eminent pianists in Europe. . . . His system of teaching is in accordance with the most approved methods."[250] Miss Lou Alley taught vocal music.

Others named on the "Board of Instruction" were Miss Mary Daniel, principal of the Art Department; Mrs. A. J. Russell, matron; Mrs. S. N. Newman, assistant matron; and Miss Fannie Taliaferro, currently a junior student, librarian.[251]

NEWMAN COLLEGE'S CURRICULUM FOR AN AB DEGREE

FRESHMAN YEAR: Latin (Caesar, Sallust, Grammar); University Algebra (completed); Geometry; Plane Trigonometry; Natural History; English Analysis; Morals and Manners; Rhetorical Exercises; French and German: First Series; Greek: Optional

SOPHOMORE YEAR: Latin (Virgil, Cicero de Senectute et Amicitia, Prose Composition, Grammar); Spherical Geometry; Spherical Trigonometry; Surveying and Navigation; Composition; Rhetoric; Botany; General History French (Grammar; Classic Readings; Written Exercises; Conversations); German (Second Series; Written Exercises; Conversations)

JUNIOR YEAR: Latin (Horace; Livy; Composition); Analytical Geometry; Conic Sections; Literature; English Classics; Chemistry; Astronomy; French (History of French Literature; Written Exercises; Conversations); German: Verb Drill; German Literature; Daily Conversations

SENIOR YEAR: Latin (Tacitus; Prose Composition); Mechanical Philosophy; Mental and Moral Philosophy; Butler's Analogy; Evidences of Christianity; English Classics; Rhetorical Exercises; Logic

DAILY: calisthenics, required chapel, Bible study, room inspection.[252]

EXTRACURRICULAR RULES AND INCENTIVES

In the same catalogue, a section on Moral Culture delineated the strong religious expectations of the faculty for the young ladies.[253] The General

Regulations cover a wide range of "musts," including punctuality, scrupulous neatness of dress and of room, very limited shopping (on Saturdays with faculty members only), infrequent visits home, and gaining the permission of faculty members for anything outside academic work; this permission was strictly administered and by no means a given.[254]

A section on rewards—Medals—read: "A gold medal will be given to a member of the Senior Class for the best essay. Thought, diction and all the elements of style, together with reading, will be taken into account. A prize is also offered for neatness, to be determined by the highest grade, in private room, in dining-room and in personal appearance."[255]

WOMEN TRUSTEES

Along with numerous men, two women served as trustees of Newman College: Mrs. E. A. Taylor of Knoxville and Mrs. Henrietta Sarah Cody Burnett of Del Rio.[256] Mrs. Burnett was the mother of several children, including Edmund Cody Burnett, coeditor of *The Carson Index* and a future faculty member, and Jesse McGarity Burnett, future faculty member and president. Later she moved to Mossy Creek and became the matron of the first Young Ladies Home.

There would be a time gap of almost ninety years before another woman would serve as a trustee of the merged Carson-Newman College.

A CHANGING OF THE GUARD

Extant sources do not reveal when talk of consolidating the two schools began. But the fact that W. T. Russell purchased a new campus for Newman College in mid-1887 makes it unlikely that any such talk was serious at that time. The issue must have gained traction in 1888. Apparently, as discussion of a merger grew more serious, Dr. Tindell did not feel he was the right person to take the lead for a combined school for both men and women. He resigned as president of Carson College on August 20, 1888, just a few days before the start of the fall session.[257]

Dr. Tindell moved to Harriman, returning to preaching and continuing his keen interest in Tennessee Baptist history. He also took an active part in the temperance movement and lived to be ninety-five.[258]

STABLE LEADERSHIP IN A PERIOD OF TRANSFORMATION: W. A. MONTGOMERY, TENTH PRESIDENT (1888–1892)

After President Tindell's surprise resignation, Carson College trustees selected William Allen Montgomery (1829–1905) as the new president. He was no stranger to the school, Carson having honored him with an honorary DD in 1870. He had told the students he could never refuse to respond to the calls of Carson College.[259] Apparently this mindset extended to the invitation to become president and to teach metaphysics and theology there. He also agreed to serve as part-time pastor of the Mossy Creek Baptist Church.[260]

Born in Jefferson County, Montgomery had probably attended Maury Academy in Dandridge. An honor graduate of the University of Tennessee, he studied law and was admitted to the bar in 1851. Like many Tennesseans, he moved westward to Texas in the late 1850s to plant cotton, a lucrative source of income until the Civil War devastated the South. He served in the Confederate Army, where he was licensed to preach to the troops. After the war ended, he returned to East Tennessee penniless.[261]

At that point Montgomery turned to the ministry for his livelihood, serving several churches in Tennessee, Virginia, and Georgia as pastor. "Preaching was his forte. He had preaching gifts in an eminent degree. . . . He preached on great subjects, handling them masterfully, his full-orbed mind illuminating them on all sides . . . with a mental intensity that was electrical in its effect."[262] He also took on several unifying roles for Tennessee Baptists.

Montgomery's biographer knew him well and revealed his "dark side" in 1919: "He was not a Pharisee and made no claims to perfection. If he were alive, I doubt not he would have me paint him as he was. So, in candor I would have to say, he was always strong but not always sweet. . . . He was sometimes caustic. . . . He was ambitious and proud and had an infirmity of temper which he, no less than his friends, deplored."[263]

A Rising Tide Toward Consolidation

President Montgomery was in office only a short time before Carson College was challenged to move in a new direction—combining with Newman College. Already a close relationship existed between the two schools, as noted in the proximity of their respective properties, their recent shared history, and the fact that they had some founders in common. Also, President Russell of Newman College had taught at Carson College. He and some other trustees served on both boards at the same time.

The leaders in the consolidation movement were practical men. They knew President Montgomery and President Russell operated respectable programs for a small number of students in each institution. They felt that the time had arrived to strengthen and enlarge facilities, but to endow money for one would be to take money away from the other. There was not enough wealth among East Tennessee Baptists for both Mossy Creek schools to grow and flourish separately.

Presidents Montgomery and Russell agreed that Carson and Newman Colleges should be consolidated. Co-education was growing in practice across the United States, and Baptist leaders in Tennessee had begun to accept the idea as sound philosophically and economically.[264]

That Newman College had already been in operation seven years near Carson College led many area Baptist laymen to accept the idea that the change was not a radical one. They endorsed consolidation, knowing that the economic benefits of the merger would help the denomination.[265]

CONTEXT: 1889 EVENTS IN WORLD HISTORY

Benjamin Harrison became the twenty-third US president and named Frederick Douglass Minister to Haiti. The 1889 Exposition Universelle (World's Fair) in Paris featured the newly completed Eiffel Tower. George Eastman began selling Kodak film, and the German firm Bayer patented aspirin. Pennsylvania's Johnstown Flood took the lives of 2,209 persons. *The Wall Street Journal* began publication, and Barnard College was founded in New York City after Columbia University refused to accept women.

CONDITIONS OF THE AGREEMENT

The two boards of trustees met in joint session April 3, 1889, and unanimously agreed on the union of the two colleges, which would be consolidated under the charter of Carson College. The new entity would be called Carson and Newman College. Men and women were to be admitted on a basis of complete equality. The properties of the two colleges were to be used for the best interest of Carson and Newman College. New buildings and expansions were to be built on property owned by Newman College, which would transfer its properties to the new institution.[266]

All members of Carson's trustees and Newman's trustees would serve at least the first year of the combined Carson and Newman College. In addition, Newman College would name four new members to the board. The combined trustees were to elect the faculty for the new entity, effective in the coming collegiate year. The official union of the colleges was to take effect when the respective trustee boards accepted, adopted, and ratified the consolidation documents that would be legally drawn up.[267]

THE "WEDDING CEREMONY"

When Carson College students got wind of the "secret" meetings being held to negotiate the consolidation of their school with Newman College, their anticipation was at fever pitch until the confirmation of agreement on both sides was finally announced. Ben W. Hooper, a lively junior, and his roommate hastily improvised plans to celebrate the union of the two schools. They organized a grotesque version of a mock wedding, choosing all male friends to represent the bride, groom, and bridesmaids (representing other East Tennessee colleges). Before going over to the Newman campus to present their drama, they rehearsed songs, dialogues, and elaborate gags.[268]

Much later, in 1951, an older Ben Hooper gleefully recalled, "Dr. Montgomery, like most of the village, was watching what was going on. He came down and said to me in a fatherly tone, 'Now, Mr. Hooper, give the young ladies a nice serenade, but see that nothing improper occurs.' Of course, I reassured the doctor."[269]

As the drama unfolded in 1889, the groom was shy and hesitant, but the bride was overly affectionate and obviously eager for the wedding-night festivities. The modest young ladies of Newman College were disgusted with the display.[270]

A year after the mock wedding, Hooper became a proud alumnus of the Class of 1890, among the first to hold a degree from Carson and Newman College. He remained a staunch supporter of the school and later was named a trustee. He also served as a two-term governor of Tennessee (1910–1914).[271]

Newman College's last graduating class in 1889. Miss Tennessee Jenkins is seated center; she later became a legendary history professor at Carson and Newman.

NEWMAN COLLEGE'S GRADUATES

In June 1889, the last Newman College graduation was held; Lavinia Tennessee Jenkins was among the six graduates.[272] Later she would become a longtime, revered professor of history and department chairperson at Carson and Newman.

In all, twenty-three young women graduated from the four-year curriculum of Newman College (under varying school names) between 1881 and 1889.[273] However, graduates of the music and art curricula only were not counted as Newman alumni, receiving certificates rather than diplomas.

The Two Became One

The consolidation document was completed on August 20, 1889. On the formal ratification of the agreement by the two boards of trustees, Newman College was legally dissolved. All of its assets, containing thirteen acres with all brick, lumber, and other materials on hand for erecting a new college building, plus its interest in the ten acres of Campus #1, were transferred to Carson and Newman College. The new entity assumed all Newman College indebtedness.[274]

The combined trustees elected W. A. Montgomery of Carson College as president of the combined colleges and W. T. Russell of Newman College as vice-president. Professor John T. Henderson was named the treasurer; and his brother, Robert A. Henderson, now on the faculty teaching English and Latin, became the secretary/registrar.[275]

The new college held all of its classes in Carson Hall. The young women lived in the Newman Dormitories or came from their homes in the community. Additionally, some faculty members hosted young women in their homes. The young men roomed in homes in the community.[276]

Beginning with the fall semester in 1889, Carson and Newman offered an improved curriculum to its thirty-three collegiate students. The thirteen students enrolled in the classical AB program were required to master Latin, Greek, and a modern language (French or German) in addition to mathematics, science, literature, and philosophy. Debates, essays, and orations, among other courses, were added during the senior year.[277]

The eighteen students completing a Latin-Scientific course had similar requirements along with an additional concentration on science courses; they received BS degrees. Two students were registered for the English-Scientific course, which omitted Latin as a requirement. They studied the Normal (Education) course, which provided instruction for those intending to teach or serve as bookkeepers.[278]

William Cate Newman lived long enough to see the merger of the men's and women's colleges. He had championed the men's college, beginning as an Oak Tree Five member in 1849, and donating money for the original Newman Dormitories. He also championed the fledgling women's schools and actively supported Newman College for women students. Described as "a zealous friend" to Carson and Newman, he donated an estimated total of $10,840 to the two colleges. Far from regretting the loss of that sum, he cheerfully told a friend late in life, "My money was spent in a good cause."[279]

The 1892 faculty of Carson and Newman College. William A. Montgomery, president 1888–1892, is seated, center. Pictured to his right is Mrs. Hassie Brown, English professor. To her right is John T. Henderson, math professor. Standing between Brown and Henderson is Edmund Cody Burnett, professor of Greek and modern languages. The others cannot be positively identified.

Philomathean Literary Society members, congregated in front of the grand administration building.

RATIONALE FOR "THE UNION OF THE COLLEGES"

"The demand of the age for the higher culture of women has brought educators face to face with the practical problem of how this demand is to be best met. . . . Nothing will answer but institutions with buildings and endowments fully equal to those given to the colleges for males. This involves a double outlay of capital, always too limited to meet our educational wants, and, at present, we believe, entirely out of the reach of the denomination in East Tennessee.

"By uniting Carson and Newman Colleges into one institution, open alike, and on equal terms, to males and females, we believe the problem as well, and even better solved. This gives us the opportunity to concentrate the entire strength of our denomination on one college, thus enabling us to bring it up to the highest standard of excellency. . . .

"Besides, in our judgment, there are peculiar advantages connected with co-education, difficult, if not impossible, to attain in any other way. Among these, the stimulus to study from the desire of each sex to excel [over] the other; the refining and elevating influence upon both . . . and the better knowledge of each other to be obtained nowhere so well as by long years of contact in the classroom, thus preventing foolish and inconsiderate marriages, are some of the most important.

"Co-education of the sexes is not an experiment. Its advantages have been demonstrated through many years, at Michigan and Cornell Universities, at Oberlin and other leading colleges, North and South. We believe it will prove equally satisfactory at Carson and Newman.

"The utmost diligence on our part will be used to give all the advantages, and avoid all the disadvantages, of the commingling of the sexes, which will be allowed only so far as is necessary to carry out the purpose of co-education. We believe girls are mentally and physically capable of as high attainments as boys. We propose to put them in Carson and Newman on exactly equal footing, and verify, as we confidently believe we shall, the truthfulness of our conviction."[280]

TOWARD EQUALITY: LITERARY SOCIETIES FOR WOMEN

For the first two years after the consolidation, the women students of Carson and Newman socialized with each other by attending the Palladian

Reading Club, a holdover from Newman College. On Friday evenings, they all met to deliver or listen to recitations, selected readings, dialogues, original essays, and criticisms, also learning the fundamentals of parliamentary law.[281]

In 1891, the faculty saw the need for two women's literary societies, equal in every way to the Philomathean and Columbian Literary Societies for men. Professor John Henderson called together all the women students and proposed the idea; they agreed at once. He selected Tennessee Jenkins and Ida Lawrence, both earning second degrees at that time, to be the leaders of their societies. Each one alternately selected a female classmate until all the young women were chosen.[282]

The two societies began meeting weekly to debate and engage in literary exercises, much like their male counterparts. They also occasionally performed plays, to the delight of all Carson and Newman students.[283]

By student-led democratic process and discussion, the two societies chose names from classical history and literature. Tennessee Jenkins's group became the Hypatian Literary Society, with the motto "Add to Virtue Knowledge." (Edmund Cody Burnett was professor of Greek and modern languages at the time. He suggested the name referring to Hypatia, a famous female Grecian mathematician and lecturer in Alexandria, Egypt, while Egypt was under Greek control.)[284]

Harkening back to mythology and the Nine Muses, the other society's name referred to Calliope, the muse of epic poetry and music. The Calliopean Literary Society, led by Ida Lawrence, adopted the motto "Remember Lot's Wife."[285] (The motto's focus was on working toward a good future and not reliving past mistakes.)

In the early days, a rivalry ensued between the two groups, with members of one society always walking on one side of a particular tree on campus and the members of the other consistently walking on the opposite side.[286] But later the two ceased their rivalries and were considered sister societies. Both societies prospered and upheld their traditions for over one hundred years.

A NEW, MAGNIFICENT ADMINISTRATION BUILDING

To grow, Carson and Newman needed larger and more modern facilities. The time was right to begin building on the new thirteen-acre campus W. T. Russell had bought.[287] A building for classroom and administrative space topped the list of needed structures.

Calliopean Literary Society members, engaged in a musical performance.

An architect designed a beautiful three-story elegant structure for a central building on the highest point of the new property. In the spring of 1890, local citizens witnessed the laying of the cornerstone. As had been true of Campus #1 in the 1850s, the building project on Campus #3 made good use of local resources. Clay dug from the earth on the site yielded excellent handmade bricks.[288]

The exterior would be completed first, with roofing and windows securing the work. The interior of the building would be finished over a period of years, floor by floor, as there was not enough money on hand for the entire project. Once the exterior was complete, work on first-floor classroom space was the priority.

The total cost of the building was estimated at $45,000. But with donated labor and materials and careful management, the eventual final cost was $33,000.[289] President Montgomery decided to launch a financial campaign to help pay for the building, but remembered his earlier fundraising attempts for the Tennessee Baptist Convention as unsuccessful. He placed Professor John T. Henderson in charge of solicitations for the administration building, and Henderson proved to be a productive fundraiser.[290]

The grand structure began to take shape on the hill, stretching ever higher against the sky. Its main entrance faced Branner Avenue, but students could enter on any side. Bedford stone trim enhanced the brickwork; arches, porches, turrets, and a soaring tower were impressive architectural details. A large bell in the tower rang out class period changes. The first two floors were completed by 1892, the third floor in 1897.[291] The building became a source of great pride for all of Mossy Creek.

W. A. MONTGOMERY'S DEPARTURE

During the spring semester of 1892, President Montgomery apparently felt that the college had reached a point of stability and would be in good hands without him. Then age sixty-three, he submitted his resignation as president, effective after the 1892 commencement. Subsequently Montgomery served several churches as pastor, the last in Georgia, and wrote many effective articles and editorials for state Baptist newspapers, including Tennessee's *Baptist and Reflector*.[292]

Indeed Carson and Newman would be in good hands after Montgomery's resignation. The next several presidents would be dedicated to the growth and prospering of the college. A sophisticated understanding of "high finance" would take on a new importance, and the student population would skyrocket to formerly unimaginable numbers. Correspondingly, the campus on the hill would sprout several new buildings designed for the students' well-being and serious study. Carson and Newman was poised to enter the twentieth century as a strong and thriving educational institution.

CHAPTER FIVE

The Building of a Campus and a Generation of Scholars
1892–1911

"The instrument of culture is the idea. The rude boy becomes the cultured man thru the instrumentality of ideas. Every means of communicating great ideas is a means of culture and has its place in college life. Art is such a means—and music. Such a means is the voice of the living teacher. But after all the greatest instrument of culture is the book. Because in books are the greatest ideas of all times and countries. The study of the great literatures of the world, and of the great books of these literatures, ought to be the central and essential thing in college life."
—Jesse M. Burnett[293]

While the new campus bustled noisily with activity—saws singing and hammers pounding as classrooms took shape on the first floor of the beautiful administration building—a group of men met quietly to determine the next leader for Carson and Newman. The trustees hoped to agree on the choice of a new president from within the faculty.

Deciding that Professor John T. Henderson was the right person for the job was not a huge leap of faith for them. Even before his graduation from Carson College in 1883, Henderson had been on the faculty as librarian, treasurer, and professor of mathematics.[294] After graduating, he had served as professor of higher mathematics and metaphysics, trustee, and financial agent. He had excelled in carrying out all his responsibilities.

John Henderson did not really want to be president, reluctantly agreeing only to be named chairman of the faculty for one year. A year later, he did acquiesce to take on the full responsibility of serving as president, to the lasting benefit of the college.

John T. Henderson, president 1892–1903.

The Right Person for the Time

GUIDED BY A KEEN INTELLECT AND AN ORDERLY MIND: JOHN T. HENDERSON, ELEVENTH PRESIDENT (1892–1903)

John Thompson Henderson (1858–1946) was a native of the Tellico Plains area in Monroe County. A graduate of Cedar Bluff Academy there, he then taught for two years at Maury Academy in Dandridge.[295] Since his father was a native of Jefferson County and he still had relatives in the area, attending Carson College was a natural step for the young scholar.

As a graduate of the college himself, Henderson related strongly to the students. He gave them his personal attention, helping them establish confidence in themselves and thereby gaining their respect, cooperation, and loyalty. They affectionately called him "Professor John" and his brother, Robert, their Latin teacher, "Professor Bob."

Later, as president, Henderson developed an astute grasp of the importance of money. But he did not use his knowledge to improve his own finances. Instead, the well-being and operation of the college was his primary concern. When the financial Panic of 1893 and the subsequent monetary depression occurred, Henderson took a pay cut along with all the faculty members. He refused additional pay for serving as president even though he spent about thirty hours per week teaching.[296] Faculty morale reached a new high because of his understanding and sacrifice.[297]

Serving as his own financial agent, he led numerous successful campaigns to raise money for Carson and Newman's needs, present and future. His fundraising motto was "Talk it up, pray it up, pay it up."[298] He presented the needs of Carson and Newman's students to potential donors so gracefully that he made lasting friends for the school.

John Henderson's magnetic personality impacted Christians all over the South. Between 1892 and 1902, he served as president of the Tennessee Baptist Convention. He wrote several books on tithing and the stewardship of life, money, and influence. In 1908 he began a thirty-year "side career" with the Laymen's Missionary Movement, a men's missions organization that later became known as the Baptist Brotherhood.[299] It was inspired by the success of the Woman's Missionary Union and the need for a corresponding missions organization for Baptist men.

In 1917, Carson and Newman conferred an LLD degree on him in recognition of his many contributions to the college and the denomination.[300]

An In-Depth Look at Campus Changes

FIRST INTERIOR PHASE OF THE ADMINISTRATION BUILDING

August 30, 1892 was a day highly celebrated at Carson and Newman as students gathered in the new administration building for the first time. Enough rooms had been completed on the first floor for classes to be held there during the fall semester. As chairman of the faculty, John Henderson called everyone together at 10:00 a.m. in a makeshift auditorium for the first-day convocation. Faculty members and students joyfully sang the majestic Coronation Hymn together in praise and gratitude for their new building.[301] During Henderson's presidency and beyond, the Coronation Hymn (or the alternate hymn tune, Diadem) became the college's "theme song" and was sung on special occasions:

> All hail the power of Jesus' name!
> Let angels prostrate fall;
> Bring forth the royal diadem,
> And crown Him Lord of all.[302]

The magnificent administration building, 1890-1916.

A Knoxville pastor and trustee wrote of the day: "The institution . . . today has set up housekeeping in a building that will meet all the conditions of successful college work. The building is indeed magnificent, well appointed, substantial and beautiful. They only need now that some friend of higher education should give them $5,000. And perhaps no better place could be found for such an investment."[303]

Thanks to John Henderson's excellence and persistence in fundraising, the building's auditorium was finished in time for the 1893 commencement. It was described as "one of the most elegant audience halls in the country."[304] Located on the second floor, it provided seating space for about twelve hundred movable chairs. It also had a stage of sufficient size for a small basketball court, where informal basketball games were played.[305] More classrooms, offices, and other spaces would be added as money became available.

STUDENTS ON THE MOVE: RESIDENTIAL LIVING SPACES

During the summer of 1892, Carson Hall was renovated for use as a dormitory for women students. It was temporarily renamed the Young Ladies

Home (later a new building would assume the same name). For several years, Mrs. Henrietta Sarah Cody Burnett lived there as matron; she was in charge of food service and a true mother figure to the young women.[306]

The young ladies apparently were expected to be better housekeepers than the men; they were graded on how nicely they kept their rooms. The grading was to be done by a committee of ladies who were liable to enter the rooms at any time between 8 a.m. and 9 p.m.[307]

Three of the four small houses east of the home were available to women who wished to save money by self-boarding. A family lived in the fourth, available to help the young women in any way.[308] These accommodations were about six unpaved blocks from the new campus. In inclement weather, the distance must have seemed miles away!

Somewhat more expensive rooms for women were available in private homes. But on the plus side, most of these homes were much nearer to campus. Of course, a female student and a male student could not reside in the same home unless they were brother and sister.

Now the Newman Dormitories on the old campus beside Mossy Creek were available for men students. There, the young men could board themselves, bringing their own cooking utensils.[309]

THE BEGINNING OF ORGANIZED SPORTS AT THE COLLEGE

As early as 1892–1893, Carson and Newman began promoting athletics on the condition that "all work must precede play." The first organized athletic event held on campus was a field day on June 3, 1893, with contests such as dashes, races, and jumps. Senior student Luther Birdwell DeArmond, the elected president of the Athletic Association and a future faculty member, supervised the event.[310]

Baseball was the first organized sport played at Carson and Newman. The baseball field was close to Carson Hall in the area where George Street is now, encompassing its connections with East Jefferson and East Ellis Streets. In 1895, the baseball team of Carson and Newman played its first intercollegiate match with the University of Tennessee and defeated them four to three. Football was also organized on the campus that year.[311]

AN OLD STORY: MONETARY WOES

The small size of Carson and Newman's endowment at this time was a serious concern, especially considering the financial Panic of 1893 and its lingering negative results. In 1893, two new monetary requirements were imposed on students entering the school, seeming to indicate significant losses of goodwill investments in students from the past:

(1) At matriculation, ministerial students who received free tuition had to sign a document stating that if they did not pursue the ministry as their career after graduation, they would repay the school the amount of their tuition for all four years.[312]

(2) The following statement applied to all other students: "It is thought that any student leaving home for college should be able to bring enough money to pay his tuition for at least one term. Students as a rule can better afford to borrow the money, if necessary, to pay the small tuition fees, than the Faculty can afford to wait. From generous indulgence, the Faculty now has scores of accounts out, of from one to ten years standing. For the good of both parties we adopt this policy."[313]

Exuberant students celebrating a patriotic occasion in front of the administration building.

A new emphasis on endowing scholarships began at this time and proved successful. Over the years, the number of endowed student scholarships grew by leaps and bounds, benefiting students and relieving the college of monetary overextension for this purpose.[314] There had always been scholarships for ministerial students, but now every effort was made not to turn away any worthy student.

In the 1894–1895 catalogue, Henderson included a special word of thanks to two trustees, W. W. Woodruff and Dr. L. W. Davis, "without whose liberal gifts the College could not have survived the last two years of financial stringency."[315]

MEDALS AWARDED AT COMMENCEMENTS

Various individuals and companies began donating medals to students achieving academic excellence in the 1880s. By commencement time in 1895, the number of medals awarded had reached twelve. They were given for diverse accomplishments—for example, the best essay prepared and read by a senior woman, the best oration delivered by a male undergraduate, the student making the most progress in music, and the most outstanding student in a particular field.[316]

1895 proved to be the final year of medals for a while. They were discontinued due to dissension on the part of judges and faculty, resulting in wounded feelings among the students and the perception of injustice.[317]

Important Carson and Newman News Items

OF THE MODERN ERA: THE BUSINESS COLLEGE

The popularity of that newfangled mass-produced machine, the typewriter, introduced an additional curriculum to many colleges. In fact, numerous specialized business colleges had been born (mostly in cities) to take advantage of the situation. Many students foresaw a stable career for themselves in secretarial work—using shorthand, taking dictation, and typing. Courses in bookkeeping and accounting appealed to other students.

Beginning in 1892, classes in stenography and typing were offered at Carson and Newman. They proved so popular that over several years, the business curriculum grew steadily. In 1898, the very modern Carson and Newman Business College and School of Shorthand and Typewriting were officially added to the curriculum. Courses offered included bookkeeping, shorthand, penmanship, commercial arithmetic and banking, accounting, commercial law, typing, and telegraphy (the latter once the school purchased a telegraph machine).[318]

1893 graduate Luther Birdwell DeArmond tutored students in penmanship, later adding accounting to the courses he taught in the business school and becoming the business school's superintendent in 1900.[319] (By 1903 he was able to combine this job with his first love: he was also named director of athletics and manager of the football team.[320]) DeArmond contacted a number of persons who had hired Carson and Newman business graduates, gladly hearing their commendations of former students. Using good marketing strategies to promote the business college, in later catalogues he listed these graduates and their positions in business offices across the United States.

SPOTLIGHT: SEVERAL OUTSTANDING PROFESSORS

Edmund Cody Burnett, Class of 1888, taught Greek and modern languages at Carson and Newman from 1891 to 1894 and was also one of Carson-Newman's first librarians.[321] Afterward, he studied at Brown University, thanks to the influence of Dr. S. W. Tindell. At Brown he earned the MA and PhD degrees and taught Greek to Brown undergraduates.[322] After teaching stints at other colleges, E. C. Burnett had a longtime career at the Carnegie Institution of Washington, DC, doing historical research and prolific writing. Among his works is the eight-volume acclaimed series of books *The Continental Congress.*[323]

Miss Tennessee Jenkins was the first professor in the new School of History in 1896 and longtime chair of the History Department.[324] She had earned a classical degree in 1889 from Newman College and another from Carson and Newman in 1893, serving as a tutor to undergraduates. At various times throughout her long teaching career, "Miss Tennie" taught English literature and French as well as history. As a lifelong learner, she sometimes took undergraduate classes in art and piano to learn new creative skills. She touched the lives of generations of students.

William Powell Hale, Class of 1898, began teaching elocution (speech) classes at Carson and Newman upon his graduation. A longtime and well-respected professor for decades, he also taught oratory, expression, and dramatics.[325] During the 1890s, he coached students on debating skills as well. A feature of commencements during the Henderson years involved "live" debates between two Hypatian and Calliopean young women and, separately, two Columbian and Philomathean young men. The students debated at least one interesting question at each commencement.[326]

Miss Blanche Thomas began teaching oil, pastel, crayon, watercolor, china, and free-hand drawing in 1896. The school of art immediately began attracting many quality students. So popular were her classes that a large hall in the administration building was set aside as an art studio for her use. Miss Thomas also began organizing art exhibits for her students at commencement exercises; these were much admired and "the talk of the town."[327] In a few years, she married W. Powell Hale. Upon Mrs. Hale's resignation to begin a family, **Miss Blanche Ellis** (Newman College's Class of 1887) served as the longtime art director.

Mrs. Hassie Brown was a beloved English professor who taught at Newman College (1884–1889) and then at Carson and Newman (1890–1895). She also served as the young ladies' physical drill instructor until she became seriously ill in 1895. Few could match her dedication to Carson-Newman; among her final words were "I die interested in the college."[328]

W. S. (William Samuel) Gass was Hassie Brown's successor, beginning his teaching career as an outstanding senior student when Mrs. Brown resigned due to illness. In 1896, his peers wrote in the student newspaper: "It is with no small degree of pride and pleasure that we as students greet W. S. Gass as a member of the faculty the coming year. Don't forget that you were once a student when you get in authority, '*squire.*'"[329] Gass would serve as the English professor at Carson and Newman for eleven years.

BROADENING THE MUSIC CURRICULUM

In 1896, the three Maples sisters of Mossy Creek—Nora, Bertie, and Lydia—all graduated from Carson and Newman with music degrees.[330] Subsequently, all three earned further degrees and teaching certificates at the Cincinnati Conservatory of Music.[331] Lydia then married and moved to Florida, but her sisters returned to Mossy Creek to live.

Nora Electra Maples (later Rankin) became the first woman given the title of director of music at Carson and Newman, lending a new breadth and sophistication to the school's music program.[332] Bertie (later Butler), an able instructor, assisted her sister in teaching music. The Misses Maples were highly respected in Mossy Creek for their accomplishments, assembling outstanding piano and vocal musical programs for commencements.

Musical groups on campus grew by leaps and bounds. In the late 1890s a fourteen-member brass band debuted on campus; it was considered "one of the chief attractions of the college." The instruments were the property of Carson and Newman, "which makes the band permanent."[333] And later a college orchestra was established! Within a few years, the college offered three degrees in music: MG (musical graduate), MB (bachelor of music), and MM (master of music).[334]

MODERN MARVELS: A TELEPHONE FOR CAMPUS (YES, ONE!)

Big news in Mossy Creek! "We now have eight trains per day that carry passengers, four each way, all of which stop at Mossy Creek. The vestibule going each way now stops here. Postal and telegraphic facilities are good. We have both the East Tennessee and People's Telephones in our town. The former has an exchange here with a telephone in the College."[335]

Moving the College into the Twentieth Century

NEW AND RETRO HOUSING SOLUTIONS

At the 1897 commencement, with the administration building all but completed, the trustees decided to proceed with the construction of a first-class dormitory for women students, the "official" Young Ladies Home. They chose to save money on the new building by tearing down the three original buildings beside Mossy Creek and recycling the bricks. The college still owned Campus #1 with its ten acres, but it would be over sixty-five years before the college made use of the land again.[336]

The new three-story women's dormitory was completed in 1899. It had a slate roof, a wraparound porch, wonderful stairways, and lovely wood trim. Students loved living there. Planned originally for fifty occupants, it

The Young Ladies' Home/Henderson Dormitory, 1899–1968.

later accommodated seventy with three to a room. The thirteen chimneys were built to take care of all the coal and wood stoves required to heat the building. This system proved unworkable, and two years later steam heat was installed. Water was first supplied from cisterns, then from a well behind the building.[337]

Dr. L. W. Davis of Knoxville, a trustee and 1882 Carson College alumnus, suggested to his wife, Nola, that the Baptist women of East Tennessee take on the project of furnishing the rooms. She was the first to pledge the furniture for a room.[338] Each room had a bedstead, mattress and springs, bureau, washstand, washbowl and pitcher, chairs, shades, large center rug, and table. Pictures show double beds. The décor was considered elegant.[339]

In 1927, the Young Ladies Home was given the Henderson name in honor of a Knoxville businessman, a trustee unrelated to John Henderson.[340] In future years, the building would variously be called Henderson Home, Hall, or Dormitory.

Once the Young Ladies Home provided living quarters for women, Carson Hall on Campus #2 was reopened as a men's dormitory in the fall of 1899. (This probably seemed like a "déjà vu" event for anyone who recalled Carson College students occupying Carson Hall as their classroom building twenty years earlier.) But finding dependable boarding facilities for the men was a problem at the turn of the century. Eventually, a large kitchen and dining room were built adjacent to Carson Hall, and for eighteen years this dining hall was in continuous use.[341]

YESTERDAY'S NAMES ON TODAY'S CAMPUS BUILDINGS

So many names of persons from the early twentieth century are still displayed on campus today! Here's the key to identifying those names on buildings:

HENDERSON HUMANITIES BUILDING was named for John T. Henderson.

BURNETT RESIDENCE HALL memorializes Jesse McGarity Burnett, professor and later president whose home was located at the site of the dormitory.

STEPHENS-BURNETT LIBRARY honors two intermarried families of multigenerational students and faculty members, including Charles Stephens (Class of 1896) and his wife, Annie Burnett (Class of 1897). Among Annie's brothers were professors Edmund Cody Burnett and J. M. Burnett, and their mother was Henrietta Sarah Cody Burnett, matron.

MAPLES CAFÉ, a section of MAPLES LIBRARY (1949), is named for D. C. Maples, a trustee; his wife, Sallie; and their children, including faculty members Nora and Bertie. Darius Leonard (D. L.) Butler, a 1901 alumnus who married Bertie, donated the money for the building in appreciation of his wife's family. The library was renamed Stephens-Burnett in 1989.

The funds to build BERTIE MAPLES BUTLER HALL, the main part of which was completed in 1954, were also donated by the Butlers. Built as a women's dormitory, it now houses male students and the welcome center.

BUTLER-BLANC GYMNASIUM was named for its two outstanding donors, trustees D. L. Butler and Henry D. Blanc. Generations of Blanc family members would become alumni and important supporters of the college.

INSIDE THE REMARKABLE ADMINISTRATION BUILDING

In local parlance, the elegant administration building would be known as "the College." When the building was finally completed about 1897, sufficient classrooms were available to accommodate a student body of about six hundred. This was a decision of great optimism; collegiate enrollment had increased greatly but was just over three hundred at this time.[342]

The first floor housed Alumni Hall, which also served as the president's office for a while. The alumni had raised money to furnish this meeting room. Each alumnus was asked to send a portrait of himself or herself to be hung on the walls. The college library and an adjoining reading room were housed on this floor, as were the business office and a small bookstore. Classrooms were available for the studies of English, history, ethics, psychology, economics, and science. A chemical laboratory was placed beside the science classroom.[343]

The auditorium was located on the second floor; its stage served a second purpose as a small basketball court. Four large rooms were assigned to the literary societies. Each society's alumni furnished their meeting area according to their own taste and budget. The Hypatian and Calliopean literary societies moved to the second floor of Sarah Swann Hall in 1905, acquiring even more lovely accommodations.[344] Their former spaces in the administration building were reconfigured into classrooms for mathematics, foreign languages, and Latin. One additional classroom was used for the preparatory division.[345]

The third floor held the large art studio, the Business Department, the school of elocution (speech and dramatics), and two meeting halls for large organizations such as the Young Men's/Young Women's Christian Association (YMCA and YWCA).[346]

College administrators wanted to keep the lovely new building as clean as possible, which was not easy in the era of unpaved roads. Students were admonished: "Both young ladies and young gentlemen are expected to wear overshoes during muddy weather, and to remove them before entering the recitation rooms."[347]

MEETING THE CHALLENGE: ENDOWMENT NEWS

In 1900, as a new century began, John Henderson was thankful that two major building programs for the administration building and the Young Ladies' Home had finally been completed and the college was debt-free.

Now he turned his attention to building Carson and Newman's endowment for the future. At this time the endowment consisted of about $35,000.[348]

The American Baptist Education Society supplied a challenging goal. They proposed to donate $15,000 to Carson and Newman, providing the college would raise another $60,000 in gifts and reliable pledges—by June 1, 1901! (The Society's $15,000 gift came from John D. Rockefeller, who was in favor of supporting worthy Southern schools.) The Society's stipulation was that $50,000 of the money raised should be held as endowment, while the other $10,000 could be used for general purposes.[349]

Henderson plunged into the endowment campaign with vigor. He used all of his persuasive skills—and all his spare time, no doubt—to contact persons from all walks of life and all areas of the country who might help Carson and Newman financially. Pages of testimonials about Carson and Newman's academic excellence and personal interest in cultivating students began appearing in the catalogues, as did handy forms for persons wishing to bestow a monetary gift or to leave their estate to the college.

Surely Henderson reflected on Jesse Baker's thirty-five-hundred-mile ride just thirty years before, raising $6,000 to cover the college's entire debt. How the value of money had changed in this new era of big banking! Now he was working to acquire ten times Baker's amount with the same brief deadline—one year. At this time, Jesse Baker was in the last year of his life; undoubtedly the two men discussed their experiences.

On Commencement Day, May 31, 1901, Henderson announced with joy that $60,000 in good-faith pledges and gifts had been secured. Of that amount, about $25,000 was already productive. Jesse Baker led the attendees in a prayer of thanksgiving. Again the grateful faculty and student body celebrated by singing the Coronation Hymn together.[350]

Henderson then decreed that money from pledges must be in Carson and Newman's hands by June 1, 1905, giving ample time for good intentions to be exchanged for productive cash. However, he sought additional funds as "insurance."[351] He well knew that unexpected events can happen over a span of time, thus some pledges might be reduced or never paid. For example, Jonathan Nelson Newman's gift of real estate valued at $4,000 lost a full thousand dollars of its worth due to the cost of litigation after his death.[352]

A NAME CHANGE FOR MOSSY CREEK

By the turn of the century some in the area, especially businessmen, were promoting a major change for Mossy Creek. They considered the name too quaint, not progressive enough for a thriving town. Sometimes local residents were called "Moss Backs," a term of derision. John T. Henderson supported a name change, although there was strong opposition from many townspeople. In February 1901, the three neighboring towns of Mossy Creek, Carsonville, and Frame Addition were merged and incorporated as Jefferson City, honoring Thomas Jefferson.[353]

The End of President Henderson's Tenure

Ironically, President Henderson's years as a faculty member and president were bookended by two smallpox epidemics—the first in 1883, when he was a senior student and assisted Professor Tindell in rounding up students. With the second epidemic in 1903, a yellow flag went up at the Hendersons' modest home on Russell Avenue—the signal that there was at least one case of smallpox within.[354] President Henderson's wife had contracted the deadly disease. Thankfully, she survived.

Knowing firsthand how smallpox spread by direct, one-on-one contact, Henderson determined to do what he could to stop the disease's advance. Thus he thought it wise to cancel commencement exercises that year since the occasion normally brought many visitors from out of town, and Jefferson City townspeople faithfully attended the ceremonies.

But this prudent move proved controversial. At their May meeting, the trustees criticized Henderson for dispensing with commencement. Also, some students who were concerned about becoming ill had returned home without finishing the semester. Henderson was criticized for not trying harder to keep them in school. Yet another point of contention surfaced regarding the employment or retention of certain faculty members.[355]

He did not take the criticism lightly. He resigned and accepted the presidency of Virginia Institute, later called Virginia Intermont College, a two-year Baptist college for young women in Bristol. His resignation was a blow to the students, alumni, faculty, and supporters of Carson and Newman, all of whom gave Henderson credit for the marvelous growth and development of the college during his years as president.[356]

A CHALLENGE TO JOHN HENDERSON'S TRUTHFULNESS

Soon after John Henderson moved to Virginia, he received word of false rumors circulating about him in East Tennessee. Wounded that his integrity was under assail, he published a response in a local newspaper:

"I learn that the report is circulated in Jefferson City that I have written letters to girls in that town and community requesting them to attend Virginia Institute. I hereby pledge myself to give One Hundred Dollars to Carson and Newman College for every such letter produced by a girl who resides in that community."[357] Clearly, John Henderson's commitment to Truth was rock solid. Apparently his response was the end of the matter.

Fortunately for all concerned, when Henderson returned to Tennessee from Virginia eleven years later, he held no grudges against anyone related to Carson and Newman. Living in Knoxville, he agreed to undertake several fundraising projects for the college over the years, with great success. When he died in 1946, he was still an active trustee of Carson and Newman.

By any measure, President Henderson's administration towered high in wonderful tangible achievements. But perhaps his most important legacy was to give the college a lasting, inspired spirit and morale. The quality of his character and his loyal, varied, longtime service to the school place him in the same high vanguard of Carson and Newman presidents as his predecessors Robert Reedy Bryan, Jesse Baker, and W. T. Russell—truly outstanding Christian men of character and excellent educators.

The Selection of an Optimistic Counselor-Administrator

Even the trustees who differed with John Henderson conceded that the scholar-president had created a desirable momentum at the college. No one wanted a vacuum to obstruct that momentum. The trustees moved swiftly to find a successor, choosing one from within their own ranks.

Millard Jeffries had been serving as the pastor of Broadway Baptist Church in Knoxville since 1893, and the church's membership had experienced impressive growth. After he introduced tithing to the congregation, they were able to complete the largest sanctuary in the city at that time. No doubt the trustees hoped he would inspire the same kind of growth at Carson and Newman. And, indeed, Jeffries became a pastor-president who would advance Carson and Newman's interests.

A FORWARD-THINKING, STUDENT-CENTERED ADVOCATE: MILLARD D. JEFFRIES, TWELFTH PRESIDENT (1903–1911)

Born and educated in Culpeper, Virginia, Millard Dudley Jeffries (1855–1936) followed an uncle into the field of medicine and graduated from the medical college of the University of Virginia in 1875. While practicing medicine, he experienced a call to the ministry and enrolled at The Southern Baptist Theological Seminary in Louisville, Kentucky, receiving a divinity degree in 1881.[358]

Dr. Jeffries's ensuing pastorates were all in college towns: Blacksburg, Virginia; Chapel Hill, North Carolina; Louisville, Kentucky; and then Knoxville. He enjoyed having contact with college students and probably felt that leading the college would offer him a different kind of ministry opportunity and challenge.

From the outset, he loved Carson and Newman and sensed the Goodness present there, developing a passion to see the college grow and progress. He longed to see new, useful buildings constructed on campus, made possible by donors who believed in the school. And he asserted that the college should exert every effort to increase its enrollment.[359]

He soon became one of the most-traveled presidents in the college's history. He visited in homes, speaking and preaching at every opportunity. The increase in enrollment attested to the success of his efforts. He proved to be very effective as a recruiter, and parents were impressed by

Millard D. Jeffries, president 1903–1911.

his warm, friendly approach. Jeffries understood that students did not come to a college on the basis of its reputation alone; they desired to feel personally wanted there.

In the school year 1906–1907, the total enrollment was 482.[360] The next year it reached 529, well above any previous enrollment. (These figures included the Preparatory Department.) Ever optimistic, Jeffries declared that with the school's growing popularity, there was no reason why seven to eight hundred students could not soon be attending Carson and Newman.

His youngest daughter, Rose Jeffries Hart, recalled later: "Father traveled all through the mountains getting pupils. . . . Then he traveled a lot trying to get funds to aid the college. He went several times to New York to interview men of wealth."[361]

Because his priority was on traveling for the college, Jeffries realized that he needed someone to leave in charge of the academic program and to handle discipline when he was away from the campus. He hired the first dean the college ever had, choosing Horace L. Ellis, the popular Latin professor who held his students to the highest standards.[362]

Jeffries apparently served as his own financial agent as well as student recruiter, philosophy professor, and president. He came to learn the hard truth of John Henderson's warning about financial campaigns: extra money beyond the goal amount would be needed to cover pledges that, however well intentioned, could never be redeemed.

CONTEXT: 1904 EVENTS IN WORLD HISTORY

The Louisiana Purchase Exposition (World's Fair) was held in St. Louis; while it was open, ice cream was created and debuted in a cone, and the first Olympic Games in the United States were held there.

In East Tennessee, the devastating New Market Train Wreck occurred just a few miles from Jefferson City on September 24, when two trains collided at high speed. One train was carrying some tourists back from St. Louis. At least fifty-six deaths and 106 injuries occurred. At the time, it was the worst train wreck that had ever occurred in the United States.

Also in 1904, the world auto speed record was set at 65.79 mph. The Russo-Japanese War began. Several notable first stage performances were held, including Giacomo Puccini's opera *Madame Butterfly* in Milan, James M. Barrie's play *Peter Pan* in London, and Anton Chekhov's play *The Cherry Orchard* in Moscow. Theodore Roosevelt was the twenty-sixth president of the United States, which purchased the Panama Canal Zone for $10 million. New York City began building Grand Central Station and held the first New Year's Eve celebration located in Times Square.

Positive Developments Early in the Twentieth Century

BEAUTY CAME TO LIVE ON CAMPUS: THE SARAH SWANN HOME

The college needed more student housing in order to grow. Trustee A. R. (Alfred Reuben) Swann, a businessman of means in nearby Oak Grove, wanted to make a large contribution to meet this need. Swann had been interested in the college's going coed in 1889. In 1904, he offered to construct a dormitory for young ladies, to be named for his mother, Sarah Austell Swann, if others would raise $10,000 for a men's hall.[363]

Obtaining the lot he wanted for the building was a complicated process, especially because he specified that he, not the college, would own the lot for the first ten years. Mrs. Nola Davis currently owned the lot—the one Mossy Creek Baptist Church had previously intended to build on, starting a cemetery behind it. (The renamed First Baptist Church of Jefferson City would move to its current location in 1909.[364])

Mrs. Davis sold the lot to the college for $1,000, which became the seed money for Davis Hall, the men's dormitory named in memory of her husband. The college then deeded the lot to A. R. Swann.[365] A treasured memory of living in Jefferson City for the Jeffries children involved walking to the campus at night and watching the bricks being burned for Sarah Swann Home.

Mr. Swann personally supervised the construction of a stunningly beautiful example of Georgian architecture with majestic Corinthian columns. His vision called for two lovely social rooms, a large lobby, and a kitchen and dining room on the first floor. An elegant stairway rose on either side of the lobby to the second and third floors. Society halls for the Calliopeans and Hypatians occupied part of the second floor. The third floor of Sarah Swann contained all dormitory rooms. There were basement rooms, too, used in various ways over the years.[366]

The first residents moved into Sarah Swann Home during the fall of 1905, even before it was completely finished. It was furnished with electricity and steam heat. Swann provided a ten-thousand-gallon water tower that supplied abundant water from a nearby spring to all campus buildings.[367] This tall, cylindrical reservoir was situated behind the present-day Bertie Maples Butler Hall.

Mr. Swann had a particular vision for the way Sarah Swann Home would operate. In contrast to the Young Ladies Home across the street, where the more affluent residents could pay their own way, he wanted Sarah Swann to serve young ladies who needed to work to earn their college degrees. His residents would use the Mount Holyoke plan, earning their room rent and a reduced cost for board by sharing in the work of the dormitory. The one hundred or so residents were divided into groups of ten and rotated through kitchen, dining hall, and various housekeeping duties. (The chief cook was a college employee.[368])

Sarah Swann Hall for women, an early picture.

The college already owned a small house utilizing this plan, and for a time both buildings were called "industrial homes." The building of Sarah Swann Home marked the beginning of a home economics program called Domestic Science, which covered such subjects as cooking, sewing, and laundry.[369]

In 1914, Swann deeded the dormitory to the college as he had promised. The "club" or "cooperative" system, as the Mount Holyoke plan was later called, was discontinued in 1951 with the approval of the Swann family.[370]

SARAH SWANN RESIDENCE HALL THROUGH THE YEARS

In 2004 the college celebrated the one hundredth anniversary of the beautiful dormitory's construction. Forty former residents came back to spend a night in Sarah Swann, and centennial ceremonies were held to commemorate the occasion.

The residence hall received major upgrades in 1919, 1965, 2002, and 2017.

In 2017, after much effort by many individuals, Sarah Swann Hall was added to the Tennessee Historical Register. An official state marker was placed at the southeast corner of the Sarah Swann property, with an official dedication ceremony held at homecoming.

Davis Hall for male students.

CLASSIC HOUSING FOR MEN: DAVIS HALL

A vigorous funding campaign was launched for Davis Hall, the new men's dormitory completed in 1906. (At that time, all dormitories for men were called "halls," while those for women were called "homes.") Located on the western edge of Campus #1 and facing Branner Avenue, Davis Hall was a three-story brick building clearly visible from the main campus. In addition to rooms for eighty students, it contained an apartment for a faculty supervisor and a kitchen and dining hall for food service. It had steam heat, electric lights, and community bathrooms.[371]

Between this building and Carson Hall, the college could house 140 male students.[372] Now the young men could play baseball, Davis Hall versus Carson Hall. Later another men's dormitory, Blanc Hall, was built adjacent to Davis Hall. Together, Davis and Blanc dormitories acquired the nickname "The Barn" because a head resident kept chickens and a cow behind the buildings. (And sometimes students brought them into the residence halls.) Davis Hall survived sixty years of sheltering high-spirited young men. In 1967, "The Barn" gave way to newer accommodations for men on the same side of the campus.

THE MILITARY COMPANY

In 1905, a new extracurricular activity was offered for several years—a military company, with uniforms and a gun supplied to each young man in the company. Participation was strictly voluntary. The existence of this group reveals the global anxiety of the pre–World War I era.[373]

EDUCATIONAL EXPANSIONS

Despite the fact that the bachelor of science degree had ceased to be offered since 1900, the science curriculum continued to be strengthened and enhanced.[374] Courses in physics, biology, and chemistry were added, as were faculty members skilled in teaching these subjects.[375] A sophisticated chemical laboratory was available for student use, thanks to scientists and others who had sent the college equipment and supplies they no longer needed.

At this time, Carson and Newman students were given more flexibility in course selection; several elective classes were available each year. For the first time, students could take a few classes outside the prescribed curriculum.[376]

In the 1909–1910 school year, a new Bible Department used the English-language Bible as the textbook. Previously, those studying the Bible had done so in the original Hebrew or Greek languages. Professor Jesse M. Burnett taught four new English-language classes, which numbered among the available electives for students.[377]

The grade required to pass any course was seventy-five out of one hundred.[378]

A TYPICAL COMMENCEMENT IN THE JEFFRIES ERA (CONDENSED VERSION OF THE 1906 EXERCISES)

Wednesday, May 30, 10:30 a.m., President Jeffries, Presiding
Doxology; Invocation; Oratorio (sung by 2 females and 2 males); Scripture Reading; Prayer; "Come Jesus, Redeemer" by Bartlett (solo); Announcements; Sermon; Hymn, "All Hail the Power of Jesus' Name" (Diadem); Benediction (*continued*)

Wednesday, May 30, 2:30 p.m., Professor Hale, Presiding
"My Heart at thy Sweet Voice" from *Samson and Delilah* (male solo); Declamation, "She Sang to Him of Heaven," by a Philomathean; Reading from Jules Verne's *Michael Strogoff* by a Hypatian; "Magnetic Valse" by Arditi (female solo); Declamation, "Old Seth Peter's Opinion," by a Columbian; Reading, "How the LaRue Stakes Were Lost," by a Calliopean; "Come Buy My Flowers" (cornet solo)

Wednesday, May 30, 8:00 p.m., Senior Music Recital, Miss Joy Bond, Directing
Part I, a Liszt Evening of piano music: Rhapsodie Hungroise XI; "Hernani" Aria and Cantabile; Rhapsodie Hungroise II; "Love Is Tyrant" from *The Singing Girl;* Rhapsodie Hungroise XII; "The Toreador Song" from *Carmen;* Delivery of Diplomas and Certificates by Professor T. A. Miles;
Part II (vocal solos except where noted): "Duo" by Wieniawski (2 violins); "Bird Song"; piece from *Der Frieschutz*; "Serenade" by Gounod; "The Spinning Song" by Litolff; Aria and Cantabile from *Faust;* "Flower Song" (in Italian); Polonaise by Chopin (4 female performers); "Swiss Echo Song" by Eckert; "Last Hope" by Gottschalk (2 pianos)

Thursday, May 31, 9:30 a.m., Professor R. A. Henderson, Presiding
Invocation; Valse (3 pianos); "Serenade" by Schubert (4 pianos); Essay, "The Beautiful in Life," by a Calliopean; Oration, "Some Real Summits," by a Columbian; "Valse de Concert" by Chopin, 4 pianists; Essay, "The Mission of Humor," by a Hypatian; Oration, "Imperialism versus Democracy," by a Philomathean; "Highland Gems" (dedicated to Goldeck) (4 pianos)

Thursday, May 31, 10:30 a.m., President Jeffries, Presiding
Invocation; Piece from *Il Trovatore* by Verdi (4 pianos); Literary Address; "The Dying Poet" by Gottschalk (4 pianos)

Thursday, May 31, 2:30 p.m., President of Alumni Association, Presiding
Orchestra; Alumnal Essay by a female graduate; Music; Alumnal Address by a male graduate; Music

Thursday, May 31, 8:00 p.m., Pay Entertainment
Featuring Professor Hale, Miss Bond, and assistants from the Elocution and Music Departments

Friday, June 1, 10 a.m., President Jeffries Presiding
March performed by the Orchestra; Invocation; Overture, performed by 8 pianists on 4 pianos; Delivery of Diplomas, Departments of Elocution and Business; Oration, "Our Country's Call for Young Men," by the salutatorian; "Serenade" by Schubert, sung by a female and a male; Valedictory Address (no title given); Thesis, "Influence of Greek Philosophy on the Thought Life of the Ages"; "Die Lorelei" (3 female singers); Conferring of AB and AM Degrees; Music; Announcements; Benediction.[379]

Good Intentions That Resulted in Regrets

THE LIBRARY THAT WAS NEVER BUILT

Carson and Newman's library facilities had always been housed in each successive administration building. Previous presidents had done their best to solicit monetary contributions and had donated books to upgrade the library's offerings; for example, W. A. Montgomery gave his extensive personal library of books to Carson and Newman late in his life.[380] Each literary society had a small library composed of books their own alumni had provided, and A. R. Swann had placed a select reading library within Sarah Swann Home.

In Jeffries's mind, the time had come for the college to have a separate building for library resources. He was well aware that Andrew Carnegie, an American millionaire-philanthropist originally from Scotland, had begun a foundation that built libraries to promote literacy and reading.

Bolstered by the knowledge that the Carnegie Foundation was investing in new library buildings all over the world, Jeffries wrote to the staff and presented Carson and Newman's needs. By 1905, the Foundation had given a favorable response, offering $10,00 for a Carnegie Library if the college could raise an additional $10,000 for ongoing maintenance.[381]

Enthusiastically, Jeffries presented the opportunity to the trustees, who suggested combining a gymnasium with the library building. They considered the possibilities for a time. But eventually they turned Jeffries down, citing other financial needs they considered more pressing.[382] According to Jeffries's daughter, his inability to obtain a Carnegie Library was his greatest disappointment at Carson and Newman.

FOOTBALL "TIME OUT"

To the dismay of many, football was suspended after the 1907 season. That year, a fatal injury was dealt to a player from the Bingham Military Institute at Asheville, North Carolina, in a game with Carson and Newman.[383] The realization that a Carson and Newman player had caused a death, however unintentionally, was a bitter pill to swallow. Interest in football then waned at Carson and Newman for several years.

MINING PROMISES AND PROBLEMS

In 1910, the trustees agreed to allow a nearby mining company to extract zinc deposits beneath the campus; they believed the resulting income would net the college hundreds of thousands of dollars. W. T. Russell was assigned the thankless job of managing the college's interests in this area.[384]

This experiment proved to be a major disappointment and a future problem stretching all the way to the present. Not only did the college realize very little income from the mining operations, but also a number of sinkholes have occurred all over campus from the drilling process. Mining has caused great difficulty in the school's ability to get footings for new buildings.

Unfortunately, this mistake was to occur again in ensuing years.

An Abrupt End to Jeffries's Presidency

In 1909, Dr. Jeffries addressed the Nolachucky Baptist Association, mentioning that he would soon be traveling a great deal. The trustees had instructed him to raise an additional $100,000. There is no further word on the level of his success with that assignment.

In the spring of 1911, the trustees instructed Jeffries to close out all pledges made ten years earlier during the endowment campaign of 1901.

They wanted the unfulfilled pledges replaced with cash or interest-bearing notes. These subscriptions had been past due since 1905, but a few were still trickling in.[385]

Also in 1911, A. R. Swann issued a new challenge for the college. If others would contribute $25,000 for the endowment, he would give a matching amount. This offer may have been the impetus for the trustees' direction to close out the 1901 campaign pledges.[386]

Jeffries was given a deadline of September 2, 1911, to report his financial efforts to the trustees. He did so on that fateful day, specifying several categories of the income he had been promised. He had acquired $9,000 in cash and cash pledges and had also secured $4,025 in interest-bearing notes, $1,300 in real estate, and $4,720 in noninterest-bearing notes, for a total of $19,045. He also reported a pledge of $12,000 in "land notes," payable annually for twenty-four years without interest. More simply stated, the donor's pledge to give $500 a year for the next twenty-four years was backed by a lien on land he owned.[387] Together, all of this income would more than meet Mr. Swann's challenge.

The trustees' executive committee discussed the report and then decided to adjust the value of the notes and pledges downward—apparently to a severe extent. Whatever else was said among the group is a mystery. But before the meeting was over, Jeffries had resigned. The termination took effect immediately, even though the fall semester had just begun.[388]

A representative student group composed a body of resolutions describing their sadness about the loss of their "beloved Dr. Jeffries." He wrote a heartfelt response: "I acknowledge with tender appreciation the receipt of your resolutions. . . . You young people occupy a place in my heart's love that shall never be vacated."[389]

Jeffries and his family moved to South Carolina, where he led churches in Edgefield and Spartanburg as pastor.[390] For the last eighteen years of his life, he served as chaplain of the Baptist medical complex in Memphis—a position that combined his dual careers of medicine and ministry.

Rose Jeffries Hart later recalled her father's abiding interest in the college: "He never forgot Carson and Newman. During his last illness in Memphis, when he was in the hospital and his thoughts were mixed up, he sometimes thought he was back at the college. He would ask what the lights were doing on in the 'auditorium' (the building next to the hospital, a medical school). The college was sort of like a child to him. He wanted so badly to do [well] for it and have it amount to something fine."[391]

The Henderson and Jeffries administrations, which bookended the turn of the twentieth century, had much in common. In a sense, both men were father figures for the institution they loved, sowing integrity and security across the campus. Both worked hard to enrich Carson and Newman, by endowment funds and by a broader curriculum, and both left under the shadow of conflicts with trustees. In the next decade, the peace and progress they had engendered were threatened by a heartbreaking fire, a tempting offer to relocate the school elsewhere, and the First World War. Again, Carson and Newman would survive daunting challenges, thanks to strong leadership and the quality of its "righteously proud" alumni. By the summer of 1911, the sixty-year-old college had graduated 308 worthy men and women.

CHAPTER SIX

Rollercoaster Years of Upheaval, Loss, and Restoration
1911–1919

"Work went on. Sometimes it seemed . . . that work was the only certainty, the only lasting truth in a human world of fitful change. Work and the mountains remained."
—Wilma Dykeman[392]

A well-dressed, slender man with observant eyes and a neatly brushed mustache strode across the Carson and Newman campus to meet his first class of the day on September 2, 1911. Those who passed him were not surprised to see a small stack of books under his arm; students and faculty alike knew his habit of using any spare ten or fifteen minutes to delve into a book.[393] Jesse McGarity Burnett had been the professor of Greek and modern languages since 1894, and he was not limited to reading English-language books. In 1911, he might have been reading the newly published *The Phantom of the Opera* by Gaston Leroux in either English or French.

Burnett's life was about to change. When the college trustees terminated Millard Jeffries's presidency that day, they called in J. M. Burnett and asked him to become chairman of the faculty for the remainder of the school year. He hesitated because he loved teaching and disliked the idea of fundraising.

Trustee W. C. Hale of Carson College's Class of 1888 agreed to serve as Burnett's financial agent.[394] Hale's immediate challenge was the $25,000 gift offered by A. R. Swann if the college could raise a matching amount. Over time, Hale was only able to raise $12,500, but Swann agreed to match the amount. The college was grateful to receive the gift of $12,500.[395]

Burnett did accept the presidency along with a reduced teaching load—only Greek and German—and was given a salary increase of $400 for the extra work involved.[396] The next year, the trustees elected Burnett president for a term of five years at a salary of $1,800 dollars per year.[397] Interestingly, this was the first time a president had been hired for a specific length of time.

The Pre–World War I Years

A CALM PRESENCE IN A PERIOD OF CHANGE: JESSE MCGARITY BURNETT, THIRTEENTH PRESIDENT (1911–1917)

Jesse M. Burnett (1870–1947) had been born to a highly literate and gracious family from Del Rio, Tennessee. John T. Henderson, a classmate of Jesse Burnett's oldest brother, Edmund, described the Burnett family as unusually refined and cultured.[398] As president Henderson had hired first Edmund, then Jesse as professor of Greek and modern languages.

Jesse and Edmund were the oldest sons of Rev. J. M. L. (Jesse Montreville Lafayette) Burnett, a well-known East Tennessee minister and farmer, and Henrietta Sarah Cody Burnett, a charming woman with a keen intellect.[399] Their eight children were educated at home by a governess until they were old enough to go to boarding school.[400] After being widowed, Mrs. Burnett served as Carson and Newman's matron of the Young Ladies Home for several years while her younger children attended the preparatory school or college.[401]

Frances Burnett, the oldest daughter, had married A. R. Swann in 1881.[402] Thus, Mr. Swann was President Burnett's brother-in-law. However, Swann's generous donations to Carson and Newman were not tied to this relationship. His benevolence to the college began before Burnett's presidency and would continue afterward.

Young Jesse M. Burnett attended the preparatory school at Carson and Newman, then earned a BA in 1891 from Richmond College in Virginia with an outstanding record. Next he studied for the ministry at The Southern Baptist Theological Seminary in Louisville, Kentucky, from which he graduated in 1894 with a master of theology degree and a high rank of achievement.[403]

In the fall of 1894 Jesse began seventeen satisfying years as a Carson and Newman professor; the college awarded him a DD in 1906. As president,

Jesse M. Burnett, president 1911–1917.

he continued to teach Greek, German, and/or philosophy in turn, leading the school well through six tumultuous years.

First Yearbook: The Swann, *1912*

Excitement ran high on campus in 1912 when students and faculty were able to hold in their hands the very first yearbook of Carson and Newman College. The annual was bound in a luxurious, soft tan leather cover with its title, *The Swann,* imprinted in gold. Elegant maroon moiré was used for the endpapers. Inside, accompanied by a photograph, the book's dedication read: "To Maj. A. R. Swann, one of the best friends Carson and Newman College has ever had, we lovingly dedicate this, our first annual."

Portraits of Millard Jeffries, who began the 1911–1912 school year as president and doubtless approved the yearbook's publication, and J. M. Burnett, current president, adorned early pages. Nine faculty members were pictured, as was Ben Hooper, Tennessee's current governor. He was an 1890 Carson and Newman alumnus and a trustee at the time.

"THE COLLEGE AND CULTURE" BY JESSE M. BURNETT

"I believe that everything about a college should have some cultural value. . . . Nothing should be given a place in college life, from a course of study down to the amusements or entertainments, that has not some element of culture. Certainly nothing should be admitted there that is vulgarizing or destructive of culture. . . . The college is primarily an institution for human culture.

"What is culture? Two ideas enter into it. Some of you had your early home in some secluded valley. The world went by on the other side of the mountains. You knew nothing of the great current of the world's thought and activity. For you the first step in culture was to come out of the narrow environment of your life down to the edge of this stream and see the world go by. The first element of culture is to get a broadening vision of the world, to have some knowledge of and some feeling for the ideas that are moving in the great world, and to feel that I am a part of this great world and have to do with the things with which it has to do. Culture is set over against a narrow provincialism. . . .

"The ideas with which culture deals must also have a certain *quality* and *magnitude*. Culture is the life of the pure and the good, the noble and the great. Culture brings one in touch not only with the great world but with the great world of great and noble ideas. Culture is set over against vulgarity; it is reaching out after the ideal. Idealism is the breath of its life. This is the work of a college, to create such an atmosphere of ideas and idealism in which young men and young women work and live for a few years, until this life has become their life."[404]

But most of the annual's pages clearly belonged to the 432 students, twenty-three of whom were proud seniors. Their pictures and four-year lists of activities were accompanied by individual, fitting lines from literature. On the other end of the spectrum were the numerous preparatory students, called "Subfreshmen."[405] Each literary society was represented along with its branches, such as an orchestra or glee club. Student fun clubs abounded, including "The High-Eater Club," "The Red-Headed Fraternity," "The Leap Year Club" (all women, whose occupation was proposing), and "The Smith Club" (for all whose last name was Smith).[406] Of course, more purposeful groups were pictured as well, such as the "Tennis Experts" and the staff of *The Carson-Newman Collegian*, the student newspaper.[407]

The Swann was so expensive to produce that the college's budget could allow no further yearbooks to be published until five years later. In the meantime, the May issues of *The Carson-Newman Collegian* served as mini-annuals, with senior portraits and all types of student memories in its pages.[408]

STUDENT PUBLICATIONS

After *The Carson Index* folded in 1886, there was a lapse of ten years before *The Carson and Newman Magazine* began. It was published monthly by all four literary societies. Like its predecessor, it contained scholarly essays by students and faculty and news items about campus events and personalities.

The next student-led newspaper seems to have been *The Karnuargus*, of which only one issue (1908) is extant in the Carson-Newman archives. Interestingly, its editor-in-chief was senior student J. I. (Joseph Isaac) Reece, future dean of Carson and Newman. The title appeared to be a student-inspired combination of the Hebrew word *karn*, meaning shining or radiant, and the Greek word *argus*, a one-hundred-eyed mythical creature.

In 1911, *The Carson-Newman Collegian* took up the reins of providing an enlightening glimpse into student perspectives of its day. This truly excellent monthly magazine lasted through May 1916, and *The Orange and Blue* began publication in the 1916 fall semester, lasting through 2010.

"Sane Athletics"

Some schools of the early twentieth century described their sports programs as "sane athletics."[409] They had allowed teams of various sports to form, then saw that athletics in general could get out of hand; some students overemphasized sports to the exclusion of their studies. The administration of Carson and Newman wanted athletics to assume a properly balanced part of college activities, with student-athletes devoting sufficient time to their studies to master them and graduate on time. For several years, the sports available had included only basketball, baseball, and tennis; the football program had been canceled in 1907 due to the death of a player on a rival team.

Interest in resuming football on campus began to pick up during 1912. By 1913, football was officially a sport at Carson and Newman once again.[410]

THE RETURN OF FOOTBALL

The outstanding student leader in the movement to renew football was Spencer Tunnell, who was appointed manager of the 1913 team. He made the schedule for the fall 1913 games and handled the team's finances.[411] He also had a great sense of how to draw crowds to watch the games.

On the morning of the game with Cumberland College, a three-inch snow fell in Jefferson City. The game was almost canceled, but Tunnell said he would manage the situation. He stacked piles of logs around the playing field, talked all the local store owners into closing during the game, and spread the word that there would be fires at the game. The largest crowd of the season attended.[412]

Football proved very popular overall. Expenses, including the purchase of new football uniforms and other necessary equipment, were successfully met.[413] (Tunnell later became the pastor of First Baptist Church in Morristown and a supportive college trustee.)

Perceiving the need for a professional coach so the football team could have winning seasons, President Burnett and the trustees added a $3 student fee per semester to enable the college to employ a full-time coach in 1913. Phil M. Utley, a recent graduate of Wake Forest College, was Carson and Newman's first football coach.[414] In 1914, James Barnett, a graduate of Richmond College, succeeded Utley as football coach and director of athletics.[415] (That year, Barnett met the daughter of W. T. Russell, Mary, an instructor on the music faculty. The couple married a few years later.)

In 1915, John Kilpatrick, who had played baseball, basketball, and football at Carson and Newman, took over full coaching duties in the Athletic Department.[416] But in 1917 and 1918, as the United States fought in World War I, no coach was employed at Carson and Newman. All sports on campus were curtailed.[417]

DANA X. BIBLE, CLASS OF 1912

Dana Xenophon Bible, a lauded football player in high school in Jefferson City, was a son of treasurer and Professor Jonathan D. Bible and his wife, Cleopatra. He entered Carson and Newman at precisely the wrong time to play college football. The school had canceled its football program just before his freshman year, and the sport returned the year after he graduated. In 1912, he was captain of both the basketball and baseball teams and president of the tennis club as well as athletic editor of *The Carson-Newman Collegian* and Columbian president.

Bible helped coach the new Carson and Newman football team the year after his graduation. East Tennessee friends recognized his potential: "Bible . . . not only can play football, but he can teach it."[418] His subsequent career certainly proved this statement true.

Dana X. Bible coached football for thirty-three seasons at five different colleges and became one of the outstanding football coaches in the country. His brilliant career was spent at Mississippi College, Louisiana State University, Texas A & M, the University of Nebraska, and the University of Texas. He also served several of these schools in administrative roles such as athletic director. Bible was inducted into the College Football Hall of Fame in 1951 with 198 career wins as a head coach. The same year, Carson-Newman awarded him an honorary DD.[419] He passed away in 1980.

OTHER CAMPUS SPORTS

Baseball had been played at Carson and Newman since 1895; football was introduced later the same year. Basketball and tennis became recognized college sports in 1908. About 1911 a campus "first" took place: Teams in basketball, baseball, tennis, and track were organized according to the students' college classifications to compete for a cup given to the class winning the most points on Field Day in May.[420] This seems to have been the first time track was recognized as a campus sport; the 1913–1914 catalogue contains the earliest picture of the track team.[421]

The Tennis Club was organized in 1911 with thirty-five members, both men and women. There were not enough tennis courts for practices, so an

"The Invincibles," undefeated 1912 baseball team.
Dana X. Bible is seated, center.

agreement was made: a club member and his or her partner would locate an area on campus suitable for a court and clear it off. That space would be theirs all year.[422]

The baseball team almost always won a large percentage of its games. In 1911–1912, the undefeated baseball team dubbed themselves "the Invincibles." That same year, the men's basketball team was undefeated, quite an achievement.[423] The varsity basketball teams of both men and women practiced on the platform of the auditorium. Since the platform was not regulation basketball court size, "the team was handicapped by playing on the small home court and then playing on larger courts on the road . . . Carson-Newman had comparable material [talented players] to other schools, but the lack of a gymnasium prevented the development of good team work."[424]

The next year, Carson and Newman's basketball coach was former student P. M. (Pryor Mynatt) "Humpy" McElveen, a local young man who had played for the Brooklyn major-league baseball team—first the Superbas, then the Dodgers—for three seasons. Later, he would play in the minor leagues for several years. Primarily a third baseman, he played every position but pitcher for his teams.[425] His basketball team at Carson-Newman won all but one game.

In the spring of 1912, the East Tennessee Athletic Association was formed for college-level competitors. Four area colleges joined Carson and Newman as participants. The association directed and regulated the sports of football, baseball, basketball, and track. Unsurprisingly, women could not participate in Association activities, but they were encouraged to continue participating in their school's athletic program.[426]

Notable Campus Activities of the Burnett Years

As with every college, some faculty members had only short stints. But those who stayed long enough to win their students' hearts were beloved and mourned upon leaving. For example, the May 1914 *Carson-Newman Collegian* was dedicated to Horace Ellis, the beloved Latin professor of six years. Ellis left to teach at Maryville College, near his home, that fall. In the same issue is an appreciation of Professor Shelby E. Jones, who had died unexpectedly. Jones had taught science, mathematics, and philosophy since 1882.

About this time, the first gold medals since 1895 were awarded on campus. The Ready Speaker's Medal went to the top two speakers. D. L. Butler and T. H. Campbell provided the medals "to arouse an enthusiasm for ready speaking and to quicken a keener interest in better expression on the part of the student body."[427]

Carson and Newman began sending their debate teams to compete with Maryville and Tusculum Colleges. In 1915, six young men from Carson and Newman won a complete victory in the Triangular Debate among these schools.[428] "Long before the advent of radio, political debates and speeches were a leading form of entertainment. Holding the attention of audiences was an indispensable political skill, and college debating societies ranked above sports as an undergraduate diversion."[429]

THE PROBLEM OF INADEQUATE WATER

When A. R. Swann built Sarah Swann Home, he took steps to provide a water system for the entire campus by constructing a concrete reservoir near Sarah Swann Home and pumping water from a spring near Mossy Creek. This system was enforced and extended from time to time.[430] But none of these efforts relieved the inadequate water pressure on the top floors of Sarah Swann and the administration building. The fact that the local water was hard did not help.

In 1913, the trustees recommended that the college sell water to a new utility company in Jefferson City. Thus for a time, Carson and Newman's water tower furnished the water supply for all of Jefferson City. But cisterns for laundry and other uses still had to be maintained. The water pressure problem was not solved until 1921, when the city established a municipal system.[431] To this day, however, the hard water is difficult to manage and filter.

B. CARROLL REECE, CLASS OF 1914

Brazilla Carroll Reece from Butler, Tennessee, later a Congressman for thirty-four years, was a scholar-athlete and lauded YMCA chapter president at Carson and Newman. Carroll's impressive speaking skills were honed while he attended college. He and a partner participated in the intercollegiate debate against Maryville College and won twice. As the valedictorian of his class, he was also the student commencement speaker.[432]

Carroll Reece also served as a soldier in World War I. Under the leadership of General John J. Pershing, he was a member of the AEF (American Expeditionary Force) beginning in 1917 and serving through 1918. He fought in France under extremely challenging conditions. Upon his return, he actively supported Carson and Newman and was a frequent visitor to campus, speaking about his war experiences and the college's need for financial help (*The Orange and Blue,* October 1, 1920 and April 1, 1921).

Located at East Tennessee State University in Johnson City in Reece's home congressional district, the B. Carroll Reece Memorial Museum contains his personal library and historic documents as well as many artifacts of Appalachia. Reece died in 1961.

NOTES ON THE FINE ARTS

A Normal (teaching) course had been established on campus for students doing postgraduate work in piano, voice, and music theory. And after years of fruitful work, Carson and Newman's music program had been

The art studio hosting a visitor—President Burnett at far right.

upgraded to Conservatory status. Located in the Young Ladies Home, the Carson and Newman Conservatory of Music was aligned with various prestigious music schools, including the Cincinnati Conservatory of Music.[433] Carson and Newman's Conservatory was well supplied with instruments in suitable practice rooms. The crown jewel of the music program was a concert grand Steck piano, placed in the auditorium for recitals and public entertainments.

A graceful art studio in the administration building was the domain of Miss Blanche Ellis, the art professor. A fascinating book about one of her students of this era, Zula Pangle, reveals the range of Miss Ellis's teaching. Zula was proficient in oil painting, wood carvings, watercolors, china painting, ceramics, and creating jewelry. Zula Pangle never became famous for her lovely landscapes or still-life creations; but in the spirit of a simpler time, she used her artistic abilities to beautify her own home and those of others. Her daughter wrote of Zula's generosity: "I have often admired paintings on the walls of friends and relatives, only to be told, 'Why, your mother painted that.'"[434] No doubt Blanche Ellis's teaching gave lifelong pleasure to many art students.

THE COLLEGE CULTURE

Although student enrollment began a slow slide during the Burnett years, new courses and clubs were still formed. Sociology was taught for the first time and a new outdoors club, the (John) Burroughs Nature Club, began.[435]

COMMENCEMENTS AND HOMECOMINGS, THEN AND NOW

In this era, homecomings were not a part of Carson and Newman's calendar; alumni came to commencements to see one another and reminisce. Joseph Robinson, an English professor, wrote a wonderful article for *The Carson-Newman Collegian* about the significance of commencement ceremonies. In so doing, he paraphrased a comment by John Burroughs, a then-popular naturalist, about the final day before leaving a beloved retreat setting: "When you come to break camp, after you have packed up everything, you still have a feeling of having forgotten something. In vain you puzzle yourself to find what it is, till in thinking about the happy sun-lit hours you have spent by the clear-flowing stream where your tent was pitched, it occurs to you that a part of your life has been left there. I think in somewhat the same manner the college man feels that a very beautiful and vital part of his life has been left at his Alma Mater, and so year after year he returns in quest of it."[436]

INTRIGUING LETTER TO CARSON AND NEWMAN'S PRESIDENT

Dear Jesse:

Being prone to think of things historically, I have often wondered whether the college possesses a complete set of its own catalogues. I have also wondered whether a set of the earliest college magazine anywhere exists. If you haven't a complete set of the catalogues I should think it would be well to advertise in the *Baptist and Reflector* and try to obtain the missing numbers before it is too late. One of these days the college will very much want to be able to trace its own history.

Affectionately,
Edmund C. Burnett[437]

Even now, Carson-Newman does not have a copy of its first catalogue. Many other catalogues and issues of student magazines, especially from the early days, are missing as well. This letter between the Burnett brothers highlights the sad reality that opportunities to collect every edition were missed.

THE FIRST STUDENT GOVERNMENT

Progressive educators were advocating the establishment of student governments in colleges at this time. Jesse M. Burnett was interested in inculcating civic responsibility in students and believed that a student government would help accomplish this purpose. A vocal segment of local people thought forming a student government would give students too much power, however. These critics deplored Burnett's "radical idea" and suggested that he did not know how to run the college.

But Burnett believed guarding and dominating students was a thing of the past. He asserted that students would be willing to submit to reasonable rules and regulations if given a voice in suggesting them. He further stated, "The rules of conduct are as few and simple as possible. Students are expected to conduct themselves as ladies and gentlemen. They are always treated as self-respecting men and women."[438]

In the 1914–1915 school year, the first student council was established with representatives from each class, including the Preparatory Department.[439] The first set of members admirably set the pace for succeeding generations of student government members. The council soon became an effective medium between the student body and the faculty.

A VERY SMALL CLUB

The Class of 1916 was thirty members strong. Two of its number, Isaac Newton Carr and Arlie Eugene Cate, had something else in common later in life. At various times, each of them became the dean of Carson and Newman.

Distractions from the College's Mission

THE SWEETWATER SEMINARY

For some time, citizens in Sweetwater, Tennessee, had wanted Carson and Newman to take over and operate the Sweetwater Seminary for

Young Ladies. The Sweetwater staff was ready to turn over the property to Carson and Newman if the college would assume $5,000 of its debt.[440]

In 1914, the college accepted the property on certain conditions, principally that it would assume no responsibility for Sweetwater's debts, past or future. Carson and Newman provided a principal, W. S. Woodward of the Class of 1908, and paid his annual salary of $1,000. The college would maintain a first-class preparatory school for girls and endeavor to make the school financially self-supporting, but that was all.[441]

From the beginning of the arrangement, the school ran on a deficit and the situation became progressively problematic. In 1916, the relationship between the two schools was terminated at the trustees' initiative. The Monroe County Board of Education and the town of Sweetwater purchased the property.[442] Many people were disappointed that the partnership did not work out. But Carson and Newman was simply not in a position to assume such financial responsibility.

THE MOUNTAIN SCHOOLS

Early in the century, several Baptist academies (high schools) were founded in various rural mountain communities. At one point, forty of them were scattered through the southern Appalachian Mountains. In Tennessee at this time, there were seven: Cosby Academy in Cocke County; Doyle Academy in White County; Harrison-Chilhowee Institute (in Seymour) and Smoky Mountain Academy (near Sevierville), both in Sevier County; Stockton Valley Academy in Helena, Fentress County; Andersonville Baptist Institute in Anderson County; and Watauga Academy in Johnson County, in Butler.[443]

A. E. (Albert Erskine) Brown was hired to oversee the work of these schools.[444] (Brown was a son of W. A. G. Brown, an early Mossy Creek College graduate and the onetime math professor and principal of the Masonic Female Institute.) A. E. Brown made the establishment of the mountain schools his life's work, planting schools in sparsely populated communities where "book learning" was desired but had required leaving home to attain. Carson and Newman awarded Brown an honorary DD in his later years to recognize his accomplishments in bringing quality education to rural mountain families.

More than once, A. E. Brown approached Carson and Newman about establishing a closer relationship with the mountain schools in Tennessee.

He seems to have wanted the college to take them under its wing as feeder schools.[445] But the trustees were rightly fearful of the stress this proposition would add to the college's already strained finances.

The Sevier Baptist Association asked Carson and Newman to elect a principal for the Smoky Mountain Academy and provide his salary. The trustees' response was swift and negative, "our finances not permitting."[446]

Naturally, in principle, Carson and Newman wanted to support these fledgling schools. But the college had rarely been on sure financial footing itself. Over time, most of the mountain schools were folded into the public education system as high schools. (The notable exception in Tennessee would be Harrison-Chilhowee Baptist Academy, still in operation now as a private K–12 school called The King's Academy.)

"Fire!" Disaster Strikes the College

On December 13, 1916, students returning to the stately administration building from lunch saw smoke billowing from the top floor. Several students and faculty members rushed inside to try to save valuable items from the building, some risking their lives. English professor Joseph Robinson and others rescued many books and furnishings from the library. Education professor William L. Gentry was described as displaying superhuman zeal and strength as he entered the burning building over and over, saving many desks and books as well. Fortunately, there were no casualties.[447]

The building quickly went up in flames. It was a total loss, including many valuable documents and records pertaining to the college's history. The Philomathean and Columbian literary society halls, with their libraries and furnishings, were destroyed.[448] Amazingly, according to the reports, almost all the pianos were saved. Apparently a faulty attic flue was the source of the fire.[449]

Everyone at Carson and Newman suffered an unimaginable loss. *The Swann*, the 1912 yearbook, had featured a lovely picture of "the College," as the building was popularly called, along with a poem paying tribute to the beautiful edifice and revealing the students' enduring love for it. A prophetic excerpt reads:

> We revere this splendid structure;
> 'Tis beautiful in all its parts;

The lovely administration building in ruins, 1917.

And, Time, you can never rupture
What she has built within our hearts.
Though you may willfully tear her down,
And send her back to mother dust,
Yet her instruction, good and sound,
You cannot make to even rust.[450]

On December 20, the trustees held a meeting at the nearby First Baptist Church, where they could still smell smoke from the burned building. Burnett described the amazing nature of the student body's spirit and loyalty. Offers of help had poured in from all the local churches. At once, spaces in the two women's dormitories were cleared for temporary classrooms. Incredibly, all classes resumed in temporary spaces on the morning after the fire.[451]

A SHOCKING OFFER

In the first trustee meeting after the fire W. C. Hale, President Burnett's financial agent, gave his fellow trustees a shock when he said he "loved the hills, the rocks and trees and valleys of old Mossy Creek and every foot of ground that belongs to Carson-Newman, but . . . there are other hills and valleys, trees and rocks and creeks just as good as these."[452] Some later described Hale's announcement as entering the trustees' ears like a thunderclap.

Hale was a leader of the Morristown Board of Trade, the equivalent of today's Chamber of Commerce. Morristown, he said, was ready to offer a site for a new campus and to raise money for buildings and equipment if the college would move there. The city would donate a site of sixty acres or more and erect a building as good as the one that was lost, also furnishing city water and sewage disposal.[453] No mention was made of replacing the four residence halls, however.

The trustees realized that other cities might bid for the college too. In fact, Len G. Broughton, pastor of First Baptist Church in Knoxville, wanted Knoxville to have a chance to acquire the college. The Knoxville newspaper soon carried a front-page article saying that Carson and Newman might move to Knoxville.[454]

The trustees then turned their attention to more pressing business—the immediate needs of the college. They authorized President Burnett and the executive committee to set apart space for classrooms, to salvage brick and any other usable materials from the burned building, and to clear the site. J. D. Bible, the college treasurer and a philosophy professor, reported that $23,000 in insurance was carried on the building. That amount just about covered the remaining indebtedness of the college. The trustees instructed him to pay all debts, buy some needed equipment, and erect fire escapes on all residence halls.[455]

In January 1917, the Morristown group invited the trustees to be their guests to view the advantages Morristown had as a college town. The trustees had a long, unrecorded discussion afterward. They must have considered the length of time it would take to raise money and develop a new campus and what would happen to the college if it had to try to survive several years of the present circumstances in the meantime. President Burnett and W. T. Russell spoke; both favored rebuilding on the current campus site.[456]

Dr. Rufus Weaver, the new leader of the Tennessee Baptist Education Commission, offered an alternate plan. Not a proponent of co-education, he suggested transforming the current Carson-Newman campus into a junior college for young women—with a home economics course the only program. He offered no provision for the women's last two years of college. He further envisioned a standard college for young men to be built in a centrally located city in East Tennessee.[457] In his plan, the chosen city would donate an acceptable site of one hundred acres and $150,000 for equipment. If the trustees would accept this plan, he said, his agency would raise $100,000. Also, he personally promised to raise another $100,000 for endowment.[458]

After discussion Len Broughton offered a resolution that they delay making a final decision for thirty days to give local cities time to make offers of land and money and to allow the trustees time to inspect any property offered.[459]

THE FINAL DECISION

The person present with the longest connection to Carson and Newman was W. T. Russell. No one could doubt his heart for the college, considering all the roles he had filled in the school since his graduation in 1869. As president of Newman College, he had purchased the thirteen acres that now composed Carson and Newman's main campus. By 1917, he had been a trustee for about forty years and was considered the "elder statesman" of the board, much as Jesse Baker had been for the previous generation.

When Russell rose to speak, the trustees listened. He eloquently urged them to keep the college where it was, preserving its rich history.[460]

After discussion, the trustees adopted his motion to rebuild in Jefferson City, on the campus that still reached down to the banks of Mossy Creek. A new administration building would be constructed on the site of the old one as soon as possible.[461] Dean William L. Gentry was hired as the financial agent to raise money for the new building.[462]

Everyone seemed to breathe a sigh of relief that the controversy had been resolved and, in the view of many, with just the right result. Speaking for many of his fellow students, M. B. Dale, the editor of *The Orange and Blue,* wrote for the January 15, 1917 edition: "What matters it if Jefferson City is a small town? It is the birth place of Carson-Newman and is surrounded by a valley as beautiful as any we know. We don't mind that we are not in Morristown or Knoxville and it is very little trouble to get here from either of the towns. . . . All of these things are incidental and more or less trivial. What we desire, very, very deeply and are eager to help realize is that Carson-Newman College shall be rebuilt on foundations sufficiently broad for a big and useful future."

Second Yearbook: The Larker, *1917*

Most people felt that *The Larker* was worth the five-year wait since *The Swann* had been published. The 1917 annual was dedicated to Dr. J. M. Burnett, "a man whose influence and interest among the students makes him not only popular, but loved and respected as well."[463] Pictures of the magnificent administration building, first in its heyday and then in ruins, reminded everyone how much they had lost.

The theme of "larking"—having carefree, wholesome fun—was much in evidence through the new yearbook's pages. The students had reproduced a picture of their beloved English professor, Joseph Robinson, as a child of about four years old. Titled "Baby Robinson," the picture was captioned, "Tall oaks from little acorns grow."[464] Another page noted of two seniors, "Lena Bird and Maye Burnett have taken a full course in 'Larking,' but however not to the exclusion of their school work."[465]

The "Smiles" section contains entertaining glimpses of campus life such as these: "Breakfast at the Young Ladies' Home is like Judgment Day. When the bell rings you have to go whether you are ready or not," and "[Bert Wilson] Wills has recently discovered an angel on earth and has abandoned his idea of becoming an aviator."[466] Social groups included "The Sarah Swann Larkers' Club," The Stew-Bum Club," "The Royal Order of Saintly Worts," and "The Karo Club."[467] Senior Bernie H. Moore (who would later become an outstanding university football and track coach) was recognized for his athletic prowess in football.[468] Cleverly written short fiction pieces and essays added to readers' understanding of day-to-day life at Carson and Newman.

In 1917, larking, of course, stood in direct contrast to the momentous destruction and violent battles taking place in Europe in World War I, which the United States had entered just before the yearbooks were distributed. Many changes were about to take place on campus.

A Transition at the Top

All the unexpected and complex events of recent years had worn greatly on President Burnett. The trustees received another surprise when, in an April 1917 meeting, Burnett read his resignation to them. He stated succinctly: "Under existing conditions I feel that it is going to be impossible for me to accomplish anything in the next few years in the college worth giving my life to. I therefore tender my resignation as President of the College."[469]

Burnett and his family moved to Belton, South Carolina, where he became pastor of First Baptist Church. Later he became editor of the *Baptist Courier,* the state Baptist paper. He held this position for almost the rest of his life.[470]

Many individuals on campus felt that Dean/Professor W. L. Gentry was the right choice to be the next president. He had been at Carson and Newman since 1907 and believed in the college's potential. He had demonstrated skill as a fundraiser along with his dedication as he risked his life retrieving many items from the burning administration building.

After offering the presidency to two other men who refused, the trustees asked Gentry to take on the presidency. He recognized that his administrative experience was limited, and as an insider he understood the challenges he faced. But he said yes to the job. To give Gentry as much time as possible to travel for fundraising, the board named Edward W. White, professor of mathematics, as dean.[471]

A "Graduate Course" for the Education Professor

A MIDLIFE CAREER CHANGE: WILLIAM LEE GENTRY, FOURTEENTH PRESIDENT (1917–1919)

Born in rural Union County, Tennessee, William Gentry (1867–1947) began teaching in his home county at age twenty. In 1895, he received a two-year diploma from Hiwassee College in Madisonville, Tennessee, probably by teaching in the fall and attending college in the spring. Four years later, he graduated with a BS degree from the National Normal University in Lebanon, Ohio.[472]

Like Robert Reedy Bryan, Gentry apparently had a natural gift for teaching. In 1907, he came to Carson and Newman to teach pedagogy (education) and was also placed in charge of the Preparatory Department.[473] In ensuing years, he also taught college-level science, English, Bible, and other subjects as needed, so his versatility was helpful to the college. As president, he established the credit-hour as the standard on campus.[474]

Gentry's main interest was in public education and the improvement of teaching skills. A practical educator, he had served on the Tennessee

William L. Gentry, president 1917–1919.

Board of Education and was in demand as a speaker in educational settings. He was often invited to serve on the staff of summer institutes for teachers.

William Gentry also excelled at hiring excellent professors for Carson and Newman. A case in point was Elmer W. Sydnor, who became a longtime English professor and the college's first professional debate coach in 1918. According to Sydnor, Gentry said more than once, "If you want your money to go to heaven you had better invest it in boys and girls, because their souls are the only things that are going there."[475]

The three years of Gentry's presidency were times of great stress, both on campus and around the world. The Class of 1920 dedicated its yearbook, *The Grenade*, to him: "Recent president of Carson-Newman College who has done more perhaps than any other man for the college in the same length of time, administering not only to its bodily needs but to its very soul, giving it his own life's blood, as it were; as an expression of our highest esteem and honor, this book is affectionately dedicated with an everlasting love."[476]

Campus Pluses and Minuses

Gentry's inauguration occurred the same day the cornerstone was laid for the new, beautifully designed administration building. He soon addressed the trustees with updates. Classes were held mostly in women's dormitories, where the spaces were too small and unsuitable for equipment. And it was difficult to regulate the conduct of the student body and maintain proper discipline when the young ladies' residence halls had to be used as classrooms, reading rooms, society halls, business offices, and public entertainment.[477] To recruit students to a college operating under such circumstances required a great deal of creativity.

The domestic science majors were the most fortunate of all the students. A. R. Swann purchased the small house next to Sarah Swann, the former home of John T. Henderson, for them. The domestic science group used the home for classroom space and a home management laboratory.[478]

In 1917, Carson and Newman's Business College/Department ceased to exist after about twenty-five years. In all likelihood, the business machines (typewriters, etc.) did not survive the administration building fire. Because of the mushrooming of competitive business colleges in many cities, a decision may have been made to "get out of the business" business.

GOODBYE TO CARSON HALL

In 1917, large amounts of money were needed to erect and equip the new administration building. The trustees discussed selling some college property and applying the proceeds to immediate campus needs. They decided to sell Carson Hall, a still-beautiful building used as a men's dormitory, to Jefferson City for $10,000 as the site of a public school. Seven acres surrounding Carson Hall were also deeded to the city. Of the original thirty-five acres of Campus #2, the college retained ten acres; the rest had been sold to individuals for home sites.[479]

This shortsighted plan did not actually provide much operating capital since the $10,000 was to be paid over eight years. Carson and Newman bade farewell to the property that had been such a source of pride since 1876. In the years to come, virtually everyone in Jefferson City would regret the college's loss of Carson Hall.

How Wartime Changed Carson and Newman

After the United States entered World War I in April 1917, many Carson and Newman male students enlisted or were drafted. Student enrollment in the fall of 1917 was the lowest, by far, in decades, hovering around the 170 mark.[480] This intensified the financial crisis for the college, since the loss of students' tuition money greatly affected income and the services the college could offer. Gentry began a fundraising campaign for the college, miraculously raising $45,000 in four months. But money was still very tight.

Some other colleges faced with the same problem saw a silver lining in the Student Army Training Corps (SATC), military units that set up offices in various locations around the country to train well-educated young men as officers for the war. Carson and Newman signed a contract with the government to house a unit of the SATC on campus. For one year, Carson and Newman received $4,436.68 for room and board. The government furnished army instructors and all necessary equipment.[481]

To qualify for housing a unit of the SATC, the college changed temporarily to the trimester system of eighteen weeks per session, since the army needed a year-round program. The government provided instruction and equipment. Students in Davis Hall were moved into the community for room and board so Davis Hall could be turned over to the SATC for barracks. Carson and Newman had recently purchased some property in front of Davis Hall on Branner Avenue, where a temporary hospital was built.

The other SATC units in East Tennessee were located at Tusculum College, King College, and East Tennessee State Normal College. Each unit organized a football team and played games against one another. This plan gave each college a football team and each military unit a made-to-order part of its physical training program.[482]

Carson and Newman students generously provided a service flag for the school, with a blue star for every known former student or professor serving in the war. The April 1, 1918, *Orange and Blue* featured a picture of the flag, displaying the letters "CNC" in a vertical row, plus "1918" made up of a total of eighty-four stars. A patriotic service was held to install the flag, with all eighty-four names read aloud. The service opened with everyone singing the "Alma Mater" and concluded with "The Star-Spangled Banner" sung in unison. Soon, twelve more blue stars were added for other former students in military training.

The April 1 *Orange and Blue* also contained a recognition of the first gold-star soldier, Claude O. Lowe of the Signal Corps, an aviation instructor and past Carson and Newman student who lost his life in an airplane accident. Sadly, over time, at least two more gold stars replaced those in blue.

Whenever anyone on campus received a letter from a soldier, it was shared and reprinted in *The Orange and Blue* so all could hear news from the front. For example, President Gentry received a letter from former athletic director John Kilpatrick "over there" in France. He expressed his desire to "do my part to bring the Kaiser to his knees" (*Orange and Blue,* November 15, 1918). M. B. Dale, former *Orange and Blue* editor, wrote from his training base in Dallas, Texas, where he eagerly awaited news from his alma mater. His letter mentioned the Spanish influenza prevalent all over the world *(Orange and Blue,* November 1, 1918). Coincidentally, Elmer Sydnor and others were recovering from the flu in Jefferson City at the same time.

The war was so all-consuming that any little break from war news—attending public entertainment, doing a kind deed, or hearing a joke or an uplifting spiritual message—was a relief for the soul. Everyone on campus needed the encouragement that, for most, "normal" life would eventually return.

On October 1, 1918, induction ceremonies were held on campus for new soldiers in the United States Army. The October 15, 1918, *Orange and Blue* hailed a "new era of usefulness" for the college. After chapel, the new graduates of the SATC formed lines in columns of two in front of Sarah Swann. They then marched over to Davis Hall, where a platform, a flagpole, and a United States flag had been installed. Faculty members, students, and townspeople gladly attended the program and congratulated the new army officers.

CELEBRATING THE ARMISTICE

The Armistice was signed on November 11, 1918, bringing to an end what many thought of as "the war to end all wars." Celebrations were held all over the world, including Jefferson City, Tennessee. The November 15, 1918, *Orange and Blue* reported that the men of the SATC and the women of the college marched from Davis Hall to Sarah Swann, where Dean White presided over the exercises. "America the Beautiful" and "The

SATC soldiers in training for World War I, 1918, in front of Sarah Swann Hall.

Marseillaise" were sung, followed by a prayer of thanksgiving and a stirring message of gratitude.

An officer of the SATC delivered the primary address, emphasizing the importance of continuing patriotism through the reconstruction period. A heartfelt rendition of "The Star-Spangled Banner" concluded the service. The student body then went on a hike together and stopped at the home of Professor J. D. Bible, who served refreshments to the appreciative crowd.

The $300,000 Campaign

With the war over, A. R. Swann thought it was time to issue a new monetary challenge to the college. Partnering with another trustee, Knoxville businessman J. H. Anderson, he proposed that each of them give $50,000 to Carson and Newman if $200,000 could be raised from other sources by July 1, 1919. Of the total $300,000, $250,000 was to be earmarked for the general endowment fund and the remaining $50,000 to be used for equipment.[483]

Immediately, the appeal went out to Tennessee Baptist churches. Almost everyone knew that Carson and Newman really needed this money. Trustee

J. H. Sharp was hired as the field agent to collect the donations, resigning the pastorate of his church in Sweetwater to accept the challenge.[484]

Baptist publications all over the state, including the flagship *Baptist and Reflector*, went into high gear to promote Carson and Newman's appeal. The January 15, 1919, *Orange and Blue* led with testimonials and pleas from well-known East Tennessee pastors. Whereas money had been tightly held during the war, now was the time to release it for the best possible cause.

An article by student editor J. B. Myers explained that Swann and Anderson's offer was for all or nothing; no halfway measures would be matched. Next to the article was an appealing close-up picture of Myers, who had recently returned from the war, in his doughboy uniform. His earnest expression seemed to communicate, "I was willing to sacrifice my life for your freedom; what are you willing to sacrifice for the college we both love?"

The back page showed a picture of the incomplete new administration building with scaffolding covering its front face. The accompanying caption read, "Shall this building stand as a monument of our success, or shall it mock our failure? What will you do to take the scaffolds down?"

The intense campaign came to a close on June 30, 1919, with J. H. Sharp having collected a total of $204,000 in cash and pledges from the churches. Swann and Anderson, well pleased, promptly paid their gifts of $50,000 each.[485]

A New Relationship with the Tennessee Baptist Convention

Even before the stressful $300,000 campaign drew to a close, President Gentry and the trustees realized that the occasional nail-biting campaign method of soliciting money again and again was unsustainable over the long term. Yet the college had to have frequent infusions of money in order to operate. The loss of the administration building to fire and the war had highlighted the fragile state of the college's income.

The Tennessee Baptist Convention, composed of Baptist churches across the state, offered a solution. Founded in 1874, the Convention held a percentage of the tithes and offerings collected from Baptist churches throughout Tennessee. They offered to give Baptist colleges that aligned with them large amounts of money each year. Naturally, there were conditions to be met.

On December 16, 1918, the Carson and Newman trustees signed a contract with the Tennessee Baptist Convention that would strengthen the college financially and secure its stability but would cede control of the college to the Convention. The parties mutually agreed to seven conditions of the trust, including the fact that the Convention would nominate college trustees for the next ninety-nine years. The trustees were required to convey title to the entire college property to the Education Board of the Tennessee Baptist Convention.[486] (However, the Tennessee Baptist Convention officially signed away its hold on Carson-Newman's property in 1965.[487])

According to the terms of the agreement, the Education Commission would have the right to select the amount and type of work done by students. Faculty members were to be men and women of Christian character, with no less than 75 percent active and creditable members of a Baptist church. The regular curriculum would provide required Bible classes or other distinctly Christian subjects that would be approved by the convention. The convention pledged to maintain Carson-Newman as a standard college.[488]

In case of a disagreement between the parties, the Education Board of the Convention would be an intermediary between the convention and the college. If terms of the contract were broken and noncompliance was in evidence, the commission would proceed to foreclose. The commission would advertise the college for sale and proceed to sell to the highest bidder for cash in hand. The final contract was signed on April 19, 1919.[489]

CONTEXT: 1919 EVENTS IN WORLD HISTORY

Woodrow Wilson was the twenty-eighth president of the United States. The Treaty of Versailles, ending World War I, was signed; the League of Nations and the American Legion were formed. New York City welcomed home General John J. Pershing and twenty-five thousand American soldiers.

A monument to the boll weevil was dedicated in Enterprise, Alabama, and Congress formed the Grand Canyon National Park in Arizona. They also passed the Volstead Act, establishing Prohibition, and the Nineteenth Amendment, the Women's Suffrage Bill. The United Parcel Service (UPS) was organized. The Rodin Museum opened in Paris, and the Irish War of Independence began. Jack Dempsey became the world's heavyweight boxing champion.

Slow Recovery from Wartime

To the sadness of all, W. T. Russell died on March 16, 1919. The April 1, 1919, *Orange and Blue* paid tribute to his sterling character and his many contributions to the college over the years.

At the next trustee meeting, President Gentry enumerated the college's immediate needs other than the completion of the new administration building: (1) a central heating plant for the administration building, the Sarah Swann Home, and the Young Ladies Home; (2) a heating plant for Davis Hall; and (3) a renovation of Davis Hall now that the SATC had left. The trustees borrowed the money to make these improvements.[490]

After the war ended, there was a pent-up demand for many things the students and faculty had sacrificially done without. Gentry had asked for campus improvements; the students asked for an annual. President Gentry did not think the school could afford a true yearbook, but he compromised with students. On May 20, 1919, *The Orange and Blue* issued a special one-time senior booklet, with portraits and remembrances of the 1919 graduates.

At the May 1919 commencement, Gentry's heroic work was recognized, and the college bestowed an honorary LittD degree on him. In June, he wrote in the school catalogue: "[The administration building] is now completed and will be dedicated for service at the opening of the fall term. It is a magnificent structure erected at a cost of approximately one hundred thousand dollars. It stands in the center of the campus, and contains all the lecture rooms and offices, the halls of the young men's literary societies, the art hall, a large auditorium, reading rooms and physical, chemical and biological laboratories. Rooms in the basement of this building are set apart and being equipped for the Department of Domestic Science and Home Economics."[491]

To everyone's joy, classes met for the first time in the new, classical-style administration building on September 9, 1919. Much later, in 1942, this building was named The John T. Henderson Memorial Hall Administration Building.[492] Popularly called "Henderson Hall," it was beloved by generations of students.

GENTRY'S DEPARTURE

By the fall session of 1919, the campus was getting back to normal. Enrollment was on the upswing. The new, modern central heating plant was a

Second administration building, later called Henderson Hall, 1919–1974.

reality, having cost $30,000 to erect and equip. All three dormitories had been redecorated. The trustees expressed their confidence in President Gentry and asked him to continue as president for three more years.

But Gentry was exhausted. He also felt boxed in and micromanaged. He remarked, "I cannot buy a pencil unless it is first approved by a committee of the trustees." In October, he presented his resignation to the trustees, requesting release by the end of December. At the same time he assured them of his goodwill toward the college.[493] Carson and Newman gave him a leaded crystal lamp as a gift. In January 1987, his nephew, James H. Gentry of Knoxville, presented the lamp back to the college; it is housed in the archives.

GENTRY LANDMARKS ON TODAY'S CAMPUS

In 1913, President Burnett sold Professor Gentry four lots fronting on Russell Avenue. Gentry built his home next door to the Burnetts, across from First Baptist Church. William Gentry's home is a familiar sight on today's campus: The Appalachian Cultural Center, located next to Burnett Residence Hall. Also, the main campus assembly space, Gentry Auditorium in Henderson Hall, was named in gratitude for President Gentry's many contributions to Carson and Newman.

After leaving Carson and Newman, Gentry held a variety of positions, all in Tennessee. First he returned to teaching at the East Tennessee State Normal College (now East Tennessee State University) in Johnson City. From there, he became director of public school libraries and textbooks.[494] His last position was with the Tennessee Valley Authority.

When A. R. Swann, Carson and Newman's most generous benefactor, died in 1926, Gentry agreed to complete his term as a trustee. Subsequently, he served about fifteen years as a trustee, in close contact with the college once again.

From 1851 until 1919, through President Gentry's term in office, all the threats to Carson and Newman's survival had come from outside sources—wars, epidemics, fire, foreclosure, and more. But the next threat would come from within. No one could foresee the difficulties and heartbreak that would ensue during the administration of the next president. The story of campus scandal and selective integrity in the 1920s may surprise many readers. The next chapter serves as a cautionary tale and a reminder that any institution, no matter how well founded or maintained, is at risk when the person at the top misrepresents situations and manipulates individuals for a hidden purpose.

CHAPTER SEVEN

Gathering Storm Clouds Over an Ethical Morass

1920–1927

"This is my Father's world,
O let me ne'er forget
That though the wrong seems oft so strong,
God is the Ruler yet."
—Maltbie D. Babcock[495]

Hushed tones and tender medical care prevailed around the bedside of Raymond K. Fleenor, a senior student at Carson and Newman. Raymond lay paralyzed and helpless for months after being severely injured in the first football game of the 1919–1920 season. He was a standout fullback and a well-regarded young man of character, one of the team's few reliable players among a sea of rookies. His drastic injury wounded the team, too. "This terrible accident hung over the team like a cloud all the season" as they continued to play, mostly losing games.[496] He died on April 19, 1920, just a few weeks before he would have graduated with his class.

Although World War I had made death more familiar, if no less dreaded, the student body felt keenly the loss of Fleenor and other classmates who had passed away. According to the April 18, 1924, *Orange and Blue,* later they proposed naming Carson and Newman's gridiron "Fleenor Field." (That did not happen.)

In 1907, football had been canceled as a sport when a Carson and Newman player had accidentally caused the death of a rival player. Now one of the college's own had died in an effort to attain victory for his alma mater. But in 1920, no one would cancel the football program for any reason. Instead, all sports would become a rallying point for the new administration, a focus of both promise and excess in the difficult years ahead.

Part 1, Partly Cloudy Skies: 1920

EXITS AND ENTRANCES

President Gentry's successor was Oscar E. Sams, a charming and earnest minister with personal charisma to spare. In 1918, Sams had become the pastor of Central Baptist Church in Johnson City, Tennessee, having moved there from Virginia. At once, he became active in the Tennessee Baptist Convention, meeting some of the Carson and Newman trustees and expressing an interest in Christian education.[497] At the college's 1919 commencement, when President Gentry was awarded an honorary LittD degree, Sams was one of four ministers given a DD degree.[498]

The trustees elected Oscar E. Sams as president on December 15, 1919, the day Gentry's resignation took effect, and set his salary at $4,200. Five months earlier, the board had commended President Gentry and raised his salary from $2,500 to $3,000.[499]

Oscar Sams was the first Carson and Newman president who was not expected to teach. As a minister missing opportunities to address his "flock," however, Sams decided to teach two hour-long weekly lecture courses for ministerial students. "Practical Pastoral Problems" and "The Personal Touch in Soul Winning" were his chosen topics.[500] Also, because chapel was held six mornings per week, he was able to address the student body frequently. On Sundays, he usually traveled to speak in area churches, sometimes using his Ford car and sometimes the "company" wagon led by a team of mules—prized equipment in his administration.

Sams came to Carson and Newman at a fortuitous time. The postwar boom in student enrollment was beginning; in 1921 alone, Carson and Newman's enrollment increased from three hundred to 375.[501] The new administration building was completed and occupied, and the Tennessee Baptist Convention had pledged to help Carson and Newman get out of debt as well as to provide long-term support. The endowment totaled over $300,000.[502] No prior president had begun his service under such favorable conditions. The future seemed bright.

A MOMENTOUS SEVEN-YEAR TENURE: OSCAR E. SAMS, FIFTEENTH PRESIDENT (1920–1927)

Oscar Ernest Sams (1877–1952) was born in Flag Pond, Tennessee, but "home" was nearby Mars Hill, North Carolina, where he grew up. As a boy, he helped to make the bricks for a building on the Mars Hill College (now University) campus. He attended Mars Hill, then a junior college. In 1898 he graduated from Wake Forest University with an AB degree.[503]

A baseball player at Wake Forest, he earned part of his expenses at his next school, Rochester Theological Seminary in New York, by playing semiprofessional baseball in the summer. He received his BD degree in 1902 and served two pastorates in Virginia. During World War I, he also did YMCA work in Camp Gordon, Georgia, before moving to Johnson City.[504]

Oscar Sams was a lifelong friend of Mars Hill College; the school served as a touchstone for him, no matter where he lived. As a pastor in Virginia, he had led one of his congregations to make a substantial financial contribution to build a men's dormitory at Mars Hill College, where a dining hall was named for him. In 1922, as the president of Carson and Newman, he raised eyebrows by spearheading a drive to erect a new gymnasium—at Mars Hill.[505]

Soon after Sams's election as president of Carson and Newman, he became sick with Asian flu. The flu developed into a more serious illness, variously described as meningitis or *encephalitis lethargica* (sleeping sickness). Sams, seriously ill, had a long stay in a Johnson City hospital and was unable to move to Jefferson City until late March 1920.[506] In his absence, mathematics professor and Dean Edward White was in charge of the college.

Once Sams had fully recovered, he began his work at Carson and Newman with great enthusiasm. In the fall, eight new professors were employed, including the venerable evangelist, lecturer, and author J. L. Campbell, who served as the Bible professor at Carson and Newman for eight years. The trustees hired a new dean—alumnus J. I. (Joseph Isaac) Reece, who had acquired exactly the type of academic experience they were seeking. Reece would also teach education and philosophy.

One of Dr. Sams's enduring legacies to Carson-Newman was the college's first twentieth-century intentional identification with Appalachia as an emblem of pride. He suggested *The Appalachian* as the title of the college yearbook, beginning in 1922 and continuing for its lifetime. Sams had a popular address he gave frequently, "The Appalachian Boy," in which he elaborately described the poverty and living conditions prevalent in the region. After giving this address in Boston, he was asked how he knew

Oscar E. Sams, president 1920–1927.

so much about "those poor, ignorant, depraved mountain people." He replied, "Madam, I have the honor of being one of them."[507]

THE CREATION OF THE COLLEGE SEAL

According to Miss Tennessee Jenkins (in an interview for *The Orange and Blue,* November 1, 1954), Carson and Newman had no official seal until the 1920s. Dr. James D. Bruner, professor of romance (modern) languages at the time, believed that the college would benefit from having a visual representation of its essence.[508] He paired the motto "Truth, Beauty, and Goodness" with Dr. Sams's suggestion of the word "Appalachian," set against a mountainous background with a torch to symbolize education. The seal bore the college's name and year of founding, 1851, in a round outside ring. A Carson and Newman student then painted the seal above the stage in the auditorium of the administration building (Henderson Hall) as inspiration for all who saw it.

THIRD YEARBOOK: *THE GRENADE*, 1920

The title *Grenade,* of course, is a reference to the war weapon that burst—quite literally—onto the scene in World War I. Of the Class of 1920, thirteen young men had enlisted and two had fallen in action. At least two of their professors had left to fight in the war, and one had returned—Hugh Max Kressin, who taught modern languages.[509] (The other was A. T. King, science professor, and whether he survived the war is unknown.) Chapel speakers made frequent reference to the war; some had fought in France. Although the war was over, the world felt much changed to the Class of 1920.

FROM THE MARCH 1, 1920 ORANGE AND BLUE "FUN FACTORY" SECTION

Ora Dowell: "Professor Kressin must have been in the French army?"
Jimmy Drake: "Why so?"
Ora Dowell: "He still uses the French slogan."
Jimmy Drake: "What's that?"
Ora Dowell: "They shall not pass."

The seniors dedicated their annual to the recent former president, William Lee Gentry. And the athletic editor of the *Grenade* staff, T. B. (Thomas Buford) Maston, appropriately dedicated the athletic section in memory of Raymond K. Fleenor.[510] A notable athletic picture is of the Hypatian and Calliopean basketball teams; the young women were dressed in dark bloomers. Half wore dark tops; half wore white tops with scarves.[511]

Not all the students' thoughts were of war and sadness. Fun clubs abounded, including the of-its-time "Jazz Baby Club," "Happy Go Lucky," "Noisy Octagon," "Hummer Bummer," "Lazy Daisies," "Hybochery Law School," and "G.A.R" (Grand Army of the Rejected).[512] The "Dean Dodgers" were mostly romantic couples watching out for Dean White, who strictly enforced dating rules.[513]

The Jazz Baby Club

A page from *The Grenade,* 1920, showing a club very much of its day.

From 1920 on, the college would produce an annual each year through 2007, with the sole exception in 1945 because of the shortages of the World War II era.

Joseph I. Reece's Background

One year after the contract between the Tennessee Baptist Convention and Carson and Newman had been signed, in the spring of 1920, the trustees were anxious for the school to become a "standardized college"—in other words, to be accredited—a basic requirement of the Convention. The Southern Association of Colleges and Schools, the accrediting agency, was raising the standards of education throughout eleven states. Accreditation was becoming increasingly important, especially in students' ability to be accepted into graduate schools.[514]

During Sams's extended illness, the trustees recognized the need for a strong full-time dean to share the load with the just-recovering president. Also, they wanted to free Sams from the day-to-day operation of the college so he could do what he excelled at—public relations and fundraising.

Joseph I. Reece was hired specifically for his professional and academic experience, including his knowledge of the accreditation process. As a bonus, he already knew the college and the culture of the region. He was from Butler, Tennessee, near Johnson City. Many of his thirteen siblings attended Carson and Newman.[515]

T. B. MASTON, CLASS OF 1920

Thomas Buford Maston, an outstanding ministerial student and athlete at Carson and Newman, would earn the title "the conscience of Southern Baptists" later in life. A native of New Market, Tennessee, Tom married his college sweetheart, Essie Mae McDonald.[516] Their life partnership would be exceptionally strong, producing mutual respect and many benefits.

Tom and Essie Mae moved to Fort Worth, Texas, for both to study at Southwestern Baptist Theological Seminary and possibly to become missionaries overseas. Tom earned a succession of degrees: the MRE and DRE degrees from Southwestern; an MA from Texas Christian University; and a PhD from Yale University, where he studied Christian ethics under Richard Niebuhr, an eminent theologian.[517]

The Mastons had two sons, one of whom was severely handicapped. Both Tom and Essie Mae tenderly devoted themselves to his daily care in their home as long as he lived. For seminary students, the sight of their learned professor humbly feeding or tending to his helpless adult son made a deep impression. Such students later organized the T. B. Maston Foundation to promote the life and ethical teachings of Jesus Christ as lived and taught by their mentor.[518]

Christian ethics composed the theme of Tom's professional life. He developed the ThD graduate program in Christian Ethics for Southwestern Seminary. The author of twenty-seven books on the subject, he led in the effort to include Christian ethics as a field of study in every Baptist seminary. As a result of his work, race relations, sensitivity to the poor, and the recognition of women as equals improved across the Southern Baptist Convention during his lifetime.[519]

Carson-Newman awarded T. B. Maston an honorary LittD degree in 1958 to recognize his prolific career as a writer and educator and his influence on Southern Baptists. An annual lecture series also honors his memory.[520] T. B. Maston died in 1988.

Joseph I. Reece, academic dean
1920–1924.

Joseph Reece was a 1908 graduate of Carson and Newman. In his senior year, he was editor-in-chief of *The Karnuargus,* the student newspaper of that day, and therein wrote an insightful and scholarly essay on the prologue to *The Canterbury Tales* by Geoffrey Chaucer.[521] As Reece's professor in 1908, President Burnett had regarded him as an outstanding student, and the two later corresponded several times about the possibility of Reece's coming to teach at Carson and Newman.[522] In 1920, the time was finally right for Reece, even though President Burnett was gone.

Reece had received an MA degree from both the University of North Carolina and Harvard University, also doing graduate work at the University of Chicago. He taught two years in the Mountain Schools program under A. E. Brown (probably at Watauga Academy in Butler) and several years in the public schools of Clearwater, Florida. He taught one year at Colorado State Teachers College, including summer school, then returned to Clearwater as superintendent of schools.[523]

The programs Reece developed in Clearwater had received wide attention, and the city poured in money to support his upgrading of the system.[524] In his work with the Clearwater schools and through various other affiliations, he had become acquainted with the personnel of the Southern Association of Colleges and Schools, and he understood the accreditation process.

Joseph Reece established himself early in his deanship as a person of integrity, honor, and conformity to rules. The 1921 yearbook shows a cartoon-figure student, "Mr. Doolittel," having received a letter from J. I. Reece, Dean. The letter reads, "Your connection with this college ceases Friday, Jan. 7th." The editorial comment is "Fired, by heck!"[525] Yet the students obviously liked Reece as well as respecting him.

Reece was fully prepared to guide Carson and Newman through the accreditation process and to give oversight in matters of curriculum, departmental organization, faculty procedures, and campus activities. Dr. Sams had no experience in these areas, but he had his own gifts to use in furthering the college's interests.[526] The two were meant to form a complementary team that would take Carson and Newman to the next level in every way.

Part 2, The Calm Before the Storm: 1921–1923

INTRODUCING DEAN REECE'S FAMILY

When Dean and Mrs. Reece moved to Jefferson City, their young son, Josef, was only a few months old. As he grew, little Josef took to campus life and charmed the students. The 1924 *Appalachian* mentions that on November 13, 1923, Josef attended chapel with his father. "Very delightful to have Mr. Josef Reece, Jr., with us in chapel," states the record.[527]

Laura Ruth Reece and Raleigh Valentine Reece were younger siblings of J. I. Reece, both Carson and Newman students when he returned to campus as dean. Laura would graduate in 1922 and return a year later as a home economics instructor, so she was on campus for the events of 1924 that would change her older brother's life. Raleigh graduated in 1923.

Another sibling was B. Carroll Reece, 1914 valedictorian of Carson and Newman and soon to be elected a Tennessee Congressman. A veteran of World War I, Carroll would return to his alma mater frequently in the 1920s to speak in chapel.[528] Later in life he would become a Carson and Newman trustee.[529]

In the fall of 1921, the Reeces took in Mrs. Reece's orphaned niece from South Carolina. Mary Lenora Martin entered Carson and Newman as a freshman and quickly became active in campus activities. Well-liked by her peers and a good student, Mary was elected freshman class historian;

won the Home Economics scholarship in her sophomore year; worked as an assistant in the Chemistry Department for several years; and was active in the Hypatian Literary Society. She was president of the Young Ladies' Glee Club for two years and played the forward position on the women's basketball team.[530]

Mary fell in love with a ministerial student, Fred T. Moffatt from Dundee, Scotland, and he returned her love. Although he was a year behind Mary at Carson and Newman, he was older than she was. According to family tradition, he spent four years in combat duty for Scotland in World War I with the Black Watch Royal Highlanders. He was decorated four times for bravery.

Once Fred arrived at Carson and Newman in 1922, he too participated in numerous campus activities. Chosen as treasurer of his sophomore class, in 1923 alone he represented the Ministerial Association on the Religious Council, was elected secretary of the Philomathean Literary Society, and won the Bible Scholarship Award. He was employed as gymnasium director for three years.[531] As a ministerial student he attended the religion classes Dr. Sams taught; in fact, when Fred was ordained to preach, Dr. Sams was a member of his ordination council (*The Orange and Blue*, October 19, 1923).

Meeting the Southern Association's Standards

Dean Reece's influence could be seen in the first catalogue he oversaw in 1921. For the first time each faculty member's name was followed by a paragraph listing his or her credentials and experience. He continued to expand the information given in each successive catalogue, including much more detail about each department and each course. Every year, Reece also printed the names of those who had earned degrees the previous year and a full roster of students at every level in every department. Other adjustments he made for accreditation include:

- Reece established a faculty committee for curriculum.[532] Together, he and the other members reorganized the curriculum to meet both Southern Association standards and the requirements of the Tennessee Baptist Convention. According to the latter, each student had to take at least six semester hours of Bible study before graduation. In the fall of 1920, the BS degree was restored after an absence of twenty years, with the first BS candidates awarded diplomas in 1924.[533]

- By 1924, students were required to choose a major out of an ever-expanding array of courses available, as well as a minor.[534] A new and interesting provision was made for second-semester French and Spanish students: they exchanged letters with students in France and South America once per week under the guidance of a bureau of international educational correspondence.
- Faculty salaries were uniformly too low to meet the standards of the Southern Association. It was impossible for the college to raise salaries sufficiently in one year, but an incremental increase over several years was planned. The trustees hoped that these steps would show good faith on the part of Carson and Newman and be accepted by the Southern Association before the salaries were completely in line with their standards.
- According to the Southern Association, Carson and Newman had an insufficient number of faculty members who held earned doctorates. There was only one PhD on the faculty, Dr. James D. Bruner. President Sams and religion professor J. L. Campbell had honorary degrees that entitled them to be called "Doctor." The college needed to adopt a plan for enabling more advanced faculty study and higher salaries to keep qualified professors, plus attracting more.
- Since Carson and Newman had an athletics program, the Southern Association required proper faculty and administrative oversight regarding all the college's sports and teams. They set forth sensible rules for athletics, requiring rigid adherence to athletic money management by college officials only and an annual vetting, team by team, of the players to ensure that they were bona fide students at the college. Accordingly, Dean Reece set up an Athletic Cabinet at Carson and Newman composed of five faculty or administrative members and five students (the managers of the five sports).[535] He headed the Cabinet every year; Dr. Sams was a member, of course. A Rules Committee was instituted to deal with infractions and judgments.

- There was also a Southern Association requirement that member colleges must have endowments of at least $500,000. Money had always been a problem for Carson and Newman; but fortunately, at this time the school did have $300,000 from the 1919 challenge by A. R. Swann and J. H. Anderson. A plan for an additional $200,000 was needed, which Dr. Sams later supplied with a challenge from the General Education Board of New York. Representatives from the board had toured the campus and expressed interest in helping the school.[536]

FAREWELL TO THE MASTER'S DEGREE AND PREPARATORY DEPARTMENT

One of Dr. Sams's first acts as president was to suggest that the college discontinue granting the master of arts degree. The trustees unanimously approved his recommendation.[537] Dean Reece agreed with the decision as the college was not equipped to meet the Southern Association's standards for an accredited master's degree program.

On the other end of the collegiate spectrum, the Southern Association had strict requirements for preparatory schools. Carson and Newman would have to house the preparatory school in a separate building and employ completely different teachers than college professors. The college was not in a position to meet these requirements. And fortunately, the proliferation of public high schools was negating the need for college Preparatory Departments. Carson and Newman would phase out the preparatory school over the next few years, concluding it in 1924.[538]

Thus ended seventy-three years of precollege education at Carson and Newman, harkening back to the days of master teacher Robert Reedy Bryan. The master's program and the preparatory school had served good purposes in their time. Now the college could concentrate on becoming a "standard" undergraduate liberal arts college.

THE NEW PRE-PROFESSIONAL PROGRAM

Other innovations at this time were the additions of the prelaw and premedical programs. Prelaw students could attend Carson and Newman three years; then their first successful year in law school would count as the fourth Carson and Newman year. Such students would then be awarded a college AB.[539]

Premedical students at Carson and Newman would take a heavy load of prescribed sciences for two years, after which medical schools would accept them. Their degree from Carson and Newman would follow after two years of medical school. This plan met the Southern Association standard and became a popular program.[540] Afterward, however, the American Medical Association increased the undergraduate requirements to three years for the combined degree and recommended a full four-year college program before students attended medical school.

ENTER THE SUMMER SCHOOL PROGRAM

Beginning in 1921, following a new and practical trend in education, Carson and Newman began offering summer school sessions. Summer school was especially attractive to public school teachers, who could renew their teaching certificates for two years and earn credit toward a college degree at the same time. (At that time, teachers were not required to hold an undergraduate degree before being hired to teach.[541]) An "early summer school" starting in March also helped teachers whose school terms lasted only five or seven months.

The first summer school commencement was held in 1924, with nine AB degrees awarded. There were also eight graduates in piano, eight in expression, and thirteen who earned certificates in music. That year, Coach Lake Russell conducted a concurrent, first-of-its-kind summer school especially for coaches, as recounted in the March 21, 1924, *Orange and Blue.* Dana X. Bible was one of the speakers he enlisted, and attendance was outstanding.

By 1925, the summer school program was very well organized. The college advertised twelve weeks of "Education, Inspiration, Recreation." The sessions were targeted not only to public school teachers but also to high-school students not quite ready for college and college students who wanted to make up back work or hasten graduation. A wide range of college courses in all disciplines was offered in a Christian atmosphere, with wonderful dormitory accommodations, the amenities of Butler-Blanc Gymnasium, occasional campus entertainments, and an inherent social life.[542]

Over the years, the college calendar was rearranged several times to meet the needs of summer school students, especially public school teachers. After the Tennessee public schools went to a standard nine-month school year, the college calendar stabilized again.

Yearbooks and the College Culture 1921–1923

FOURTH YEARBOOK: *THE WANEHI*, 1921

The Class of 1921 celebrated the return of alumnus and former Professor W. S. Gass to campus along with that of his wife, Elizabeth (a sister of former President Burnett), and their four children. W. S. Gass had served as the college's English professor from 1896 to 1907; now he assumed dual positions as the college's treasurer and principal of the Preparatory Department.[543] (Sadly, he would die that summer.)

The Gasses' oldest child, college senior Frances Swann Gass (named for her aunt, Mrs. A. R. Swann) was class poet, valedictorian, and coeditor-in-chief of the yearbook. She had quickly become a popular classmate the previous year, when the Gasses moved back to Jefferson City. No doubt Frances had a hand in naming the 1921 yearbook *The Wanehi:* "This volume of our College yearbook makes its appearance under a new name which carries with it an appropriate significance. *Wanehi*, an Indian word meaning 'hickory country,' was the term applied by East Tennessee Cherokees to this particular section. We use this name with the hope that we may thereby perpetuate something of the history and romance of *Wanehi*."[544]

This delightful yearbook was dedicated to President Sams: "To one whose enthusiasm for the advancement of the College has stirred us to high endeavor; whose steadfast earnestness has been an inspiration to us; and whose genial counsel has smoothed our way and warmed our hearts—to our President, Dr. Oscar E. Sams, we dedicate this volume."[545]

The yearbook included "Wanehi Worries" by the staff, an entertaining one-act play about getting the annual out. The section "Hickory Chips" covered college publications, the Student Activities Council, and the Forensic League.[546]

Nora Maples Rankin also returned to her alma mater in 1921, again as head of the Music Department (no longer called a Conservatory). The department offered a new expanse of piano, voice, and violin courses under her leadership.[547] In an unfortunate coincidence with W. S. Gass, she would also become ill and die within a few years (1925).

FIFTH YEARBOOK: *THE APPALACHIAN*, VOLUME 1, 1922

Thanks to a suggestion from Dr. Sams, the 1922 yearbook had a new title.

"The staff of the 1922 yearbook takes great pleasure in introducing to you this, the first issue of THE APPALACHIAN. We wish to extend our sincere gratitude to both the administration of the college and to the entire student body for their hearty cooperation in adopting a permanent name for our Annual.

"We feel that THE APPALACHIAN is the most appropriate name that could have been selected, since Carson-Newman is located in the heart of the great mountain region bearing this name. To attempt to give a definition of the word would be sacrilegious, since the very air we breathe is permeated with the spirit of the Appalachians, and to each of us it has an individual meaning, which meaning we hold sacred."[548]

In an unusual move, the staff dedicated the yearbook to "Our Devoted Mothers," accompanied by a photo of the painting popularly known as "Whistler's Mother" and Rudyard Kipling's poem "Mother o' Mine."[549]

Seniors included Laura Ruth Reece, essayist and home economics major described in an accompanying quotation: "She could roaste, and sethe, and broile, and frye, / Make a good soupe, and bake a pye" (from Chaucer's *The Canterbury Tales)* and Alexander Chavis, future physics professor who had interrupted his college work to enlist in the Navy during World War I.[550]

Purposeful clubs of the time included those related to the students' home locations, such as the Knox County Club; the Masonic Club; and the Biology and Chemistry Clubs, both of which had numerous members.[551] Some of the fun clubs were Eta Beta Pi Club (motto: "Never Stop Eating Until You Have Had Enough"), Ole Pals, and the Ain't-Went-Out-Much Club.[552]

SIXTH YEARBOOK: *THE APPALACHIAN*, VOLUME 2, 1923

This yearbook was dedicated to J. Hardin Jacobs, a fellow student who died suddenly in February, an event that shocked the entire campus. He had been the competitive orator of 1922, the 1922 editor-in-chief of *The Orange and Blue,* and was the business manager of the current yearbook.[553]

There were many debate and forensic triumphs to celebrate, as reflected in the yearbook. Elmer Sydnor had become "the winningest coach in the South" in the area of public speaking; the traveling Carson and Newman students he had developed won an amazing 85 percent of their contests (*Orange and Blue,* October 19, 1923).

Both Elizabeth and Frances Gass were now employed by the college. Elizabeth was warmly welcomed as matron of the Young Ladies Home (*Orange and Blue,* September 21, 1923). Frances was serving as a teacher in the preparatory school, imparting math and Latin to young students.[554] Elizabeth's role recalls that of her mother, Henrietta Sarah Cody Burnett, as matron of Carson Hall when it was a women's dormitory in the 1890s. Elizabeth's employment with the college ended in 1926, when her mother became ill and needed her daughter's ministrations. Frances taught until the Preparatory Department ended in 1924. Later in life, she wrote the definitive book on her mother's family: *A Burnett Family of the South* (1964).

In fun observations, the style of the day for anyone wearing glasses was the classic round frame only. A copy of *The Appalachian* cost $4. And pictures of the student body were panoramic in this era. Occasionally, mischievous students on the end of one side, having been captured by the camera, would run behind the photographer to the other side and pose again, thus appearing on both sides of the picture!

Property Projects

AN EXPANDED SPORTS PARK

In June 1921, the college bought a five-acre tract fronting on Branner Avenue, between Davis Hall and what is now Davis Street. Purchased from a group of Branner heirs, the tract filled in the missing part of the college's rectangle of land between Branner Avenue and Mossy Creek. In addition to the current primary campus, the college still owned the ten-acre Campus #1, on the edge of which Davis Hall had been built. The new five acres became known as Alumni Athletic Field, part of what President Burnett had called the college's Sports Park.[555]

THE BUTLER-BLANC GYMNASIUM

While Dean Reece molded the college toward academic accreditation, President Sams gave attention to buildings and athletics. He combined the two interests by actively advocating for a gymnasium. Realizing that no funds were available for this much-needed building, he expressed the hope that Baptist individuals and groups would donate funds for the cause.

At the May 18, 1921, commencement, he announced that Henry Blanc, a Knoxville trustee in the lumber business, had offered $10,000 to build a gymnasium if another individual would match the amount. (Blanc's son Adrian was a football player at Carson and Newman.) Trustee D. L. Butler met the challenge, and Sams announced that construction would proceed "as rapidly as brick would be available." Blanc personally supervised the construction process, and everyone easily agreed that the new gymnasium should be named for both men.[556]

The 1922 yearbook carried an architectural drawing of Butler-Blanc Gymnasium as it would look when completed, accompanied by the following appropriate statement: "The fundamental business of the college is, and always will be, intellect; but the personal business of every student is to see to it that he has a body which will serve intellect."[557]

The Blanc-Butler Gymnasium was completed in time for the 1923 spring commencement. The gym was a marvel, the showplace of the region. The gym "proper" had a floor space of sixty by eighty-eight feet, with a running track on the second floor and a court for basketball and indoor baseball. The basement floor contained lockers, showers, areas for visiting teams, and a *swimming pool* (italics from the original description).[558] Butler-Blanc's swimming pool was the only indoor pool in the area and used a filtering plant to keep the water constantly purified.

Butler-Blanc Gymnasium.

Included in the new gymnasium were two suites of rooms for athletic directors. Because the college had only one athletic director, Dean Reece and his family moved into the apartment at the front entrance to the gym in 1923.

ANOTHER TRY FOR A LIBRARY

Like Millard Jeffries before him, Oscar Sams saw the need for a campus-wide library. He hoped alumni would make a substantial initial investment and the Carnegie Foundation would donate the rest. He had a sketch drawn of the proposed building for the 1923 yearbook, showing an elegant, classical-style building topped by a large dome and anchored by columns on the front. It was to be called the Alumni Library.[559] But plans were dropped by the end of 1923; money was needed for other projects, and the Carnegie Foundation declined to invest in the building.[560]

1922 UPDATE ON CARSON HALL

One of the trustees' primary regrets was having sold Carson Hall, a lovely and treasured mansion on Campus #2, to the town of Jefferson City in 1917. By 1922, they realized their mistake; absence had indeed made their hearts grow fonder. More rooms for male students were desperately needed at Carson and Newman.

When it became known that Jefferson City was about to sell the Carson Hall property—the acreage had been deemed unsuitable for public schools—the trustees saw a chance to regain Carson Hall. They debated whether the school could afford to repurchase it or whether they should try to rescind the original contract. (The full purchase price had not yet been paid to the college since the purchase term was for eight years.) According to professional advice, likely the college would not be able to collect the remainder of the debt from the town.[561]

But while they deliberated, a surprise awaited. A private buyer surfaced, clearing up the debt and purchasing the property from the city.[562] The new owner, M. L. (Martin Luther) Beeler, an architectural contractor who had attended Carson College's preparatory school in the 1880s, began renovating Carson Hall inside and outside to transform it into a single-family mansion.[563] No longer did it look like the Carson Hall of yore.

The former Carson Hall would never belong to the college again.

THE FIGHTING PARSONS

The September 30, 1921, football game against the Athens School (now Tennessee Wesleyan University) yielded both a distinct win (20–0) and a new team name. During the game, "player Ira Dance, a ministerial student, hit one of the Athens players and knocked him unconscious for several hours." The Athens fans were so angry that Ira Dance had to be hidden until their player recovered. Recounting the incident, the Knoxville paper referred to the Carson and Newman team as the "Fighting Parsons," and that name stuck.[564] The 1923 *Appalachian* said of Ira Dance: "He is the man who gave the team the name of Fighting Parsons and he is really all that the name implies."[565]

The new team name not only stuck, but it also spread. "The strength of the team attracted widespread attention, and the ginger with which that strength was applied won for them the distinguishing pseudonym, 'The Fighting Parsons.' This cognomen followed on into basketball, track, and baseball, and it now looks like a permanent fixture to all Carson-Newman teams."[566]

The team's quarterback that year and future captain, Sam B. Holt, had a nickname that stuck too. Coach McCown had plucked the talented young athlete from his hometown of Newport, Tennessee, where a grocer named Taylor had given Sam the nickname "Frosty" for no apparent reason (*Orange and Blue,* March 20, 1965). Sam "Frosty" Holt would become a legendary coach and athletic director at Carson-Newman, training generations of athletes.

Iconic cartoon of "The Fighting Parsons," 1921–1931.

Sports 1921–1923, a Revolving Door for Coaches

During the early 1920s, a stable athletic program was hard to develop, partly because no coach had been hired during the war years. Afterward, the new coaches struggled to mold winning teams with inexperienced, sometimes lightweight players. Such coaches stayed only one year at the college.

Former coach John T. Kilpatrick returned from military service in France to resume teaching athletics at his alma mater for the 1920–1921 season. The "green" football players of the previous year developed and matured under Kilpatrick's leadership.

Local physician and sports enthusiast Dr. R. M. McCown coached both football and basketball as a volunteer during the 1921–1922 school year.[567] An experienced volunteer coach, he helped get the college's athletic program on track. "Dr. R. M. McCown freely gave us his influence and service as football coach. A number of players of experience and promise flocked the gridiron, and the thud of the pigskin was a song of optimism to the cheerful supporters of *The Orange and Blue.* Coach McCown sifted his material and turned out a well-ordered machine."[568] The 1921–1922 year was widely regarded as the turning point of athletics at Carson and Newman.

The development of the basketball teams, both male and female, was greatly aided in 1923 by the completion of the new gymnasium. No longer did the basketball teams have to practice on less than a regulation-size court (as in the former administration building) or have to dodge the posts on their usual practice area, the third floor of the Minnis-Zirkle Store in downtown Jefferson City.[569] By 1924, the women's basketball team would be known as the Parsonettes, with future physical education professor Mae Iddins as their star center.[570]

Carson and Newman students were excited to learn that Tom Moran would be the football coach for the 1922–1923 school year. He had been a football star for the Praying Colonels team at Centre College in Danville, Kentucky. Even better, Tom was the well-coached son of the Praying Colonels' coach, Charlie Moran. Under the senior Moran's leadership, little Centre College of Danville, Kentucky, had "shocked the world" by defeating Harvard.[571]

Mae Iddins in her Parsonette uniform, circa 1924.

On December 4, 1922, Coach Charles Moran of Centre spoke in chapel at Carson and Newman, describing the origin of the Praying Colonels—a good counterpart to the Fighting Parsons. The students were delighted with both father and son. Tom Moran stayed at Carson and Newman through the fall 1923 semester and coached some of its greatest football victories. Student Lake Russell then assumed coaching responsibilities until finishing his degree in 1926.

President Sams, quite a sports enthusiast, was thrilled at the upsurge in athletics at Carson and Newman. He had given a great deal of his attention to athletics, both for its own sake and as a public relations tool for the college in his three years in Jefferson City. Now that the Butler-Blanc Gymnasium was completed, the college could work toward a full athletic program. He announced in 1923:

> "I came to realize last year that Carson-Newman was fast heading toward a girls' school. This was due to the fact that we are better equipped to care for girls. . . . More than one young man informed me that he was not interested in Carson and Newman since it was a school for preachers and girls. So with eyes wide open, I launched into athletics, and most of you are acquainted with the fact that we had football and basketball teams that were willing to meet any school on any ground. . . . Our recognition of athletics and the completion of the gymnasium have put us on the map in the eyes of young men of this section. No money that we spent on advertising has counted more for the future of Carson and Newman College. We now appeal to young men."[572]

Although Dr. Sams had been a ministerial student himself, he had also been a standout baseball player in his youth. He saw sports as a sure way to attract more male students and was eager for the college to have winning athletic teams. His younger son, Conway, later recalled his own childhood interest in sports while the family lived in Jefferson City: "I was perhaps more concerned with sports than most, due the presence of college teams and Dad's interest in sports. The presence of Frosty Holt, my idol, colored that somewhat."[573]

A Disastrous Decision

As time went on, the athletic program consumed more and more of Dr. Sams's thought process. He dreamed big for the college's teams. Yes, they were all much improved. But if they won their games all the time, they would become champions! Everyone would be talking about Carson and Newman's players. What would it take to win even more games and bask in the glory of undefeated seasons?

Quietly, without anything being said, over time Dr. Sams had developed an aversion to Dean Reece. The struggle was one-sided; no evidence has been found that Reece opposed Sams or even realized that Dr. Sams had a problem with him. The only known reason for this aversion is that Dean Reece, a stickler for conforming to rules, would have been an obstacle to the president's wanting to bend the rules of athletic procedures to attain consistently winning teams. There may have been other reasons; but if so, they are lost to time.

SAM "FROSTY" HOLT, CLASS OF 1927: A CARSON-NEWMAN LEGEND

Even in his student days, Samuel Boyd Holt from Newport, Tennessee, showed his athletic prowess. He was captain of the football, basketball, and baseball teams, and the assistant to Coach Lake Russell.

Sam and Bonita Sharp were judged the most popular student couple on campus. (Bonita was the daughter of pastor and fundraiser J. H. Sharp.) They later married, spending most of their lives in Jefferson City in the service of Carson-Newman. Holt Fieldhouse on campus was named for him. According to the 1927 yearbook:

"'Frosty' Holt, assistant football coach, Parsonette coach, and baseball coach, is one of the most all-round athletes Carson-Newman has ever produced. He has won honors in all branches of athletics, and his teams have proven his ability. . . . What he doesn't know about football, basketball and baseball, and everything else related to sports can be . . . hidden in the eye of a needle.

"Besides being such a mentor of the athletic world, he is also a student that makes the hearts of the profs glad. He is reputed to have pulled down an A in Bible, and the chances are that he will turn out to be a preacher—about the time the Gulf of Mexico turns to buttermilk."[574]

Dean Reece was far from being against athletics. He attended most games and was an enthusiastic supporter of all the teams, as students had observed with appreciation. As chairman of the ten-member Athletic Cabinet, and because he had been hired specifically to move the college toward accreditation, he would have done nothing to jeopardize Carson and Newman's athletic standing.[575] The Southern Association required their colleges to uphold high standards in all areas, including athletics.

Whatever Dr. Sams's complaints against Dean Reece were, he carried them home to his wife. Like many wives, Mrs. Sams knew only her husband's side of the situation. Together, they brooded about how they might be able to get rid of Dean Reece at the college. Sams did not want to confront Reece, and he had no basis for asking the trustees to dismiss him. Reece was popular with the students, faculty, and townspeople; he had recently been elected to serve as a city alderman.

So what could be done? They would find a way to get him to resign. They resorted to a drastic and outrageous attempt at ousting the dean. Together, they wrote an anonymous letter accusing Reece of immoral relations with Mary Martin, his wife's niece, knowing there was no truth to this statement. But would others believe it? If so, Dean Reece would be forced to resign. They dated the letter December 21, 1923, the last day of classes before the Christmas holidays, and mailed it.[576] Then they waited to see what would happen.

Part 3, The Eye of the Storm: 1924–1926

INJUSTICE PREVAILS

Dr. and Mrs. Sams did not have to wait long to find out Dean Reece's response to their letter—and it was a scenario they might not have anticipated. On January 7, 1924, when classes had resumed and the students and faculty were assembled in chapel, Dean Reece and Dr. Sams were both onstage. Dean Reece read the letter aloud, adding that he thought he knew who the author was because the handwriting was the same as that on a Christmas card he had received. He had also recognized some of the phraseology in the letter, he said.[577]

There must have been a horrified gasp from the audience. President Sams then stood up and asked all those who supported Reece to stand. The assemblage arose as one. Doubtless Laura Reece, Mary Martin, and Fred Moffatt were all present.

Two days later, on January 9, the trustee executive committee met in the president's office. Whatever Dr. Sams told them must have satisfied them. At commencement exercises in May, the trustees gave the following affirmation of Dr. Sams, leaving no doubt where their sympathies lay: "The trustees, after careful deliberation and prayer, have selected a President of the College in whom they have unbounded confidence. . . . The President is placed at the head of this institution. . . . For four years he has led us with such wisdom, tact, and consecration that our college has experienced unparalleled growth and progress. Today we thank God for President Sams. We reassert our steadfast confidence in him and pledge him our united loyalty and support."[578]

There was a further statement of expectations: "The trustees expect for the President of Carson and Newman College the hearty cooperation of every member of the faculty and the unreserved loyalty of every student in the college."[579] Extant issues of *The Orange and Blue* for that time period do not reveal anything overt about the situation. But the articles student staff members wrote about President Sams's campus or outside activities changed in tone. No longer flowery or flattering, they were simply respectful and reported the facts.

The students came to Dean Reece's defense insofar as they were able. In the February 1, 1924, issue, *The Orange and Blue* ran a front-page feature article on Dean Reece, "Still Waters Run Deep," with a two-column picture, pointing out that it was Reece working behind the scenes who was responsible for much of the college's progress and calling him "our beloved Dean Reece": "As dean of Carson and Newman College his motto has been service to the institution. No individual has done more to systemize and standardize the work of the college, raising it to a higher scholastic standing among the schools and colleges of the South. . . . He has been so honest and fair and square with everyone. . . . He is a Christian gentleman. And we believe that no college has a greater Dean than Carson and Newman has."

Then came the annual spring revival. In an evening service after the minister's call for confessions, Dr. Sams said that he had a statement to make. His confession was that Mrs. Sams had written the letter without his knowledge. He did not retract the statement in the letter or apologize for it but instead proceeded into self-justification, saying that everything he had ever done had been in the best interest of the college, that he would give his right arm before he would do anything to hurt the school.[580] This was the first time the Samses' name had been injected into the public forum, and it was Dr. Sams himself who did so—though many might have already surmised his involvement. Mrs. Sams may have offered to take the blame in order to protect her husband, and the letter was probably in her handwriting.

This was apparently the first time Mary Martin had heard that the president could be involved in the attack against her uncle, with her reputation as collateral damage. In shock, she collapsed. Fred Moffatt carried her out of the church.

Afterward, Dr. Sams apologized to Dean Reece on behalf of his wife. Reece generously accepted the apology and continued as dean. Both men hoped the matter was cleared up and settled.[581] But after the Samses' name was associated with the scandal, some faculty members left at the end of the year, not wanting to be embroiled in the controversy.

The town did not want to let go of the scandal. Dr. Sams's apology did not stop the rumors and the divisiveness. In fact, the campus and the town began dividing into pro-Sams and pro-Reece camps.[582] Apparently President Sams held private conferences with some student leaders, seeking their support.[583]

The trustees assembled in April for the first of their two spring meetings. A year's leave of absence was approved for Dean Reece, who said he would use it to study school administration at the University of Chicago.[584] There is no indication whether the leave was Dean Reece's idea or whether the trustees proposed it. Reece apparently was led to believe that his job and his apartment would be waiting for him when he returned. Trustees suggested strongly that if Mary Martin would complete her work at another college, Carson and Newman would accept the transfer of her credits and award her a degree.[585]

Joseph I. Reece stayed at Carson and Newman through summer school in 1924 and was back on campus for the first football game of the season; students expressed their appreciation for his presence there. He spoke in chapel before returning to Chicago. Education professor John Dawson Everett would serve as acting dean in Reece's absence.[586]

Mary Martin bravely rejected the idea of going to another school, choosing instead to continue her studies and her job as chemistry assistant. She moved into Sarah Swann Home and made new friends, one of whom was Janie Swann Huggins, who would graduate in 1926 and later become a legendary English professor at the college. But the joy had gone out of Mary's college experience.

In obvious votes of confidence, when the four classes organized at the opening of the fall 1924 session, Mary Martin was elected president of the senior class, and Fred Moffatt was voted president of the junior class.[587]

When the trustees held their May 1925 meeting—at which they usually elected the faculty for the coming year—Congressman Carroll Reece asked for ten minutes on their agenda to discuss his brother's role as dean. The trustees heard him out. Then on Dr. Sams's recommendation, they dropped Dean Reece and elected Professor Arlie E. Cate as dean. (Arlie Cate "inherited" Dean Reece's apartment in the gymnasium as well. He was a lineal descendant of the Newman family so important in founding and supporting Carson and Newman.) Reece was not offered any position with the college.[588]

In the meantime, Mary Martin was under increasing pressure from the controversy on campus. Reece's de facto dismissal added to her burden. Finally, her health broke. She left school, even though the semester would not end for a few more weeks, and went to Johnson City to stay with Dean Reece's mother. She may have completed her college courses in Johnson City.

Under the circumstances, the faculty voted to award her degree at the June commencement. Mary then wrote to ask that her degree be awarded at the summer school commencement, presumably when fewer suspicious eyes would be upon her. The trustees approved this plan.

The rumor mill became active once again on the news that Dean Reece was coming to town to confer with Dr. Bruner that summer, speculating that Mary wanted to graduate in the summer because Reece would be there. Would they live together in Jefferson City? On the date of Reece's expected return, Reece-watchers were on Depot Street waiting to see if he got off the five o'clock train.

One who heard the rumor was Fred Moffatt, who was livid at the damage still being done to Mary's reputation. He took the bold step of calling on the president, saying he wanted to talk to him as a younger minister to an older one. As Dr. Sams warmed to the conversation, and in his effort to explain his position, he finally told Fred that he and Mrs. Sams had worked on the letter together for three weeks, weighing every word in it—all in the interest of the college.

Fred Moffatt was astounded by the confession and the contradictions. He must have thought of all that had been done to Mary, changing her from a bright and happy person to a pale shadow of herself, when she was completely innocent of any wrongdoing. And these events had happened at the hand of their college president, a minister who taught religion courses and championed the cause of Christ at every opportunity.

As for Dr. Sams, when he thought over the afternoon's interview, he realized what he had done. For the first time, he had confessed his role in the writing of the accusatory letter to Dean Reece. He had to find a way to smooth the situation over. That night, about nine o'clock he made his way to Blanc-Davis Hall, where Fred had a ground-level room. He went to Fred's window and called to him. Moffatt answered him: "For your own safety's sake, go away."

That fall Fred stayed in school but took little part in campus activities, only attending his classes and working his job as gymnasium director.[589]

After graduating, Mary Martin accepted a teaching job in her home state of South Carolina. Dean Reece, knowing that his excellent academic reputation had been ruined by falsehoods, searched for a new line of work. He moved back to the Johnson City area with his family and started an insurance business.

Everything seemed quieter at Carson and Newman, and President Sams and the trustees felt relieved. But the unseen divisions were deep and wide. In addition to faculty members, trustees, alumni, townspeople, and potential donors, there were 575 students from sixteen states and three foreign countries who knew about the controversy.[590]

The $200,000 Challenge of 1924–1925

In 1924, the college moved to enlist the personal support of Tennessee Baptists in their urgent need to secure $125,000 by July 1, 1925. J. H. Sharp, who had successfully raised the money needed for the $300,000 challenge in 1919, was again employed as fundraiser. Since the General Education Board of New York had pledged to give the college $75,000 if $125,000 additional monies were raised, the combined total of $200,000 would complete the accreditation requirement of an endowment of $500,000.[591]

A plea went out to Baptist church members to put money earmarked for Carson and Newman into their collection plates: "The very life of the college depends on this money." Thankfully, just before the deadline Sharp reported $128,000 in hand.[592] All debts were paid by August 31.

The Tennessee Baptist Convention had assumed responsibility for notes totaling about $60,000 for the college and was annually applying the college's pro rata share (5 percent) of Cooperative Program receipts as payment. After the notes were paid off, the pro rata share would be available for operating expenses. This arrangement was satisfactory to the General Education Board.[593]

Stately Miss Tennessee Jenkins,
revered history professor.

Recognition for Longtime Professors

W. Powell Hale returned to the college in 1924 after an absence of several years, having traveled while doing Lyceum work. (Lyceums were public cultural events that took various forms, such as concerts, lectures, historical celebrations, comedic presentations, and plays.) He would teach Expression and the Dramatic Arts for years to come, and occasionally he gave public entertainments at the college. Carson and Newman would benefit greatly from Hale's expertise.

The Forensic League led by **Elmer W. Sydnor** was reaching great heights in various regional contests. In 1924, Carson and Newman students won nine of eleven intercollegiate debates, and the college was awarded the top medal in the Tennessee Inter-Collegiate Oratorical Contest (*Orange and Blue,* April 25, 1925).

The 1925 *Appalachian* was dedicated to **Miss Tennessee Jenkins:** "The patient teacher, the sincere friend, the eminent thinker, whose lifelong service has been instrumental in making Carson and Newman College the great institution it is today."[594] She was also widely considered "the Sweetheart of Carson and Newman."[595]

Blanc Hall, in front of Davis Hall, "The Barn."

Changing the Campus Landscape

THE GREATLY NEEDED BLANC HALL

The college was still woefully short of housing for male students since Davis Hall could accommodate only sixty-eight young men. Dr. Sams's vision of attracting male students depended on the college's ability to house them as well as to place them on sports teams.

In April 1924, Knoxville businessman Henry D. Blanc issued a second challenge. He offered $20,000 to build a dormitory for men if others would give $10,000. The other trustees accepted the offer and authorized the executive committee to proceed with plans and construction. Blanc Hall was not to cost over $40,000. Again, Henry Blanc supervised the construction. Blanc Hall opened in the fall of 1925 and was connected to Davis Hall by a covered walkway.[596] Together, Blanc and Davis Halls became known as Blanc-Davis or "The Barn," beloved by generations of male students.

SEEING DOUBLE: TWO SIDE-BY-SIDE SARAH SWANN HOMES?

On April 9, 1926, A. R. Swann, Carson and Newman's most generous benefactor, died at his home near Dandridge. In his will, he left $35,000 to the college to build a matching dormitory next to Sarah Swann Home.

First college-owned president's home, the former home of W. T. Russell.

He had already donated the home then called the "Practice House" (formerly belonging to John T. Henderson) next door for the college's home economics students.

THE FIRST COLLEGE-OWNED PRESIDENT'S HOME

Carson and Newman had never owned a home for its presidents, but the trustees decided to take this step in 1924. Dr. Sams and his family, who had been living in a basement apartment in Sarah Swann Home, would be the first to occupy a college-provided president's home.

W. T. Russell's lovely former home was purchased and renovated. By spring 1925, the Sams family was living there. In 2002, Conway Sams recalled the "vast yard . . . at the brow of the hill on Russell Avenue."[597] His memories also included the flower garden his mother created there and a sea of poppies in the yard.

Located across the street from present-day Fite Administration Building, the home was later razed to pave a parking lot for Bertie Maples Butler Hall.

Sarah Swann Home had been built for $35,000 in 1904–1905.[598] A. R. Swann had estimated that a matching building would cost $70,000 now. According to his will, the college had two years to raise the matching $35,000. If the college was not able to raise the $35,000, they were to use his bequest to renovate and refurnish Sarah Swann, then invest the balance in an endowment fund for maintenance of the residence hall.[599]

The faithful Henry D. Blanc offered to give the first $10,000; however, there is no record of any other effort to raise the remaining $25,000. By default, the college chose to exercise Mr. Swann's second option. But it is interesting to speculate why, especially since Dr. Sams had reported in 1925 that some young women were being turned away from the college due to lack of dormitory space.[600] Considering President Sams's concern that Carson and Newman was attracting primarily women and preachers, did he fear that adding residence space for about one hundred more women would unbalance the gender enrollment for years to come?

BY THE NUMBERS:
1919–1927 ENROLLMENT AND GENDER COUNTS

In 1923, Dr. Sams noted the perception that Carson and Newman was primarily for women and ministerial students, which he set out to change by developing winning athletic teams. The following annual statistics reveal that female students did not significantly outnumber male students until 1924 and beyond.[601]

Blanc-Davis Hall accommodated 150 men beginning in 1925, while Sarah Swann Home and the Young Ladies Home (named Henderson Home in 1927) had a combined capacity for 180 women on campus.

1919: Men 145, Women 110, Total 255. **1920:** Men 166, Women 155, Total 271. **1921:** Men 185, Women 191, Total 376. **1922:** Men 172, Women 202, Total 374. **1923:** Men 212, Women 229, Total 441. **1924:** Men 240, Women 287, Total 527. **1925:** Men 252, Women 323, Total 575. **1926:** Men 225, Women 331, Total 556. **1927:** Men 257, Women 333, Total 590.

Athletics to the Fore, 1924–1925

Nationally, one nickname for the 1920s was "The Golden Age of Sports." The nation's attention was on standout baseball players such as Ty Cobb, Lou Gehrig, and Babe Ruth; world heavyweight champion Jack Dempsey; golfer Bobby Jones; and winning football coaches such as Knute Rockne of Notre Dame and Alonzo Stagg of the University of Chicago.

In spring 1924, Oscar Sams reported on Carson and Newman's own Golden Age. The year was one of superlatives in athletics: "We had the greatest football team in the history of the college and a basketball team that would have held its own with any five in the state."[602]

WINNING FEVER

As far back as the turn of the century, Carson and Newman catalogues carried statements about the college's high standards for athletics: "None but bona fide students, actually studying in our college, will play on our teams."[603] The 1920s catalogues continued to print the same kinds of statements; but behind the scenes, changes were occurring. Winning became everything.

Previously, the college's business office had exercised control over all aspects of athletic finances, collecting all athletic funds and paying the related bills. This was the proper way to handle athletic funds. However, in the fall of 1924—while Dean Reece was in Chicago on leave—with Dr. Sams's help and blessing, a local booster club was organized to support the football team. This group was composed primarily of townspeople who had no personal connection to the college. They simply loved football and attended the games with enthusiasm. President Sams turned over the management of all athletic gate receipts and donor funds to the boosters club, which was taboo.[604]

Since Carson and Newman was not yet accredited, there was no oversight in such matters above the level of the president. The Southern Association would not have allowed such a procedure to occur—nor would have Dean Reece.

Matters came to a head in 1924, when the football team was scheduled to play Centre College on October 11. Centre had beaten Carson and Newman 7–0 the year before. The Fighting Parsons were ready to take on the Praying Colonels this time, and students were very excited and hopeful about winning over their rival.

Two illegal football players had been secretly registered under assumed names and hired to play football at Carson and Newman.[605] The local boosters club, of which Dr. Sams was an active member, had secured the two enormous young men to play for Carson and Newman. But they were not students at the college. They were "Ringers," football players who had no real interest in getting an education but who were available for hire at various colleges to help win games. In 1980, looking back to his student years at Carson and Newman, Sam B. "Frosty" Holt remembered seeing Ringers getting off the train. Calling them "mooses," he recalled, "They weighed 230, 240, 250 . . . and I said, 'Oh man, murder, murder.' I weighed about 145 to 150 pounds."[606] (Holt's weight was typical at the time.) Ringers had no legitimate or legal business at any college, especially not at a Christian institution.

According to procedure, the acting dean, Professor John D. Everett, was to certify the list of players as bona fide students. He had just occupied the dean's office for a few weeks and could not find the two student athletes' admission records. Because he could not verify the players in question, he took the matter to Dr. Sams. The president directed him to go ahead and sign the eligibility statements. Everett had no idea he was approving irregular players.[607]

GAME DAY AND REPERCUSSIONS

The football team left for Danville, with almost the entire student body at the train depot to see them off. But Centre College's coach, Charlie Moran, learned that Carson and Newman would be using two illegal players, registered under false names. Centre canceled the game, forfeited it, rather than play Carson and Newman. An investigation followed, and the Ringers were dropped from the team.[608]

Coach Lake Russell took much of the heat and the blame for the brouhaha. But the incident reflected negatively on all of Carson and Newman. It would take a while for the college to live down the incident due to all the criticism and finger-pointing. The trustees were vocal in insisting on a completely clean athletic program.[609]

After that football season, Coach Lake Russell wrote: "We can face the seasons to come without fear of shame, because irregularities which having heretofore caused us embarrassment have been abolished, and a possibility of a recurrence of any of these has been far removed. . . . The 'cleanup' has swept away many of our best athletes out of school, but it left us those with the proper morals, willing hearts, and those with the Carson-Newman spirit."[610]

The Christian Atmosphere on Campus

Carson and Newman had always been openly and decidedly Christian and Baptist. But in the 1920s, Christian organizations on campus seemed especially conspicuous and fervent. To name one, the Chambliss Society (named for the beloved John A. Chambliss, Carson and Newman's first full-time Bible professor who had died in 1916) carried the motto "Carson-Newman Out and Out for Christ." Dr. Sams and Dr. Campbell were the sponsors.[611] The Volunteer Band, the Definite Service Band, and the Mission Band were also among the popular college organizations for devout young men and women.

Nearby First Baptist Church and the college encouraged students to join the BYPU (Baptist Young People's Union, the forerunner of Training Union). Collegiate young women joined the "Glad Girls" Sunday School class (a reference to the popular book *Pollyanna* by Eleanor H. Porter). Students were expected to attend chapel daily except on Sundays, when they were to attend church services and then, in the afternoon, study the Sunday School lesson for next week.

Revivals occurred frequently in Jefferson City; *The Orange and Blue* documented one in the March 21, 1924, issue with the headline "Carson and Newman Experiences Modern Pentecost." The article contained a summary of revival meetings in which God moved powerfully and students felt convicted about their sins. At Dr. Sams's suggestion, bonfires were lit afterward at Davis Hall and Sarah Swann Home for the burning of playing cards, cigarettes, and other items of temptation.

Combining his twin passions for religion and sports in fervent language, Dr. Sams commented that Carson and Newman students "rooted" as hard for Christ as for football, athletes included. But it seemed to many that the college had a Christian identity crisis at this time. Was Carson and Newman a place where faith triumphed over sin and adversity, or a place where sin was covered over with a Christian gloss?

Reaping the Consequences

A LAWSUIT FILED

With Dr. Sams having confessed to Fred Moffatt his involvement in the letter-writing scheme, Mary Martin, teaching in South Carolina in 1925, filed a lawsuit against Dr. and Mrs. Sams in the Jefferson County Circuit Court.[612] Although Dean Reece was not an official party to the suit, no doubt Mary had consulted with him and Mrs. Reece, her aunt. Mary and the dean were the two foremost persons whose lives had been forever changed by the letter's accusations, and apparently no one who perpetrated or extended the scheme had expressed any type of apology to her.

The charge in the November 17, 1925, lawsuit was slander, and the proposed remedy was $25,000. Immediately, the attorney hired by Dr. and Mrs. Sams asked for the suit to be dismissed since the statute of limitations for slander (eighteen months) had expired. Just as swiftly, the request was denied.

A long list of subpoenas was issued, and depositions were taken. The list included faculty members, dormitory matrons, trustees, students, and townspeople and was not limited to Tennesseans. The trustees met on Thursday, May 27, 1926, and discussed the lawsuit, but took no action. The case was set for 9:00 a.m. on May 31, to be heard in Circuit Court.[613] (May 31 was the Monday after the college's commencement on Friday, recognizing Carson and Newman's seventy-fifth anniversary. The anniversary celebration must have been limited due to the circumstances; little was written about it. That fall, the descendants of Dr. Richard Scruggs, Carson and Newman's first four-year graduate in 1855, presented the college with a handsome portrait of him to recognize this milestone in its history.)

AN ALUMNUS'S HELPFUL MEDIATION

With the trial rapidly approaching, Dr. J. I. (James Isaac) Huggins, who was neither a trustee nor an employee of the college, foresaw ruin for Carson-Newman's reputation and future. Huggins, an honor-roll student at Carson and Newman in the 1890s, attended Vanderbilt Medical School and became a highly respected medical doctor in East Tennessee. An ardent supporter of the college, he probably received a degree from Carson and Newman after he graduated from medical school, according to the educational custom at the time.

Dr. Huggins regularly attended commencement exercises and the annual alumni meeting. He was a dear friend, neighbor, fellow church member, and personal physician of A. R. Swann, the college benefactor who had died only seven weeks earlier. He also currently had eyes and ears on campus as the father of student Janie Swann Huggins, who described Mary Martin as "a very special friend of mine." (Janie's middle name was a result of the close friendship between her father and A. R. Swann.)

Greatly concerned for Carson and Newman, Dr. Huggins decided to intervene between the parties involved in the lawsuit. He called two trustees—J. H. Anderson and A. R. Swann's son, Alfred Austell Swann (Alf)—and asked them to meet him at the college on Sunday afternoon, less than twenty-four hours before the scheduled court hearing. Dean Reece was also present at the meeting on Mary Martin's behalf. She may have been on her way to Jefferson City from South Carolina.

Asked what it would take to settle the court case, thereby saving the reputation of Carson and Newman, Reece answered in effect: "Only one thing can make this case go away. That is a full and honest public confession from both Dr. and Mrs. Sams and a statement of sincere remorse on their part." Dr. Sams had thus far been able to avoid a public confession of his own involvement.

Years later, Janie Swann Huggins described the meeting: "They met here on the campus, and they said this thing has got to be settled. It cannot go any farther. It will ruin the college. Daddy said, 'This just has to be done.' So the dean made the Samses rescind the charge. It was terrible. Dean Reece was definitely hurt, and the Samses were too."

A RETRACTION ISSUED

The next morning, the Samses and their attorneys, Mary Martin and her attorney, and many of the subpoenaed witnesses and spectators appeared in the courtroom at nine o'clock. The judge announced that an agreement had been reached by the parties that would "settle with binding finality the matters at issue and in controversy."[614] He then issued a consent decree that contained a statement by the Samses. It read in part: "We, O. E. Sams and Mrs. O. E. Sams . . . regret that the anonymous letter of December 21, 1923, reflecting upon the character and reputation of Dean J. I. Reece and his foster daughter, Mary Martin, the plaintiff in this case, was ever written and we hereby acknowledge that any accusation

The Class of 1926. Janie Swann Huggins is far left, third row from the top. Fred Moffatt is in the fourth row, third from the right. Mae Iddins is far left, seventh row. Lake Russell, coach and student, is beside her, slightly elevated.

and innuendo contained therein and all other accusations and innuendo following therefrom have no foundation in fact and the same are untrue and we hereby completely and fully without reservation or equivocation retract the same."[615] The judge declared the case dismissed.

AN OFFICIAL APPLICATION FOR ACCREDITATION

With the court case resolved, the trustees resumed their concentration on requirements for accreditation. Dean Reece had taken care of the college's academic requirements for accreditation during his tenure. The financial requirements had now been met. President Sams and the trustees were satisfied that, at long last, the college was ready for accreditation. The Southern Association met annually in December to evaluate schools applying for accreditation. In 1926, Dr. Sams and the trustee president traveled to the meeting site and presented the case for Carson and Newman's accreditation with confidence.[616]

To the disbelief of the two men, the unthinkable happened. The Southern Association members vetoed the college's application for accreditation.[617] Apparently neither Sams nor the trustees realized how far the ripples from the Sams-Reece problem had spread or how significantly they loomed in the evaluations of many.[618] Reece was well known to officers of the association and had many friends among members from other colleges. "Several of them felt that Dean Reece had been greatly mistreated, persecuted, and abused," wrote Dr. Isaac Newton Carr, who was present at the meeting. Carr, the dean of Mars Hill College at the time, later recorded the experience in his history of Carson-Newman.[619]

Dejected, Dr. Sams then had to return to Carson and Newman and report the rejection. Just afterward word came to him that Joseph I. Reece was considering filing a lawsuit against Carson and Newman's trustees for breach of contract—their failure to honor the agreement that Reece could return to Carson and Newman after his leave of absence. (J. I. Reece never filed such a lawsuit.) Sams justifiably concluded that the college would never gain accreditation as long as he was president. And he did not want to be the cause of a lawsuit against the trustees or to permanently ruin the college's reputation.

Over the Christmas holidays, President and Mrs. Sams discussed the situation and agreed that he should leave at the end of the school year.[620]

Their decision was made exactly three years after they had composed the anonymous letter to Dean Reece. The years between Christmas 1923 and Christmas 1926 had been bruising and left lifetime scars for all involved.

CONTEXT: 1927 EVENTS IN WORLD HISTORY

Charles Lindbergh made the first solo air crossing of the Atlantic Ocean, New York to Paris, in *The Spirit of St. Louis.* In baseball news, Babe Ruth became the highest paid player ($70,000), and Lou Gehrig was named Most Valuable Player. The Academy of Motion Picture Arts and Sciences was created in Hollywood. Calvin Coolidge was the thirtieth US president. In Nashville, a previously unnamed radio program became known as the Grand Ole Opry. Henry Ford produced the last Model T car and the first Model A, which sold for $385. Meanwhile, the first Volvo car premiered in Sweden. Chiang Kai-shek formed a revolutionary government in China, and Joseph Stalin became the leader of the Soviet Union.

Part 4, Aftermath of the Storm: 1927

RESIGNATION OFFERED AND ACCEPTED

Oscar Sams submitted his resignation to the trustees in early 1927, saying, "I go from your midst . . . without the slightest semblance of feeling against anyone living. It has been my privilege to pray daily for those who have judged me so harshly. The members of the executive committee have been loyal to their task and have given me all the support and cooperation one could ask."[621]

He then expressed alarm over the fact that only three room reservation fees had been sent in for the next year, whereas the previous year there had been paid reservations for almost every dormitory room by that time. The trustees accepted his resignation, effective July 1, 1927.[622]

DIBRELL HICKS, CLASS OF 1927

A different Carson and Newman tragedy occupied the hearts and thoughts of college faculty and students in February 1927, due to the sudden death of Dibrell Hicks, the senior voted "Most Popular Man." The 1927 *Appalachian* was dedicated to Hicks: "To our leader, our friend, our pal, our classmate, who died a real man, and whose memory will ever be cherished by those who knew him, we lovingly dedicate this volume."[623]

Hicks had joined a crowd of curious onlookers in downtown Jefferson City to witness the arrest of murderer W. B. Johnson, who had barricaded himself on the second floor of a house. Johnson shot out of a window, presumably aiming at one of the police officers present. An innocent bystander, Hicks was shot in the forehead and died instantly.[624]

In his final report to the trustees, Dr. Sams listed the major accomplishments of his administration, including: (1) construction of Butler-Blanc Gymnasium and Blanc Hall; (2) addition of a president's home; (3) elimination of indebtedness; (4) enlarged and strengthened faculty; (5) improvement of salaries; (6) growth of the endowment from $315,000 to $500,000; (7) elimination of the preparatory school and the master's degree program; and (8) exponential growth of student enrollment.[625] Concerning accreditation, Sams said, "Every condition has been met for entering the Association of Colleges, and with my going, there should be no difficulty experienced in gaining entrance next December."[626]

He included some personal comments in the report, saying that he had had only two vacations of two weeks each while he was president. During his presidency, he had worn out three Ford cars traveling for the college and had never charged Carson and Newman a cent for gasoline or repairs. "My holdings today are very little, if any, larger than they were on the day I came to the college," he said.[627]

The trustees' official acceptance of Dr. Sams's final report took the form of a recommendation for future employment: "The trustees consider Dr.

Sams eminently fitted for an important pastorate or the presidency of a college and would congratulate any community that may be so fortunate as to secure his services in either capacity. President Sams leaves the college with the highest esteem of the trustees and with their best wishes for his future."[628]

At the June 1927 commencement, Dr. Sams presented 64 AB diplomas. Oscar Ernest Sams, Jr., was one of those graduates; he had served as the editor-in-chief for the 1927 *Appalachian* yearbook.[629] Dr. Sams also presented fifteen BS diplomas and twenty-two special diplomas and certificates in art, music, and expression. Dean Arlie Cate would preside at the summer school commencement in August on behalf of sixteen more graduates.[630]

Some years later when the Samses visited Jefferson City—possibly at younger son Conway Sams's graduation from Carson-Newman in 1934—Dr. Sams sought out Dr. J. I. Huggins. In a positive turn of events, Dr. Sams thanked Dr. Huggins for his help in halting the 1925–1926 lawsuit.

Life After Carson and Newman

Oscar Sams assumed the presidency of Bluefield College (now University) in Bluefield, Virginia, later in 1927.[631] The junior college did benefit from his three-year stay. Under Dr. Sams's leadership, Bluefield developed a new summer school program and an Aviation Department. The school also gained accreditation in the American Association of Junior Colleges, a milestone event.[632]

The Samses then went "home" to Mars Hill College, where Dr. Sams was known and loved. He was brought back as vice-president, a title he would hold until his death. Dr. I. N. Carr, still dean at Mars Hill at the time, said Sams had no assigned duties, but administrators hoped he could secure financial support for the college. His health began to fail, however, and ultimately he was permanently disabled.[633]

At Mars Hill, Dr. Sams was well remembered as a dynamic leader in his earlier years. Despite his progressive illness, partial paralysis, and eventual inability to speak, he was regarded as an icon on campus.[634] Decades later, Conway Sams remembered, "There never was a kinder man."[635] Oscar Sams died in 1952.

Joseph I. Reece succeeded well in his insurance business in Johnson City, at one time serving as the Tennessee Commissioner of Insurance. He and his family eventually moved to his wife's home territory of Pickens County, South Carolina, where he died in 1970.[636]

Josef I. Reece, the adored "campus child," became a career Marine. He served in both World War II (including assignments at Iwo Jima, Saipan, and Okinawa) and the Korean Conflict. Josef Reece died in 2018 at age 98.[637]

Mary Martin and Fred Moffatt married in June 1926. Fred furthered his education at Union Theological Seminary in New York and Princeton Theological Seminary in Connecticut. After leading a number of small churches, in 1937, he accepted the pastorate of the First Baptist Church of Frankfort, Kentucky, from which he retired in 1961. Fred and Mary had three sons, one of whom was given Reece as a middle name. Fred died in 1970, and Mary survived him by several years.[638]

During the low points of the 1920s on the Carson and Newman campus, Truth sometimes suffered from neglect, Beauty might be deemed artificial, and Goodness seemed only a distant memory. According to Dr. I. N. Carr, the scandals recounted in this chapter had left scars that would take twenty years to heal.[639] Fortunately, the next leader of the school would serve for exactly that amount of time, rebuilding stability and the essential Carson-Newman spirit. The seventy-five-year-old college would again thrive and begin new chapters in its unique heritage.

CHAPTER EIGHT

National Challenges Met and Sacrifices Made

1927–1948

"O God, I cried, give me new birth! . . .
I know not how such things can be;
I only know there came to me
A fragrance such as never clings
To aught save happy living things . . .
And, through and over everything,
A sense of glad awakening."
—Edna St. Vincent Millay[640]

"Wanted: a forward-thinking Baptist educator, administrator, peacemaker, and healer who can bind up broken hearts and dreams while inspiring others to excel. Anyone committed to sports above academics need not apply. A strong intellect and consistent integrity, with justice for all, are 'must' credentials for a successful candidate. Gifts in public speaking, money management, and promotion are definite pluses. Above all, any applicant must maintain a scandal-free administration." Imagine the Carson and Newman trustees placing such a classified advertisement in 1927 for a new president!

This scenario is pure fiction, of course. The trustees chose not to advertise the presidential vacancy or even to invite applications. Instead, a subcommittee began discreetly surveying the persons suggested by its own members.

Moving swiftly to secure a new president who could begin leading the college during the summer months, the subcommittee soon narrowed their focus on James T. Warren, currently an administrator at the Tennessee College for Women—a Baptist school in Murfreesboro. The trustees elected Warren in time for him to attend Carson and Newman's commencement at the end of May, warning him to guard the college's finances and to avoid deficits. His presidency began on July 1, 1927, and his salary was set at $4,200.[641]

First Steps: Making Positive Long-Term Decisions

CARSON AND NEWMAN'S FIRST TWENTY-YEAR LEADER: JAMES THOMAS WARREN, SIXTEENTH PRESIDENT (1927–1948)

A native of Corinth, Mississippi, James T. Warren (1884–1948) was a small child when his family moved to rural Sharon, Tennessee (close to Martin). James was the oldest of ten children, most of whom died before reaching adulthood. Raised on a farm, he acquired a strong work ethic at an early age. As a boy, he attended public schools and performed all the manual labor involved in farm life; but above all he longed for a great education. His mother told him that he was going to college "if she had to sell the bed she slept on" (*Orange and Blue,* September 17, 1927).

He was elated when educational opportunities opened up for him. He graduated from Hall-Moody Institute in Martin—a junior college—and earned the BS and MA degrees from George Peabody College in Nashville. In 1929 Georgetown College in Kentucky would give him an honorary LLD.[642]

Academic administration proved to be his forte. Before coming to Carson and Newman, Warren served as professor and vice-president of Hall-Moody; superintendent of public schools in Rockwood, Tennessee; and vice-president of Tennessee College for Women in Murfreesboro.[643] His diverse experiences included overseeing various phases of college life, including finances, teaching, curriculum, faculty, students, and campus activities.

Warren was an active Baptist layman who was often invited to address Baptist congregations, associations, and other similar groups. Possessing a personable manner and a natural dignity, he had an inviting way of speaking to large audiences. His own dedication to the cause of Christ led to an atmosphere of consecration on campus and in other settings.[644]

Dr. Warren actively demonstrated his devotion to family members who needed him. He brought his youngest sister, fourteen-year-old Gladys Elizabeth Warren, to the president's home after their mother died; Gladys graduated from Carson and Newman in 1929. (In 1935, he hired her to

James T. Warren, president 1927–1948.

teach English, French, and history for a year; the practice later deemed nepotism was not a factor then.) Warren and his wife also took in another sister's children, three orphaned nieces who lived with them and graduated from the college.

President Warren took several steps to encourage more social interaction among the students. For example, when enrollment was relatively small, he arranged for male and female students to dine together, to their delight (*Orange and Blue,* November 22, 1930). He also encouraged the matching of female/male literary societies—the Calliopeans with the Columbians and the Hypatians with the Philomatheans.

Warren believed that Carson and Newman should remain a college and not become a university. In his view, the faculty and administration could maintain personal care and concern for each student if enrollment were limited to five hundred maximum. Also, he valued the intellectual depth of the classes a smaller educational institution could offer. However, in his twenty years as president, he was to see the college enrollment increase to well beyond five hundred.

THE COURAGE OF EARL STALLINGS, CLASS OF 1943

As pastor of the First Baptist Church in Birmingham, Alabama, in the early 1960s, the Rev. Earl Stallings had an open door policy. On Easter 1963, Andrew Young and two young black women entered the church to see how they would be treated. Many members of the all-white congregation stormed out, but Pastor Stallings welcomed the three as children of God. Martin Luther King, Jr. praised him for his gracious welcome to the visitors, but Stallings was vilified in the press—both local and national.

As a college student, Stallings had had a strong personal relationship with Dr. Warren, calling him "the father I did not have." For the rest of his life, he never doubted that he did the right thing in Birmingham, crediting Carson-Newman for giving him a social conscience. "I had the courage to stand for righteousness and justice because it was planted in my heart by the men and women who were the faculty and administration of Carson-Newman College," he said in 2003. Earl Stallings passed away in 2006.[645]

GAINING ACCREDITATION AT LONG LAST

The first item on President Warren's agenda was to accomplish the college's long-delayed accreditation with the Southern Association of Colleges and Schools. Some Carson and Newman students applying to graduate schools had been rejected because their degree was from an unaccredited institution.

Knowing that having the goodwill of former dean Joseph I. Reece was key to securing the Southern Association's approval, Warren and D. L. Butler, trustee and longtime benefactor, asked to meet with Reece in late 1927. The conference went well; Reece agreed to write a letter to the Southern Association stating that matters relating to him at Carson and Newman had been settled to his satisfaction. In addition, he generously urged the Southern Association to accept the college into its membership.[646]

At the annual meeting of the Southern Association in December 1927, the college's request for membership was approved. Another accrediting body, the American Association of Colleges, admitted Carson and Newman into full membership soon afterward. Now both technical and professional schools would accept Carson and Newman graduates for work on advanced degrees.[647]

That was the good news. Somewhat negative, though not surprising, news came in its wake. The Southern Association sent a follow-up letter noting several weaknesses that should be addressed right away: (1) Not enough faculty members held a doctorate; (2) The college should have a written policy of helping professors get advanced degrees; and (3) Salaries needed to be larger so professors could afford to undertake graduate studies. The college was to report the specific steps being taken to address these weaknesses.[648]

In 1928, the salaries of full professors were raised $300 per year, bringing them to $2,700. That was still $300 below the minimum set by the Southern Association, but now Carson and Newman could point to progress in this area.[649] Also, some professors were taking steps to further their graduate training. But efforts to employ professors who already had doctorates were unsuccessful; Carson and Newman salaries were not high enough to attract them. At this time, the college began to base faculty salaries on rank, experience, and tenure, and set an incremental course toward raising faculty salaries to the required levels.[650]

To balance the new necessary expenditures, scholarships for children and relatives of faculty members were abolished. Warren also dispensed with the team of mules and wagon President Sams had used.[651] Most significantly, he raised college fees. These had always been kept as low as possible in order to accommodate poor but worthy students.

STUDENT EXPENDITURES FROM THE EARLY 1930S

Tuition and fees for a year cost about $126. Room and board costs varied according to dormitory: Sarah Swann, where residents worked to supplement costs, $165; both Henderson Home and Blanc Hall, $203; Davis Hall, $198. For a year, a student spent a total of $291 to $329.[652]

HIRING FACULTY AND STAFF MEMBERS OF EXCELLENCE

Dr. Warren was gifted at choosing faculty and staff members who would stay a long time and make many contributions to the college. His first such hire was **Roy Myers** in 1928 as the college's treasurer and business manager. A former Carson and Newman student who had acquired broad educational and business experience, Myers also had a proven track record of integrity—an even more important asset. The Warren-Myers partnership saw the college through some of the most difficult financial times in its history: the Great Depression and World War II.

Also in 1928, President Warren recommended the addition of a qualified woman to direct physical education for female athletes, who had been neglected. **Mae Iddins,** a talented athlete of the Class of 1926, was hired to head the women's division of physical education and given special training. Thus began Iddins's long and effective tenure. Since female athletes were not allowed to participate in intercollegiate activities at the time, she developed a popular point system for intracollegiate contests for women. Her students proudly wore their well-earned letters on sweaters and other garments.[653]

The college hired **Sam "Frosty" Holt,** star athlete of the Class of 1927, as athletic director and football coach when Lake Russell resigned in 1929. Holt had been working at a high school in Bristol, Virginia, since his graduation. But no one in Jefferson City had forgotten him, and he was "unquestionably the choice of the alumni and students" (*Orange and Blue,* February 23, 1929).

LONGTIME FACULTY AND STAFF WITH STAYING POWER

Warren's hires who stayed twenty years or more, noting the year each began, included Carl Tabb Bahner, chemistry, 1937; William W. Bass, English, 1934; Bernice Carter, dean of women, 1945; Elizabeth Clark Cates, art/education, 1938; Joe A. Chapman, biology, 1947; James O. Conwell, modern languages, 1947; Edgar M. Cook, psychology/education and dean of men, 1934; Sam B. "Frosty" Holt, 1929; Janie Swann Huggins, English, 1940; Mae Iddins, physical education, 1928; Mildred Iddins, librarian, 1944; Charles H. Jones, music, 1946; Roy Myers, treasurer, 1928; Oscar L. Rives, Bible/religious education, 1947; Albert R. Sloan, mathematics and treasurer, 1936; L. Dan Taylor, Bible/Greek, 1946.[654]

Culture Captured by the Student Newspaper

The Orange and Blue was an excellent, balanced newspaper and effectively communicated several dimensions of American culture to its readers during the Warren years. It reflected the current trends of the country as well as the pulse of current events and moods on Carson-Newman's campus. Below are examples from issues of *The Orange and Blue,* as noted in parentheses.

Chapel Accounts (October 28, 1928): Popular biology professor Judson Dunbar Ives spent 1923–1952 teaching at Carson-Newman. "Romans 12:13 was the basis of the message brought to us by Prof. Ives [who] developed this subject in a very attractive manner. . . . He showed us that the student who placed a tack in his classmate's seat was not being peaceful with all men."

Sorrows (December 8, 1928): When Bible professor J. L. Campbell died, an editorial paid tribute to his work ethic and consecration: "His class room was the HOLY OF HOLIES of the College. In every class . . . there was held a spiritual feast."

Traditions (various issues): Armistice Day was celebrated each year with a parade, chapel program, and literary society presentations close to November 11. The chapel program included a salute to the United States flag, a patriotic address, thirty seconds of silence to remember victims of the war, and the retiring of the colors. One literary society presentation involved a reading from *All Quiet on the Western Front* by Erich Maria Remarque and a dramatization of a soldier's leaving for the war and then his return home. Fireworks lit up the nighttime sky on November 11.

Natural Disasters (March 21, 1930): A tornado struck Jefferson City on March 18, 1930. No one was hurt, but property damage was extensive. Trees on campus were felled. The skylight of the administration building smashed into fragments on the ground. Windows shattered in Sarah Swann. The top of the smokestack on the 1919 central heating plant was blown off, and the remainder was "left standing like the leaning tower of Pisa."

Alumni News (October 13, 1931): Horace L. Jones, Class of 1898, was the head of the Greek Department at Cornell University. He was also the author of an eight-volume series, *The Geography of Strabo,* and the textbook *Poetic Plural of Greek Tragedy in the Light of Homeric Usage.* Dr. Jones wrote:

"One of the prides of my life is that my father's name, like that of the good and great John T. Henderson, is inseparably associated with the greatest and best little college in all the world!" Horace's father was beloved professor of mathematics Shelby E. Jones (Class of 1877), who taught from 1882 to 1914.

Campus Improvements (November 24, 1931): In 1931, Jefferson City paved its streets for the first time, including Russell and Branner Avenues. Shortly thereafter, the campus walkways were improved too—either tarred with cinders or covered with concrete. Students rejoiced: "We have no excuse for 'run-down' heels now that we have concrete walks and 'tarred walks,' and we no longer have a dusty road near us to complain of."

Student Accidents (December 8, 1931): On November 18, student Ernest Horton was performing an experiment in the chemistry lab when his apparatus exploded. Flying glass pierced his left eye. At first doctors thought he could recover naturally, but a week later his eye was removed at a hospital in Bristol. Horton returned to school soon afterward, a hero to his classmates.

Concerts (February 16, 1932): The Zimmer Harp Trio presented a magnificent concert in the auditorium, with a baritone assisting in the program. "The audience was spellbound to the end. . . . The best program the college has had this year, it was deeply appreciated."

Senior Receptions (April 19, 1932): President and Mrs. Warren would soon entertain the seniors at a Leap Year party; girls were to invite boys. "The girls are already planning to wear the most 'fatal' dresses possible and the boys are buying books on 'what to say under all circumstances.'"

Radio (October 11, 1932): By the 1930s, radio had become a primary form of entertainment. An *Orange and Blue* reporter titled his column about campus romances, activities, study woes, and personalities "The Campus Shadow" after a character on a radio program. The mysterious, anonymous crime-fighting character "The Shadow" knew everything about everybody.

Literature (February 14, 1933): A student editorial praised Edna St. Vincent Millay's portrayal of her honest and complicated feelings in her poetry and declared her the poet of their generation.

Dramatic Performances (January 17, 1933): "The Dramatic Club will present the play 'Esmeralda,' a comedy in four acts written by Frances Hodgson Burnett and William H. Gillette. . . . [Mrs. Burnett] is a relative of former President J. M. Burnett and Mrs. A. R. Swann." Frances Hodgson Burnett, who had lived in nearby New Market when she was young, was most famous for writing *A Little Princess, The Secret Garden,* and *Little Lord Fauntleroy.*

New Campus Organizations (September 25, 1934): A student marching band with drums and drum major was formed at Carson-Newman. (It would end in 1938 but return anew in 1945.)

Memorials (April 30, 1935): Nora Maples Rankin, the first female director of the Music Department, left $300 in her will for improvements to the auditorium stage before she died in 1925. After the upgrades were made in the 1930s, the new luxurious stage curtains bore her name in large embroidered letters. A newcomer's question "Who is Nora Maples Rankin?" gave friends and students an opportunity to remember and describe her.

Oddities (October 15, 1935): There were twenty-one sets of twins on campus as well as many sets of sisters and brothers.

Hypatian Literary Society (November 19, 1935): The Hypatians took an imaginary trip to Norway during their recent meeting. The speakers gave a travelogue of the country, highlighting its musical and playwriting culture.

Missionary Alumni (January 28, 1936): "Dr. W. H. Tipton, Class of 1900, recently returned to his work as editor of Sunday School literature for the China Baptist Publication Society. He has served more than 30 continuous years in China. He received a D.D. from Carson-Newman at Commencement when his son, Bryson, graduated."

Philomathean Literary Society (November 24, 1936): The Philos discussed "Some Famous Women of History" on November 6. Joan of Arc, George Eliot, and Marie Curie were among the women studied.

Christmas Events (December 14, 1937): W. Powell Hale presented his own theatrical version of Charles Dickens's *A Christmas Carol* on December 16 at Carson-Newman. Hale made a remarkable success with his popular rendition of the Christmas classic, adding touches of humor to the Dickens story.

Inspiration (November 19, 1940): A prayer room in the administration building was dedicated to the memory of mathematics professor and former dean Edward W. White, who had died in 1937. White, nicknamed the "Grand Old Man," began his teaching career at Carson-Newman in 1917.

Calliopean Literary Society (April 1, 1941): The Callies presented a pantomime of Longfellow's *Evangeline* with ten members portraying various characters.

Columbian Literary Society (April 1, 1941): "The Columbian quartet [was] so well received . . . for its rendition of 'Let the Church Roll On.'"

Humor (April 15, 1941): "Dr. Bahner: 'What happens when the human body is immersed in water?' Student: 'The telephone rings.'"

Sports (March 23, 1944): "The 'Holt Machine' continues to develop in Roy Harmon [Class of 1944], who recently became the head coach at Young High School in Knoxville." In less than ten years Roy Harmon would be coaching for his alma mater under the leadership of Sam "Frosty" Holt. Every issue of the newspaper covered the latest news about the athletic teams—wins, losses, comments from the coaches, interesting observations, statistics, and so forth.

May Day Celebrations (April 26, 1944): Professor Janie Swann Huggins brought the May Day tradition back to campus in the 1940s. The graceful winding of the May Pole, the creating of May baskets, and a coronation for the May Queen and her court were part of the pageantry. During World War II, a naval review was added to the program. (This rite of spring was celebrated on campus until the mid-1960s.)

Tributes (September 2, 1947): T. C. (Thomas Carlyle) Hutton died in 1947, having taught Latin and Greek at Carson-Newman since 1919, and also served as registrar. A former student wrote of him: "For him there was no time but eternity—he went backward easily and transferred the ideas of the ancients to the present, he plucked the treasures which would outlast all time."

The Modern Portia Club (January 16, 1948): "Founded in 1925 . . . the club emphasizes the study of modern fiction, giving its members the opportunity of reading the best novels written by living authors and contributing the works studied to a special collection in the library. The club meets twice a month under the sponsorship of Miss Janie Swann Huggins, a charter member."

Christian Organizations (various issues): The Life Service Band, the Volunteer Band, the Definite Service Band, the J. L. Campbell Ministerial Association, the Baptist Student Union—all were popular groups that helped college students to follow Christ or dedicate their lives to Christian service.

A HYPHEN PUNCTUATES THE COLLEGE'S NAME

In 1930, Carson and Newman officially became Carson-Newman College thanks to a change in the charter. The hyphen had sometimes been used informally before 1930, but not in official college documents.[655]

New Things Under the Sun: Progress in the Early 1930s

A NEW IDENTITY AND MASCOT FOR THE ATHLETIC TEAMS

The name "Fighting Parsons" had been attached to the athletic teams, particularly the football team, since 1921. However, by 1930, many on campus had second thoughts about the name. Other colleges tended to assume that all male athletes at Carson-Newman were ministerial students, which was not true. The name gave Coach Holt trouble in recruiting athletes. Also, there was growing unease about the connotation of fighting combined with "parsons."

"Frosty" Holt held a campus-wide contest to determine a new name, offering a $10 gold piece to the person who proposed the winning name. The winner was Miss Tennessee Jenkins for her suggestion of "The Fighting Eagles."[656] Since the eagle is the national bird, strong and swift in attacking its prey (or opponents), this designation was deemed apt. Thus, in 1931, the Fighting Parsons became the Fighting Eagles.

Just as the female basketball team had been called Parsonettes in the 1920s, the 1931 women's basketball team was renamed the Shegles. This designation only lasted one year, eventually giving way to Lady Eagles.[657]

Soon the college installed two pairs of concrete eagles on the Russell and Branner Avenue sides of the Administration Building. Seeing these mascots every day inspired thoughts of victory for both athletes and other students.

"IT GETS FOGGY AT MOSSY CREEK"

Coach "Frosty" Holt raised the level of school spirit surrounding outdoor sports, especially football, by coining the phrase "It gets foggy at Mossy Creek."[658] Having been a student athlete in the 1920s, doubtless Holt had witnessed firsthand the phenomenon of fog rising over the sports field from nearby Mossy Creek, confounding visiting teams who could not see to play well. But Eagles accustomed to playing in the fog could often use the "cover" to their advantage.

Exactly when the first football game was won thanks to this misty "secret weapon" is lost to the proverbial fog of time. But Frosty Holt was fond of reminding his teams that even if they lost away games, the tables might be turned when rival colleges played at Carson-Newman.[659] (Even today, Carson-Newman students often tap into the local legend of weather favoring the Eagles by chanting jubilantly, "It gets foggy at Mossy Creek!")

THE SNAKE DANCE (*ORANGE AND BLUE*, OCTOBER 31, 1931)

After the football team's homecoming victory over Tennessee Polytechnic Institute in October 1931, campus residents pulsed with the need to celebrate. The celebration took the form of a long line of students in the shape of a snake with "wiggles, squirms, and shouts . . . into the road of freedom between Sarah Swann and Henderson Hall. There the snake unwound himself . . . and stretched out to his full length. With grace and marked rhythm he wiggled his way across the C. N. campus: with a twist, a turn, a graceful curve of the body, he slid by Henderson Hall, the Ad Building, and at length slid down the embankment to Main Street. Undazzled by the lights of the city and the noise of traffic, the snake unstealthily and openly . . . made his way down the highway, disregarded the stoplight . . . and was soon not only sending up yells to the skies but songs—in all of which 'C. N.' and 'team' seemed to be the outstanding words . . .

"The trip was too much for the snake. Having spent his energy . . . his body severed its relations and was seen in many small parts slipping hesitantly and slowly back to its confinement."

THE INAUGURAL HOMECOMING CELEBRATION

Carson-Newman's first homecoming for alumni was held in the fall of 1930. Previously commencements in May or June had been the only natural chances for graduates to see one another, but the addition of homecoming to the fall school calendar added a second opportunity. Also, a new pattern was set: organized class reunions were now held every 10 years at homecoming.

Plans for the second homecoming on Saturday, October 3, 1931, were described in the September 15, 1931 *Orange and Blue.* Saturday classes would cease at 10:00; a brief program of music and general entertainment followed. The expected large crowd of alumni and friends would enjoy fellowship on campus, with lunch served by the Home Economics Department at a nominal cost. Afterward the campus buildings and society halls were to hold open house before everyone gathered to watch the football game.

THE ORGANIZATION OF THE A CAPELLA CHOIR

Luther Carter, the professor of voice in 1932, was quite taken with the quality of the voices in the Glee Club. Under his direction, the Glee Club was transformed into the A Capella Choir, traveling on school breaks to perform without accompaniment in many locations under the years. (In 1940, the Glee Club was reintroduced as a choral group, distinct from the A Capella Choir, according to the April 30, 1945, *Orange and Blue.)* The A Capella Choir still amazes listeners with the beauty of the singers' voices, and the annual spring concert and homecoming concert are favorite events on campus.

The A Capella Choir of 1946–1947. The director, Charles Jones, "Fessor," is on the top row, center.

THE ANNUAL SUMMER PREACHERS' SCHOOL

In addition to regular summer school sessions, in 1931, President Warren and his friend A. F. (Albert Franklin) Mahan—trustee, East Tennessee pastor, and former Carson and Newman student—organized the college's first Preachers' School for East Tennessee Baptist ministers. They did so at the urging of William D. Hudgins, head of the Education Department at the Tennessee Baptist Convention at the time. Hudgins had observed that many Baptist pastors had not been able to attend college and did not own many books; they greatly needed educational opportunities.

That first year, about fifty-five Tennessee preachers came to Carson-Newman for a week to hear some of the great Bible scholars of the day, such as A. T. Robertson and W. O. Carver of The Southern Seminary in Louisville, Kentucky. Other distinguished professors and pastors gave special lectures (*Orange and Blue,* September 15, 1931). Practical topics such as English grammar, ministerial dress, and table manners were also addressed.

The scholarship, inspiration, and fellowship among this group proved such a strong draw that the program was expanded to four weeks during the summer, with ministers choosing one week to attend each year. Classes for women began in 1942. The summer preachers' school lasted until 1999.[660]

Practical Additions to Academics

THE THIRD DEGREE

The college already offered the BA and BS degrees. In 1931, Carson-Newman began a new four-year curriculum major leading to a BS in commerce (business). Fred Noe, a new faculty member, taught the commerce classes in addition to serving as Coach Holt's assistant in physical education.[661]

EXPANSION AND EXCELLENCE OF HOME ECONOMICS

The home economics program was growing in reputation and enrollment. One advantage Carson-Newman had in this area was the Practice House, the former home of President John T. Henderson and a gift of A. R. Swann in 1917. Senior home economics majors were required to live in the

In the foreground, the "Practice House" of home economics students, former home of John T. Henderson. In the background is the observatory, originally built as a water tower for Sarah Swann Hall (out of picture at left).

Practice House for nine weeks in groups of five or six. They did their own planning, buying, and work, learning about home life and home management problems in practical ways under the supervision of an instructor.[662]

Within a few years, an additional curriculum in home economics was begun for future teachers of home economics. The Home Economics Club was also established, quickly becoming an outstanding organization on campus.[663]

CAMPUSOLOGY

An informal class to orient new students to life at Carson-Newman was called "Campusology," held on Sunday afternoons. Campusology offered no college credit and was not mentioned in the catalogues, but was popular and must have been of great personal value to students.

Campusology classes expanded when Wade H. "Dad" Bettis, a janitor at the college, took over the teaching. A much-beloved figure, Bettis probably covered Carson-Newman history, traditions, activities, and organizations so that students felt comfortable making good choices. As evidenced by his nickname, "Dad" Bettis was a faithful and reliable friend to all students (*Orange and Blue,* October 11, 1932). In later years, *campusology* came to refer to informal advice sessions on dating and marriage, according to the September 17, 1949, *Orange and Blue.*

Effects and Ripples from the Great Depression

The American Great Depression began at the end of 1929, but not until 1932 did it affect Carson-Newman in a major way. Administrators and trustees worked together to make decisions that would keep the college going. At stake, too, was the school's endowment—over $500,000. So many individuals and churches had made sacrificial gifts to Carson-Newman that letting the funds shrink from inflation or succumb to bank failures was unthinkable. Where possible, contracts with service providers were renegotiated for savings.

FACTS ABOUT THE GREAT DEPRESSION

Beginning after the stock market crash of October 1929, the Great Depression was the worst economic downturn in the history of the United States. The crash made paupers of most investors and led to the failure of nearly half of the banks in the United States, leaving millions of people without their savings or any recourse. Over the next several years, consumer spending dropped. Widespread unemployment followed as companies failed and laid off workers. By 1933, about fifteen million Americans were unemployed and desperate for food and shelter, lining up at soup kitchens and sharing overcrowded households with relatives or friends.

After Franklin Delano Roosevelt became president in 1933, he created new programs and jobs that eventually lifted many Americans out of dire poverty. For most of the country, the Great Depression had ended by 1939.

MANAGING PROPERTY HOLDINGS IN THE GREAT DEPRESSION

In the 1930s, the Knoxville banks holding Carson-Newman's endowment funds either closed or borrowed money from another entity to reopen. In particular, the East Tennessee National Bank, which had been regarded as a financial Rock of Gibraltar, did not reopen.[664] The Mossy Creek Bank, which had been headed by W. T. Russell in its heyday, also closed for good.

College officials disagreed regarding the overall course of action that should be taken in this crisis. Some wanted the college to accept a percentage of the endowment in cash at the current deflated prices. But others, including President Warren and treasurer Roy Myers, favored another option.[665]

The endowment funds were secured by mortgages on real estate, and the college took over multiple pieces of property that the bank had held as collateral. Some were homes; some were businesses; and they were in various sections of Knoxville. By renting the properties, paying the taxes, and keeping the property in good repair, Carson-Newman benefited from collecting the rent payments. Under this plan, the college held the properties until property values had recovered enough that no loss in endowment funds would be sustained. Then the college would sell them. Some properties were held for as long as ten years; but in the end, the endowment was saved and even enhanced.[666]

The college employed a skilled repairman as superintendent to choose responsible tenants for all of the properties, collect rents, and make repairs. This arrangement proved successful.[667]

After the crisis finally passed, the trustees commended President Warren and others for their handling of the endowment funds. Warren had proved his financial acumen and justified the confidence the trustees had placed in him.[668]

FOUR-LEGGED "SUMMER SCHOOL" CAMPUS DWELLERS

Despite the unkempt appearance to the campus, in the summers the college rented the baseball field and recreation areas for pastureland. Milk cows were led across campus every morning to the grazing area.[669]

A SECOND FRUITLESS TRY AT PRODUCING INCOME FROM MINING

Mining beneath the college property had been occurring since 1910 with minimal benefit to Carson-Newman. During the Warren years, the college signed a contract with the Universal Exploration Company to mine zinc ore under the athletic field. The Universal Company subleased the property to the American Zinc Company, which constructed a shaft, installed machinery, and procured a railroad line to the entrance. Optimists thought that the income from this source might be as much as $100,000, and they planned for most of the money to go into the college's endowment.[670]

Carson-Newman received a total of about $4,000 from the new contract.[671] But no more substantial income from mining operation was ever realized, and the college was left with uneven grounds that would limit expansion for decades.

TRIMMING THE ART DEPARTMENT

In 1932, the college discontinued the Art Department due to small student numbers. However, the next catalogue mentioned that the art professor of twenty-six years, Miss Blanche Ellis, would teach five college-level art classes in her home.[672] Apparently this arrangement did not prove successful; after 1933, the college did not have any art classes until the 1939–1940 school year, when a new two-year curriculum for elementary schoolteachers was established. The two art courses in that catalogue were for future elementary school teachers only.[673]

By 1947, however, art had been restored as a department, with seven classes taught by Elizabeth Clark Cates (Class of 1936). Two of those courses were still designed for elementary education majors; the other five were based in the fine arts and personal creativity.[674]

Wishing on a Star: How Carson-Newman Gained an Observatory

The December 19, 1932, *Orange and Blue* revealed an inspiring story taking place on the Carson-Newman campus. Alexander Chavis, the physics professor, had taught an astronomy course for several years. He had acquired a nice telescope for students to use but was hindered in having only a tripod on which to mount it. The cost of a proper observatory was prohibitive for Carson-Newman, especially during the Depression. One fine day, Chavis had an epiphany about the abandoned water tower A. R. Swann had built near Sarah Swann Home almost three decades before. Could the water tower be repurposed as an observatory?

PROFESSOR ALEXANDER CHAVIS'S SECOND FULL-TIME JOB

Over the years, Carson-Newman graduates had been making enviable records wherever they went. The person keeping up with "wherever they went" was Alex Chavis, the outstanding physics professor who doubled as the college's first alumni secretary. A veteran of World War I and member of the Class of 1922, he began both positions in 1926. Only a detail-oriented person could accomplish both jobs with precision and success, but Chavis did so willingly.[675]

In his role as alumni secretary, Chavis coordinated updates on alumni address, family, and career changes, publishing these news items in a column of *The Orange and Blue* and the *Alumni Bulletin*. (He edited the latter.) He also served as campus liaison for homecomings and class reunions and urged alumni to contribute regularly to their alma mater. During World War II, he listed the addresses of Carson-Newman students and graduates serving overseas and encouraged alumni friends to write to them. He printed the first two invaluable alumni directories (1935 and 1940).[676] Alexander Chavis served as alumni secretary for a record-breaking thirty-one years while he taught physics, retiring from both positions in 1957 (*Orange and Blue*, October 18, 1947).

Subsequent investigation revealed that the water tower's walls were built of reinforced concrete twelve inches thick—a degree of sturdiness most desirable in an observatory. Chavis's idea was workable if money could be found to construct steps leading up to the top and to erect a revolving aluminum dome on top with windows for viewing.

Chavis, who also served as the college's alumni secretary, had an idea for a possible funding source too. Enter the Class of 1926, which had been collecting money since its graduation for an as-yet-undetermined gift to the college. Its plan had been to settle on the nature of the gift when it met for its class reunion in 1936. About halfway through the ten-year period, Chavis approached the class about this distinctive possibility. He estimated that already they had accumulated close to the amount needed for stairs, a steel guard to hold them in place, and the revolving dome.

Class secretary Ruth Banks Sedberry conducted a massive handwritten correspondence with all seventy-three class members to secure their votes on the matter. Eventually, she conveyed a positive response to the jubilant Alex Chavis.

Initial work on the observatory was completed in 1933, and the September 26, 1933, *Orange and Blue* recounted the success story:

> "The observatory is 75 feet high and 13 feet in diameter. . . . The top platform is reached by a series of concrete steps; a steel guard extends all the way up inside. The dome of the observatory revolves on roller bearings. . . . The observatory was designed by M. L. Beeler. The [college's] four-inch refracting telescope will be mounted in the observatory. Plans are already being formulated for the purchase of a larger telescope.
>
> "In addition to a mounted telescope, the observatory, when completed, will contain other astronomical equipment such as a transit, a celestial clock, and a Foucault pendulum. This pendulum will be the best of its kind in the state. The length of the suspension will be 64 feet.
>
> "The observatory offers an ideal situation for such a pendulum, since there will be no disturbing air currents when the lower door is closed. The rotation of the earth on its axis can be shown by means of the Foucault pendulum."The observatory is being built by the Class of 1926 as a class memorial. The formal dedication will be in the spring of 1936, when the class has its tenth-year reunion."

Meanwhile, as mentioned in the September 24, 1935, *Orange and Blue,* Dr. Chavis gladly gave alumni and guests nighttime tours of the observatory during homecomings and commencements.

CONTEXT: 1937 EVENTS IN WORLD HISTORY

The Appalachian Trail was completed, covering two thousand miles from Georgia to Maine. The Golden Gate Bridge in San Francisco opened. Congress established the National Gallery of Art, and Arturo Toscanini conducted the first "Symphony of the Air" over NBC Radio. The Boston Red Sox acquired the contract of nineteen-year-old Ted Williams. To the nation's dismay, aviators Amelia Earhart and Fred Noonan disappeared during a flight over the Pacific Ocean.

The coronation of Great Britain's King George VI took place in London, as did the publication of J. R. R. Tolkien's book *The Hobbit.* Toyota Motors in Japan became an independent company. Joseph Stalin, the Soviet Secretary-General, conducted sham trials of his enemies. Francisco Franco, Spain's general and dictator, made several offensives in Spanish cities. The Buchenwald concentration camp opened in Germany. The famed *Hindenburg,* a German airship, exploded in flames over Lakehurst, New Jersey.

Campus Events of the Late 1930s

COLLEGIATE FORAYS INTO THE WORLD OF RADIO

Enterprising student Herbert Diggs, who desired a career in radio, put Carson-Newman "on the ether waves" on March 14, 1938. The thirty-minute program, announced by Diggs himself in a sort of audition with radio station WNOX in Knoxville, opened with the college orchestra playing "I Love Thee Truly." Diggs gave a brief historical sketch of the college, followed by President Warren's describing Carson-Newman's ideals of Christian character and thorough scholarship.

Grayce Reynolds, a piano instructor, accompanied various student vocal numbers: a male quartet, a female solo, and a male solo. Then, Coach Holt set forth the college's athletic ideals and achievements. The orchestra closed the program with "Marchita." Thus, a wide audience of listeners heard a promotional summary of Carson-Newman's purpose, history, and excellence, according to the March 15, 1938, *Orange and Blue.*

Nine years later, Carson-Newman participated in weekly radio programs hosted by Station WCKR in Morristown. A sampling of the college's diverse topics included an address by Dean I. N. Carr, a concert by the A Capella Choir, a thought-provoking forum on global affairs from the International Relations Club, and a program of organ music performed by the music faculty (*Orange and Blue,* November 1, 1947).

TRAGEDY FOR THE BASKETBALL TEAM

On February 1, 1938, the outstanding Eagles basketball team had just traveled through Bulls Gap on their way to play the East Tennessee Teachers in Johnson City. Their bus was involved in a tragic crash that broke many hearts on campus and beyond, as recounted in the February 8, 1938, *Orange and Blue.*

Approaching the bus was a car with a trailer attached. The driver was trying to pull around a parked car but the trailer smashed head-on into the bus, killing two basketball players and injuring several others. The bus driver, Howard Jarnagin, managed to stop the bus just short of a power pole, even though he was injured. But Roy Roberts and James "Jimmie" Grissom, seated behind Jarnagin, were killed by shattered glass and flying debris. Their teammates reported that both the bus and the trailer seemed to explode on impact.

Roberts, a senior and star guard, had just been voted Most Intellectual Boy earlier that day. Also a Carson-Newman baseball player, he was president of the Boosters Club and the Science Club. Grissom, a sophomore and guard, had hoped to earn Roberts's prominent place on the basketball team after the latter graduated. *The Orange and Blue* reported: "Roberts and Grissom . . . have been integral parts of the greatest basketball machine Coach 'Frosty' Holt has ever produced—a team that in one year swept all opposition aside and finished undefeated in the Smoky Mountain Conference. This same machine working every bit as smoothly as last year was treading exactly the same path until this recent tragedy shattered the Eagle Combination."

Services for Roberts and Grissom were held two days after their death in chapel for their campus family. Later, a plaque was placed on campus in their memory—first at Butler-Blanc Gymnasium, then in Holt Fieldhouse.[677]

Carlyle Marney, Class of 1938, noted Baptist scholar and minister.

CARLYLE MARNEY, CLASS OF 1938

Most Popular Boy, football player, varsity debater, in the band, on the Baptist Student Union council—these are just a few of Leonard Carlyle Marney's varied activities at Carson-Newman. He also had the title role as "The Bat" in the 1938 Philo-Columbian play, a mystery by Mary Roberts Rinehart.

A native of Harriman, Marney entered Carson-Newman on a football scholarship and felt a call to preach while in college. After graduating, he earned a master's degree and doctorate in theology from Southern Seminary in Louisville. His long-term Baptist pastorates were in Austin, Texas—where he also served as professor of Christian ethics for Austin Presbyterian Seminary—and Charlotte, North Carolina. He lectured and preached at Duke, Princeton, Harvard, and Yale. In addition, he held seminars for active-duty Navy chaplains and wrote many books and articles on the Christian life.

In 1967, Marney established Interpreter's House, an ecumenical study center for ministers and laypersons at Lake Junaluska, North Carolina. He died suddenly in 1978.[678] For years, Carson-Newman has sponsored an annual lecture series in his honor.

STIRRINGS OF WAR

Like the rest of the United States, Carson-Newman students and faculty were caught off-guard by Orson Welles's radio broadcast of "The War of the Worlds" on October 30, 1938. Most listeners were accustomed to hearing the truth on the radio, so some were taken in by Welles's fictional account of Martians invading earth, based on a novel by H. G. Wells. An editorial in the November 15, 1938, issue of *The Orange and Blue* scoffed at those who believed Welles's broadcast.

However, a different type of war was approaching, and it was real. Early the next year, Adolf Hitler's German Storm Troopers marched through Prague, the capital of Czechoslovakia, revealing his intention to conquer other nations by force. Carson-Newman students noted that the prime ministers of Great Britain and France, who had acquiesced to Hitler's demand for a bit of Czechoslovakia in exchange for peace, had lost face. "What is to come, and how will this end?" they asked with foreboding (*Orange and Blue*, March 21, 1939).

A DREAM THAT CAME TRUE: THE WARREN BUILDING

As the nation was finally beginning to recover from the Depression, President Warren became convinced that the college needed to erect a science building. With the college's increased enrollment and student demand for scientific training, a new building could house the biology, chemistry, and physics departments, and thus release scarce space in the administration building for classrooms in other disciplines and for enlarging the library.[679]

Some were skeptical that enough money could be collected for the new building; the college appealed to Tennessee Baptists for funding. Henry D. Blanc, who had spearheaded the erection of the last major building on campus—Blanc Hall in 1925—wrote the first check for $5,000. After collecting funds for two years, the college had $19,000 committed to the new science building. Most pledges would be paid within months after construction began.[680]

A. R. Brown, a loyal trustee recently killed in a tragic car accident, had left a large amount of money to the college in his will. His bequest raised the total substantially. President Warren believed that others would be inspired to make contributions once construction began, and he was right.[681]

The newly constructed Science Building,
later named for President Warren.

JUST HOW CROWDED WAS THE ADMINISTRATION BUILDING?

Before the Science Building was completed in 1939, the 1919 administration building housed all campus offices for administrators and most faculty members, the library, space for mailboxes, cases for trophies, offices for *The Orange and Blue* and *The Appalachian,* and classrooms/laboratories for the following disciplines: accounting, art, Bible, biology, chemistry, commerce, home economics, dramatics, economics, education, English, expression, French, German, geography, Greek, history, Latin, mathematics, organ, philosophy, physics, piano, political science, psychology, public speaking, sociology, Spanish, violin, and voice. Only physical education classes were held elsewhere—Butler-Blanc Gymnasium or outside.

D. L. Butler purchased the construction materials and donated much of his time to oversee the construction, thereby saving the college at least 40 percent of the construction cost. The building was completed at a cost of $40,808.57, including the architect's fees.[682]

But the almost $41,000 did not include the expensive modern scientific equipment necessary to fulfill the building's purpose, which was purchased for an additional $20,000. Classes began meeting in the almost-completed building in the fall of 1939.[683] President Warren's belief in the need for a science building was vindicated in 1939 and deemed visionary just a few years later.

The first floor became the home of the Physics Department, containing classrooms, storage rooms, and the alumni office—a boon for alumni secretary/physics professor Dr. Chavis. The Biology Department occupied the second floor, and the Chemistry Department was located on the third floor.

The 1939 building (officially named for James T. Warren in 1959) served the science departments well until 1972, when the Dougherty Science Center was constructed. Today the Warren Building houses the Art Department.

Starts and Stops in the Early 1940s

A NEW ENDOWMENT CAMPAIGN FOR NEEDED BUILDINGS

In 1940, with the science building finally completed, a new endowment campaign was launched. Within the past ten years, interest rates had decreased. Alarmingly, income from the endowment had been cut by more than half. Without additional income the college could not continue a satisfactory program, much less construct other needed buildings on campus.[684]

Unfortunately, the campaign had to be delayed indefinitely when the United States entered World War II in December 1941. Building materials were primarily available for war uses only. In the meantime, however, several East Tennessee Baptist associations accepted specific financial goals on Carson-Newman's behalf.

The Knox County Association's goal was $75,000, and the money was to be used to erect the Baker Building, a student center that would also house the home economics classrooms and laboratories. A cafeteria large enough to serve the entire student body was also high on the "want list." The Baker Building would house the Willson Cafeteria, honoring a large gift from the Willson family of Athens, Tennessee.[685]

The Ocoee Association targeted its financial goal for a fine arts building, with A. W. Chambliss, an associate justice of the State Supreme Court, as the major donor. The building was to be named for Chambliss's deceased father, once a Bible professor at Carson-Newman.[686]

MISSIONARY KATHLEEN MANLEY'S HARROWING JOURNEY HOME

"Kathleen Manley '28 who has spent the past three years as a missionary in Nigeria, West Africa, will arrive next week on furlough. Miss Manley expected to get home two months ago but her departure from Africa was delayed on account of an epidemic of yellow fever in the hospital where she has been superintendent. After two members of the staff had died with yellow fever, she was about to depart for home but delayed her departure in order to nurse one of the doctors who had been stricken with the malady.

"Within a few days she contracted yellow fever and was seriously ill for many days. She finally set sail . . . with two other missionaries, but the ill luck which had prevented her earlier departure still pursued her. Three days out of Lagos, she was shipwrecked. After abandoning the ship, the crew and passengers found refuge on a small island where they were stranded for a number of days until picked up by another ship and finally landed at a French port. Miss Manley and her party landed at a Canadian port this week and her friends are anxiously looking forward to her arrival in Morristown" (*Orange and Blue,* September 7, 1937).

The Holston Association pledged money for a new home for the president of the college.[687] The current president's home, which had originally belonged to W. T. Russell, was in need of prohibitively expensive repairs and updating.

Additionally Bertie Maples Butler and D. L. Butler, already generous benefactors of the college, pledged $25,000 to begin a new free-standing library—the college's first—to be named after the outstanding Maples family.[688]

By May 1944, a total of approximately $175,000 in cash had been received.[689] But as the war continued and inflation ravaged the national economy, the new buildings would cost more than anticipated.

A SOLUTION TO THE PROBLEM OF STUDENT ILLNESSES

Various illnesses hampered students' ability to stay on campus for medical treatment since Carson-Newman had no infirmary. In 1940, a full-time nurse, Mrs. G. H. Payne, was hired to dispense necessary medications and help students recover. Small isolation wards were set up in dormitories, and student fees were increased to cover Mrs. Payne's salary and medical supplies. She had a good sense of humor about the irony of her last name and also answered to "Mrs. Misery" (*Orange and Blue,* August 27, 1940).

In a few years, the college was able to purchase the Murray residence near campus for a central infirmary for all students. (Ida Lawrence Murray, the founder of the Calliopean Literary Society, had graduated in 1893. She and her husband had shared the distinctive home for many years.[690]) Now the property houses the Kathleen Manley Wellness Center, named for the alumnus (Class of 1928) and international medical missionary who later served as campus nurse.

NINETY YEARS OF PROGRESS ACCORDING TO THE MEN'S LITERARY SOCIETIES

Appropriately, the college made much of its ninetieth birthday in 1941. The first celebration belonged to the Philomatheans, whose literary society had been formed in 1851—the college's birth year. They planned an elaborate banquet at the S & W Cafeteria in March in Knoxville with the theme "Ninety Years of Progress." The keynote speaker was former Philo Harry Laws, now a graduate student at the University of Tennessee, who would give "a glorious dissertation on the theme." As part of his address, Harry delivered an article on the society's history written by Dr. Edmund Cody Burnett of the Division of Historical Research, the Carnegie Institute of Washington, DC (*Orange and Blue,* March 18, 1941).

Edmund C. Burnett was a 1888 graduate of Carson College and a former Carson and Newman faculty member. In order to give some background on him to the 1941 audience, *The Orange and Blue* reporter stated: "We don't know that Dr. Burnett is the oldest living Philo in point of age, but we do know that he has been a Philo longer than any other man now living. And we know that Dr. Burnett knows whereof he speaks when it comes to history—and Philos. He's written enough books in his day to line the walls of a young library."

At the banquet, the Philos paid "homage to a society that through ninety years has maintained the spirit and reality of progress." Also featured on the program was "the entrancing harmony of the Shallow River Boys" (*Orange and Blue,* March 18, 1941).

The Columbians, whose literary society was also formed in 1851, held a celebratory banquet at the S & W on April 12. But their events were kept a grand secret (*Orange and Blue*, April 1, 1941).

NINETIETH ANNIVERSARY COMMENCEMENT ACTIVITIES

Carson-Newman proudly invited its two oldest living graduates to attend the alumni dinner on May 12, 1941, and the subsequent commencement activities as special honored guests. Both men were from the Class of 1881, composed of twelve members. They would be observing the sixtieth anniversary of their own graduations as well as the ninetieth anniversary of the college!

William Spencer "Spence" Bryan was the valedictorian of the Class of 1881, a Columbian, and a son of Robert Reedy Bryan, the college's beloved second president and master teacher. Like his father, W. S. Bryan spent his life educating young minds. He was the longtime dean of the Oklahoma Military Institute in Claremore, as noted in the May 6, 1941, *Orange and Blue.*

Dr. Elbert P. Morgan of Fall Branch, Tennessee, also a Columbian, was the other honored guest. By 1941, he had been a medical doctor for fifty-seven years, probably an unparalleled record in his area. Incredibly, he had also served as a US Postmaster.

Both men expressed joy in being able to attend commencement and to see all the changes in the college. They had attended Carson College on Campus #2. Bryan and Morgan, both still quite active, enjoyed catching up with each other from years past. (Morgan would die the following year, 1942, at age eighty-two; Bryan would die at age ninety-seven in 1954.)

THE RENAMING OF THE ADMINISTRATION BUILDING

On March 26, 1942, Carson-Newman honored former President John T. Henderson by naming the administration building for him. Even though Henderson was still living, the formal name of the building became the John T. Henderson Memorial Hall Administration Building.[691] In addition to all he had done for the college in his eleven years as president, Henderson had played a prominent role in raising funds to construct the administration building after the earlier one burned in 1916 (*Orange and Blue*, May 27, 1944).

In other commencement-related news, the 1941 senior class performed the play *You Can't Take It with You*—a perfect topic for those about to vacate dormitories after four years. A violin performance was the last on campus; for financial reasons, the Violin Department ceased to exist afterward. And among all four literary societies, the Columbians easily won the Inter-Society athletic trophy (*Orange and Blue,* May 6, 1941).

FOND FAREWELLS TO RETIRED FACULTY MEMBERS

Professor **John D. Everett** was the beloved education professor at Carson-Newman from 1919 until his retirement in 1942. The Carson-Newman chapter of Future Teachers of America was named for him in 1936.[692] Briefly the interim academic dean between Joseph I. Reece and Arlie E. Cate in 1924, Everett had heartily recommitted himself to teaching education classes afterward.

A trio of significant faculty members retired in 1944. "Mademoiselle" **Winifred Moore** had taught French at Carson-Newman since 1928; she was an aunt of chemistry professor Carl Tabb Bahner. **W. Powell Hale,** professor of dramatic arts, began teaching in 1898, with occasional years away dedicated to public performances. But he had taught at Carson-Newman continuously since 1924. A dramatics troupe was named the "Powell Hale Players" in his honor.[693] Miss **Tennessee Jenkins** had been a revered history professor since 1895. Her tenure—forty-five continuous years, plus parts of other years—was the longest of any faculty member in the twentieth century.

The College's Involvement in World War II

When the United States entered World War II at the end of 1941, everything changed all over the nation. In 1942, numerous male Carson-Newman students enlisted in the war for the highest of purposes—to win freedom from tyranny for the world.

Three professors also left to serve in the war: Fred Noe, assistant coach and professor of commerce; Virgil A. Warren (no relation to the president), professor of modern languages; and Genter L. Stephens, voice professor and director of the A Capella Choir. The October 5, 1943, *Orange and Blue* saluted all three for their service, noting in Stephens's case: "The words of that beloved benediction of the choir are our parting words to him. 'May the Lord bless you and keep you and cause His face to shine upon you and give you peace'" (Numbers 6:24–26). All three survived the war, but only Noe returned to Carson-Newman.

"THE VIEW FROM THE ADMINISTRATION BUILDING STEPS AT NIGHT"

During wartime, a student noted a campus view that brought him a sense of peace: "The sight which meets your eye as you leave the Ad Building at night is beautiful beyond expression. . . . The black trees cast a sturdy, lacy-edged shadow against a dark blue sky. The green-cheese moon is a skiff anchored in sea foam clouds. A few stars flirt scandalously. . . .

"Who could fail to stop and drink in great draughts of chill night air and solitude? Who could fail to wonder at the beauty of the world, and marvel at man's relation to such a universe? This is our setting for peace. From the Truth of the universal laws, the Beauty of natural phenomena, and the Goodness of the Supreme Being who gives all, we should understand better the ideals of our school" (*Orange and Blue*, August 4, 1943).

THE NAVY V-12 PROGRAM ON CAMPUS

Wanting to contribute to the war effort and also needing to boost student enrollment numbers, Carson-Newman officials recalled that during World War I, a Student Army Training Corp fulfilled both needs on campus. Now they looked into the possibility of having another military training unit at the college. In December 1942, the Navy and Marine Corps had begun a program for young officer trainees called V-12. After surveying the military options for young men, a committee from Carson-Newman settled on a Navy V-12 training unit as the best fit and invited Navy representatives to visit the school.[694]

The Navy officers who investigated Carson-Newman were especially impressed with the newly completed science building. Carson-Newman had excellent academic offerings, including mathematics, chemistry, physics, engineering drawing, descriptive geometry, and history—subjects the trainees needed to master in order to become commissioned officers.

Left, Dr. Warren receiving an official plaque from a Navy officer representing the V-12 program.

Officials of Carson-Newman and the Navy signed a contract on June 11, 1943. By July 1, the first unit of men from the Navy V-12 program arrived on campus, a diverse group from all over the country. Many of them had to adjust to small-town life in Jefferson City, and the college's firm prohibition against dancing on campus was a sore point. Having had varying levels of education before joining the Navy, some were well prepared for college life and some "washed out." They took various subjects at school with an emphasis on science courses, mathematics, and history pertaining to war. The trainees came in "waves" over the next two years, some departing and others arriving.

If the trainees were nervous about being assigned to a college campus, the "civilian" Carson-Newman students were not sure how to approach them either. Generally, Southern hospitality prevailed in the students' effort to make the trainees feel welcome.

The March 23, 1944, *Orange and Blue* printed a letter from a departed seaman to the unit just arrived, urging them to approach college life with openness, make friends, and participate fully in all activities. "We missed the boat our first semester," the writer admitted, but afterward his unit found "comradeship and unbreakable friendships" with the civilian students. An editorial in the same issue chided civilian male students who did not appreciate their deferment. "Do you ever think that that guy who went in your place is living a life absolutely devoid of personal freedom—while you calmly assume your role as a 'college man'?" *The Orange and Blue* frequently promoted buying war bonds as a meaningful patriotic investment too.

Coach Sam "Frosty" Holt played a role in bringing together the two groups. He easily persuaded the naval officers to let the trainees play football for Carson-Newman rather than participate in the Navy's physical education program. However, persuading the young men who cared nothing for Carson-Newman to join the football team was quite another matter. Treating them with respect and understanding, he called for the teammates to pray together and work together to bring victory on the field for Carson-Newman. Coach Holt eventually won the naval trainees' respect and had two successful football seasons with teams formed of both naval and civilian men (*Orange and Blue,* March 23, 1944).

The Navy trainees began their own newsletter, *The Periscope*, detailing all they were learning from a military standpoint as well as their campus activities. Besides playing football for Carson-Newman and participating in the annual May Day pageant, they were heavily involved in music. They had their own orchestra called the Navy Commodores and their own choir, led by Professor Stephens, director of the A Capella Choir, before he went overseas himself.[695]

The Navy V-12 men occupied Blanc-Davis Hall, but there were not enough rooms there. Overflow Navy men occupied Sarah Swann Home, with all female students living in the Henderson Dormitory. (Male civilian students boarded in residences in town.) The female students who continued to serve meals in Sarah Swann Home to the Navy trainees kept the college administrators aware of the considerable damage inflicted on their beloved society halls there. The young ladies were able to move back into Sarah Swann early in 1945.

While Carson-Newman had the V-12 program, the length of semesters was reduced in order to have three semesters per year. With this program, the teachers had year-round employment. Carson-Newman received income, which kept it alive, and was able to render a real service to the country.

FIRE ON CAMPUS

Shouts of "Fire!" "Fire!" rang out at Sarah Swann Home in the spring of 1945, and pandemonium ensued. Young ladies hurriedly packed, threw belongings out of windows, and "mobilized boyfriends into pack mules." The problem "turned out to be the garage immediately behind Sarah Swann. With the help of the Jefferson City Fire Department and student volunteers the fire was put out but not until Mrs. Rubin and Dean Cate were each minus a car" (*Orange and Blue,* September 19, 1947).

Soon after D-Day—June 6, 1945—the Navy V-12 program was phased out. About six hundred naval trainees had received two to four semesters of college training in the two years of Carson-Newman's V-12 program. A number of the seamen who passed through Carson-Newman's halls had developed quite a fondness for the campus, their civilian classmates, and especially for the professors who had bent over backward to help them pass courses.[696] Many such seamen kept in touch with each other and Carson-Newman friends over the years.

THE TRANSITION BACK TO "REGULAR" COLLEGE

There was no *Appalachian* for 1945 due to the war, but that year, the June 23 *Orange and Blue* printed an honor roll of thirty-eight young men who would have graduated had they not answered the call of their country. The 1946 *Appalachian* printed the names of the 1945 graduates as well as their own, plus those of six former students who had given their lives for their country.

On August 20, 1945, the college opened on a full civilian basis, reverting to the two-semester school year with a summer session. Soon Carson-Newman would experience the influx of the postwar student population, some of whom would come because the new GI Bill awarded servicemen free college tuition.

POSTWAR PROPERTY INNOVATIONS

College officials stayed alert for expansion opportunities when properties near the campus became available for sale. One such site was the former home of President Jesse M. Burnett on Russell Avenue, directly across from First Baptist Church. After Carson-Newman purchased it in 1946, the house was remodeled as a dormitory for up to twenty-four young women.[697]

The postwar era also brought a need for a new type of student housing—college-owned space for parking trailers occupied by married students. The first such couple to attend Carson-Newman was allowed to park on the college's original ten acres, Campus #1, and other couples followed suit. The trailer park came to be called Eagle Village. Within a few years space was allotted for fifty trailers! Today the area is the Silver Diamond Baseball Complex.[698]

In 1946, the college community welcomed the construction of a new central heating plant to replace the damaged unit President Gentry had erected in 1919. The new plant, located behind the present-day Baker Building, contained three 150-horsepower boilers and was built with monies obtained from having the V-12 unit on campus. In addition, a warehouse building and machine shop were constructed behind the Sarah Swann Home.[699]

PROFESSOR JAMES FERNANDO ELLIS

Ellis Street (off Russell Avenue) in Jefferson City is named for this beloved man who taught history and political science at Carson-Newman from 1926 to 1947 (his death). He was the brother of Blanche Ellis, longtime art professor, and Lula Ellis, an early college librarian. A man of many interests, he surprised a student who wrote in the November 1, 1938, issue of *The Orange and Blue:* "You should have heard Dr. Ellis playing the piano over in Sarah Swann parlor the [other] night!" Dr. Arlie Cate told this story at Ellis's memorial service: "Dr. Ellis, I understand, told his students in his summer school classes on Thursday morning that he was through. Before dawn of the next day his prophetic statement had come to pass. . . . Always a student . . . he knocked at the door of another classroom and entered there" (*Orange and Blue,* September 2, 1947).

Soon after the war ended, construction materials were finally becoming available for public use. The college geared up to construct the planned new buildings, excavating the properties on which they would be built. At this time, the Practice House of the home economics program was torn down in anticipation of a new building going there.

But inflation had stealthily robbed a considerable amount of the money that had been raised. In fact, the college had less than half the money needed to construct crucial buildings—the Baker Building, the Fine Arts Building, the new library, and a new president's home. A new architect was chosen to redo and scale back the plans, delaying the start of construction even further. Guy Bettis, the superintendent of buildings and grounds, was tapped to oversee work on construction when it began. But as 1948 dawned on campus, only partial excavations marked most of the building sites.[700]

The End of Dr. Warren's Tenure

President Warren did not live to see the erection of the other buildings he had proposed and promoted. Feeling unwell, he consulted doctors; tests indicated a need for exploratory surgery. In early January 1948, just before his surgery he decided to resign, effective at the end of the school year. He wrote a gracious letter to the trustees, admitting that his hearing loss was deepening and expressing concern about his overall health. The college needed a new, younger administrator to move forward into the 1950s and beyond, he urged.[701]

A Knoxville trustee and distinguished surgeon, Dr. Herbert Acuff, oversaw the medical team during Dr. Warren's surgery on January 10. The operation revealed a malignancy in advanced stages. Warren never regained consciousness and passed away on January 16, 1948.[702] (He was the second president to die while in office; William P. Rogers, the first president, had died soon after the college's birth.) Warren's death released an outpouring of accolades for his wisdom in leading Carson-Newman to new levels of accomplishment.

The statistics of Warren's twenty-year tenure are impressive. During his presidency about fifteen hundred students graduated with a bachelor's degree—over six hundred more than had graduated from the founding of the college through 1927.[703] The net enrollment was under five hundred when he came; fluctuated between 450 and six hundred during the 1930s; and surged to 831 in his last year. In 1928–1929 there were twenty-five faculty members teaching eighteen disciplines. In 1947–1948, forty-four faculty members taught twenty-three disciplines; the number of administrators (14) was unchanged between those years. The college's endowment had not only been saved but tripled (before inflation). The library now contained an amazing twenty-eight thousand volumes and subscribed to 225 periodicals.[704]

A BRIEF BUT MEANINGFUL PERIOD: ISAAC NEWTON CARR, SEVENTEENTH (INTERIM) PRESIDENT (1948)

Dean I. N. Carr was elected to serve as acting president along with his duties as dean. He agreed to accept if Miss Tennessee Jenkins would come out of retirement to take over his history classes. Fortunately, she did.[705]

A 1916 graduate of Carson and Newman, a Philomathean and a debater, Carr was a veteran of both world wars. He earned an MA degree from the University of North Carolina, then took two additional years of study at Duke University and spent six months at the Université de Poitiers in France. For seventeen years he served as dean of Mars Hill College, leaving to enter military service in World War II.[706]

On his return in 1945, he joined the Carson-Newman faculty as professor of history, filling the place of his own undergraduate history professor, Tennessee Jenkins, who had retired. He was named dean in 1947 when Arlie Cate retired. (Cate continued to teach, however.) Over the years, Dr. Carr had visited 168 institutions of higher learning, which gave him a breadth of knowledge helpful in his new role.

During Carr's presidency, he made the decision to remove the word *Appalachian* from the college seal, citing the negative connotation of the word in the national consciousness. No doubt he also remembered that its use at Carson-Newman originated with former President Sams, who had publicly portrayed the Appalachian people as depraved and ignorant. The word would be absent from the seal for twenty years until the next president chose to restore it.

Among Carr's most significant accomplishments during his brief tenure was the elimination of the campus discipline committee, which had become an "execution body" in the minds of some students. A more positive form of administration, the "Open Door Policy," replaced it. Carr also took a special interest in the construction of Maples Library, personally choosing the type of steel used for the stacks, including the beams that ran from the top floor to the bottom as well as the sturdy shelves.[707]

Dr. Carr welcomed the incoming president in October 1948 and was relieved to resume "only" the deanship and his teaching role. The next spring, he personally planned the new president's formal inauguration. He retired in 1957 but still had an important contribution to make to the college. The trustees commissioned him to write the *History of Carson-Newman College,* published in 1959.

ACCOLADES FOR CARR'S INTERIM PRESIDENCY

The 1949 *Appalachian* effectively described I. N. Carr's ten-month presidency on the heels of a great loss to the college:

> "In appreciation—To Dean Carr, who guided the destiny of Carson-Newman through one of its trying periods. The day following the death of our late president, Dr. Carr found himself Acting President, Dean, and Head of the History Department. It was with superhuman effort and unwavering faith in the student body that he met this mountainous task.
>
> Improvements in the form of paint, benches, water fountains, tennis courts, and repairs gave the college a new face. The 'Open Door Policy' was established which meant a hearing of and cooperation with all groups. This gave the college a new attitude.
>
> Losses of faculty members became gains, for with magician-like precision, qualified faculty members were pulled out of thin air. This gave the college a more scholarly air. The smoothness of his administration gave the trustees a longer period of time in which to find our president.
>
> So to you Dr. Carr, we bow in humble appreciation for ringing true the words 'Carson-Newman Evermore.'"[708]

"We live in deeds—not years." This inscription on a sundial donated by the Class of 1939 underscored lessons students had learned on campus about the importance of relationships and sacrificial living. The atmosphere that had fostered such maturity had been planted years before by visionaries—founders, faculty members, students of excellence, and past presidents.

In just eleven years of Dr. Warren's tenure, five former Carson-Newman presidents died: Millard Jeffries (1936, age 81), S. W. Tindell (1939, age 95), John T. Henderson (1946, age 87), Jesse M. Burnett (1947, age 77), and William L. Gentry (1947, age 79). Dr. Warren himself, of course, made the sixth (1948, age 63). Their collective, sacrificial deeds on behalf of Carson-Newman sustained and moved the college forward. Now a new president and a new generation of students would build some of Carson-Newman's greatest days of academic excellence, community spirit, and Christian values.

CHAPTER NINE

Amid Forward Motion, a Grateful Look Back
1948–1963

"Through many dangers, toils and snares
I have already come;
'Tis grace hath brought me safe thus far,
And grace will lead me home."
—John Newton[709]

A common and irrational form of discrimination almost cost Carson-Newman one of its most effective leaders. At least two trustees on the 1948 presidential search committee mentally rejected candidate Daniel Harley Fite at first glance—because he was a short man. Unfortunately, seated in a low chair in his first meeting with the trustees, he appeared even shorter than he actually was. On paper he was the leading candidate for president after the committee's first choice, Dr. Charles W. Pope—a former pastor of First Baptist Church, Jefferson City, and then the leader of the Tennessee Baptist Convention in Nashville—who had declined the position.

Judge Hamilton Sands Burnett, Chief Justice of the Tennessee Supreme Court, a member of Carson-Newman's Class of 1916, and the oldest son of former president Jesse M. Burnett, headed the trustee presidential search committee.[710] He brought a biblical perspective to the task. On meeting Fite in person he thought, "This man won't do. I was looking for a man like Saul who was head and shoulders above everyone else."[711] (Saul, the first king of Israel, was a tall, striking figure; see 1 Samuel 9:2.) Henry Blanc, the trustee chairman and college benefactor, had the same reaction. Perhaps they were visualizing a leader physically like the late President Warren, who had been well over six feet tall.

Of course, the measure of a man's height is no indication of his abilities. The character and skills Dr. Fite brought to leading Carson-Newman gave the best proof of that truth. Judge Burnett later recalled that the more he and Fite talked, the more Fite "grew on him."[712] Fite's own humorous recollection was, "I got a little bigger all the time, so they invited me to campus to look around."[713]

In September 1948, the trustees unanimously elected Harley Fite as president. He began work on October 15 at an annual salary of $6,500.[714] After spending several months learning the job, he was formally inaugurated in April 1949. On that occasion, he articulated his philosophy, welcomed by the college faculty, administrators, and students: "Look behind gratefully, accept work willingly, and press on to meet the future under God, unafraid." He also set forth a fourfold plan of concentration for the college: new buildings, more teachers of quality, an increased enrollment, and an expanded curriculum (*Orange and Blue,* April 8, 1949). Achieving these goals would occupy him throughout his twenty-year presidency.

C-N's First President Born in the Twentieth Century

LEADER OF VISION AND INTEGRITY: DANIEL HARLEY FITE, EIGHTEENTH PRESIDENT (1948–1968)

Harley Fite (1902–2003), the second of seven children, grew up on a farm in Wilson County, Tennessee.[715] Many of his high standards and values can be traced to his background. Of his family Fite wrote: "Early in life we [children] learned the value of work. We were taught that work is ennobling, not degrading. . . . Parents did not have to preach honesty. The children saw them practice it."[716] He also remarked: "In the daily life on the farm, each family member had his or her own well-defined role and responsibility. Of course, we children had the privilege to pursue our own needs and desires, but these were not allowed to displace the collective needs of the group. Obligations to the family came first, and the economic condition created intense family loyalties that not only insured survival of the group but also provided a strong feeling of security and belonging for individuals."[717] Staff and faculty members at Carson-Newman—Fite's latter-day family—could easily attest to working within the same value system decades later.

HARLEY FITE'S LIFELONG WORK ETHIC

One newly hired faculty member made his way to Carson-Newman to meet the president personally. Since the professor arrived before classes began and encountered few people on campus, he approached a gardener who was pruning some bushes outside a building. "Could you tell me where I could find Dr. Fite?" he inquired. The gardener took off his gloves and extended his hand. "I'm Harley Fite," he said to the astonished professor.

Harley Fite attended a one-room schoolhouse (grades 1–8), then high school, in Auburntown, Tennessee. He was an achievement-oriented student, later recalling he was allowed to learn beyond the standard curriculum. "I studied algebra, plane geometry and geology in elementary school. This was unheard of in a day of regimentation. . . . Even in college I did not feel handicapped though my high school was small and unaccredited."[718]

Fite graduated from Middle Tennessee State Teachers College in Murfreesboro (now Middle Tennessee State University) in 1927, majoring in agriculture, sociology, and science. He then studied at George Peabody College in Nashville, receiving an MA and PhD from that institution, where he majored in education and minored in social studies. His earned PhD was the first for a Carson-Newman president.[719]

After teaching in public schools for several years, he taught at Austin Peay State College in Clarksville, serving as academic dean there until 1946. His career then took him to Tennessee Valley Authority (TVA) as an education officer and afterward to the Florence State Teachers College in Alabama (now the University of North Alabama) as head of the Department of Education and Psychology. He was in Florence when Carson-Newman came knocking at his door.[720]

Moving to Jefferson City with his wife, three daughters, and a cluster of Rhode Island Red chickens, Fite and his family moved into the "Holston Home," which the college had purchased in 1946. It was a large brick residence deemed more suitable than the previous president's home and located next door to it on Russell Avenue.[721] This house had last been

D. Harley Fite, president 1948–1968.

owned by the beloved Dr. Roger M. McCown, a physician and former coach at the college.

Fite hit the ground running at Carson-Newman; he was equal to the challenge of modernizing and equipping the college for student life in the twentieth century. During his presidency an amazing twenty-four buildings, all sorely needed, were constructed on the sixty-five-acre campus. Thus he well earned the title "The Great Builder," which he modestly protested.[722]

Just after Dr. Fite's first year on campus, *The Orange and Blue* ran a heartfelt editorial about him: "There's a Lot of Fite on the Campus" (November 5, 1949). The student writer sang the president's praises, citing the newly formed "largest financial campaign in the college's history . . . many campus improvements . . . the numerous addresses Dr. Fite had already presented to campus, civic and church groups 'that appeared to be prepared just for them' . . . and the fact that no student had 'ever entered Dr. Fite's office and been refused his undivided attention and understanding counsel.'" Harley Fite was already well on his way to being recognized as a president both ahead of his time and just right for his time.

"The Monument," topped by an eagle,
in front of Henderson Hall.

The World of Carson-Newman in the Late 1940s

THE FORTY-NINERS AND THEIR MONUMENTAL GIFT

Carson-Newman's largest graduating class thus far, that of 1949—189 seniors strong—collectively expressed their hope to be a credit to the world at large on behalf of their beloved college. The monument they chose for campus is probably the most recognized, enduring class gift to Carson-Newman. "Meet Me at the Monument" became a destination for all kinds of student meetings on campus after 1949. The fifteen-foot-tall familiar monument, situated on Russell Avenue in front of the present-day Henderson Humanities Building, is topped by a statue of an eagle in flight and weighs approximately thirteen tons (*Orange and Blue*, April 28, 1949).

THE MAJOR PROBLEM: CRITICALLY OUT OF SPACE

On Harley Fite's first visit to campus in 1948, he observed the same scene repeated almost everywhere: long lines of students. At the bookstore, the class registration tables, the post office, and especially the dining hall, which was housed in Sarah Swann Hall—there was simply not adequate room for everyone. In fact, classes scheduled just after lunchtime often began late because students could not get through the lines and finish eating on time. More dining space for the mushrooming student body was urgently needed.

Many other colleges had set aside space for student centers on campus. In such buildings, their students could gather in informal settings, check their mail, play games, dine, or sit together and talk. Carson-Newman students had no such dedicated space.

Several academic disciplines had scarce classroom space and needed buildings of their own. For example, the popular home economics program had long since outgrown its allotted space in the basement of the administration building (Henderson Hall). There was nowhere to set up and use modern equipment for homes and no "Practice House" for senior majors.

The Music Department was bursting at the seams as well. Its classes were held all over campus, wherever there was a spare room at any given time. The crowded campus library in the administration building was so filled with books and resources that few students could study there at the same time.

JOE MACK HIGH'S *THE CENTURION*

On March 18, 2019, Carson-Newman held a program highlighting ninety-four-year-old Joseph Maxwell High's original work of biblical fiction, *The Centurion: A Tale of the Crucifixion,* recently published. A member of the Class of 1949, High was a World War II veteran who took advantage of the GI Bill to attend college. He later spent many years teaching accounting and business at Carson-Newman.

In 2019, looking back on his student days seventy years earlier, "Joe Mack" recalled with obvious pleasure that Carson-Newman offered about two hundred courses and they were all free to him! Eager to learn, he took courses in philosophy and English every semester, and he studied in every discipline. "All I learned is contained in the book," he told the audience.

The housing crisis for all eight hundred students was just as severe. The college simply could not thrive and grow unless there was more dormitory space for students. Men could live in town when "The Barn" (Davis and Blanc adjoining residence halls) was full, but female students were not allowed to do so unless they were "townies" from Jefferson City and lived with their parents.

As a stopgap measure Carson-Newman purchased the King Hotel near downtown and renovated it to house twenty-four young women at a time. The former president's home, at this time called the "Powers Home," was also used as a women's dormitory. The Burnett Home on campus was designated for freshman women, three to a room. Music professor Ruth Groseclose was their matron.

A FRIGHTENING NIGHT AT THE BURNETT HOME

Collegiate security concerns are nothing new. Late one night in January 1949, the agony of studying for freshman first-semester exams gave way to terror for the young women living in the Burnett Home. During exam week, a disguised male stealthily entered the house through a first-floor window after midnight and began menacing the young ladies. Racing from room to room on both floors, he banged on doors and shone bright lights in the faces of those who opened their doors, causing pandemonium. Although he did not physically hurt anyone, he upset every Burnett resident, doubtless causing some a sleepless night and a lowered exam grade. Somehow he escaped without being caught or identified.[723]

THE SOLUTION: MULTIPLE NEW BUILDINGS

Both trustees and Fite agreed that constructing several new buildings as soon as possible was paramount to serving the growing number of students who wanted to attend Carson-Newman. Their goal was for the college to enlarge its physical facilities to care for at least one thousand students.

Thankfully, solutions to two problems were already under construction. The new **Maples Library,** the first free-standing library Carson-Newman had ever had, was dedicated at homecoming in 1949. (Maples Library's front door is now the entrance for Maples Café.)

Designed to complement the look of the Maples Library, the **Chambliss Fine Arts Building** opened in the fall of 1950. Funded by the Ocoee Baptist Association and Justice A. W. Chambliss, it was named for Reverend John Alexander Chambliss, the Justice's father. J. A. Chambliss had been the college's first full-time Bible professor from 1914 until his sudden death in 1916.[724] The college's ministerial association was named "The Chambliss Society" in his memory for several years.

The new fine arts building contained a recital hall (later named for Music Department chair Ersa Davis) with a seating capacity of 140.[725] Other amenities included a pipe organ, two electronic organs, two concert grand pianos, spaces for offices, nineteen practice rooms, a studio with recording equipment, a record and score library, listening rooms, and classrooms for music and art instruction.[726] Music students and faculty were greatly relieved to have a "home" on campus.

Obviously, to fund other buildings, monetary gifts of unprecedented amounts were necessary. Trustees authorized a goal of raising $652,500, knowing that the building process would take many years. "In 1948 the college was in a state of emergency in so far as buildings and facilities were concerned . . . and did not get out of a state of emergency, buildings and facilities wise, until 1968."[727]

Campus Student Activities of the Early 1950s

Foremost among the extracurricular organizations at Carson-Newman were the four literary societies, each of which met every Friday night in its own attractive hall. Their members enjoyed literary programs and developed skills in debate, oratory, and conducting public meetings. Almost every student on campus proudly belonged to the society of his or her choice. A number of other options available to students also set the tone for campus culture, informal learning, and fun.[728]

ACADEMIC CLUBS WITH HIGH STANDARDS FOR MEMBERSHIP

The Modern Portia Club, organized in the mid-1920s, was for young women majoring in English. The "Portia" reference was to a character in Shakespeare's play *The Merchant of Venice*—a young woman both beautiful and brainy who succeeded beyond all expectations despite the limitations of living in a man's world. The popular club's purpose was literary advancement, cultural refinement, and the study of modern fiction.

The Forensic Club encouraged its members to participate in all types of forensic contests. Teams representing this organization consistently won high honors in local, regional, and national forensic tournaments.

Membership in the **Future Teachers of America** was open to all students planning to enter teaching as a profession. They were kept informed on current developments in education and encouraged to develop a strong professional attitude toward the teaching profession.

The Dramatic Club was for students who participated in several carefully selected plays each year. These popular programs provided cultural development and entertainment for the student body and community. **Alpha Psi Omega** was an honorary dramatic fraternity open to students who had attained a high standard of work in dramatics.

The Science Club was composed of students with outstanding scholastic records who majored or minored in one of the natural sciences. Members attended frequent programs of scientific interest.

The Home Economics Club was open to all young women majoring in the subject. The club offered its members opportunities to learn about homemaking and/or entering the professional field.

The International Relations Club held monthly meetings for students specializing in social science or history. The club used materials from the Carnegie Endowment for International Peace for its programs.

The Language Clubs—French and Spanish—promoted cultural interests in France, Spain, and "Spanish America," and practiced the use of these languages. All students enrolled in French or Spanish classes were eligible for membership. **Sigma Delta Pi** honorary society members were enrolled in at least junior-level second-semester Spanish courses.

RELIGIOUS ORGANIZATIONS

Students were required to attend chapel four times per week in Henderson Auditorium, and most attended a local church on Sundays too.[729] In addition to the well-attended weekly Sunday School and Training Union classes held at Jefferson City's First Baptist Church for collegiate men and women, there were two **Young Women's Auxiliary (YWA)** groups. Female students who boarded at the college comprised one group, and the "town students" living with their parents made up the other. All YWA members learned how to support missionaries by praying and giving.

The Baptist Student Union (BSU) was composed of all the Baptist students on campus. The student body elected officers who, together with representatives from each religious organization, formed the BSU Council. The Council's purpose was to correlate all religious activities, encouraging every organization to engage fully in the activities each undertook.

The Volunteer Band met weekly to study international mission fields and missionary methods. Since standards of health and preparation for appointment by the Foreign Mission Board were very high, members sought information that would help each one make the highest possible vocational contribution. Students in the Volunteer Band regularly led in and performed mission work in the local community.

CARSON-NEWMAN ALUMNI SERVING AS OVERSEAS MISSIONARIES

The earliest known Carson-Newman graduate to become an international missionary was W. H. Tipton, Class of 1900, and many other alumni likewise spent years overseas engaged in mission work. But the highly spiritual atmosphere on campus during the Warren and Fite years contributed to an unusual number of Carson-Newman students serving as international missionaries after graduating and receiving seminary training. Representative alumni career missionary couples of this period include Dan and Betty Alice (Cowan) Carroll, Class of 1949; Carl and Mary (Pate) Yarnell, Class of 1950; and Don and Ina (Sandidge) Frazier, Class of 1951. By 1963, Carson-Newman led the nation in college student and alumni volunteering for mission work.

The Definite Service Band was formed in response to Baptist churches' calls for young people who would work as church secretaries, educational directors, choir directors, and in other nonministerial roles within churches. Such students received welcome training and fellowship.

The Life Service Band was composed of students who planned to become professionals in the secular field—lawyers, doctors, nurses, teachers, businessmen, and so forth. Within this organization, such students studied ways they could render Christian service through their chosen callings and as volunteer workers in their local churches.

The J. L. Campbell Ministerial Association was named in honor of Carson-Newman's outstanding Bible professor 1920–1928. Ministerial students and religion professors met weekly to discuss problems related to a minister's work, to study biblical questions, and to research questions of denominational interest. Every ministerial student was expected to be an active member of the group. The association encouraged its members to preach in churches as often as possible and to perform every type of mission work available within reach of the college.

Carson-Newman's Thrilling Centennial Year, 1951

How far Carson-Newman had come in one hundred years! The college's one hundredth birthday was an occasion to be celebrated with hearts full of gratitude. Indeed, faculty, staff, students, and alumni spent the 1950–1951 year looking back at all the college had achieved and those who had moved it forward over the years.

Several official publications commemorated the college's centennial. The 1951 *Appalachian* featured a fascinating mix of photos from the past and present and was dedicated to those who founded and perpetuated the college. Several pages were occupied by a carefully researched and written history of the college by Arlie E. Cate and a long article about all the C-N presidents by Miss Tennessee Jenkins. "Miss Tennie" was able to provide first-person memories, having personally known at least ten of the eighteen presidents!

The *Alumni Bulletin* contained all kinds of interesting historical information for its alumni audience of many decades. *The Orange and Blue* carried detailed articles about all the celebrations, plus reprints of Arlie Cate's and Tennessee Jenkins's articles from the yearbook.

Carson-Newman pulled out all the stops for a major celebration lasting several days at the end of the school year. Besides the usual recognitions involved in commencement exercises—the honoring of seniors and granting of degrees, a baccalaureate program with addresses and sermons, special events for alumni, musical recitals, forensic and debate contests—an elegant celebratory dinner was held for all. Ben W. Hooper contributed a colorful account of the impromptu mock wedding scenario he and his roommate had concocted in 1889, when Carson College for men and Newman College for women were joined together.[730] Ben Hooper would die in 1957 at age eighty-six.

Other notable Centennial commencement events included:

A THEMATIC PARADE OF FLOATS

On Thursday, May 24, Russell Avenue and other streets surrounding campus provided the setting for a parade of ten highly ornamental, colorful floats passing before enthusiastic crowds. The floats served dual purposes, each one recounting a specific decade of the college's history and a different phase of the college's program or organization.[731]

The three first floats emphasized area pioneer preachers and their efforts to establish an institution of higher learning; Carson College for men and Newman College for women flourishing side by side; and the combined Carson and Newman College for all students, united in 1889. Subsequent floats emphasized such aspects as music, science, and athletics; the four literary societies; student/veteran contributions to the defense of the United States in wartime; and the imagined Carson-Newman of tomorrow.

THE GRANTING OF HONORARY DEGREES

College officials had planned to grant ten honorary doctoral degrees, one for each decade of the school's life, during the centennial commencement. Outstanding friends of the college and alumni such as Dana X. Bible (Class of 1912) received these special tributes. Because one recipient was not able to be present, only nine degrees were actually granted.[732] Apparently the person unable to attend at the last minute was W. S. Bryan, an 1891 graduate and a son of former president Robert Reedy Bryan. "Spence" Bryan was Carson-Newman's oldest living graduate in 1951, living in Oklahoma.

At this occasion, Miss Tennessee Jenkins was the first woman ever to receive an honorary doctorate from Carson-Newman (*Orange and Blue*, May 22, 1951). Attendees at the ceremony, many of whom were her former history students, were thrilled to recall her stellar, dedicated teaching career at Carson-Newman.

A STIRRING HISTORICAL PAGEANT

An outdoor musical drama was widely considered the highlight of all the centennial events. "Carson-Newman College: A Century of Service" was performed on Thursday, May 24, on the lawn of Henderson Hall. Two stages had been constructed on the west portico for the presentation of interior scenes, with a spotlight moving from one side to another. Between the two stages was placed a huge frame in which costumed students portrayed persons of historical significance in the life of the college. Outdoor scenes were staged on the steps and the walkway in front of the building.

A prolific Knoxville playwright, Betsy S. Wolfe, was commissioned to write the scenes and dialogue to portray the sweeping story of Carson-Newman. Professors Janie Swann Huggins (English) and Harvey Hatcher (speech and dramatics) coordinated and directed about four hundred cast, crew, and committee members.[733] Music Department chair Ersa Davis selected and arranged all the music in the pageant and played the organ, while music professor John P. Bollinger directed the orchestra. Senior John W. Lynch served as the narrator, and a speech choir gave readings at intervals.

Setting Forth on the Next One Hundred Years

After the centennial celebration was over, Dr. Fite and the trustees worked together to rewrite the college's objectives. Wanting to remain true to the original vision of a Baptist center of education in East Tennessee but also to serve current students in the modern world, they prioritized needs and possibilities for Carson-Newman to be its best.

For alumni who graduated in the 1950s and 1960s, some of the college's best-remembered staff and faculty were hired during these years. For example, in 1951, Roy Harmon became the new head football and basketball coach. A member of the Class of 1944, he had studied athletics under Coach "Frosty" Holt and later made a name for himself as a high-school coach. He immediately charted a new course for athletic teams at the college.

Dietician and cafeteria manager Pearl McHan was hired in 1952. She improved food service at the college and mentored hundreds of students who worked in the cafeteria. When big occasions were planned at the

MAJOR HISTORICAL EVENTS PORTRAYED IN THE PAGEANT

Carson-Newman's earliest years as a college for men were captured in the legend of the 1849 planning meeting of the founding fathers, the Oak Tree Five, and the following scenes:

- the first class of Mossy Creek Missionary Baptist Seminary;
- the 1851 organization of the men's literary societies;
- the first graduation in 1855;
- the forced closing of the school during the Civil War and the Union troops who destroyed the Mossy Creek Baptist Church building;
- Robert Reedy Bryan's reopening of the school in 1868.

Other scenic highlights included the 1869 solar eclipse and President Jesse Baker's ensuring that the college would not be eclipsed by making his long trip to raise funds urgently needed;

- Native American students who attended the school 1884–1885;
- the establishment of Newman College for women in 1882;
- a more genteel version of the original 1889 mock wedding symbolizing the union of the men's and women's colleges, with Professor Tennessee Jenkins representing Newman College and retired Professor W. Powell Hale portraying Carson College;
- the formation of the women's literary societies in 1891;
- the burning of the magnificent administration building in 1916;
- the 1904 construction of Sarah Swann Home by A. R. Swann;
- the important 1927 acceptance of the college into the Southern Association of Colleges and Schools and the joyous singing of the college theme song, "All Hail the Power of Jesus' Name";
- the on-campus Navy V-12 program that allowed the college to continue through World War II;
- the portrayal of 1951 current campus activities, including clubs, publications, men's and women's athletics, dramas, the radio workshop, groundbreaking cancer research conducted by chemistry professor Dr. Carl Tabb Bahner, and musical organizations.

The triumphant finale featured Dr. Fite and the entire faculty and cast accompanied by the oldest alumni in attendance, present-day seniors, and graduates of the near future. Hearts full, the assembled crowd stood and sang the school's "Alma Mater" and listened reverently to the "Hallelujah Chorus," led by the A Capella Choir, orchestra, and organ.[734]

In future years, the pageant would be repeated during the annual Founder's Day. It was too wonderful to perform only once!

college, she served special and memorable meals in appropriately decorative settings.

Some innovative "firsts" for Carson-Newman administrators in these years included a public relations director, religious and social director, and director of development. Too, several creative programs were implemented. The results broadened Carson-Newman's horizons in various ways.

THE OFF-CAMPUS PROGRAM

In 1950 Carson-Newman began offering Christian educational courses to Tennessee pastors and laymen who could not come to Jefferson City on a regular basis. The first such class was held in Lake City. The program was so popular that 602 individuals were soon enrolled in 13 off-campus sites. In 1953 Clarence Watson became the first full-time director, overseeing the peak period for the Off-Campus program during the 1955–1956 school year, with 896 persons enrolled in 23 centers.[735]

By the 1961–1962 school year, the program had ebbed and was phased out. However, the extension program was able to reach many adults whose lives had been enriched by the knowledge and relationships gained.

TRANSFORMED COLLEGE/COMMUNITY RELATIONSHIPS

Harley Fite observed that the college's relationship with the citizens of Jefferson City could be improved. Knowing that each could benefit from a closer connection with the other, in 1953 he created the College-Community Council made up of citizens from the college, Jefferson City, and other towns in Jefferson County. Members attended periodic meetings on campus, and increasingly the college began to share its resources and facilities with the community. Student musical groups gave frequent enjoyable programs, and for several years the community was invited to attend a beautiful Easter sunrise service on the east steps of Henderson Hall, facing Mossy Creek.

Some community leaders also served on the college's new Advisory Board, a grassroots organization of about 100 persons. They excelled at their voluntary responsibilities—to study college-related problems and make recommendations to the trustees.[736]

By the mid-1950s Fite had been elected president of the Jefferson City Chamber of Commerce in addition to his "day job." Along with other key city leaders, he helped persuade the owners of the Magnavox Company to locate in Jefferson City—a boon to both the community and the college. Magnavox made cabinets for televisions and radios and provided a great industry for the area for decades.[737] Company employees were welcome to attend cultural events at the college and to take helpful night classes.

NATIVE AMERICAN STUDENTS

Since young Cherokee students had briefly attended Carson College and Newman College in 1884–1885, much about the Cherokee way of life had changed in the area surrounding East Tennessee by the mid-twentieth century. The early experiment in educating Native Americans failed for many reasons, in part because the students' learning curve in reading, writing, and speaking the English language was insurmountable on a short-term basis. There were many other cultural differences as well.

However, in the decades since, Cherokee students had received a high level of instruction that prepared them to enter college. A number successfully attended or graduated from Carson-Newman in the 1950s and beyond, including Jean Bushyhead, a daughter of the distinguished Robert Henry Bushyhead, a Cherokee Christian minister to his own people.

EAST TENNESSEE COLLEGES AND AN UNSOLVED WHODUNIT

In February 1954 one of the four beloved eagle statues that adorned Henderson Hall disappeared. The May 8, 1954 *Orange and Blue* described the missing eagle as "kidnapped by brutal hands" of a rival athletic college. The first college suspected was Lincoln Memorial University, where a few impulsive Carson-Newman student-athletes immediately headed to search for the missing eagle. Not finding it, they nonetheless brought back LMU's statue of Abraham Lincoln and displayed it on the Henderson lawn, along with a cannonball also purloined from LMU.

Dr. Fite, livid over the incident, ordered the statue returned to LMU posthaste. The students complied, learning that Carson-Newman's eagle might have been in Johnson City on the East Tennessee State College campus in Johnson City—but was no longer there. Carson-Newman students feared the worst: "Is our Eagle lying broken, mutilated, by the roadside . . . or undergoing tortures . . . or worse still, did someone take our Eagle believing it belonged to State? Any word or information concerning our Eagle would be greatly appreciated."

Before the eagle was returned, two more disappeared from campus. The December 6, 1955 *Orange and Blue* reported that all three eagle statues had been discovered in a closet at Tusculum College in Greeneville. ETSC students had recently raided Tusculum, and most people believed the eagles had been "planted" there. But the truth was never known. The wandering eagles were joyfully welcomed home and given a new coat of paint.

CONTEXT: 1955 EVENTS IN WORLD HISTORY

Elvis Presley made his first TV appearance, while "The Lawrence Welk Show" premiered on ABC. The Salk polio vaccine was approved as safe and effective. David Ben-Gurion formed the first Israeli government. Ray Kroc opened the first McDonald's Restaurant in Des Plaines, IL; in Chicago, the first "sun-powered" automobile was demonstrated.

Baseball legend Mickey Mantle hit his 550th home run. West Germany became a member of NATO. President Dwight Eisenhower raised the minimum wage from 75 cents to $1 per hour. Rosa Parks was arrested in Montgomery, AL for refusing to move to the back of a city bus; the Supreme Court ordered school integration across the nation "with all deliberate speed." Disneyland opened in Anaheim, CA. *The Return of the King,* the final volume of "The Lord of the Rings" trilogy by J. R. R. Tolkien, was published in England.

RADIO STATION WVCN

A new development of 1956 was "the voice of Carson-Newman," radio station WVCN. Since the 1930s the college had occasionally utilized radio stations in Knoxville and Morristown to promote its programs; now Carson-Newman had its own station, having invested in radio equipment.

Located in the Chambliss Fine Arts Building, the studio was entirely staffed by students under the supervision of R. Forrest Conklin, speech professor (*Orange and Blue,* September 21, 1956). The station operated from 4:30 p.m. until midnight every day, broadcasting music, discussion programs, poetry readings, several ball games, and even an eclipse of the moon.

MISS TENNESSEE JENKINS BADE FAREWELL TO THE COLLEGE

In 1953 Miss Tennessee Jenkins retired for the second and final time. The faculty and administration managed to pull off a surprise chapel recognition of her personal history with the college in February. She heard Dr. Fite, Dean Carr, and others deliver accolades about an unnamed distinguished teacher who was the object of admiration and affection of the entire campus. This professor, they said, had taught more students than any other teacher in the history of the college. No wonder, since she had the longest tenure of any professor—54 years!

Called to the stage to receive a gift, she said when the realization dawned that she was the professor being lauded, "I began to feel as though I were attending my own funeral." From memory, she quoted an appropriate poem to express her feelings and wished her many colleagues and students a heartfelt "Godspeed" (*Orange and Blue,* February 14, 1953). She continued to host the annual Hypatian teas at her home as long as her health allowed. The October 31, 1963, *Orange and Blue* would recount her life and Carson-Newman's mourning over her July 30 death; she was almost ninety-two. Ever-positive, she had hoped to celebrate her centennial birthday in 1971.

Progress in Constructing New Buildings 1951–1963

A STUDENT CENTER AND A NEW HOME ECONOMICS "PRACTICE HOUSE"

In the fall of 1951 the multipurpose **Baker Memorial Building,** named for a trustee, was opened. Its three stories housed the much-needed large Willson Cafeteria and a nursery center (first floor); the student center, post office, recreation room, canteen, bookstore, and student publications offices (second floor); and the Home Economics Department with labs and essential equipment (third floor). This structure relieved overcrowding for home economics students, supplied sufficient room for the student body to dine together, and provided space for leisure activities.[738]

With the completion of the large Willson Cafeteria, Sarah Swann's kitchen and dining rooms were no longer needed. One dining room was converted to dormitory rooms, and the other again became a parlor.

Home economics majors received a second boon in 1951. The college had purchased a **Home Management House** for hands-on practical training in hospitality, cooking, and housekeeping during their senior year.[739] The new center was the former home of the Bird family, located at the corner of Russell Avenue and North College Street.

RESIDENCE HALLS FOR WOMEN

The lack of sufficient student housing was a major concern. Annexes to the **Burnett Home** were completed in 1949 and 1952. The **Everett Home** next door was purchased in 1953 on the death of John D. Everett, the retired professor of education, and converted immediately to an adjunct dormitory for 12 young women. In 1963 the original Burnett and Everett Homes were torn down and adjoining land was purchased with an eye toward future expansion.

In 1954 the front section of a major new women's residence hall was completed and named for its major donor: the **Bertie Maples Butler Residence Hall.** Located next to Sarah Swann and behind the former president's home, this columned dormitory was arranged in suites—two rooms with an adjoining bathroom between them. Each suite housed four young women.[740]

Like other student housing of the era, Butler Residence Hall would be constructed in stages for financial reasons. In 1958 Butler's two side wings were erected, necessitating the demolition of the first president's home to extend the Butler parking lot.

Mrs. C. C. James donated a large home on Russell Avenue to the college in memory of her brother in 1956. **Duncan Hall** housed 24 young women at that time, later becoming a campus showplace for textiles and a guest home. At this time the **King Hotel** was discontinued for college use.[741]

Student enrollment continued to climb every year, usually by 100–150. In 1961 the college accidentally accepted more female students than it could accommodate, even with the added buildings. In **Sarah Swann Home** and **Henderson Home,** an overflow of young women had to be placed temporarily in unlikely spaces, such as hallways and storage closets.

HOW THE RANKIN FAMILY AIDED THE COLLEGE

While female students were not allowed to live in private homes unless they lived with their parents, young men were able to board with families in Jefferson City. One family providing that service was Sam Hull and Chlorice Bible Rankin, who had bought the former Carson Hall (Campus #2) with seven acres in 1930. (The young Chlorice Bible had attended Carson and Newman College.) "The Rankin House," as the grand home was now informally called, contained 15 rooms; the Rankins' children had grown up there. Now space was available for male students.

This was not the first time the Rankins had shared their home with Carson-Newman students. For decades the Calliopean Literary Society held formal garden parties on the lawn of the mansion. Several female Rankins were Callies in their youth. *The Appalachian* yearbooks of the 1940s-1950s show charming pictures of the Callies in their long, flowing dresses, mingling outside the vintage home and enjoying the annual event.[742]

A NEW RESIDENCE HALL FOR MEN

In 1956 the front section of a new dormitory for men, **Alumni Memorial Hall,** was erected thanks to the generous gifts of loyal alumni. This dormitory was located on the corner of Branner Avenue and North College Street.[743] By 1957 its capacity was already exceeded! Each year **Blanc-Davis Hall** was filled "to the rafters" as well.

The front façade of Alumni Hall was designed to match that of Blanc Hall. Thus a reminder of Blanc Hall still exists on campus, even though it was torn down in 1967.

HOUSING FOR MARRIED STUDENTS

Eagle Village was still in use for married couples. But with the GI Bill still in force, more room for couples was greatly needed. Two generous families with a heart for student couples donated both land and money for 14 apartments (inside five buildings) and two duplexes. Each year 18 married couples were able to live in these accommodations.[744]

A NEW ACADEMICS BUILDING

In 1958 the college took possession of the nearby property once used as the **Jefferson City Elementary School,** purchased the previous year. The academic departments of history, political science, geography, business, and mathematics were moved there to relieve overcrowding elsewhere, and adequate classrooms were available within the building for these disciplines.[745]

HEALTH AND PHYSICAL EDUCATION BUILDING

Meanwhile, Carson-Newman desperately needed a larger gymnasium. As the student body grew, **Butler-Blanc Gymnasium**—the pride of the college in the 1920s—became woefully inadequate. There was only room for the football and basketball teams to use the facility; other students were left without a place to participate in sports and recreation. Unfortunately, the college's choice of location for building a separate fieldhouse was thwarted by a familiar, recurring problem—the discovery of sinkholes from deserted mines and the inability to obtain footings.

The college was forced to purchase additional property further down Branner Avenue to build its new fieldhouse. Finally in 1959, the new facility was completed. It was named for the acclaimed athletic director and longtime coach Sam B. "Frosty" Holt in 1961. Features of the modern **Holt Fieldhouse** included not only a gymnasium but also bleachers seating over 3,000 people; classrooms; offices; sleeping quarters for visiting teams; a swimming pool; special exercise rooms for general physical education; four major sports showers; and dressing rooms.[746] For years men used this new facility, with women using Butler-Blanc.

A MODERN INFIRMARY

In 1961 the newly constructed Kathleen Manley Infirmary opened on Russell Avenue. Since 1952 Kathleen Manley had been employed as the college nurse in the former home of Ida Lawrence Murray, which was too small for the current student body. The home was torn down and a modern, well-equipped infirmary was built on its site, thanks to substantial financial help from the Nolachucky Association. The building's name honored not only Miss Manley, a former 20-year missionary to Nigeria and a member of Carson-Newman's Class of 1928, but also seven other missionaries with ties to the Nolachucky Association (*Orange and Blue,* December 5, 1961).

First Baptist Church, Jefferson City, Tennessee, as it looked in the 1940s–1950s. (Courtesy of the Tennessee State Library and Archives, Looking Back at Tennessee Collection.)

THE ANSWER TO THE NEED FOR A CHAPEL

The First Baptist Church of Jefferson City, adjacent to Carson-Newman's campus, had long provided its sanctuary for college chapel services during the week. But with Carson-Newman bursting at the seams with students, the church sanctuary was now inadequate both during the week and on Sundays. In 1962 First Baptist entered into a building program to construct a larger sanctuary.

The college administration had long wanted to build a chapel on campus, but the cost seemed prohibitive. And why build two large auditoriums less than a block away from each other that were both dedicated to religious activities? Dr. Fite worked with Dr. Charles Pope at the Tennessee Baptist Convention to negotiate a creative solution for both church and college. As a result, monies were reallocated for the church's building program in return for an official agreement allowing the college to use the church's new sanctuary for chapel services and other appropriate programs (*Orange and Blue*, December 5, 1961). This updated cooperation reaffirmed the historical "college in the church" relationship between the two friendly entities.

A "FALL FROM GRACE" IN THE NEW SANCTUARY

The last chapel of 1962 was held on Monday, December 17, when the new sanctuary was three months old. The program climaxed with Handel's "Hallelujah Chorus" and all the students rose to their feet, according to custom. About 130 students were on the south side of the balcony, where suddenly "there was a heart-stopping crack, a sound of wrenching timber, a crescendo of screams, and the balcony . . . started its downward plunge. The assembled student body stood in open-mouthed horror as they witnessed their classmates hurtling to the pews below" (*Orange and Blue,* December 19, 1962).

Reacting quickly, students in the pews below sought cover under their seats. As a result, only eight were taken to the hospital; none had life-threatening injuries. The organist narrowly escaped being hit by an 80-foot-long railing that crashed into the chime box next to her.

The reason for the balcony's collapse was determined to be faulty steel used in construction. According to the January 17, 1963 *Orange and Blue,* the replacement steel was checked five times in multiple ways.

A LONG-AWAITED CAFETERIA BUILDING

By the 1960s the Willson Cafeteria in the Baker Building had outgrown its space, completed in 1951. Once again long lines formed at every meal, and the college wanted to use the first floor of Baker for the post office and an enlarged student recreation and conversation space. Loyal supporters of Carson-Newman and entrepreneurs with a huge canning enterprise, the Stokely family of East Tennessee, came to the rescue with a large monetary gift for a new building.

The Stokely Memorial Cafeteria, completed in 1963, was a modern building that served several purposes. The name Willson Cafeteria was carried over to the largest dining room in the Stokely building, located on the main floor. Adjacent dining facilities for small and large groups could accommodate up to 2500 persons (*Orange and Blue,* September 6, 1963). Later the large basement area was finished, providing a number of classrooms and faculty offices.

Stokely Memorial Cafeteria.

The Early 1960s: Keeping Traditions, Entering a New Era

At the dawn of the new decade, the college again revised and updated its objectives. Trustees envisioned the decade as one of development and progress. Continuing with the construction of new buildings as needed, they set a benchmark capacity of 2,350 students as a campus goal for new buildings (*Orange and Blue,* November 15, 1960). The total enrollment at this time stood at 1,813.

SPORTS SPLASHES

Team sports were making headlines at Carson-Newman in the early 1960s. For example, the basketball team boasted two outstanding players who were destined to have long careers at Carson-Newman: Clark Bryan and Chris Jones. As noted in the February 21, 1961 issue of *The Orange and Blue,* Bryan was named Most Valuable Player of the Eastern Division of the Volunteer State Athletic Conference. Jones, "high-point man of the team, was named an All-Star to the Conference Team" and was the college's first All-American.

In later years Clark Bryan was a longtime and beloved dean of students at Carson-Newman. Chris Jones became the head basketball coach at the college and, for his doctoral dissertation, wrote the definitive history of sports at Carson-Newman: *It Gets Foggy at Mossy Creek* and its sequel.

THE COLUMBIANS HOST BERNIE MOORE, CLASS OF 1917

In 1962 the Columbian Literary Society held its annual spring banquet at the Mountain View Hotel in Gatlinburg. They had a very special guest speaker: Bernie Hawthorne Moore, a former Columbian who had had a longtime stellar career in coaching. Having excelled at playing varsity football and basketball at Carson-Newman, the Jonesborough native coached at the University of the South (Sewanee) before going to Mercer University as head football and basketball coach. Then Moore spent 1929–1947 at Louisiana State University as head coach of football and track and field. LSU named its track field in his honor.[747]

He accepted the post of Southeastern Conference (SEC) Commissioner in 1948 and was named to the College Football Hall of Fame in 1952. Winning several prestigious career awards, he was also inducted into the Louisiana and Tennessee Sports Halls of Fame. He remained a steadfast friend to his alma mater and a personal resource for coaches such as "Frosty" Holt.[748] Bernie Moore retired as SEC Commissioner in 1966 and died in 1967, praised for his integrity and adherence to clean sports and academic standards.

HOMECOMING 1962 "LITERAMA" EVENTS

Carson-Newman continued to be proud of its strong liberal arts programs, as well as growing in other areas. In 1962 homecoming parade floats and dormitory decorations took on elaborate and varied literary themes, as the October 20 *Orange and Blue* reported. The freshman float featured the story of the Pied Piper; the sophomore float represented *Brave New World.* Juniors pictured "The Old Woman who Lived in a Shoe" for their float, while the seniors' float revealed images of *The Four Horsemen of the Apocalypse.*

Other special floats included the Philomathean-Hypatian effort for *Ben-Hur,* complete with a moving chariot, and the Calliopean-Columbian contribution of Don Quixote tilting at windmills. The Alpha Kappa Psi business fraternity portrayed pioneer aviation with "The Spirit of St. Louis"; the Student Government's float carried a likeness of *Twenty Thousand Leagues Under the Sea.*

The exteriors of the women's dorms were also highly festooned. Sarah Swann was adorned with a *Gone with the Wind* theme, while Burnett took on the look of a set for "Hansel and Gretel." Henderson Dormitory featured an ornamental paddleboat such as Mark Twain piloted on the Mississippi River, and Butler Hall was bedecked with images from "Cinderella."

THE PRELUDE TO INTEGRATION

By the early 1960s, with civil rights a major issue across the United States, secular and faith-based colleges alike faced questions about when they would integrate their campuses. The Education Commission of the Tennessee Baptist Convention, which oversaw the three Baptist colleges in the state, decided each institution should deal with integration on its own. But the trustees at each Tennessee Baptist college would have to approve the change (*Orange and Blue,* November 29, 1960).

Much of the sentiment expressed in *The Orange and Blue* from the student body was pro-integration. Also, several Carson-Newman alumni who served overseas as career missionaries wrote to express how embarrassed they were by American segregationist policies. Imagine, they said, trying to evangelize Africans for the gospel of Christ and being asked why they should believe those whose country rejected African Americans as less than human. Sadly, when the subject of integration was broached at a meeting of trustees—an all-white body of men—a few protested.

Slowly trustee opinions began to soften. In December 1963 Dr. Fite made the momentous announcement that henceforward, qualified students would be admitted to Carson-Newman regardless of race. The very next year Carson-Newman would accept its first African American students.

To turn the pages of *The Orange and Blue* from the 1950s-1960s is to be immersed in a dizzying microcosm of change. In the peaceful postwar years, the student newspaper reflected a worldview centered on Carson-Newman's campus and a return to hope and gentle fun. April Fool's editions offered such fictions as "Famous Poet Samuel Taylor Coleridge to Speak in Chapel," "All Girls' Regulations Are Abolished," and "Fashion

Notes by Lotta Buell." Long articles detailing the weddings of Carson-Newman students and alumni dominated the newspaper's pages, accompanied by large photos of the happy couples. Opinion pieces denounced cafeteria line breakers and alternately belittled and defended freshmen students.

During the late fifties, the newspaper revealed students' newly acquired interest in national events and cultural changes. College organizations held mock political elections, inspiring passionate debates. In the sixties students mourned President Kennedy's assassination, feared the results of the Cold War, and were awed by the possibilities of space exploration. Looking ahead to the seventies, the newspaper was occupied with the complexities of the Vietnam War and, closer to home, a devastating fire in one of Carson-Newman's most beloved buildings. Whatever major events occurred around the globe and within the local world of Carson-Newman's campus, *The Orange and Blue* covered it all until its demise in 2010.

CHAPTER TEN

The Evolving Revised Standard Version of the College
1964–1977

"The dogmas of the quiet past are inadequate to the stormy present. The occasion is piled high with difficulty, and we must rise with the occasion. As our case is new, so we must think anew and act anew."
—Abraham Lincoln[749]

Patricia Crippins was consumed with trepidation as she walked the two-mile distance from her home to Carson-Newman, even though the campus was very familiar to her. She had often visited her grandfather, John Sheets, at his workplace in the maintenance building behind Sarah Swann Hall. Her grandmother and some of her aunts and uncles also worked at the college.

A 1964 graduate of Nelson Merry High School in Jefferson City, Patricia and two of her friends were the first African American students to apply for enrollment at Carson-Newman that fall. All three were accepted. Tony Mills, an outstanding student-athlete, would leave after their first semester to enter military service; he later returned. Carlette Dunwoody would marry and move away after their freshman year. Of the three, Pat alone would complete her education without interruption and make history as Carson-Newman's first four-year African American graduate.

In a 1995 interview she explained what the experience of integrating Carson-Newman was like.[750] "That first year was hard. Just like I came from an all-black high school, most of the students here came from all-white high schools. So we had four classes of people who had never had an integrated experience, education-wise. . . . The second year got a little better because students coming in behind me were coming from integrated experiences and were used to [learning with] black students.

"I had a few incidents of going into the classroom and somebody would get up and move to the other side of the classroom, or either they would see me coming down the street and cross the street. . . . As long as it was that kind of passive resistance to my presence, I didn't worry. Only once during the whole four-year period that I was here—and it was my first year—did I hear the 'N' word. It was from far away and I never saw the guy who said it.

"[A Knoxville reporter] called the president and said, 'We hear you've integrated at Carson-Newman. We'd like to come up and interview the students.' Dr. Fite said to that reporter, 'We've had three black students to enter, but they're just that, new students. If we treat them that way, we won't have problems. Sorry, no interview.' . . . Dr. Fite did let reporters come in 1968. An interview came out in the paper on Memorial Day, 1968, with my picture in there, saying 'First black graduate of Carson-Newman.' I was really proud of that opportunity to represent my family and my community as a person who had strived to get to the point of graduation."

Pat's sociology major enabled her to serve low-income persons and help meet various individual needs as manager of the East Knoxville Community Action Committee Neighborhood Center, where she worked for 28 years. The group's motto was "Helping People Help Themselves." In 1997 she became the Knox County administrator of elections. She received the Community Service Award from the Greater Knoxville Community in 2008.[751]

Pat was always generous with her time when she was asked to speak to classes and groups at the college. When an interviewer inquired how she felt about her Carson-Newman education, Pat responded: "I'm always telling students I meet that if they really want an education, a sound background in the very complex life they'll be facing after school, come to Carson-Newman. . . . While you're here you know what loving your fellowman means, and when you leave here, you have a mission, not only to succeed for yourself but also to share what you know and how you feel with other people. It's a very user-friendly place. You get beyond just being a number. You have a name, you come from somewhere, and you are of value. Those are the things they taught me here that I love."[752]

Patricia Crippins passed away in 2011.

LONGTIME FACULTY AND STAFF HIRED BY HARLEY FITE

Professors and administrators who stayed 20 years or more, noting the year each began, were Janice Addington-Strong, sociology, 1968; Louis Ball, music, 1961; Mary Charlotte Ball, music, 1968; Alma Baskerville, music, 1949; James Baumgardner, history, 1964; William Blevins, religion, 1966; Cripps Brashear, history, 1948; Imogene Brewer, library, 1965; Paul Brewer, philosophy, 1958; Clark Bryan, dean of students, 1964; John Burton, physics, 1964; Robert Burts, history, 1956; Daniel Champion, speech, 1968; Denver Childress, mathematics, 1967; Howard Chitwood, mathematics, 1957; Freddie Clark, guidance/psychology, 1953; Earl Cleveland, art, 1964; Will John Cloyd, biology, 1956; James Coppock, 1961; Henry Dickenson, biology, 1953; Louise Dickenson, French, 1959; Rosemary Edens, Spanish, 1966; Edward Freels, geography/geology, 1961; Joan Frisbee, business, 1958; Libby Hudson Gardner, physical education, 1968; John Gibson, education, 1963; Verner Hansen, mathematics, 1962; Jerome Harper, Spanish, 1966; Carey Herring, mathematics, 1967; Joseph M. High, business, 1951; Charles Hobbs, English, 1965; Karen Hutton, French/Spanish, 1960; Henrietta Jenkins, English, 1959; Ann Jones, music, 1967; Charles King, physical education, 1968; Ray Koonce, psychology, 1956; Jeff Daniel Marion, English, 1966; Barbara McDougal, home economics, 1956; Pearl McHan, dietician, 1952; Frances Morgan, Spanish, 1965; Albert Myers, chemistry, 1954; Gerald Naylor, biology, 1961; H. T. Niceley, art, 1965; Thomas O'Neal, physics, 1963; Truett Patterson, chemistry, 1964; James Pethel, music, 1962; Louise Snodderly, library, 1967; Sue Swilley, music, 1965; Thomas Teague, music, 1962; Robert Turner, English, 1955; Ruth Turner, English, 1959; Sherman Vanaman, mathematics, 1956; Clarence Watson, religion, 1953; John Welton, speech/dramatics, 1960; Bruce Whitney, French, 1966; Martha Wilson, physical education, 1964; Robert Wilson, physical education, 1964; David Young, history, 1962.[753]

The State of the College 1964–1968

EDUCATIONAL PROGRAM AND FACULTY

In 1964 Carson-Newman celebrated the 75th anniversary of the merging of Carson College with Newman College in 1889, publicizing all the advantages of a Christian college education in an eight-page special edition of the *Knoxville Journal*.[754] The college's illustrious history, wide-ranging liberal arts curriculum (music, literature, science, religion, home economics, drama, debate, and much more), and strong athletic program were all on display. The self-contained newspaper section highlighted an energetic and likable president, an ever-growing campus, and a priority for each student to flourish as a well-rounded, knowledgeable, perceptive, and caring citizen of the world.

Carson-Newman employed very capable faculty and staff members, skilled in their respective academic disciplines. Because many of them were alumni of the college themselves, they deeply understood the school's traditions and values. Thus a high percentage had known one another for decades; among them they had a close bond of rapport and shared memories.

SPORTS OVERVIEW

In 1964 Roy Harmon was the director of the Health and Physical Education Department. Every student was required to take classes within the department and to pass swimming. Harmon's understanding that some students aren't suited for competitive physical activities motivated him to create a program that allowed each student to compete on the level of his or her abilities. He would die of cancer in 1969 at age 51.[755]

Under Mae Iddins' leadership of women's physical activities, Frances Roden taught synchronized swimming classes in the 1950s and 1960s. Using Esther Williams's films as her inspiration, Mrs. Roden choreographed kaleidoscopic patterns of swimming for young women.[756] Observers were charmed by their efforts.

In 1964 Sam "Frosty" Holt, Carson-Newman's athletic director and head baseball coach, hired Robert "Bobby" and Martha Wilson for the college's physical education faculty team. Bobby, who had won four letters in football and baseball at the University of Mississippi, would serve dual roles. He was hired as football offensive coach and Holt's assistant coach for the baseball team. Within a year, Holt retired from coaching and Bobby Wilson, a former professional baseball player, would oversee the baseball team.[757] Martha Wilson would teach diverse physical education classes, later serving as department coordinator. Both would remain at Carson-Newman until retirement and afterward continued as beloved members of the community.

Football had a succession of head and assistant coaches, including Dalmuth Shealy, a Class of 1960 alumnus who was respected by all (*Orange and Blue*, April 16, 1966). He worked hard to successfully turn around the Eagles' losing streak in football.

Gene Mehaffey, the head basketball coach, became athletic director in 1968, with Bobby Wilson as his assistant director (*Orange and Blue*, March 13, 1968). In the fall of 1970 Chris Jones, Class of 1962, would return to Carson-Newman as assistant basketball coach (*Orange and Blue*, April 8, 1970). Later Jones would become head basketball coach at his alma mater, always willing to help players—or indeed, anyone—who wanted his assistance.

RUMBLINGS OF UNREST, 1960S-STYLE

The general trend toward unrest and questioning among young people in the early- to mid-1960s was slower to reach Carson-Newman than in some American universities. Most Carson-Newman students were church members who attended frequent required chapel programs with little resistance and enjoyed the atmosphere of the traditional literary society meetings. They even put up with having to attend classes on Saturday mornings, although most colleges had eliminated weekend classes.

Nevertheless, by the late 1960s, required chapel programs became problematic for some students. Some speakers were considered dull or repetitive. Also, one issue had risen to student protest level: the lack of dances on campus. Many Baptists considered dancing sinful, but most students saw dancing as a social issue—a chance to have fun and get to know other people—and small Jefferson City did not offer dances. President Fite responded: "The administration believes the school social program should not run counter to the accepted mores of the people who own it. . . . [Tennessee Baptists] are not fanatics, but sincere, honest people who think dancing is a MORAL ISSUE" (November 11, 1967 *Orange and Blue;* the capitals are Fite's).

He continued: "A few years ago, with trustee approval, we began permitting folk games (also called folk dances) on the campus [as part of the physical education program]. We were called to task for this in several places, the objection being 'This is only a forerunner, a foot in the door, to social dancing.' Those of us in the administration had to try to justify this type of recreation in three associations in Tennessee and in another state from which we get many students. This consumed days of time that should have been put to better use." Fite also said prophetically, "I suspect many of these people . . . would take the matter to the floor of the [Tennessee Baptist] Convention in its annual session if the college sponsored dances or permitted students to plan and promote dances off the campus."

The Great Builder's Last Construction Projects

As Harley Fite entered the last five-year phase of his presidency at Carson-Newman, there was still much to be done as student enrollment continued to soar and several new buildings were needed "yesterday." In the September 18, 1967 *Orange and Blue* he pointed out that since 1948, every building on campus had been built or remodeled except four: Butler-Blanc Gymnasium, the Warren Science Building, Henderson Dormitory, and Blanc-Davis Hall. The latter two would soon be demolished. In the meantime, he saw several more buildings finished under his watch, with two other major projects (a new library and a new Science building) in the advanced planning stages but to be completed by his successor.

ACADEMIC AREAS ADDED TO STOKELY MEMORIAL

In 1964 construction additions were made to the ground level of the Stokely Building for education and psychology classrooms and offices. By 1966 after further construction, the areas of history, political science, geography, and geology were housed there as well (*Orange and Blue,* September 17, 1966).

NEW RESIDENCE FOR MEN

In 1964 the older section of the former Jefferson City school property off Branner Avenue was demolished to make way for the first wing of a sorely needed third men's residence hall. Lacking a name, the new dormitory was simply called "New Men's."

In 1967 two additional wings were completed, one called "Blanc-Davis Wing" to commemorate the old combined Blanc and Davis dormitories ("The Barn"), torn down the same year. The new building was the college's first electrically heated, completely air-conditioned residence hall, with a housing capacity of 450 men (*Orange and Blue,* May 13, 1967). Nine years later in the December 10, 1976 *Orange and Blue,* dean of students Clark Bryan noted the irony that this residence hall was still called "New Men's." It has since been renamed as Heritage Hall.

THE FATE OF THE OBSERVATORY

While students were away from campus for Thanksgiving holidays in late 1965, a storm devastated one of the campus's most visible landmarks. Gale-force storm winds blew down the dome of the observatory so prized by the college. According to the December 4, 1965 *Orange and Blue,* "The refracting telescope located in the observatory was damaged beyond repair when the dome hit it as it was blown off. The dome landed within 20 feet of the north wing of Butler Dorm. Another piece of metal landed only two yards from the parlor."

The telescope was valued at a $400 replacement cost, and neither the observatory nor its contents were covered by insurance. A smaller telescope was borrowed so the semester's astronomy class could be completed. But future astronomy courses would be offered infrequently until a new science building was erected. The useful days of the observatory, constructed in 1904 as a water tank for Sarah Swann Hall, were over.

WOMEN'S RESIDENCE HALLS

The Calliopean and Hypatian literary societies had been meeting in Sarah Swann Hall since 1905, when the residence hall was built. In 1965, due to renovations in Sarah Swann to relieve overcrowding, the female literary societies were moved to the Administration Building, Henderson Hall. Two new rooms were built there for their use.[758]

A new four-story Burnett Hall was constructed on Russell Avenue in 1966 and dedicated to former president Jesse M. Burnett.[759] The residence

Bertie Maples Butler Hall, built as a women's dormitory.

hall accommodated 286 female students and fulfilled a great need for more dormitory space (*Orange and Blue*, January 29, 1966).

In 1968 the final wing of Bertie Maples Butler Hall was completed across the back of the building (*Orange and Blue*, September 28, 1968). The remains of the observatory were removed to make way for this construction.

The same year, according to the September 28, 1968 *Orange and Blue*, Henderson Dormitory was torn down to make way for a new future library building. This first women's dormitory on the current campus had been built with bricks recycled from the college's three original buildings beside Mossy Creek (Campus #1). The 1899 stately dormitory with its wraparound porches had once housed the college's Conservatory of Music and sheltered generations of young ladies.

NEW SPORTS FACILITIES

Carson-Newman's seating for outdoor games of all types left much to be desired. At homecoming one year in the mid-1960s, at least 1,000 people had no seat for the big football game. A major upgrade, the Burke-Tarr

Fite Administration Building.

Stadium, was completed in 1966 with a 4,000-seat capacity. With an unobstructed view from any area, the new home of the Eagles contained a 50-foot press box, snack bars, a new scoreboard, and a president's section (*Orange and Blue,* November 12, 1966).

Brand-new tennis courts were also built on Branner Avenue where "the Barn" had been located.

A CHANGE OF ADDRESS FOR THE HOME MANAGEMENT HOUSE

The Home Management House, located on Russell Avenue, was razed in 1967 for a faculty parking lot. The Duncan House across the street became the new Home Management House where senior home economics majors could practice, in a homelike situation, the knowledge and skills they had learned in their course work. The women lived there for 12-week periods (*Orange and Blue,* November 11, 1967).

THE FITE ADMINISTRATION BUILDING

The influx of student growth stretched the Administration Building, Henderson Hall, to the limit. It could not be enlarged or fireproofed, and there was simply not enough room for the larger group of professors and administrators who had been employed and needed office space.

In 1967 a new modern Administration Building was completed on the corner of Russell and North College Streets and named for Dr. Fite. The lobby boasted a state-of-the-art campus switchboard. This building also provided long-needed protection for valuable college financial records and student academic records (*Orange and Blue,* September 18, 1967 and September 30, 1967). Yet some valuable records were allowed to remain in Henderson Hall, which became a major regret in 1974.

1965 Glory Days: Two National Championships

SPORTS NATIONAL WINNERS: BASEBALL

In May 1965 the air was electric in St. Joseph, Missouri, as the final two college baseball teams played each other for the national championship. Carson-Newman and Omaha University were the teams vying for the prize at the 1965 National Association of Intercollegiate Athletics (NAIA) tournament composed of eight southeastern states. The winner was Carson-Newman College!

Winning the national title was no fluke. Carson-Newman had a baseball team of true excellence; 5 of its players were placed on the All-Tournament Team of 14, and senior pitcher Clyde Wright was named the Most Valuable Player among the players of more than 480 schools that belonged to the NAIA. As detailed in the September 18, 1965, *Orange and Blue,* that year Carson-Newman had won thirty-three games and lost only three in their normal season, capturing the state Volunteer State Athletic Conference (VSAC) title.

Two coaches deserved special credit for building up the team. Sam B. "Frosty" Holt, Carson-Newman's longtime baseball coach and athletic director, had just retired from coaching (*Orange and Blue,* March 20, 1965). He had excelled at spotting talented young high-school athletes, including Wright, recruiting and training them for Carson-Newman. The current baseball coach, Bobby Wilson, who had just completed his first season with the team, was named NAIA Coach of the Year (*Orange and Blue,* October 16, 1965). What a way to begin his career at Carson-Newman!

Left-handed pitcher Clyde Wright was a standout in his four years at Carson-Newman, hurling the school's first no-hitter and chalking up

The 1965 national championship baseball team.

a phenomenal 35–4 pitching record. After being named Most Valuable Player in 1965, Wright was drafted by the Los Angeles Angels and played for them eight years. He pitched the first no-hitter ever thrown at Anaheim Stadium and won over one hundred major-league games, later pitching for teams in Wisconsin and Texas and for three years in Japan.[760]

ACADEMIC NATIONAL VICTORS: DEBATE

In May 1965, another dream came true for Carson-Newman. The outstanding debate team of students John Wittig and Barnett Pearce won the National Championship Debate held at West Point, New York. The topic given them was "Resolved: That the Federal Government Should Establish a National Program of Public Work for the Unemployed." Each team participating had to be prepared to defend either side of the proposition.

According to the May 5, 1965, *Orange and Blue,* Wittig and Pearce were up against formidable teams from notable universities such as Harvard, Northwestern, Massachusetts Institute of Technology (MIT), and the University of Southern California (USC). Past Carson-Newman teams had placed at this fierce competition, but none had won it all. Carson-Newman welcomed the young academic champions back with joy.

Speech professor and debate coach R. Forrest Conklin had chosen to train his team in the British style of debate, which emphasizes logic and

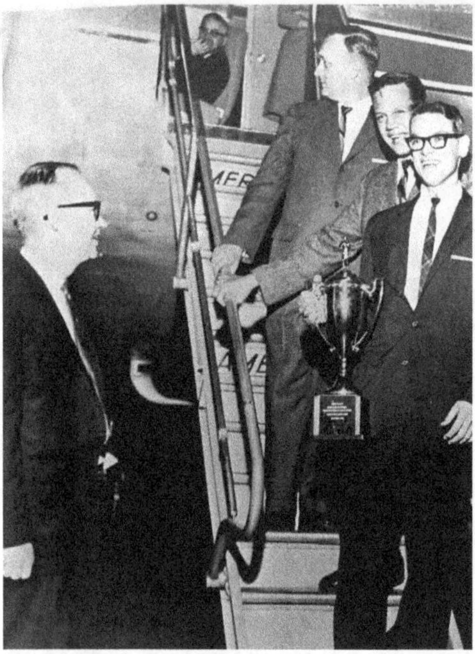

The 1965 national debate champions, John Wittig and Barnett Pearce, deplaning with their coach, R. Forrest Conklin.

rhetoric and the ability of the debaters to think fast on their feet to use these devices. Another aspect of this style is based in humor, to try to poke fun at the opponents' case (May 5, 1965, *Orange and Blue*). The American style of debate, which is the more common, leads its proponents to memorize vast amounts of relevant material—quotations and other forms of sources—to offer these points at the most judicious time possible. Conklin's choice had paid off.

Following the top ranking of the debate team, in December 1965, Forrest Conklin was named national Debate Coach of the Year (*Orange and Blue*, December 4, 1965). Carson-Newman's Communications Department still gives the Forrest Conklin Top Debater Award to its best debaters. There is also an Elmer W. Sydnor Leadership Award, honoring the college's first debate coach, for excellence among their communications majors.

RATS PAY THEIR DUES TO ATTEND CARSON-NEWMAN

For decades, freshmen at Carson-Newman, popularly called "Rats" by upperclassmen, were deemed the lowest form of humanity—in fun—maybe. In the September 18, 1967 *Orange and Blue,* academic dean Walter Guyton set forth guidelines for upperclassmen regarding acceptable challenges they could issue to "lord it over" freshmen for three weeks. A sampling of activities included: (1) reporting any Rat not wearing the identifying orange beanie between 6:30 a.m. and 10:00 p.m.; (2) requiring a Rat to sing the *Alma Mater* from memory—standing up, of course; (3) ensuring that Rats addressed upperclassmen as "Sir" or "Madame" to show proper respect; (4) demanding that a Rat recite the current Eagle football schedule from memory on request; and (5) conscripting a Rat to carry his or her textbooks across campus to class.

The Benefits of a Coalition of Colleges

In the 1960s, several small private colleges in Tennessee, Kentucky, and Virginia formed a cooperative endeavor, the Mid-Appalachian College Council, for the cultural and academic advantages the partnership brought to Appalachia (*Orange and Blue,* December 5, 1969). One activity was the block booking of artists, which enabled small schools to host performers they could not otherwise afford.

For example, famous British actor Basil Rathbone came to Carson-Newman on his world tour to deliver his sophisticated program of literary classics, "In and Out of Character" (*Orange and Blue,* October 10, 1963). Musicians who made appearances at Carson-Newman during this period included Jerome Hines, American bass opera star; Ravi Shankar, India's leading concert instrumentalist; Mary Costa, soprano opera star originally from Knoxville; and Pierre Cochereau, organist of the Notre Dame Cathedral in Paris, France (*Orange and Blue,* March 18, 1964, and April 1, 1967).

Another wonderful accomplishment of the Mid-Appalachian College Council was the establishment of an undergraduate training center dedicated to biological fieldwork. The MACC colleges worked together to select a seventeen-acre site in East Tennessee for the study of fresh water and marine life, plus other aspects of nature. This laboratory opened in 1968 (*Orange and Blue*, March 3, 1972).

Each summer in the late 1960s and 1970s, the best biology students from each MACC school were invited to attend a ten-week summer session at Norris Lake near LaFollette, Tennessee. The facilities included a twenty-two-foot floating laboratory, a thirty-five-foot landing craft, a floating dock, and choice study equipment. Each student paid about $100 per week to take one course at a time, spending all day and well into each night in lectures and research. Classes included geology, forest ecology, limnology, vascular botany, and ornithology. Joe Chapman, Carson-Newman's representative, considered the project a great success and a wonderful opportunity for biology students (*Orange and Blue,* December 1969).

Significant 1968–1970 Retirements

Retirement became a tricky subject for President Fite when he approached the age of sixty-five in 1967. He had spearheaded the college-wide rule that when individual faculty and staff members reached sixty-five, they must retire. Few exceptions would apply. As a person of integrity, he also planned to retire at sixty-five. However, the trustees were adamantly unwilling to let him go. Everything was progressing so well at Carson-Newman that they wanted him to continue indefinitely.

President Fite stayed one extra year to appease the trustees, with his last day scheduled for July 31, 1968 (*Orange and Blue,* January 20, 1968). He became the most active retired president in Carson-Newman's history. For the first eleven years of his retirement, he served as vice-president of a Morristown bank, where his vast knowledge of people made him a valuable asset. For the same reason, the trustees asked him to work "free-lance" for Carson-Newman in the area of deferred giving. He also wrote for many educational and church-related magazines and self-published five books.

Also in 1968, **Ersa Davis** retired after more than forty years of excellence in the Music Department (*Orange and Blue,* January 20, 1968). Athletic director **Sam B. "Frosty" Holt** retired as well after thirty-nine years spent at Carson-Newman (*Orange and Blue,* March 9, 1968). Together, the three retirees had contributed one hundred unforgettable years to Carson-Newman's unique history.

A MAN FOR ALL SEASONS— FOOTBALL, BASEBALL, BASKETBALL . . .

In a series of articles in *The Orange and Blue* in the 1960s, Coach "Frosty" Holt paid tribute to several 1920s coaches who had taken him under their respective wings and given him formative sports advice. The first was **R. M. McCown,** who saw the young athlete's potential and invited him to finish high school at Carson-Newman's preparatory school, then attend college while playing sports. "He became the greatest friend to me and the athletic department. . . . It pleased me and thousands of others when the athletic fields were named McCown Fields" (October 20, 1962).

"**Lake Russell** . . . was a second Dad to me. . . . He was one of my closest friends during my college days and later became my coach. . . . I give him credit for keeping me in Carson-Newman" (November 10, 1962).

Pryor "Humpy" McElveen "was my first college baseball coach and . . . taught me some of the basic fundamentals about the game of baseball. I remember some of these things until this day" (November 10, 1962).

What Frosty Holt had been given, he paid forward to generations of young men he coached. They loved him dearly. In 1960, a group of his former lettermen pooled their money and gave him a car. He received a number of awards; in 1962, he received the American Baseball Coaches Association's Distinguished Service Award and was inducted into the NAIA Coaches Hall of Fame. In 1965, he was elected to the Helmes Baseball Hall of Fame. But to Coach Holt, "The chance to attend college and especially Carson-Newman College was the greatest step in my life" (November 10, 1962). Sam B. "Frosty" Holt passed away in 1986.

In May 1968 **Richard Pettigrew**, an excellent English professor, received the first Distinguished Faculty Award.[761] Dr. Pettigrew taught by the Socratic method, asking layered questions that caused students to think before answering. The next year he was compelled to retire because he had reached age sixty-five, much to the displeasure of many students who considered his classes among the best at the college. After retiring from Carson-Newman, he returned to teaching at Catawba College in North Carolina, where he had served on the faculty earlier.[762]

THE FINAL LOSS OF HARLEY FITE

Harley Fite remained in good health most of his long life, dying at almost 102. At his memorial service in early 2004, many stories were told about his character and leadership. Those in attendance were especially captivated by a grandson's remembrance of a significant childhood experience with his grandfather. The story he related was so like the Dr. Fite they had known and loved!

An apple tree heavy with fruit stood behind the president's home. Standing beside it, Dr. Fite and his young grandson—Paul Roden, Jr.—surveyed the tree's bounty, wishing for a juicy bite of the delicious fruit. But neither could reach even one apple.

Dr. Fite studied the situation and broke the silence. "I believe that if we cooperate with each other, Paul, we might be able to achieve what we both want," he began. "Suppose I lean down and you climb on my shoulders. Then I'll straighten up and you reach as high as you can for a couple of apples. Working together, maybe we'll both be able to enjoy an apple." The plan worked, and the boy learned a memorable, far-reaching life lesson from his wise educator-grandfather.

Pettigrew's esteemed colleague in the English Department, **Janie Swann Huggins**, joined him in retirement in 1969. The two had co-sponsored the student literary publication *The Eagle's Quill* and an organization for students interested in creative writing, the Scribblers Club. According to the April 29, 1969, *Orange and Blue*, "[Miss Huggins] has never been a 'yes-woman' but has retained a genuine independence of mind." She taught at Lincoln Memorial University for three years afterward.

An October 15, 1976, *Orange and Blue* profile of Miss Huggins highlighted her founding of the Panathenees Honor Society for women at Carson-Newman in 1958.[763] Hoping that eventually the national Mortar Board organization would approve Panathenees as a chapter of Mortar Board, she was elated when that occurred in 1974.

Meanwhile, the Class of 1926 Carson-Newman alumnus continued to read and love literature; "I'm electrified by Walt Whitman," she commented. She expressed gratitude that many former students appreciated her having required them to memorize select literary passages, affirming, "It gives you something beautiful to think about when you're growing old." The lifelong learner summarized her current state of contentment: "The teacher is retired; the student is thriving" (*Orange and Blue,* October 15, 1976).

The longtime dean of women, **Bernice Carter**, also retired in 1969, as did **Edwin Richardson**, a beloved religion professor (*Orange and Blue,* April 17, 1969). All four 1969 retirees planned to work actively after retiring from Carson-Newman, feeling they still had much to contribute elsewhere. The following year **Mae Iddins** retired after forty-two remarkable years spent overseeing women's physical education at Carson-Newman.[764] The Olympic-sized swimming pool in Holt Fieldhouse was named in her honor (*Orange and Blue,* February 11, 1979).

An Era of Rapid Changes

A LEADER SWIMMING IN TROUBLED WATERS: JOHN ALBERT FINCHER, NINETEENTH PRESIDENT (1968–1977)

Originally from Union County, South Carolina, John Fincher (1911–2002) won the only college scholarship in his county, enabling him to graduate from the University of South Carolina in Columbia in 1933 with a BS in education. After spending one year as an elementary school principal, he returned to the university for a master's degree in biology. He earned his PhD in biology at the University of North Carolina in Chapel Hill.[765]

In 1939, he served as a research fellow at Highlands Biological Laboratory in North Carolina, then taught at Cumberland College (now the University of the Cumberlands) in Williamsburg, Kentucky; Millsaps College in Jackson, Mississippi; and Howard College in Birmingham, Alabama, which became Samford University in 1965. He served as assistant to the president of Samford for three years, becoming academic dean in 1957.[766] He had settled into that position when the Carson-Newman presidential search committee came calling in 1968.

Fincher was surprised at Carson-Newman's interest in him as he was already fifty-six. But the committee had done its homework in studying resumés with an eye toward matching a candidate with experience needed at the Tennessee Baptist school.

John A. Fincher, president 1968–1977.

Of major importance to them were two criteria that Fincher met: (1) an administrator who had dealt successfully with the climate of unrest in the current generation of college students; and (2) a scholar who was also a true academic. Regarding the former, Fincher's description of how Samford had successfully involved students more closely in the governing process, thereby gaining their trust, was reassuring to the Carson-Newman representatives. His solid background in teaching biology and having an earned doctorate in that field fulfilled the second criterion. John Fincher was inaugurated as Carson-Newman's president in 1969.

A lovely home off campus was built for the Finchers. Called "The Columns," it served to remove the president from easy access during his private time.[767] Trustees felt that on-campus living was too demanding for the college leader. Two subsequent presidents lived there as well.

The new president advanced his previous Samford policy at Carson-Newman, encouraging students to participate in the Student Government

Association (SGA). Fincher knew that change was inevitable. He noted that this generation of students desired to participate in the decision-making processes of the college, not simply to be recipients of it. At first he was complimented on his willingness to listen to students (*Orange and Blue,* April 25, 1970). Clark Bryan and Suzanne Matheny, dean and assistant dean of students, had more long-term success at maintaining reputations for openness and fairness.

In later years, Fincher reflected to a friend, "I felt like I hopped aboard a train going 100 miles an hour." A vocal minority of students, which grew in number and peer influence year by year, seemed to want the Baptist school to give them all the freedoms of a state university. The dancing controversy heated up, and other problems surfaced in the 1970s that would have been unthinkable before. These included complaints about chapel, panty raids, food fights, students dismissed for possessing marijuana, a lack of understanding between black and white students, athletes seeming to receive preferential treatment, and women wanting to live off campus. A streaker ran across the entire length of the basketball court before a game, his entrance timed so a spotlight was on him in the darkened gymnasium.

In 1974, both *The Orange and Blue* and *The Appalachian* reached a height of biting satire and accusations of administrators' ineffectiveness at Carson-Newman. The latter was withheld from students and withdrawn from public viewing for years.

No women had been part of the Carson-Newman trustee board since Newman College was a separate entity. In a welcome move, Fincher named Martha Henderson Ashe as a trustee in 1970, almost ninety years later.[768] Mrs. Ashe was the granddaughter of former president John T. Henderson.

President Fincher vowed to strengthen the academic program at Carson-Newman. Thanks in large part to Walter Guyton, the creative academic dean during most of Fincher's years in office, academics were greatly repurposed in the 1970s. Required chapel attendance was reduced to once per week (*Orange and Blue,* September 1969).

Retiring at the end of the 1976–1977 school year, President Fincher and his wife returned to South Carolina. Eventually they made their way back to Birmingham, Alabama, where they lived the rest of their lives.

Part 2 of the Dancing Controversy

The fact that dancing was not allowed on campus was the single hottest point of contention between students and the administration. In 1970, Dr. Fincher took the matter to the trustees, especially since some students who had attended dances off campus had been injured coming back late at night. He framed it as a matter of student safety and a social matter, which the students appreciated. He also pointed out that some off-campus dances were held in circumstances that were far from ideal for student safety. The trustees agreed to let the school try holding dances. The students were elated, and occasional dances were scheduled on campus.

However, as word spread across the state that Carson-Newman students were dancing, the news caused a furor among many Tennessee Baptists. The Tennessee Baptist Convention questioned Dr. Fincher's control of his students, suggesting that he be removed for overstepping his bounds or was "in over his head." Several churches asked that their contributions to Tennessee Baptist colleges be withheld.[769]

In November 1970, the matter was addressed at the annual meeting of the Tennessee Baptist Convention. A clear majority of ministers and church representatives were most emphatic: dancing should not be allowed at any Tennessee Baptist college. An official ban on dancing followed, and Carson-Newman's trustees affirmed the ban.[770] Students were crestfallen.

There was a food fight in the cafeteria that evening. Despite the amount of clean-up required and the cost of the food wasted, Pearl McHan understood the students' frustration and did not complain. Some administrators were angry about the food fight since they had sided with the students and felt their own jobs were now on the line.

The November 13, 1970, *Orange and Blue* carried a black-bordered "Obituary for Student Dancing, 13 months old. Death was attributed to suffocation." A letter to the editor of *The Orange and Blue* (October 1, 1971) pointed out the irony that dancing was outlawed on campus, but killing was implicitly permitted by the military presence of the Reserve Officer Training Corps (ROTC).

The issue surfaced over and over during the 1970s, when occasional dances were scheduled off campus. One dance was held literally in the street behind Butler-Blanc Gymnasium. Signs advertising off-campus dances carried creative messaging such as "D____e to be held" or "Foot Function Ahead." The April 23, 1974, *Orange and Blue* carried a photograph of an impromptu dance occurring inside the Baker Building (Student Center) as students simply moved to the music playing.

Reaching across the Integration Gulf

As the late 1960s turned into the 1970s, more African American students entered Carson-Newman. But they still felt distinctly in the minority and misunderstood. Some were from other countries.

In 1966, Valentin Mbong, an international student from Cameroon and a talented soccer player, entered Carson-Newman. He was named Joe College for homecoming and proved to be a valuable addition to the soccer team. Tony Mills returned and was a standout basketball player for Carson-Newman. They wanted to be known as individuals, not just as athletes.

Carson-Newman held programs to raise awareness of the different perspectives of white and black students. According to the September 1969 issue of *The Orange and Blue,* the showing of the film *Black History: Lost, Stolen, or Strayed* was well attended, but the discussion afterward revealed a deep chasm in the black versus white reactions to it.

In the February 27, 1970, issue of *The Orange and Blue,* black student Dennis Reed understandably objected to the traditional singing of "Dixie" before sporting events at Carson-Newman. In an effort to bridge the gap of differing perspectives, he recommended that white students read some black literature and try to understand the black point of view.

By 1974, Black Awareness Week was held on campus, featuring several types of activities to help educate white students about the history and perspectives of blacks. The Black Cultural Society had been added to the list of organizations on campus: "It is a club in which black students can keep in touch with black reality. . . . Most blacks do not want to be the token in a group," wrote Tyrone Fritz, urging more open communication between white and black students (*Orange and Blue,* October 17, 1975).

President Fincher was questioned many times about why there were no blacks on the faculty or in the administration. His answer was that efforts had been made in that direction, but Carson-Newman could not compete moneywise with state colleges or larger universities. Not until 1992 was a full-time African American faculty member—Gladys Sheets Clay, an aunt of Patricia Crippins—hired at the college. Her specialty was teaching English and education; she was director of academic skills development.[771]

A DAY WHEN GOODNESS REIGNED ON CAMPUS

On October 23, 1970, Carson-Newman held a "Clyde Wright and Frosty Holt Day" in chapel when Clyde Wright came to town. Clyde had had a banner season pitching for the Los Angeles Angels, and he was famous. Frosty Holt, on the other hand, had been retired for two years; half the student body did not know him. Most Carson-Newman students excitedly came to see Clyde Wright, an alumnus who had made good, but they considered Frosty a tag-along because he had been Wright's coach.

Clyde Wright discussed his pitching career, praised Frosty Holt, and then turned the program over to him. "Frosty spun many yarns of his times with Clyde at Carson-Newman. In fact, he told us more about Wright than Clyde did." But he also told the attentive audience about the long-ago changing of the athletic teams' name from Fighting Parsons to Eagles, his World War I days in the U.S. Navy, and countless other topics. "By the time Frosty was finished you felt as if he was your best friend. . . . The man's electricity made the crowd realize the major impact that Holt has had at Carson-Newman and more than justified his being honored."

"The crowd came to see Wright but most left remembering Holt. . . . This is by no means an indictment of Wright, who deserved the recognition of his alma mater, but rather the overshadowing achievements of Holt, whose years of dedication have made it possible for all of the Clyde Wrights in Carson-Newman's history," wrote student Tom Ficara (*Orange and Blue*, October 29, 1970).

Overheard as the students left chapel: "Clyde Wright may be sex, but that old Frosty Holt is love."

Coach Sam "Frosty" Holt, mentoring young football players.

Innovative Academic Changes

After new academic dean Walter Guyton's "assessment semester" at Carson-Newman in the fall of 1967, he lost no time making adjustments.[772] Across his seven years at Carson-Newman, his most significant changes included:

Saturday classes were eliminated by lengthening classes on Tuesdays and Thursdays.

Classes began three weeks earlier than before (in August) so the fall semester would be completed by Christmas holidays. Students would take exams before they left for break rather than after they returned. Spring exams and graduation would occur in early May.

Students could take one optional mini-term course in May—three weeks of daily classes for either three or four hours credit—from a limited choice of class offerings. Some classes were more creative than conventional.

Basic curriculum requirements were lowered so as to give students more chances to take elective classes. Minors were no longer required, but students had to take a specified number of courses outside their major.

Students could be exempted from some basic academic courses by passing a proficiency exam.

In some academic areas, the number of required courses was lowered.

Juniors and seniors were allowed to take one course per semester on a pass/fail basis.

A C average in the major field was required for graduation.

The Washington Intern Program offered a student the ability to obtain fifteen hours of credit in political science and history by residing in Washington, DC, for one semester and working for a senator or representative who subscribed to the program.

An interdisciplinary semester in London was added as a spring option.

A study-abroad semester in Latin America was added.

A new academic hierarchy grouped seventeen departments into five divisions: humanities, fine arts, applied arts and sciences, social sciences, natural sciences, and mathematics.

The Honors Program was initiated for the brightest students. The Faculty Honors Council was established to administer the Honors Program.

A "no major" major was allowed, called General Studies.

Panathenees, a leadership honor society for college women, was upgraded to a chapter of the National Mortar Board in 1974. Beginning in 1978, the group included outstanding male students in its membership.

A new Reserve Officer Training Corps (ROTC) on campus allowed students to acquire a good education and also to train to serve their country in a military setting.

Five national honor societies were established at the college.

Carson-Newman was approved to give the Algernon Sydney Sullivan Award, one of the most outstanding national collegiate awards, to two seniors and one other person on an annual basis.

The Individual Directions program was offered to self-motivated students, supervised by the Faculty Honors Council.

An Honors Day program was held at the end of each school year.

All college committees had at least one student representative.

A counseling program was offered to freshmen.

A Career Opportunities Day was held each spring to help students seek employment opportunities by meeting employers in their fields.

New courses were offered in a number of disciplines.

Outreach to Hancock County

In the 1960s, President Lyndon B. Johnson's "War on Poverty" effort turned the nation's attention to the dire living conditions in parts of Appalachia. Carson-Newman representatives explored ways the college could help relieve the widespread poverty of its neighbors. The results of their work centered on nearby Hancock County, Tennessee, one of the nation's poorest counties in per capita income. According to the September 17, 1966, *Orange and Blue,* several Carson-Newman students from Hancock County helped to develop and distribute a questionnaire to about six hundred families in the county about their greatest needs and struggles.

Many inhabitants of Hancock County were part of a dark-skinned people group of mixed origins who had settled the region before white men moved in. The white settlers called them Melungeons, derived from the French word *mélange,* meaning mixture or medley. Because of severe prejudice against them, Melungeons had been run off their farms and forced to move higher into the mountains with poor soil, few jobs, and limited ability to feed their families.[773]

Outdoor dramas such as *Unto These Hills*, a play about the Cherokee Indian Nation, had become a tourist draw in the general area. Carson-Newman, the Tennessee Valley Authority (TVA), and other community leaders decided to launch a similar effort to tell the story of the Melungeon people. An outdoor theater was constructed in Sneedville, Hancock County's largest town, in time for the July 1969 opening performance of *Walk Toward the Sunset* by Kermit Hunter. An amazing 10,185 persons attended the first twenty-five performances of the play (*Orange and Blue,* August 1, 1970).

Carson-Newman played a large role in the success of *Walk Toward the Sunset*, which ran for six seasons. John Lee Welton, the college's drama professor, oversaw the crew members and directed the cast, composed of community performers and Carson-Newman students (*Orange and Blue*, December 1969). Many audience members had never heard of Melungeons before, but were touched by their plight after watching the play.

Even those who actively helped Hancock Countians reach a more sustainable way of life were surprised by some developments that unfolded:

1. The self-esteem of individual Melungeons was raised as they saw themselves through the eyes of others who did not look down on them. They began to hold large conventions celebrating their heritage and researching clues to their mysterious origins.
2. Hancock County government officials used *Walk Toward the Sunset* as a rationale for road improvements to make their remote area more accessible to the outside world.
3. Improved roads, in turn, helped the county to persuade several new businesses to locate in Sneedville.
4. Economic development followed, including the operation of a craft store where the residents could market their wares. Notably, Alex Stewart, a cooper, was later featured in the Smithsonian Crafts Bicentennial Show on the Mall in Washington, DC.[774]
5. For a number of years, Carson-Newman offered its students an ongoing chance to travel to Hancock County weekly, boarding buses to tutor individual Melungeon children. Due to this outreach, the education of both groups was enriched.

Encore Buildings of the Early 1970s

A NEW LIBRARY OF EXCELLENCE

By the mid-1960s, the Maples Library was completely out of space. The administration and library staff considered various locations on campus for a new library, but wound up constructing the new library adjacent to Maples, literally building on their previous investment.

Head librarian Mildred Iddins loved to visit other libraries while on vacation with her sister, Mae. While the new facility was in the planning stages, Mildred visited many libraries across the country to see their facilities and to gather ideas, paying her own expenses as she traveled. As a college librarian, she was often permitted to go into the "inner sanctum" of such libraries. Mildred Iddins's goal was to make Carson-Newman's new library an outstanding one.[775] Other members of the library staff were invited to visit nearby colleges with her on day trips.[776]

The new Learning Resource Center, as it was called briefly, was open by the end of 1970. It had four full floors and a major innovation: an elevator! It would be accessible to all students, including those physically disabled.

PENNIES AND DOLLARS FOR A NEW SCIENCE BUILDING

While the Warren Science Building had been furnished with the very latest scientific equipment in 1939, it was sorely out of date almost thirty years later. Too, the number of science students and majors had grown exponentially since then. Estimates for an adequate new Science Center ran at 3.2 million dollars, so creative means of fundraising were needed for the building to be constructed without any government monies.

In 1966, the members of 531 Tennessee Baptist churches committed to donate a penny per day to the building fund. At the completion of the "Penny-a-Day Campaign" three years later, they had contributed over $800,000 to the project.[777] Of course, other gifts were welcome, too. The September 17, 1966, *Orange and Blue* reported that Magnavox donated $30,000 for the new building; and as time went on, other donors sent large gifts as well.

Appeals were personified in the name of the beloved biology professor who doubled as the college's alumni coordinator, Joe Chapman, whose office was in the basement of the Warren Building. "Get Joe out of the basement!" was the rallying cry on campus (*Orange and Blue,* September 28, 1968). An auction was held in Burke-Tarr Stadium to fund the physics laboratory, which was named for Roy Roberts and James Grissom, the basketball players who had perished in a bus accident in 1938 (*Orange and Blue,* October 1, 1971). Roberts had been president of the Science Club at the time of his death.

The new building, opened in 1972, was named the Dougherty Science Center after the late Thomas Hunter Dougherty (Class of 1911) and his wife, Nan Meek Dougherty. Their family gave a major gift in memory of the educators. Dougherty Science Center's lobby contains artfully placed plaques noting all of the science and mathematics professors in Carson-Newman's history, beginning with Shelby Jones, who taught 1882–1914.

Dougherty Science Building.

THE REPURPOSED WARREN BUILDING

Two Fine Arts Departments were given space in the old science building because the Chambliss Building was completely out of space. The basement and top floors were allotted to the Music Department; the number of music majors had increased by leaps and bounds. Individual practice rooms, faculty offices, and a large rehearsal room occupied the fourth floor. In the basement were a band practice room and a room for equipment.

The Art Department used the first (ground) floor for a creative workspace for art students, while the second floor was converted to individual art studios for seniors, offices, and a large gallery space where exhibits were held. A large classroom had an adjacent projection room. (A small metal building behind Bertie Maples Butler Hall contained the ceramic studio and kilns.)

CONTEXT: 1972 EVENTS IN WORLD HISTORY

Elvis Presley recorded a live album at New York City's Madison Square Garden. For the first time, the Winter Olympic Games were held in Asia—in Sapporo, Japan. Apollo 16 astronauts landed on the moon. Sandy Koufax, Yogi Berra, and Early Wynn were named to the Baseball Hall of Fame. On "Bloody Sunday" in Derry, Northern Ireland, the British Army shot twenty-seven unarmed civilians during a civil rights march; fourteen died. Transit fares in New York City rose to thirty-five cents. United States president Richard Nixon made a groundbreaking trip to China. "M*A*S*H" debuted on television, and the musical *Grease* opened on Broadway. In California, the Alcatraz Prison closed. Secretary of State Henry Kissinger declared, "Peace is at hand in Vietnam," and the Watergate cover-up began.

Title IX and Resulting Changes on Campus

In the 1970s, at the same time the Equal Rights Amendment was being debated, a far-reaching act of Congress began creating a virtual seismic shift at Carson-Newman. Title IX of the Educational Amendments of 1972 had a direct impact on women's sports at colleges and universities across the country, prohibiting sex discrimination in any education program or activity receiving federal financial assistance.

Carson-Newman does not receive federal monies *per se,* but some federal assistance goes directly to students in the form of scholarships. Thus, Title IX prompted a self-examination at the college regarding inequities of all kinds between men and women students (*Orange and Blue,* February 1, 1975). Suzanne Matheny, assistant dean of students, chaired a committee highlighting the status of women on campus.

Regarding athletics, all females at the school knew that the quality of their physical education facilities did not in any way match those of men. Scholarships for female athletes were scarcer and lower than those for male athletes. Women's athletic uniforms of the time reflected the modesty and femininity expected of them.

But the main differences were in the overall campus rules. Carson-Newman administrators had always taken seriously their responsibilities *in loco parentis* (Latin for "in the place of a parent"). In 1971, the legal age of adulthood changed from twenty-one to eighteen, meaning that almost all college students were adults and responsible for themselves. But at Carson-Newman, little had changed for women. For example, women students were required to sign out when leaving campus; on their return, they had to be in their residence halls by a certain hour. Male students did not have to sign out, and they had no curfew. They could have cars on campus; women students could not.

At many US colleges and universities, Title IX ushered in the advent of coed dormitories. Carson-Newman's female student leaders did not ask for coed dorms, but they did want answers to the broader questions of women's rights.

Over time, significant progress was made in equalizing the ways men and women were treated at Carson-Newman.

A Sudden, Sad Farewell to Henderson Hall

Over the years, Henderson Hall, the onetime Administration Building (until Fite Administration Building was completed) and the main classroom building of the Humanities Division, had become a liability to the Fite and Fincher administrations. Completed in 1919, Henderson Hall was greatly loved by alumni, students, and professors, but the despair of some administrators. The building's outdated codes, antiquated fixtures and furnishings, quirky spaces, and limited access for physically disabled students were drawbacks that hindered plans for upgrading the building to serve more students.

The completion of the Fite Administration Building relieved some space pressures, but not all. Renovations on the auditorium were made in 1973, and insurance on the building was updated as well. Reluctantly trustees met in early January 1974 to approve plans to renovate the rest of Henderson Hall at great expense.

In the early-morning hours of January 16, 1974, the campus came alive to shouts of "Fire! Henderson Hall is burning!" Some male students rushed across campus to the scene, while female students were confined inside locked dormitories but crowded around the front windows to watch the building burn. The night sky glowed as flames leaped above the burning

Henderson Hall burning in 1974.

building and through its windows. Many felt like they were watching a horror show—but the horror was real. Everyone was in disbelief.

Within hours the building was gone. "Firemen, hampered by the strong west-to-east winds, were unable to contain the blaze which spread rapidly throughout the predominantly wooden structure. . . . Due to the late hour and the speed at which the fire spread, the only articles that were saved from Henderson Hall were some chairs, trophies, and an antique piano from Philo Hall. When asked about the possibility of retrieving the marble plaques of the four literary societies, Dean Clark Bryan said, 'The stones are down there, but they're in a million pieces'" (*Orange and Blue*, January 25, 1974).

All the buildings close to Henderson were at risk for the fire spreading to them, but none more so than Sarah Swann Hall, full of women students and built in 1904 with an abundance of wood. Thanks to the heroic efforts of fire fighters, the fire did not reach any other buildings. Daylight brought the fearful sight of the decimated building, with its still-smoking pillars; the entire remains smoldered. Many remembered with sorrow the irreplaceable panoramic class pictures of the past that had hung in the hallway of the basement. But few students realized that the fire was the second one on that site. Most did not know about the school's first administration building, erected in the 1890s and destroyed by fire in late 1916.

The campus and community soon learned of the significant losses of faculty members whose offices were in Henderson. None was more tragic than that of L. Dan Taylor, a longtime religion professor whose lifework of decades—a manuscript of his own original, painstaking translation of the New Testament from the Greek—had burned. Most professors lost their personal libraries, class lectures and notes, and various belongings; some lost their doctoral dissertations and master's theses.[778]

Too, papers and documents in the offices of the five humanities departments—Religion, English, Foreign Language, Speech, and Drama—vanished overnight. The Drama Department lost its theater for small productions, the Drama Den; every prop and costume that had been accumulated over the years; and all the photographs of the department's productions for the past twenty years.

Rehearsals were already underway for the spring 1974 play, *The Remarkable Mr. Pennypacker* (*Orange and Blue,* February 8, 1974). After willing students did the hard work involved in cleaning out the old Tarr Chevrolet Building in downtown Jefferson City, the play was held there. The building was dubbed "the Phoenix Theater," referring to the bird that rose from the ashes of fire in Greek mythology.

Speculation began immediately about the cause of the fire. Investigators found clear indications of arson; fires had been set in several distinct areas. The college offered a $3,000 award for information leading to the arrest and conviction of a person or persons who set the fire. No one was ever arrested.

Earliest estimates of the loss of Henderson Hall itself were set at $2,000,000. Treasurer Albert Sloan calculated that at least $50,000 more would be needed to rebuild (*Orange and Blue,* January 25, 1974).

Meanwhile, administrators sprang into action to find rooms to hold the dozens of classes in the humanities—not just for the remaining weeks of the spring semester, but for years while construction of a replacement building was ongoing. Available space was limited on campus, but many college employees made sacrificial adjustments to help. For example, the library staff gave up their lounge and other "corners" of their relatively new building for makeshift classrooms.

The biggest offer of help came from Jefferson City's First Baptist Church, whose Sunday School and Training Union classrooms stood empty during the week. Once again, as in the early days of Mossy Creek Baptist Seminary, "college in the church" would be held as the partnership continued between Carson-Newman and the church beside the campus.

A Tangible Look at Carson-Newman's Past

One week after the fire, the trustees met to plan a replacement building. They deliberated carefully about what spaces the new building should contain. They would retain the footprint of the old Henderson Hall, but the first floor would be ground level. The exterior front stairs would have a landing as well as a porch. However, the interior would be very different. The building would carry forward the name of former president John T. Henderson; the complete name would be Henderson Humanities Building.

Months of disappointing delays ensued as an architect was hired, new blueprints were drawn up, and insurance adjustments were debated, negotiated, and accepted. Groundbreaking ceremonies for the new building were not held until spring 1975. Meanwhile, on March 7, 1974, a crowd assembled in front of Fite Administration Building to watch the opening of the cornerstone from two buildings that had been destroyed by fire—the first laid in 1890 and the second in 1917. The latter had not been opened since 1917. One of the distinguished guests was Lone Sisk, Class of 1922, who had helped assemble materials for the cornerstone of Henderson Hall in 1917, when he was a student (*Orange and Blue,* March 22, 1974).

The 1890/1917 cornerstone was later placed in the front (west) entrance to Henderson Humanities Building, containing new items from a 1976 dedication. (Its previous contents were placed in the special collections room of the library.) The walls in both the west and east entryways are covered with clay bricks salvaged from the 1919 Henderson Hall.

Three Concurrent Anniversaries

1976 was a banner year for anniversaries in Jefferson City. It was the nation's bicentennial; the 125th anniversary of Carson-Newman's founding; and the seventy-fifth birthday of Jefferson City, whose name had changed from that of Mossy Creek in 1901.

In anticipation of Carson-Newman's 125th anniversary, the cover of the 1975 *Appalachian* featured drawings of Harvey Carson, for whom Carson College was named, and William C. Newman of the family for whom Newman College was named. Much of the college's history was highlighted inside its pages as well.

During the national bicentennial celebrations in 1976, Pearl McHan gave an extraordinary dinner at Stokely Cafeteria, serving dishes that had been favorites of several United States presidents. In the fall, a homecoming float represented Carson-Newman's 125 years, and the 1976 *Appalachian* also contained several historical features. Jefferson City celebrated its seventy-fifth birthday with several key local events, including *Heritage '76*, a play in 12 acts.[779]

CONTENTS OF THE COMBINED 1890/1917 CORNERSTONE

A fascinating group of objects emerged from the old cornerstone: an envelope containing unspecified materials from the 1890 cornerstone; a copy of Dr. Len G. Broughton's address given in 1917 at the cornerstone ceremony; a written prayer given by the Rev. J. L. Dance at the same occasion; 1917 coins; a Carson and Newman catalogue for 1917–1918; a November 8, 1912, issue of William Jennings Bryan's paper *The Commoner,* bearing the headline "Congratulations to President-Elect Wilson"; a King James Version of the Bible; a list of alumni; a list of East Tennessee Baptists who helped pay for the building; manuscripts of the *History of Carson and Newman* by W. T. Russell; a September 13, 1917 *Baptist and Reflector;* a September 15, 1917, *Knoxville Journal and Tribune,* containing stories on Russia as a new republic, British forces penetrating into France, and the allotment of a "great war hospital" to Memphis by the federal government; a September 1917 *Royal Service Magazine;* and an ear of corn from A. R. Swann's farm (*Orange and Blue,* March 22, 1974).

The Decline of the Literary Societies

During most of the 1960s, the four literary societies held on to a strong membership among Carson-Newman students. The societies had been the anchor of social life on campus for decades. But as the years went by, fewer students joined the traditional literary societies. Some would have preferred to join chapters of national, primarily social fraternities or sororities, of which there were none at Carson-Newman. The mushrooming of diverse campus activities and clubs affected the membership levels as well; students could choose organizations that aligned with their own interests. The traditions of the literary societies seemed archaic to students who were not interested in learning about them.

LETTER TO THE EDITOR— FEBRUARY 11, 1977, *ORANGE AND BLUE*

"The loss of Henderson Hall in 1974 was, indeed, a tremendous blow to the students, faculty, and alumni of Carson-Newman College. Many precious objects of both monetary and sentimental value were destroyed. Before the disaster, each of the C-N literary societies had its own personal hall, decorated in its particular colors and lushly furnished in the taste of its members. It was particularly devastating to these societies when all of their belongings, some dating back as far as the 1800's, were burned. These belongings, including baby grand pianos, were supposedly insured, but a controversy over the insurance policy has made it impossible for the organizations to receive funds for replacing them. . . .

"It was decided that the societies would have to share two rooms. . . . This edict was disappointing but was not considered unreasonable by the four societies. However, the administration has classified the two meeting halls as multipurpose lecture rooms and refuses to allow the societies to personalize them in any way. Any objects which are put on display for meetings must be packed away immediately at the meeting's end. Also, without any consideration for the wishes of the societies' members, the administration ordered a large number of gold chairs, which almost fill the meeting room from wall to wall. These meeting rooms cannot compare in any way to the beautifully furnished, personal halls that the societies were so graciously granted in the past. They are little better than classrooms. . . .

"An institution which is so proud of its impressive past could make room for four organizations which have played such active roles in its history. It is not only the convenience of the Callies, Columbians, Hyps, and Philos that is at stake here; it is the tradition of Carson-Newman College."

Respectfully,
Harriet A. Miller,
Calliopean Literary Society

The literary societies still met on Friday evenings. The first administrative step that negatively affected them was the elimination of Saturday classes in 1968. Students were free to leave campus for the weekend after their Friday classes were concluded. And as more parking lots were built on campus, restrictions were gradually eased on students having their own cars. Chapel was moved from Fridays to Tuesdays.

Then the loss of Henderson Hall to fire in 1974 heralded the death knell since it had held all four society halls. For three years Philomatheans, Hypatians, Columbians, and Calliopeans had no meeting places. Many members drifted away to other organizations and clubs. Student Harriet Miller wrote an earnest letter warning that an irreplaceable loss was underway.

Sadly, Harriet's articulate plea for the consideration of all four literary societies went unheeded. In 1980, the Callies lost their charter due to lack of interest (*Orange and Blue*, September 17, 1985), as did the Hyps in 1987. Both women's societies rechartered later in the 1980s as Greek sororities, and the men's societies did the same. But during an eight-year period between 1997 and 2005, the Hypatians, Philomatheans, and Columbians ceased to exist.

Of all four literary societies, only the Callies still operate. Keeping the motto "Remember Lot's Wife," today's Callies are known as Chi Lambda Delta, a Christian service organization for women.

The Henderson Humanities Building

The long-awaited Henderson Humanities Building was occupied for the spring semester in 1977. Its exterior appearance was similar to the former Henderson Hall, but not identical. The ground-floor entrance and the installation of an elevator ensured that disabled students could easily access all floors of the building.

The auditorium had a new name: that of former president William Gentry, whose family had remained strong supporters of Carson-Newman (*Orange and Blue*, January 28, 1977). Sharing the first floor with the five-hundred-seat Gentry Auditorium was a small theater, classrooms, the speech and drama departments, and a faculty lounge furnished partly through gifts from Martha Henderson Ashe (*Orange and Blue*, February 11, 1977).

Henderson Humanities Building, completed in 1977.

Besides the balcony level of the auditorium, the second floor housed the Religion and Philosophy Department, classrooms, and two multipurpose rooms initially used for the literary societies, with a capacity of one hundred persons each. The English and Foreign Language Departments occupied the third floor (*Orange and Blue,* January 28, 1977). At first the fourth floor was used for storage, but it has since been developed to serve a number of uses.

William C. Houston, an art professor, prominent landscape painter, and member of the Class of 1973, was commissioned by the Class of 1975 to paint a portrait of the former Henderson Hall. It hangs in the first-floor main hallway of its replacement building. The framed painting, large and luminous, beckons alumni to come close and to recall memories of special times spent in that building with great friends and favorite professors of the past.

In January 1977, a distinguished alumnus came back to Carson-Newman for a semester. T. B. Maston, Class of 1920, served as a visiting professor of ethics, occupying the chair of Southern Baptist Studies. By now he was retired after a long and distinguished teaching career at Southwestern

T. B. Maston, Class of 1920, noted
Baptist ethicist and professor.

Baptist Theological Seminary in Fort Worth, Texas. Maston, a prolific writer, had often been on campus in the summers as a speaker for the Preachers' School.

Interviewed for the February 25, 1977, *Orange and Blue,* he recalled meeting his wife, Essie Mae McDonald, at the college. Sarah Swann Hall was the only building still standing from his student days; the presidents of his era had been Jesse Burnett, William Gentry, and Oscar Sams. He remembered the first administration building at the center of campus, and now he taught in the third building on the same spot.

Maston's advice for Carson-Newman students: "Attend classes regularly, be serious in seeking truth and knowledge, know that God wills a certain quality of life, and seek the will of the Lord concerning the direction in which you are going to go." Those are excellent words for college students of any generation.

CHAPTER ELEVEN

A Vision for Greatness with a Commitment to Place

1977–2000

"'Appalachian' is the fourth word on the college seal, along with 'Truth, Beauty, and Goodness,' the college motto. . . . Give us men (and women) to match our mountains."
—Frieda Burts[780]

"Our college seal calls us . . . to act locally as we think globally, to learn to live well among these communities and rivers, these hills and valleys. To live well with each other in a place may be the one virtue the world needs to learn most if humanity and the earth are to survive the 21st Century. At Carson-Newman, we can teach this virtue because it is our Appalachian heritage and identity. 'And the Word became flesh and dwelt among us.' Likewise, may our ideals as a college become flesh and dwell here in our Appalachia."
—Guy Larry Osborne[781]

The decade of the 1970s was a dizzying period of change at Carson-Newman, indeed across the United States. But in 1977, the Carson-Newman community was given a unique, tantalizing glimpse of just how much the college had changed since the turn of the previous century. In November, ninety-nine-year-old Miss Charlotte Young from Black Mountain, North Carolina, visited the college she had known as Carson and Newman as a freshman and sophomore in 1898 and 1900–1901. She had eagerly absorbed the study of classical literature and Latin; the latter was no longer even taught at Carson-Newman.

While on campus in 1977, she spoke to various groups and read from her books of poetry. "The giving spirit of my professors was a hallmark in my early life," she commented.[782] Her fourth book, *Day of Miracles,* was dedicated to three of them: *To the memory of Jesse Burnett, Shelby Eliot Jones, and "Professor Bob" Henderson, each a devoted scholar, saint, and seer, representing the spirit which is Carson-Newman College.*[783]

Young had spent most of her life teaching English in rural schools in North Carolina and East Tennessee. In her sixties, she completed her undergraduate degree at Western North Carolina College (now University); an undergraduate degree had not been required to teach high-school students until then. She taught until she was eighty-five.

In her sixties Charlotte Young began writing poetry, having loved the art form all her life. Her poems manifested her appreciation of world literature, deep religious convictions, and love of humanity. "I'm the last leaf on the tree," she said wistfully to Carson-Newman students in a creative writing class—an allusion to O. Henry's short story *The Last Leaf*—"but fine young people are an inspiration to me."[784]

Miss Young's memories of her long-ago days at Carson-Newman amazed many who met her in 1977. At a dinner in her honor, she asked the English professor seated beside her, Jeff Daniel Marion, whether Mossy Creek still sprouted the long, graceful green fronds of moss she remembered so well. He regretted having to tell her they had disappeared decades ago when mining was practiced beside the waterway.

As Miss Young spoke of lessons learned from her family and from the classroom, her unquenchable and vibrant spirit impressed her listeners. One audience member asked how she had attained such a depth of understanding of life. In reply, she described witnessing a young girl, entranced with a small bird, who clasped it so hard in her hands that she crushed it. "I learned not to hold any living thing too tightly," she said, "and to be willing to let go."[785]

Incredibly, Charlotte Young returned to Carson-Newman at age 105 and was able to meet a young woman to whom she had given financial support. She was "still quite alert and active," taking one day at a time in deep appreciation of life but ready to go whenever the Lord called her (*Orange and Blue,* October 14, 1983). Charlotte Young died in 1985 at age 107.

Matching the College's Needs with a Presidential Candidate

In 1977, Carson-Newman was still a quality college, but during the 1970s it had stagnated in some ways. Student enrollment had dropped; the college had acquired significant debt; and faculty morale was low. The presidential search committee focused on the need for a strong Christian leader who could balance support for Carson-Newman's liberal arts traditions with the demands of a world on the brink of a new millennium.

The trustees found their choice of candidate in the president of Anderson College (now University), a Baptist school in Anderson, South Carolina. Cordell Maddox was somewhat familiar with Carson-Newman, having occasionally mentioned "that little college in the mountains" to his wife, Brona, and commenting that it was a fine school. He was still relatively young, but experienced enough to have a reservoir of management skills. A good public speaker, he had already proven himself a capable fundraiser.

Maddox had a down-to-earth view of being a college president: "A college president isn't someone in an ivory tower. He is beating the bush, being aggressive, and not getting discouraged when someone says no."[786] He also understood Carson-Newman's twin priorities: "The primary objective of Carson-Newman is learning" and "Carson-Newman's foremost goal is Christian commitment . . . and advancing the interest of Christianity" (*Orange and Blue,* September 19, 1984). He began his work at the college on September 1, 1977, and was inaugurated in April 1978.

Carson-Newman's Longest-Tenured President

A STRONG ADVOCATE FOR EDUCATION AND CHRISTIANITY: JESSE CORDELL MADDOX, TWENTIETH PRESIDENT (1977–2000)

Even as a boy growing up in LaGrange, Georgia, Cordell Maddox (1931–2018) was a standout as a student-athlete. At Furman University in Greenville, South Carolina, on an athletic scholarship he played basketball, tennis, and football, qualifying him as a triathlete. He lettered in all three sports and was known as "Iron Man Maddox" because he sometimes played more than one sport on any given day. (Too, at the time football players often played all four-quarters, both offense and defense.) He was named an All-American athlete in both football and tennis.[787]

Studying religion and English to prepare for a career in ministry, Cordell served as president of the student body, was a member of the Blue Key leadership organization, and participated in ROTC. After graduating, he attended The Southern Baptist Theological Seminary in Louisville, Kentucky, earning two divinity degrees—the BD and the MDiv.[788]

Returning to South Carolina, he worked for the state Baptist Convention—first as Royal Ambassadors coordinator and then as director of the Brotherhood Department. He also served eight years in the US Army Reserves as a chaplain. When Furman invited him back, he answered the call, serving in various administrative roles—director of alumni affairs, director of development and public relations, and assistant to the president.[789]

Next he served as executive vice-president of Anderson College in Anderson, South Carolina for one year before becoming president in 1971. There, he established an excellent relationship with students, faculty, and staff. His fundraising skills helped Anderson College achieve many goals, and he served on several boards in the field of higher education. He also became president of Anderson's Chamber of Commerce and provided leadership in founding the Anderson Arts Council.[790]

When the Carson-Newman presidential search committee came calling, Maddox was interested. Ambitious for the college from the beginning, he later said, "The more I studied it, the more I saw it as a sleeping giant, and we needed to wake it up."[791] On his first visit to campus, he immediately noted the inadequacy of the Baker Building as a student center, a limitation that bothered him for years: "I want the student center to be the hub of the campus. Now it is merely a place that people pass through" (*Orange and Blue,* April 28, 1978).

Over time Maddox grew in depth of maturity and judgment. He had the ability to see things as they were, but also to envision improvements in a way that combined solid business practices, positive relationships with individuals, and forward thinking. Personable, diplomatic, and blessed with a good sense of humor, he nonetheless stood firm on matters crucial to a college, such as academic freedom.

In later years, he received honorary doctorates from the Baptist College of Charleston (now Charleston Southern University) and Furman; the latter also inducted him into their Athletic Hall of Fame in 1986.[792] A few years after he went to Carson-Newman, Maddox was invited to take

J. Cordell Maddox, president 1977–2000.

what once had been his "dream job"—Furman's presidency. But he passed up the opportunity and stayed at Carson-Newman, thus becoming the college's longest-serving president ever, with a tenure of over twenty-two years.

Vision '80: A Campaign for Greatness

In the fall of 1980, the college set in motion a three-year financial campaign with an ambitious title, calling for vision and aspiring to greatness. The effort proved both practical and inspirational, with a goal of ensuring that every program at Carson-Newman would be of high quality. According to the September 26, 1980, *Orange and Blue,* the $4 million campaign outlined specific projects and needs for the next ten years, designed to meet both current and long-range development.

Fulfillment of the base goal, $2.5 million, would cover several objectives for the present: retirement of the college's debt, including the cost of the new music building; renovations needed for several existing buildings; more scholarships; enrichment of the academic program; and making the energy system cost-efficient. Objectives in the challenge goal, the remaining $1.5 million, included completing the fourth floor of Henderson Humanities Building; renovation of the Stokely Building's ground floor; rehabbing recreation and intramural facilities and tennis courts; funding to start up a computer system; library acquisitions; and faculty development (*Orange and Blue*, September 26, 1980).

Sherry Shurden, editor-in-chief of *The Orange and Blue* for the 1980–1981 year, wrote a wise student-centered comment in the April 29, 1981 issue: "Vision '80 for Carson-Newman must go farther than raising money. 'Greatness' for Carson-Newman should mean that every student that comes here is directly challenged to 'greatness.'"

REFLECTIONS ON STUDENTS IN RECENT DECADES

The April 23, 1982, *Orange and Blue* carried an interesting cartoon by David Norris, Class of 1980, from the College Press Service. There were three frames labeled 1962, 1972, and 1982; they made a statement without any accompanying caption.

The 1962 frame showed a crowd of students—clean-shaven young men, some with crew cuts or wearing football helmets, and smiling young women neatly dressed with pageboy haircuts and hairbands. The 1972 frame showed the same faces, but the students had transformed into hippies. Men wore beards along with "granny glasses" and Clapton T-shirts. Their long, scraggly hair was ringed by bandannas around their foreheads. Young women wore wrinkled T-shirts and carried protest signs. The 1982 frame was identical to that of the 1962 frame, suggesting that students of the two decades were alike.

While the 1970s protest era did change the college landscape significantly, the 1980s did not bring a return to the quiet and complacent early 1960s. American college students had changed forever. They now arrived on campus armed with more knowledge than ever before, having been raised in a somewhat more permissive atmosphere. They were more independent and less hesitant to challenge authority and norms. They placed a greater priority on relevance to the current world.

Through Vision '80, the college conducted nine intensive mini-campaigns in various areas of Tennessee, reaching out to alumni and friends in each region. By fall 1981, students were already seeing a difference in increased scholarships and in facelifts for various campus buildings (*Orange and Blue,* September 25, 1981). By early 1982 alumni had given $1.7 million to Vision '80, and the overall goal was extended to $5 million. The final mini-campaign would be centered in Knoxville in 1983, according to the October 22, 1982, *Orange and Blue.*

As recounted in the April 15, 1983, *Orange and Blue,* a grateful Cordell Maddox announced, "Vision '80 has been the most successful campaign in the 132-year history of Carson-Newman. I interpret this success as a vote of confidence from our various constituencies. Through their gifts they are saying, 'I believe in the quality Christian education that is available at Carson-Newman.'" By Thanksgiving, an amazing final total of $5,707,824 had been received (*Orange and Blue,* November 17, 1983).

Ongoing Controversies

From the beginning, Cordell Maddox wanted to support students: "Every deserving student should have the opportunity for a college education" (*Orange and Blue,* October 22, 1982). But the students did not always make it easy for him; nor did he always accommodate them. Right away they asked to hold dances on campus, but he knew the history of that controversy with the Tennessee Baptist Convention and declared the issue too minor to reconsider. Students continued to attend dances held off campus.

Female students continued to press for the same freedoms male students had. Restrictions gradually eased for women to bring cars and to live off campus, and in 1978 women who lived in the residence halls were finally released from having nightly curfews.[793]

Even the location of commencement ceremonies became a tug-of-war issue between seniors and administrators some years; should the college hold an outdoor graduation with open space or a crowded indoor ceremony with air-conditioning? Proponents of each side "won" intermittently.

TENSIONS REGARDING THE ATHLETIC PROGRAM

For years there had been a perception that administrators favored athletes over other students. In 1978, the Supreme Court of the Student

Government Association found a football player guilty of breaking into a concessions machine. He was given a penalty of social probation, which disqualified him from playing for the rest of the season. When Maddox softened the sentence, enabling him to play, an outcry erupted from the students. The president soon addressed six areas of contention on campus, one of which concerned the football player. Maddox assured students that the result would have been the same if the student involved had been on the debate team (*Orange and Blue,* November 17, 1978).

Tensions over athletics continued. Questions often arose about athletic scholarships—why some were bigger than academic scholarships, and why male athletes were awarded more scholarships than female athletes, for example?

RACE RELATIONS

Relationships between black and white students definitely needed improvement. Black athletes, wanting to be known as whole persons, were often stereotyped as talented only in athletics. Some white students were slow to accept blacks as equals or to offer their friendship to African Americans. Therefore, black students tended to band together for social interaction.

Some of the racism on campus could be considered subtle; however, some was overt. When Venyke Cleveland entered the Miss Carson-Newman pageant in 1981 as a black contestant, she received threatening phone calls warning her she should withdraw. According to the March 27, 1981, *Orange and Blue,* her campus room was vandalized while she was out; obscenities and Ku Klux Klan slogans were written in lipstick throughout her room. No one was ever convicted of the incident.

Knowing that there was anti-black sentiment in colleges across the nation at the time did not help; Carson-Newman students should have risen above this pattern and behavior. Various faculty members tried to lead in this effort by example and activism.

CHAPEL VARIATIONS

By the standards of yesteryear—required chapel attendance six days per week plus church attendance on Sundays during Carson-Newman's first one hundred years—students of the late 1970s "had it made." They only had to attend ten chapels per semester, and church attendance was encouraged but not required. In early 1979, chapel was rescheduled from Fridays to Tuesdays, easing the way for students to leave campus for the weekend. But student complaints and extreme rudeness toward chapel speakers continued, embarrassing faculty and administrators every week.

In 1981, a Furman University professor spoke in chapel and experienced the rudeness firsthand. He suggested to administrators that Carson-Newman try some options that would provide some flexibility and lessen the stigma of required chapel. Beginning in January 1982, students were given a list of about twenty-five chapel programs that would meet at various times during the semester. They could choose any ten to attend and did not have to sit in assigned seats. Students liked the plan, and "chapel anxiety" eased (*Orange and Blue,* January 22, 1982).

In the mid-1990s, chapel became a pass/fail "course" under the Community Life and Worship program (*Orange and Blue,* April 28, 1995). Students still had to attend ten chapels per semester, but they could earn credit-hours for attendance—one per year, four maximum over the course of their time at Carson-Newman. The negative aspect came into play if they did not attend ten chapels per semester. In that case, they received an F that impacted their cumulative grade-point average.

Campus Building Changes in the 1980s

A NEW MUSIC BUILDING

The Chambliss Fine Arts Building had long been inadequate for the rising number of music students. Tentative plans called for the enlargement of Chambliss until late 1977, when local trustee Lonas Tarr advocated persuasively for a completely new building for music students. The Chambliss Building became home to the Psychology and Sociology Departments, and a site for a new music building was chosen—the entire block bordered by Russell, South College, and Swann Streets (*Orange and Blue,* September 15, 1978).

Two older homes stood on Russell Avenue in that block and were now "in the way of progress." In the center was Miss Tennessee Jenkins's former home; she had willed it to the college with the stipulation that her house could not be torn down. At the end of the block was "the Johnson Home," once owned by 1930s Bible professor John R. Johnson. For years, the college had rented both homes. (In the 1940s the Johnson home had

An excited crowd attends the grand opening of the new music center at homecoming 1980. The A Capella Choir performed a concert on the front porch.

temporarily housed several women students and was lovingly nicknamed "Johnny's," according to the October 10, 1986, *Orange and Blue.*) The Johnson house was torn down, and the Jenkins home was moved around the corner on the opposite side of South College Street.

The other impediment to replacing the music building was, of course, lack of money—the familiar root of many problems. The new building was envisioned as an impressive structure that would serve 150 music majors and three hundred additional students in general music courses. A new recital hall with perfect acoustics would be the focal point of the building and would also serve as a small auditorium for many needs. The cost was estimated at $2.5 million, of which the college could now pay $1 million. The Vision '80 campaign would pay for the rest (*Orange and Blue,* September 15, 1978).

Construction began in 1978, and the building was completed by the end of 1980. The lobby was named for Ersa Davis, retired longtime department chair, and the large rehearsal room for Charles Jones, director of the A Capella Choir, according to the March 27, 1981, *Orange and Blue.* The two hundred and fifty–seat recital hall was named for donors J. D. and Mildred McNees Thomas. At the dedication Mrs. Thomas commented, "I was a student here at Carson-Newman 60 years ago. At that time we arrived by train and walked from the station up the hill to the campus, where there were about four buildings" (*Orange and Blue,* October 14, 1983).

GENERATIONS OF MUSIC STUDENTS HONORED "FESSOR"

Before Charles Jones retired in 1983, his thirty-eight-year tenure as music professor had earned him many devoted "fans"—especially among the students he had directed and mentored in the A Capella Choir. In 1998, Jones's former students contributed over $210,000 for an endowment supporting the A Capella Choir at Carson-Newman in the name of their beloved "Fessor" (*Orange and Blue,* October 30, 1998). Charles Jones passed away in 2007.

In 2003, the music building, a grand showplace, would be named for Lonas Tarr's mother: The Mabel Lewallen Tarr Music Center. The structure continues to provide excellent facilities for all types of presentations.

A DEVASTATING FIRE AT THE FIRST BAPTIST CHURCH

In the early-morning hours of December 2, 1985, flames were spotted near the pulpit of First Baptist's sanctuary. Firefighters climbed into the building but were unable to locate the fire's source at first. Unfortunately, winds were at forty-five miles per hour. When smoke began pouring from the roof and it ignited, residents of Burnett Residence Hall were evacuated into the cold night. Shortly the steeple crashed into the sanctuary, and the columns supporting the entrance collapsed (*Orange and Blue,* December 9, 1985).

Just as First Baptist had come to Carson-Newman's rescue during the loss of Henderson Hall to fire in 1974, now Carson-Newman gladly helped the church—reverting to "church in the college." Sunday morning church services were held in Gentry Auditorium, with some Sunday School classes meeting in Henderson Humanities Building. Sunday night and Wednesday night services were held in Thomas Recital Hall in the music building.

Carson-Newman was affected by the loss of its weekly chapel space; the number of required chapels decreased from ten to seven for the spring semester. Gentry Auditorium, the new chapel site, was not large enough for everyone, so chapel had to be on a first-come, first-served basis during

First Baptist's rebuilding process (*Orange and Blue,* December 9, 1985). The new sanctuary was completed in 1988.

A FINAL GOODBYE TO CARSON HALL

Known as "the Rankin House" to students of the 1930s–1980s, the former Carson Hall (Campus #2) had been the home of the Rankin family until its sale in the 1980s. The widowed owner, Chlorice Bible Rankin, had hoped Carson-Newman would want to buy back the former home of Carson College; but it was deemed too far from campus and too expensive in light of more pressing matters. She sold the stately house to the Esso (now Exxon) Corporation, which built a gas station beside the home.

Despite the home's excellent condition and historical importance, in January 1987 it was razed (*Orange and Blue,* January 26, 1987). It occupied the space where Taco Bell and Burger King now operate between Highway 11E and East Jefferson Street.

A NEW NAME FOR THE LIBRARY

On May 11, 1989, Carson-Newman's library was officially renamed the Stephens-Burnett Memorial Library in honor of two distinguished families long associated with the college. Charles Burnett Stephens, a contractor and highway engineer from Morristown, had set aside a most generous gift to Carson-Newman in his will.[794]

His sister, Katharine Anne Stephens, was present at the naming ceremony to acknowledge their family's love and support for Carson-Newman. The siblings' parents, longtime Carson-Newman trustee Charles Snapp Stephens and Anne Elliott Burnett Stephens of Morristown, had met and married when they were Carson-Newman students.[795] Anne was a sister of former Carson-Newman president Jesse M. Burnett and distinguished American historian Edmund Cody Burnett; the latter was one of the college's first librarians in the 1890s. The library's new name perpetuated an awareness of the college's history and educational traditions.

Outreach Ministries

Barnabas House was established at Carson-Newman in 1981 as a ministry to support persons in church-related vocations. Named after the New Testament–era Christian who counseled and encouraged early ministers

The Stephens-Burnett Library, 1989.

such as Paul and John Mark, Barnabas House offered services such as confidential counseling, workshops, seminars, a journal, and research on the unique problems ministers face.

William Blevins, the director and a religion professor, noted that ministers sometimes felt unable to discuss their stress factors and problems with friends, church members, or even family members, since a minister's family was supposed to be perfect in the eyes of his congregation.

"This is one way Carson-Newman can 'give back' to the pastors and churches who support our college. When pastors can find help for their own problems or sharpen their skills, then the local churches are enriched. Barnabas House exists for that purpose," Blevins commented to Don Garner, his colleague in the Religion Department (*Orange and Blue*, October 5, 1984).

Appalachian Outreach was founded in 1985 by Kerry and Karen Castle Smith, Classes of 1983 and 1985. As students they learned that helping the poor was at the very heart of Christian service; Jim Wilson, the campus minister at Carson-Newman (Class of 1970), mentored them in serving mountain people. Appalachian Outreach was formed as a community ministry with volunteers providing services that might not otherwise be available, such as home repair—for example, patching or replacing roofs and restoring plumbing—or help in obtaining utility services (*Orange and Blue,* November 12, 1985).

Samaritan House, which began operating in 1987 as a student-led ministry, offered temporary shelter to persons experiencing a crisis in sudden homelessness (from fire, evictions, or foreclosures). In 1997 alone, forty-seven families and 109 individuals were given emergency shelter, food, and clothing (*Orange and Blue,* September 26, 1997).

Appalachian Outreach and Samaritan House now operate as one organization, called the Appalachian Ministries of the Smokies. In 2020–2021, the Appalachian Ministries saw a surge of need related to the Covid-19 pandemic, with greatly increased local demand for temporary housing and donations of food and money. Students who volunteer for these ministries are well versed in serving others.

Innovative Curriculum Advances

THE BIBLE SCHOOL

In the fall of 1979, Carson-Newman founded a two-year program for men and women who had been called into church-related vocations but who lacked the college or seminary training needed. This program replaced the summer Preachers' School dating from the 1930s, with a longer and more deliberate focus for adult students. Called simply "the Bible School," it was affiliated with Carson-Newman but technically not part of it. However, the college awarded an associate in arts degree to its graduates (*Orange and Blue,* September 12, 1979).

The curriculum included Bible, Baptist history, and English courses—classes designed to help adults minister in a small-church setting. The Bible School provided an invaluable service to the Southern Baptist denomination.

GRADUATE COURSES IN RELIGION

In 1980, Carson-Newman partnered with The Southern Baptist Seminary in Louisville, Kentucky, to offer two graduate-level religion courses each semester. Southern Seminary professors traveled to Carson-Newman each week to teach the courses, which benefited many students. According to the October 26, 1979, *Orange and Blue,* the courses would count for either seminary credit or as senior undergraduate classes.

CONTEXT: 1982 EVENTS IN WORLD HISTORY

The World's Fair in Knoxville opened to good reviews but lower attendance than expected. Coach Paul "Bear" Bryant ended his legendary career at the University of Alabama. Michael Jackson's album *Thriller* debuted, and the first compact discs (CDs) were released to the public in Germany. Samuel Morse's painting "Gallery of the Louvre" sold for $3,250,000. The first issue of *USA Today* was published. Great Britain's William, the future Prince of Wales, was born to Prince Charles and Princess Diana. Hank Aaron and Frank Robinson were elected to the Baseball Hall of Fame. Dr. Michael DeBakey performed the first heart transplant. The Vietnam Veterans Memorial Wall opened in Washington, DC; Ronald Reagan was the US president. Sally Ride was named the first American woman astronaut, and Native American athlete Jim Thorpe's gold medals from the 1912 Olympics were reinstated posthumously.

THE NURSING PROGRAM

In 1982, a desire to start a nursing program at Carson-Newman coincided with a public need for more professional nurses. Academic Dean Roy Dobyns headed a committee that developed a cooperative arrangement with East Tennessee Baptist Hospital in Knoxville to offer students an innovative BSN along with practical, supervised training in a hospital setting (*Orange and Blue*, September 10, 1982). In 1985, when the hospital withdrew from the arrangement, Carson-Newman began its own nursing program.

Accreditation did not occur until after 1987, when the college was able to house the program in its own new home, the renovated Jefferson Elementary School building. In 1991, the building was named for Hannah Hylton Pederson, who had headed the public nursing program in Knox County. In 1997, the division began offering a master's degree in Nursing (MSN). Today Carson-Newman also offers a graduate degree in becoming a family nurse practitioner.

Following a sudden destructive fire at the Pederson Nursing Building, the new Drama and Ted Russell Center, a state-of-the-art facility, will house the nursing program and serve as the campus hub for health sciences.

NEW MAJORS AND DIVISIONAL CHANGES

In the late 1970s and early 1980s, several new majors were added. The new communications major replaced the separate speech, drama, and media majors. The Home Economics Department initiated the Child and Family Studies major in 1982. A public administration major was added as well (*Orange and Blue,* October 22, 1982).

Later, new degree programs were offered in photography, medical technology, and data processing. The History Department was the first to include a world perspective with classes focusing on China and Japan. The Religion Department added classes taught by a missionary-in-residence. The significant changes in the college curriculum led to an expansion in the number of divisions from five to eight (*Orange and Blue,* April 15, 1983).

A RETURN TO GRADUATE SCHOOL

In its early history, Carson-Newman had offered a master's degree program, but this practice had ended in the early 1920s. In 1987, the college perceived a new demand for a master's degree program in education, and two graduate programs were set in motion. These were the master of education (MEd), with emphasis on curriculum development and leadership skills, and the master of arts in teaching (MAT), designed for those who had not pursued licensing qualifications as undergraduates (*Orange and Blue,* February 13, 1987).

In 1993, a master's program was added for teaching English as a second language (*Orange and Blue,* November 23, 1992). Later, other graduate degrees were added. Today, Carson-Newman has a healthy enrollment of over one thousand graduate students who are studying to receive any of the numerous graduate degrees offered—some at the main campus, some at the Knoxville center, and some online.

INTERNATIONAL PROGRAMS

Carson-Newman began venturing into an international approach when students took advantage of study-abroad programs. In 1985, an education professor, Ronald Midkiff, led a team of teachers to Zhengzhou, China, to conduct a four-week oral English workshop for Chinese English teachers. In 1986, the Chinese Cross-Cultural Institute was formed, allowing Chinese students to study at Carson-Newman.

From this beginning, an active partnership with international students was initiated. The former residence of Kathleen Manley on Russell Avenue is now home to the Center for Global Education, which administers such programs. Manley, a career missionary to Nigeria for many years before she served as nurse at Carson-Newman, doubtless would approve of the international focus of her onetime home.

The English Language Institute at Carson-Newman is housed in Miss Tennessee Jenkins's former home. There, international students strive to improve their English-language proficiency to the level needed to enter colleges and universities in the United States. Students who graduate from the Institute and earn six credit-hours at Carson-Newman receive twelve credit-hours in English as a second language, which can be used as foreign-language credit.[796]

The Strategic Plan

By 1985, much had improved at Carson-Newman since the Vision '80 Campaign for Greatness, and indeed the campus had seen steps toward greatness. Such steps included:

- a need for a winter commencement, held for the first time in December 1985 with forty-seven graduates (*Orange and Blue,* December 9, 1985*);*
- a steady gain in student enrollment, from 1518 in 1977 to over two thousand in 1988 (*Orange and Blue,* September 20, 1988*);*
- annual budgets in the black since the late 1970s;
- a willingness to accommodate physically disabled students on an individual basis *(Orange and Blue,* February 27, 1990);
- new buildings constructed and older buildings renovated;
- many new majors and academic programs added.

In 1987, the trustees commissioned an objective look at Carson-Newman from a consulting company, Barton-Gillet. Their consultant George Keller, a specialist in higher education, spent quality time on campus, evaluating programs and structures and talking with numerous people at the college. He presented a perceptive look at both strengths and weaknesses of the college. More significantly, he proposed a strategic plan, to be divided into two components over time, and suggested an overall goal for the college: "to become the best small Baptist college in America." At first the time frame for reaching this goal was 2000, the new millennium; soon it was adjusted to 2001, the college's 150th anniversary (*Orange and Blue,* November 29, 1988).

Specific goals Keller gave the college included building a new student center; increasing the number of computers; updating scientific equipment; improving the library collection; awarding more student scholarships; strengthening the honors program; increasing faculty salaries; starting a chapter of Phi Beta Kappa; and improving the architecture on campus (*Orange and Blue,* January 30, 1990).

Carson-Newman's perceived weaknesses included the athletic program, which Keller said was not worth the high cost to the college. In a related observation, Carson-Newman's academic standards were too low for admitting students. Some students admitted specifically for their athletic prowess did not have the background or the willingness to mount a rigorous academic challenge. Yet they were often given large scholarships, which decreased the scholarship pool of money for motivated academic students. High-school athletes often considered Carson-Newman their "fallback" school—they could be admitted there if nowhere else (*Orange and Blue,* March 28, 1989). Carson-Newman was already working on higher academic standards for admitting students.

As for strengths, Keller found many. But most significantly, he identified four areas in which Carson-Newman already excelled but had the potential of achieving national recognition. In a nod to the college's religious orientation, he called them the "Steeples of Excellence" (*Orange and Blue,* November 29, 1988). The college mounted an all-out effort to lift up these four areas in order to become the best small Baptist college in America by 2001.

Steeples of Excellence

APPALACHIAN STUDIES

Carson-Newman proudly touted its home in beautiful East Tennessee, a part of Appalachia and the home of the diverse people of the mountains. Appalachia included areas of grinding poverty; the grandeur of the

Biltmore Estate in Asheville, North Carolina; and everything between. With the word *Appalachian* on the college seal, Carson-Newman had been intimately involved with Appalachian communities and issues for many years. In the last twenty years, especially, the college had made major commitments to the mountain people to increase their pride in their heritage. Those commitments were about to amplify in both substance and number.

WILMA DYKEMAN, AN APPALACHIAN TREASURE

No stranger to Carson-Newman's campus, Wilma Dykeman (1920–2006) returned in 1993 to receive the Outstanding Educational Service to Appalachia award. Dykeman was an extraordinary writer who concentrated on Appalachia as the focus of her books, both fiction and nonfiction. Raised in Asheville near the French Broad River, she married into the Stokely family of Newport, Tennessee, where the river was her neighbor again. Her first book, *The French Broad,* was a collection of vivid facts, stories, and concerns about the river's history and health as pollution and contamination increased. Ultimately becoming part of the Rivers of America series, the book won her both attention and awards.

A subsequent work of fiction, *The Tall Woman,* drew attention to the plight of Appalachian women and the lack of education prevalent in the mountain communities. As an author, professor, public speaker, syndicated columnist, and state historian, Dykeman was ahead of her time in raising awareness about societal and environmental issues through well-written literature.

Michael Carter, vice-president for academic affairs, and Guy Larry Osborne, dean of academic special programs, actively engaged in helping students and faculty learn more about the area where they lived and worked (*Orange and Blue,* October 4, 1991). As an outgrowth of their work, an Appalachian Heritage Week was celebrated every fall on campus, with pertinent demonstrations, programs, and exhibits designed to educate participants about Appalachian culture.

Heritage Week activities included crafts demonstrations (basket weaving, butter churning, and so forth); reading Appalachian literature; performances of Appalachian-based plays or an examination of how Hollywood depicts Appalachian culture in films; clogging; and traditional mountain music. The cafeteria held an Appalachian dinner for students and a potluck for the faculty (*Orange and Blue*, November 19, 1990). English professors R. R. and Ruth O. Turner taught a course in Appalachian folklore in the May mini-term and concluded the course by holding a wide-ranging Appalachian meal for students (*Orange and Blue*, October 4, 1991).

In 1988, Carson-Newman began awarding an annual Outstanding Educational Service to Appalachia award to persons who had made significant, long-term contributions to Appalachia. They included Bill Landry, WBIR-TV creator and narrator of *The Heartland Series*, which highlighted notable history, places, and people in East Tennessee; Guy and Candy Carawan, social justice activists and folk singers at the Highlander Center; and Eliot Wigginton, teacher and author of the *Foxfire Project*, which gained a national following for its depictions of Appalachian rural life. For several years education professor Sharon Teets taught a popular summer course for teachers in the Foxfire method of educating young students.

The Mossy Creek Reader, Carson-Newman's annual literary publication that had begun as *The Eagle's Quill*, refocused its content on regional literature. The editor, poet-in-residence Jeff Daniel Marion—himself from East Tennessee—selected writers who were from Appalachia or whose work revealed Appalachian culture. Each issue had a relevant theme (*Orange and Blue*, February 14, 1992).

In 1991, Carson-Newman's Appalachian Center opened in the yellow frame house next to Burnett Residence Hall. Originally built as the home of former college president William Gentry, the house had been more recently occupied by retired dean I. N. Carr and his second wife, Freda West Blanc Carr.

The newly christened Appalachian Center served as both a museum and a place where Appalachian writers, scholars, artists, and musicians could discuss their Appalachian connections with the community. Center director Jeff Daniel Marion hosted semester-long exhibits and varied programs charting all facets of Appalachian life—photographs, quilts, literature, music, and more. He was "adamant about preserving Appalachian culture, not only because it is his roots, but because the area has always been misunderstood" (*Orange and Blue*, December 7, 1990). Today's

Appalachian Cultural Center maintains a warm sense of place and purpose on campus.

BAPTIST STUDIES

Even before the Tennessee Baptist Convention chose Carson-Newman as its repository for Baptist documents regarding East Tennessee, many invaluable Baptist historical materials had been donated to the archives in Carson-Newman's library. Also, Carson-Newman's Religion Department already offered related courses in Baptist history, theology, and contemporary faith life. The combination of classwork and available study material convinced George Keller that Carson-Newman could become the leading Southern Baptist college in focusing on Baptist Studies.

With the emphasis on Baptist Studies leading the way, Carson-Newman offered special seminars and lecture series, student and faculty research into Baptist history, and the compilation of an archive of papers, books, and correspondence pertinent to Baptist history and heritage. Additionally, the Religion Department added the Oxford Term, in which two highly motivated students at a time were chosen to do extensive research in Baptist history in preparation for a semester of research at Oxford University.[797]

Today, the Baptist Archives are housed in the Stephens-Burnett Library to preserve Middle and East Tennessee's Baptist heritage.[798] The collection contains the minutes, records, annuals, and histories of various churches and associations; ministers' and laymen's papers, diaries, letters, and sermons; and the collections of various missionaries. Also included are early Tennessee Baptist newspapers, Tennessee Baptist Convention annuals, regional state newspapers, and selected Southern Baptist journals. Books of Baptist history, doctrine, missions, and biography are part of the collection (*Orange and Blue,* October 17, 1997).

CHURCH MUSIC

The accomplishments of Carson-Newman's Music Department in the area of church music were impressive. The department had developed a church music library, sponsored the commissioning of new church music, maintained a catalogue of outstanding choral music, and brought outstanding musicians to campus for its students to meet and hear.

In the 1980s, the Louis and Mary Charlotte Ball Institute of Church Music was established at Carson-Newman. Louis Ball was a former

Music Department chair, and his wife, Mary Charlotte, was a beloved music professor. The Institute named for them serves two purposes: to benefit the college's church music program and to serve ministers of music and other scholars as they guide the development of church music on a national and international basis.[799]

Today, the Ball Institute is still active in promoting, conducting, and publishing scholarly research in sacred music. It also preserves a growing collection of piano and instrumental literature, offers workshops for worship leaders, and commissions new works.

WELLNESS

The wellness emphasis centered on the concept of being intentional about maintaining health rather than having to treat illness as a result of neglect. Tom Cronan, chair of the Physical Education Department, advocated lifelong fitness. In his view, Carson-Newman should graduate students committed to a lifelong program of physical health (nutrition, exercise, and so forth) and mental health. He encouraged faculty and staff members to adopt healthy lifestyles, too (*Orange and Blue*, October 21, 1988). The walking trail in Jefferson City's Centennial Park, behind the campus, was used as part of the Wellness Steeple.

The Kathleen Manley Infirmary became the Wellness Center. With a hospital and a number of medical offices nearby, a "sick bay" was no longer needed for students. The Manley Building was reworked to house services in counseling, health, and eventually disabilities. But an additional building was needed for a fitness facility housing all types of equipment for all types of students.

The Holt Fieldhouse served team athletes well, and the Butler-Blanc Gym was still used. But George Keller had advocated de-emphasizing athletics at Carson-Newman. To no one's surprise, the athletic program was not cut. However, Cordell Maddox had always wanted a great student center for all Carson-Newman students. Could a new vision for the student center accommodate wellness fitness facilities too?

Student Activities Center

Initial plans for a new student center called for it to be constructed next to the Holt Fieldhouse. However, discussions resulting from the Wellness

The Maddox Student Activities Building, 2000.

Steeple paved the way for a new plan: one large, multipurpose building that would house a new student center, new intramural facilities and other amenities for all students, and the Holt Fieldhouse for varsity athletes—all combined under one roof. Thus a traditional view of a single-use building gave way to a much greater vision.

The Holt Fieldhouse underwent large-scale renovations in order to better serve its more targeted focus on varsity athletics. The other half of the complex, completed in 1993, was the Student Activities Center that Maddox had envisioned when he first visited campus, "writ large." Dedicated on October 15, 1993, the building was a dream come true for Maddox (*Orange and Blue,* October 29, 1993).

Now truly the hub of the campus, the Student Activities Center contains over ninety-six thousand square feet for the campus post office and bookstore; a market; a Chick-fil-A Express; a TV lounge and the Grand Hall; three full-sized gymnasiums; an indoor running track; game rooms; a weight room; a cardio room; a gymnastics room; meeting rooms; the swimming pool; locker rooms; spaces for intramural sports; walking tracks; classrooms; and numerous offices.

Sports Personalities, Pinnacles, and Programs

Early in his presidency, Cordell Maddox endorsed Carson-Newman's athletic program: "A good sports program is important to the life of the college. . . . We are living in a competitive world, and athletic competition is good and healthy. A strong athletic competitive spirit in all sports is what is needed. . . . Good programs give us visibility and publicity" (*Orange and Blue,* September 16, 1977). He noted, however, that the college was spending a quarter of a million dollars on the athletic program; therefore, careful stewardship of the resources in that area was needed.

In 1979, with **Ron Case** as football coach, the Eagles dedicated their season to **Sam "Frosty" Holt,** fifty years after he began coaching at his alma mater. The team did well (*Orange and Blue,* September 12, 1979). After Frosty's death in 1986, memorials to him abounded. None topped student Andy Rines's column about him in the October 14, 1989, *Orange and Blue.* Rines described a football game against Mars Hill College when Frosty was sixty-five. A Mars Hill player accidentally knocked Frosty down. "Frosty got up slowly, hitched his pants in a way that had become trademark for him, and said, 'Nobody from Mars Hill is tough enough to take me out.' C-N won 14–12."

Rines opined: "Frosty's influence was as deep as his fire was bright. . . . Frosty was also a pioneer. At the end of his era, C-N was the first private liberal arts school in the South to break the color barrier. . . . Frosty Holt was C-N's answer to Bear Bryant, and when he died we said goodbye to a legend."

THE ATHLETICS HALL OF FAME

In 1984, homecoming activities included the installation of a brand-new Athletics Hall of Fame: "Eagle Athletic Heritage . . . Then and Now." There were eight initial inductees: Dana X. Bible, Bernie W. Moore, Ernest Tucker (a Class of 1924 baseball and tennis standout and an innovative career high-school coach), Mae Iddins, Lake Russell, Sam "Frosty" Holt, Milas "Slim" Shoun (an outstanding 7'3" basketball player in the Class of 1927), and Roy Harmon (*Orange and Blue,* October 5, 1984).

In 1980, **Ken Sparks,** Class of 1967, became head football coach. The following year, Cordell Maddox was questioned about why football was allotted such a high percentage of the college's athletic budget. "Football brings in more money than any other sport; therefore, football will get the emphasis over other sports," he answered (*Orange and Blue,* December 4, 1981).

In 1990, the Eagles won their fifth NAIA football championship (out of seven tries). The same year they had an undefeated season, 10–0, their first in fifty-four years (*Orange and Blue,* November 19, 1990). Sparks became an icon with the longest tenure of any Carson-Newman football coach.

Chris Jones, head basketball coach, tendered his resignation in February 1988, but in 1989 he attended the homecoming game to be honored with other Carson-Newman Hall of Fame members at halftime. He later completed a successful career at Lincoln Memorial University, but never lost his love for Carson-Newman and continued to be a strong supporter of the college.

In 1987, **Bobby Wilson** retired from coaching baseball; his jersey and number, 38, were retired as well. In 1986, he had been inducted into the NAIA Baseball Hall of Fame after winning the title Tennessee Valley Athletic Conference Coach of the Year (*Orange and Blue,* April 27, 1987). Both he and his wife, **Martha Wilson,** continued to teach physical education courses at the college for several years. Bobby Wilson passed away in 2008, Martha Wilson in 2022.

By the 1990s, Carson-Newman's sports program had expanded well beyond the traditional football, basketball, and baseball. Other sports played were volleyball, tennis, cross-country, wrestling, soccer, track, softball, and golf. Athletics moved from the NAIA to the NCAA for its advantages in prestige, visibility, and financial benefit (*Orange and Blue,* October 31, 1991). But the move had a negative side as well—the increased level of difficulty in competitions.

Jean Love, a Carson-Newman senior in 1983, became Carson-Newman's first All-American in women's tennis (*Orange and Blue,* March 31, 1983). With a 3.88 GPA, she was a model for any athlete to follow. After earning graduate degrees at Vanderbilt University and the University of Tennessee, in 1988 she returned to her alma mater as tennis coach, following in the footsteps of her mentor, **Libby Hudson Gardner**. In 2018, Love stepped down as head tennis coach after thirty years but continued to teach physical education for several years.

Vickee Kazee-Hollifield, also from the Class of 1983, returned to her alma mater in 1985 as the women's softball coach. By 1995, her team had won the South Atlantic Conference for the fourth time in six years, and in 2013 the softball complex at Carson-Newman was renamed for her—popularly called "the Vick." In 2014, she logged an amazing one thousand victories with her teams.[800] She retired from Carson-Newman in 2018 after thirty-three years of coaching.

Special Events

TENNESSEE HOMECOMING '86

Governor Lamar Alexander declared 1986 the year for Tennesseans to celebrate their home and heritage, including those who had moved away. All kinds of homecomings, large and small, would be held in various parts of the state during the year.

Carson-Newman's alumni director, Nelson Ross, had suggested to Alexander that on January 1, 1986, all kinds of bells should be rung at the state Capitol and throughout Tennessee. To the governor, the bell ringing signified "not only ringing in the new year, but also the calling home of Tennesseans from across the nation" (*Orange and Blue,* January 28, 1986).

Jefferson County was chosen as a pilot community for the statewide celebration. Editions of *The Orange and Blue* detailed several local homecoming events. On May 19, the Tennessee Homecoming Special train made a whistle stop in Jefferson City. On July 26, a county celebration was held on the grounds of Henderson Humanities Building, with a new county cookbook for sale. And in October, Carson-Newman's traditional homecoming celebration was expanded to a three-day event and reunited all classes of alumni. Tennessee flags were displayed all over campus.

Students had fun decorating their residence halls for homecoming '86. Butler Hall occupants placed a quilt on "Granny Butler's Feather Bed" for their front yard, with the name and hometown of each resident written on a quilt square. Alumni Hall inhabitants followed a Civil War theme and constructed a Union cannon and Rebel camp on their lawn. A float decorated New Men's yard. The front of Burnett Hall was transformed into a log cabin, complete with a wishing well and an outhouse. Sarah Swann Hall residents dressed in old-fashioned apparel and decorated their home with a picket fence, lemonade stand, and tire swings (*Orange and Blue,* October 10, 1986).

A ROUSING DEBATE

On October 16, 1995, an old-style British debate was revived at Carson-Newman for a match-up between Carolyn Blevins, religion professor, and John Wells, political science professor. Their topic—"Men and Women are Different, and These Differences are Sufficient to Demand Same-Sex Institutions of Higher Learning"—was designed to elicit student emotions and reactions about same-sex schools versus coed schools.

John Wells took the "pro" side and Carolyn Blevins the "con" side. The debaters were in top form, and students were stirred to think and evaluate the facts and implications of each side. After the opening arguments were set forth, two long lines—pro and con—of enthusiastic students formed to speak. Students were invited to change lines as they changed their minds. A student vote for choice—whichever type of school one chooses—closed the evening, and many expressed the wish for more such debates (*Orange and Blue,* October 27, 1995).

AN HONORARY DOCTORATE FOR DOLLY PARTON

On October 21, 1990, Carson-Newman bestowed an honorary doctoral degree on one of the best-known and hardest-working figures in Tennessee: Dolly Parton, acclaimed singer, songwriter, and actress. Having had an illiterate father who struggled to provide for his large family in Sevier County, Dolly realized the value of education and literacy from a young age. "I don't want my people to be ignorant anymore. I want them to have every opportunity," she said. "Today the world has gotten smaller through communication and transportation. Everyone needs to be fluent in the language of that new world, and fluency comes through education" (*Orange and Blue,* October 26, 1990).

Two years after her Dollywood theme park became a resounding success, Dolly created the Dollywood Foundation in 1988, offering college scholarships to local high-school students. At the time Carson-Newman honored her, she was meeting with educators concerned about the 35 percent dropout rate in Sevier County. These conversations led to the Buddy

Program—her plan to motivate local high-school students not to drop out by presenting them a sizable check after graduation.

Today, the Dollywood Foundation is the inspiration behind Imagination Library, which provides preschoolers with free age-appropriate books each month. Dolly Parton is legendary for her outstanding commitments to advancing education in Tennessee and beyond.

Of Minds and Miracles

The Strategic Plan adopted in 1987 necessitated a bold, unprecedented financial campaign that was initiated in the fall of 1991. Called "Of Minds and Miracles," the campaign would double Carson-Newman's resources with a mind-blowing goal of $50 million—ten times the goal in the "Vision for Greatness" campaign in 1980. Every gift would matter greatly.

The campaign was targeted to achieve many milestones. Strengthening the college's endowment, paying for the impressive new Student Activities Center, and increasing faculty salaries to retain excellent professors were only a few of the objectives. Those leading the charge also knew that funds would be needed for future uses: "We are now at the point where we must educate people in what nobody knew yesterday, and prepare them for what no one knows today, but what they must know tomorrow," Cordell Maddox said, quoting Margaret Mead (*Orange and Blue,* January 30, 1998).

"Of Minds and Miracles" successfully concluded in 1997 with $51.6 million given by 8,882 donors. In his inspiring twenty-first state of the college address, presented at the January 1998 faculty meeting, Maddox looked to both present and future: "The dawning of a new century must challenge all of us to shake loose from apathy and to take hold of those things that really matter. And I believe that Carson-Newman matters, that Christian education matters, that teaching values in a Christian environment matters, and that a quality liberal arts program such as this college provides is not a luxury but a necessity" (*Orange and Blue,* January 30, 1998).

Having used in his speech the motif of a clock about to strike midnight for the new millennium, 2000, and the college's upcoming 150th anniversary in 2001, he concluded, "The state of Carson-Newman is strong and when the clock strikes twelve the college will be prepared, ready, and eager for the challenges and opportunities of the next 150 years." Surely the triumphant, indeed miraculous, conclusion to this financial campaign resulted in one of the college family's greatest outpourings of Truth, Beauty, and Goodness in its long history.

NEW GATEWAY ENTRANCE

Since the Carson-Newman campus had no formal entrance, a spot between the Butler-Blanc Gymnasium and the Warren Building was chosen to meet this need in 1992. Located alongside Ken Sparks Way, this gateway is marked by steps leading to prominent white columns, symbolizing academia.

Computers: "The Wave of the Future"

From a vantage point well into the twenty-first century, looking back to the days before computers were common seems almost comical now. But just a few decades ago, computers were the equivalent of science fiction. The few that existed in the 1970s were almost the size of a room, used reels to process and record information, and made weird grunting sounds. But no one minded because the "someday" potential of computers seemed miraculous.

The first computer on Carson-Newman's campus was housed in the Dougherty Science Center, and adding more was a high priority. The library received the next one in 1982; the same year registration for the fall semester was accomplished by computer rather than in person. Generally the process went well, but there were some glitches. For example, classes were assigned on a first-come, first-served basis, without regard to whether the student was a freshman or a senior. The necessary adjustments were made, and overall students were thrilled with the new system. However, long lines were not abolished yet; students still had to line up in the treasurer's office to pay their bills (*Orange and Blue,* September 10, 1982).

Thanks to Vision '80 and a large donor gift that enabled the college to offer a major in data processing, changes continued. In 1985, Carson-Newman received a five-year grant from the Pew Trust for $50,000 each year, to be used for computer instruction for the faculty. Physics professor

John Burton took a leave of absence to earn a master's degree in computer science, then returned to help the faculty develop computer skills.

In 1986, amid renovations to Stokely Memorial's ground floor, a new computer lab was installed with twenty-four AT&T terminals and eight printers. An April 7, 1986, article in *The Orange and Blue* stated that, at present, only 4 percent of Carson-Newman students had computers, but that number was expected to rise. Individual computers were first used in Carey Herring's statistics classes (*Orange and Blue,* November 29, 1988).

Thanks to another grant from the Pew Foundation, Carson-Newman's mainframe computer system was placed in the annex to the Dougherty Science Center (*Orange and Blue,* October 4, 1988). An excited President Maddox predicted that computerization would revolutionize student living. Students would access academic information online and prepare term papers from their rooms. The entire campus would be wired; students could go to any computer and log on. Electronic mail would become popular. Eventually students could use the computer resources in the library instead of the massive card catalogue cabinets.

In 1994, the World Wide Web was born—the Internet as we know it today—and students quickly took to it. In the library, a new computer lab opened in 1996. The following year, *The Orange and Blue* reported that students now used the Internet for everything—research, entertainment, shopping, and so on (February 14, 1997).

CARSON-NEWMAN HIGHLY RATED

The forward strides taking place at Carson-Newman brought the college new positive attention from influential college ratings publications. In 1996, *Money Magazine* rated it "one of the best college buys now" (*Orange and Blue,* October 11, 1996); the student writer commented that such ratings helped students appreciate their school.

By the fall of 1997, Carson-Newman was "the only liberal arts college in the south to be recognized on all three lists (quality, value, and cost efficiency) in the 1998 *America's Best Colleges Guide,*" a publication of *U.S. News and World Report* (*Orange and Blue,* September 26, 1997).

In 1998, emeritus chemistry professor Carl Tabb Bahner donated an eight-station computer lab to the English Language Institute on campus. Dr. Bahner had long been involved in exacting cancer research and was an icon on campus. Also having been interested in foreign missions since childhood, Bahner was thrilled to learn that a lab was needed to support international students at Carson-Newman, knowing his resources would allow him to fund such a gift. As a longtime scholar and eminent scientist, the ninety-year-old Bahner made the leap into "the computer age" look easy for anyone of any age (*Orange and Blue,* September 25, 1998).

New Campus Chapters of National Educational Programs

BONNER SCHOLARS

Carson-Newman began participating in the Bonner Scholars program in 1991, just one year after the four-year national scholarship program was launched. The forty scholars complete 280 hours of community service annually as a strong team, with ten incoming students accepted into the program per year. The students also complete a cornerstone project during their four years and are given several opportunities to lead a group. Topics discussed and researched during peer meetings include time management, conflict resolution, poverty reduction, and education reform.[801]

Over sixty-five college and universities nationwide now have a Bonner Scholars Program on campus; Carson-Newman's chapter was one of the first.

LABORATORY FOR LEARNING

In 1992, Carson-Newman was selected as one of seventeen colleges in the nation to broaden the understanding of learning within the college community by forming a Laboratory for Learning. The founder, Ernest Boyer, a specialist in higher education, maintained that students in American colleges should be unified by more than parking grievances and football rallies. He saw everything students did on campus, from academics to athletics to dining to late-night gatherings in the residence halls, as interwoven.

Twin hallmarks of the Laboratory for Learning were (1) an understanding that learning can occur anywhere, and (2) a recognition that relationships among participants contributed to the learning process. Students learned how to connect classroom instruction with issues related to life.[802]

Laboratory for Learning participants at Carson-Newman formed teams of students, faculty, and staff to implement programming within their respective areas. For example, biology students teamed with their professor, Bob Trentham, and Tennessee Valley Authority (TVA) staff members in an effort to clean polluted Mossy Creek and to learn more about water life (*Orange and Blue,* December 8, 1995). An English professor, Andy Hazucha, took his students on a field trip to Emert's Cove in the Great Smoky Mountains, a rural generations-old settlement containing a graveyard where some Revolutionary War veterans were buried. There a colleague of Hazucha's read aloud his poem about the sights, atmosphere, and meaning of Emert's Cove.

The concept of the Laboratory for Learning seemed to undergird a remark Cordell Maddox had made about education years earlier: "I really believe . . . that a diploma is not going to be worth much in the future unless you've got an education to go with it" (*Orange and Blue,* November 20, 1984). The Laboratory for Learning was a factor in Carson-Newman's goal to become the best small Baptist college in America.

College vs. University

In 1995–1996, the faculty and staff of Carson-Newman considered a major change of direction, that of becoming a university rather than remaining a college. As a sign of the times, numerous other colleges were making the switch to become universities.

At Carson-Newman, a task force carefully considered the definitions and implications of both possibilities, with some group members favoring a change and others preferring for the school to continue operating as a college. In the end, after much discussion, the consensus was for the school to remain a college (*Orange and Blue,* September 27, 1996). This decision held until 2013, when Carson-Newman became a university.

A Retirement Full of Surprises

Students had been teasing Cordell Maddox that he would never retire, but in the spring of 1999 he announced that July 31 would be his last day as president. Viewing Jefferson City as home after twenty-two years, he would continue to live in the area. "I have had the blood transfusion to blue and orange," he said with a smile (*Orange and Blue,* March 2, 1999). He would relinquish to his successor the honor of steering the college during its 150th anniversary in 2001—the deadline for all his hard work in striving to make Carson-Newman the best small Baptist college in America.

The college held a banquet in his honor in June 1999 and, as a surprise, named the Student Activities Center after him. While he and guests were inside dining and enjoying the program, workers outside were busy replacing the sign on the building to read "Maddox Student Activities Center."[803] On hearing of the honor before seeing the sign, he was speechless.

The other surprise for Maddox was that he continued serving as Carson-Newman's president into the new millennium. The next president was not able to begin his service until January 31, 2000, so the trustees asked Maddox to serve as his own interim president for a few more months.

FINALLY, A STUDENT HAD THE LAST WORD

As a senior, Angela M. Blair, the editor of *The Orange and Blue* 1998–1999, wrote a significant column in the November 20, 1998 issue: "The past four years of my life have been an incredible journey that have brought me to this place and shaped me into the person that I now am, or am becoming . . . I will tell anyone who asks that I love this place, that God brought me here against my will for a reason, and I am thankful that He did, because—in my opinion, this is already the best small Christian college in the world."

Carson-Newman's identity as a Baptist college had always been essential to President Maddox, but a point of controversy with Baptists emerged toward the end of his tenure. Originally in the history of Carson-Newman, the trustee board had nominated and chosen successors when vacancies occurred.[804] But this practice changed when the college aligned with the Tennessee Baptist Convention in 1919. The state convention disallowed naming anyone outside Tennessee to the board and reserved the right to approve or deny any persons nominated as trustees.

In light of ongoing disagreements about education and theological issues among Tennessee Baptists, in April 1998 Carson-Newman's trustees voted to return to the college's original charter of self-perpetuating trustees.[805] They wanted the option to select some trustees, especially alumni, living outside of Tennessee who supported Carson-Newman's historical mission. Their desire for stability and growth for the college drove the issue.

As a compromise with Tennessee Baptists, they proposed that all new trustees be active members of Baptist churches, with no more than 25 percent located outside Tennessee. Several Baptist colleges elsewhere had reached similar agreements with their state conventions.

The Tennessee Baptist Convention supported Carson-Newman with $2.4 million annually, but that was a relatively small percentage of the college's budget. The money was primarily used to fund student scholarships.

Meeting in November 1998, a substantial majority of messengers to the Tennessee Baptist Convention voted to withhold any contribution to Carson-Newman until a satisfactory agreement could be negotiated.[806] "Our academic integrity is not for sale," declared Maddox (*Orange and Blue,* November 20, 1998). The matter remained unresolved until his successor took office.

CHAPTER TWELVE

Carson-Newman in the Twenty-First Century—Coming Full Circle

2000–2018

On December 31, 1999, the world braced for a new century, uncertain of what was to come at the dawn of a new era. This was true for those in New York City, watching the ball drop in Times Square, but it was also true on the campus of Carson-Newman College. The next two decades would test the college's mettle while also providing exciting new opportunities for expansion.

Since the meeting of the Oak Tree Five in 1849, Carson-Newman has undergone many changes, but always at the heart of the college's mission has been to give men, and later women, a solid Christian educational foundation from which they could be a force for good in their communities. Even in the early days, the Mossy Creek Seminary placed a heavy emphasis on the quality of learning—students took classes in Greek, Latin, and rhetoric while also enrolling in courses that emphasized practical skills like bookkeeping. One thread running continuously throughout the college's history is its dedication to Christian higher education with a liberal arts foundation. This foundation would be tested many times throughout the college's history, but each time the institution emerged from these challenges with a renewed sense of purpose and dedication to this cause.

In this sense, the first two decades of the twenty-first century provided many continuities with the past, while also presenting new challenges and opportunities for the college. As we look forward, Carson-Newman University has in many ways come full circle from its beginnings as Mossy Creek Seminary. Although Carson-Newman is now a university with a wide variety of majors, minors, and emphases along with thriving graduate school curricula, that original mission still fuels the faculty, staff, and students who work, live, and study in Jefferson City, Tennessee.

Carson-Newman in the Wider Baptist World

Carson-Newman is certainly a special and unique place, especially for its former students, and it also belongs to a wider community of Christian colleges and universities. These relationships are incredibly important for the health of the college, but they also exist within a wider network of Baptist affiliations. Carson-Newman first signed an agreement with the Tennessee Baptist Convention (TBC) in 1919. As part of this relationship, the TBC grants funds to Carson-Newman each year through their Cooperative Program; and in exchange, the TBC appoints members of the college's Board of Trustees from a list of nominees provided by the college. Naturally, the TBC wants Southern Baptists to serve on the board, and thus Carson-Newman always nominated Southern Baptists for those seats.

However, by the mid-1990s many of our sister schools in the Baptist world wanted to change the way their trustees were elected. Namely, they wanted to choose their own board members, so that they could elect members to the board who had special connections to their campus but were not necessarily affiliated with a Southern Baptist church. This desire stemmed from a practical need to expand their abilities to fundraise—for example, many major donors/alumni might not be Baptist but wanted to participate in the future direction of their school. It was also an ideological issue, as universities such as Samford argued that state Baptist associations were becoming too aggressive in their attempts to force both board members and faculty to publicly announce their fealty to certain theological positions, such as biblical inerrancy.

Throughout the 1990s, colleges broke away from their state Baptist state associations in rapid succession. Baylor, Furman, Mississippi College, and Samford were just a few of the schools that severed ties in order to have more control over their board, while also ensuring academic freedom for their faculty. Each of the schools that broke away had to make a choice—did they want to completely sever ties, or did they want to maintain those relationships but keep the power of choosing trustees for themselves? In April of 1998, Carson-Newman chose the latter option under the leadership of President Maddox and the Board of Trustees. When they announced this decision, the press release emphasized that the change "in no way signifies a lessening of Carson-Newman's commitment to Tennessee

Baptists or a shift from its strong Baptist heritage and roots."[807] The college would still have Baptist trustees, but now they could be Baptists from other states; and they would be chosen by the board rather than at the state convention.

Despite these assurances, there were still concerns, particularly among more conservative elements of the TBC, that this change was part of a broader shift at Carson-Newman away from Baptist orthodoxy. However, it must be remembered that this was not just a fight about Carson-Newman, but part of a broader conflict about the nature of Baptist life and governance. Groups such as the Concerned Tennessee Baptists worried that too many moderates were being elected to important positions within the TBC itself. They feared that this lack of conservative voices at the highest echelons of power allowed the various institutions of higher education too much leeway to pursue certain strands of intellectual inquiry. Religion departments were a lightning rod for attention for these groups and their monthly newsletters. Ultimately, this was not a fight about Carson-Newman, but the college was an important symbol in this larger conflict about faith and freedom within Baptist life.

President Maddox strongly defended the right of the college to maintain its standards regarding academic freedom. In an interview with the *Knoxville News-Sentinel,* he said, "We are a liberal arts college, which means we're seeking truth, wherever it leads. And some of the conservative people are not happy with that and they would like for us to be another type of institution."[808] In the same article, the president of the TBC, Rev. Doug Sager, responded by highlighting the importance of accountability to the convention because the college received significant funding from the Cooperative Program every year. Sager argued, "It's not about any takeover, only about having a say in where and how the convention funds are used."[809] The TBC confirmed this stance the very next month during its annual meeting in Kingsport. There, the convention voted to hold Carson-Newman's yearly contribution in escrow until the college backed down and reverted to the old system of trustee appointments.

New Leadership and Old Problems

In the spring of 1999, Dr. Maddox announced he would retire in July, and the Board began the search for his replacement. In the interim, Dr.

Maddox continued to serve, remaining in office until January 2000. After an exhaustive search, they chose Dr. James Netherton to be the college's twenty-first president. Dr. Netherton came to Carson-Newman from Samford University, where he worked as provost. Prior to his work at Samford, Netherton served as vice-president and chief operating officer at Baylor University. Each of these schools dealt with controversy surrounding their relationship with their respective state conventions, and the board believed that these experiences made Netherton an attractive candidate for president. In their first interview after his appointment, Netherton and board chair, Dr. Marvin Cameron, both highlighted his ability to repair the strained bonds between convention and college. As Dr. Netherton put it, "We're talking about a refinement. We're not talking about a divorce."[810]

As part of his program of refinement, Netherton's first step was to return money given to the college by various Tennessee churches that had supported the school's bid for self-appointed trustees. The college returned this money to the convention as a *mea culpa* for its original decision. The next step was to amend the college's bylaws, which the board did in November of 2000. This revision removed the April 1998 language and reinstated the TBC's right to appoint trustees, with certain provisions protecting board members from removal of their post by the convention. In response to these actions, the TBC released the funds they had held in escrow since 1998. Despite the importance of the funds to the operations of the college, Netherton maintained that in the end this was not a fight about money. "This is about the proper form of a relationship. And if you get the relationship right, the money takes care of itself."[811]

However, there were still problems with the relationship, namely a group within the TBC still worried about Carson-Newman's ideological position on a host of theological and scientific questions. Some were also worried that the convention did not have enough power to remove trustees and faculty who did not adhere to the ideas expressed in the Baptist Faith and Message, which had been revised in 2000. The first Baptist Faith and Message was released in 1925 and laid out the doctrinal positions of many in the denomination while also reaffirming the importance of spiritual liberty within the Baptist tradition. The newest version of the document highlighted issues that many within the SBC felt were of paramount importance at the turn of the century—namely gender, Scripture, and polity.

James Netherton, president 2000–2007.
(Courtesy of Hester Photography.)

Because Baptists are a non-creedal people, the Baptist Faith and Message (BFM) is primarily an explanatory tool, rather than a regulatory one. Despite this historical understanding, some wanted to use the BFM as just that—a regulatory tool designed to enforce orthodoxy in Baptist institutions of higher education. There were fears that these kinds of tactics would be used at Carson-Newman, but Netherton provided assurances that the academic freedoms enjoyed by professors and students would not be stymied in any way. This allayed fears in the short-term, but questions of academic freedom and integrity would reemerge periodically throughout the following decade.

Tragedy Strikes

The fall of 2001 was supposed to be a special time on Carson-Newman's campus. The college prepared to celebrate its sesquicentennial, 150 years of academic excellence and student life. Our motto for this celebration,

"A Heritage of Faith, a Future of Excellence," aptly captured the feeling on campus as students and faculty returned in August. On the morning of September 11, 2001, that celebratory feeling disappeared as news reports began covering the attacks perpetrated by al-Qaeda. Terrorists hijacked four airliners, flying two planes into the north and south towers of the World Trade Center in New York. The third plane crashed into the Pentagon and the fourth plane, destined for Washington, DC, crashed in Pennsylvania after brave passengers fought back against their attackers. The first plane crashed into the North Tower at 8:46 a.m. and the second plane hit the South Tower at 9:03 a.m. Within two hours, both buildings collapsed.

As this terrible day unfolded, Carson-Newman students and faculty members were preparing for the Founder's Day Chapel, and many of them had not heard about the attacks. Dr. Netherton led the student body in prayer after announcing the terrible news. His prayer called for wisdom, unity, and mercy for our nation and the world. Both students and faculty were dumbfounded by the events, and it was hard to understand how to move forward—how would faculty talk about the tragedy with students? How would students respond to this attack? How did our international students and their families feel? President Netherton and Provost Michael Arrington decided to keep the college open because they believed it was part of Carson-Newman's unique mission as a Christian college to minister to students in the midst of this tragedy. The planned birthday celebration for the college turned instead into a candlelit prayer vigil, which gave students an organized space and time for their prayer concerns and grief.

New Challenges

Despite achieving the milestone of 150 years of service as a college, Carson-Newman faced serious problems heading into the new century. As a tuition-driven school, the college needed to grow its student body to maintain its yearly budget needs. Unfortunately, the upcoming years were to be lean ones, with consistent drops in student enrollment each fall, which led to harsh budgetary constraints. It would be up to President Netherton to steer the college through these stormy waters, while also dealing with continuing questions concerning academic freedom on campus. In addition to these problems, a rift began to develop between faculty and administration. Many faculty members were concerned about a lack of communication among the president's office, the Board of Trustees, and faculty. The next four years would be spent dealing with these problems, while also setting forth a strategic vision for the campus and working on re-accreditation in partnership with the Southern Association of Colleges and Schools (SACS).

A STUDENT'S LIFE AT C-N

Jennifer Sauceman came to Carson-Newman to run cross-country and study biology in 2000. CNC, as it was still called then, felt like a welcoming place, full of sports opportunities, campus activities, and academic rigor. C-N's dedication to the liberal arts appealed to her own wide-ranging intellectual interests, as did the vaunted honors program, under the direction of Dr. Mark Hussung. Her experiences at C-N reflect how well the college exceeded her expectations. As an honors student, she took Faith and Freedom, a team-taught class that delved into the life and theology of Dietrich Bonhoeffer to examine how faith confronts evil. She also studied Baptist history at Regent's Park College at Oxford University, which certainly fulfilled her wish for academic rigor and liberal arts studies! Although the college experienced bouts of turmoil during her time as a student, her professors remained dedicated to her education above all else. C-N's cross-country team also excelled, competing in the Division II National Championships during her four seasons of competition. After graduation, she went on to medical school and is now a practicing pediatrician in the area.

In 2001, the college began a year of self-study that would culminate in a report presented to SACS. That study, and SACS's response to it, would determine CNC's accreditation status; therefore, it was extremely important to present a full accounting of the state of the college. Drs. Jim Coppock and Mark Heinrich worked closely with administration to develop the self-study, but there were many hurdles to overcome before re-accreditation could be secured. One problem immediately facing the team tasked with making the report was the college's lack of a strategic plan. Netherton's background in academia left him well prepared for certain aspects of leadership, but he preferred a freewheeling style of leadership with less formal planning in terms of written documents. This, combined with the college's murky financial situation, did not please SACS, and the college was placed on probation, with a revisit scheduled for the 2011 school year.

This setback did not ease tensions between college personnel and the president, as faculty continued to meet with each other and in formalized listening sessions to explain their concerns about the future of the college. Their priorities were declining enrollment, lack of financial clarity, and concerns regarding academic freedom. Each of these problems was clearly articulated, but the disconnect between faculty and administration remained firmly in place, in addition to a general lack of communication between faculty and the Board of Trustees. The issue came to a head in 2005, as direct action against the administration became more widespread and organized. Faculty, both current and retired, as well as alumni, began meeting to discuss the future of the college and its leadership. They also formed two groups, Friends of Carson-Newman College and Concerned C-N Alumni and Friends, which appealed directly to the board and the president for a change in direction. Neither group directly called for Netherton's removal from office, but they did highlight the very serious problems facing the college—namely, declining enrollment and the college's financial health. From 2000–2005, student enrollment declined 11.9% while other colleges and universities saw increases during the same time frame. Because the college relied so heavily on tuition as a revenue generator, the salaries of faculty and staff stagnated, which contributed to a general sense of low morale across campus.

For most of the 2005–2006 school year, these two groups tried repeatedly to find solutions for the college's problems. They met with the president and provost directly, they connected with trustees, they created a website to air grievances; but it seemed that little progress was being made. On October 2, 2006, the faculty council met and discussed voting on a resolution of no confidence against President Netherton. A memorandum was sent to faculty and staff laying out the plans for this vote, which would take place on Thursday, October 5. In this memorandum, the council detailed the myriad ways it had attempted to work with administration for the betterment of the college, but it saw no discernible action to fix problems. Therefore, its only option was the vote of no confidence.

The vote was held on a sunny morning, with local press standing outside the Tarr Music Building to hear the results and attempt to get quotes from faculty and staff. The text of the vote highlighted the several key items of concern for faculty and staff—the financially precarious nature of the college, declining student enrollment, lack of strategic planning, the fearful climate of retribution created by administration, low morale, and a failure to maintain "a sense of Christian community and professionalism." Retired faculty and alumni also passed votes of no confidence in solidarity with faculty and staff. In response to the vote, both the board and President Netherton released public statements. The board acknowledged that certain problems needed to be addressed, which should happen within a constructive framework for both faculty and administration. Netherton sought to transform the conflict into one that would turn negative judgments into constructive processes. The local press interviewed several people connected with the college community, with Netherton highlighting the recent success of a capital giving campaign, and others arguing that this vote was not against the president personally, but rather a forcible call to deal with the college's problems before it passed the point of no return.[812]

After the vote of no confidence, the board instituted a series of listening sessions, and in the new year Dr. Netherton gave several conciliatory interviews to local news outlets. The listening sessions were for faculty, staff, and alumni and were held throughout the spring 2007 semester in various locations throughout the region. These listening sessions made clear just how long-standing these grievances were, with some faculty members seeking no confidence votes as early as 2002, but having held off until they felt the situation had reached a tipping point. Recent alumni also spoke about the care and nurturing their professors exhibited, even amid the chaos surrounding the vote. Despite their love for these professors, young alumni worried about the state of the college, because even with the best professors, it was clear that the state of classrooms was falling woefully behind in this new era of technology.

President Netherton's response to media in January of 2007 sounded quite different from the listening sessions. In interviews, he focused primarily on the achievements of CNC during his tenure, while pointing to lack of faculty and staff raises as the primary problem facing the college. His first statement came in the local paper and focused on the ways he planned to change in order to become the president that "Carson-Newman needs me to be."[813] The article also highlighted the recent financial donations given to the college and the president's explanation for the recent drops in enrollment, which led to no faculty raises, which he believed to be the heart of the problem.[814]

At their February meeting, the board announced that they would have a final decision ready by the end of March 2007. In the meantime, listening sessions would continue and some members of the faculty became more willing to air their grievances publicly. Religion professor Dr. Wade Bibb provided several examples of what he saw as incompetence from administration, and several faculty members went on the record to discuss the conflict between professors and the president."[815] In response, Netherton echoed his earlier sentiments that this was not really about his leadership so much as it was about lack of raises for faculty. But many argued that this was not a single-issue vote about faculty raises, but rather the cumulative effect of years feeling dismissed by administration and being rebuffed when they attempted to voice alternative opinions or ideas. It was about a love for Carson-Newman, not personal animosity toward any individual.[816]

This maelstrom ended abruptly on February 16, when Dr. Netherton announced that he was leaving Carson-Newman for a position at Mercer University. The news of his imminent departure meant that no real resolution emerged from this years-long process, and it meant that Carson-Newman needed a new president, one who could bring back stability and trust in the administration and its process.

Familiar Faces

To lead Carson-Newman through these stormy waters, trustees turned to a man uniquely suited to the task—Professor Joe Bill Sloan—the son of a legendary math professor, alumnus of the college, professor in the Political Science Department, and associate provost. Professor Sloan spent his youth on campus and enrolled as a student in 1963. He returned to his alma mater as a professor in 1969, and spent the next forty years shepherding students through the intricacies of law and public policy. Professor Sloan had a foot in both camps, he was widely respected by faculty across campus, but he also had a deep understanding of the administrative challenges facing the university in the wake of President Netherton's departure. As one professor put it, "He knows the faculty and staff; he knows the campus issues, and he understands the internal nuances. Besides, he's not aligned with any faction. He brings no personal agenda except to put C-N on a sound academic and fiscal foundation for the new president." He was an obvious choice for the post, but the first few months of his tenure were, in his own words, "very challenging."

Professor Sloan had been contemplating retirement when the call came for his promotion to interim president, but he took on the responsibility of righting the ship despite any misgivings. One of his first responsibilities as interim was to brief the faculty at their next meeting about the true state of affairs with regard to the college's financial health. This report was not a happy one, but President Sloan delivered a full accounting and received a standing ovation from the faculty as thanks for his honesty. He and Michael Arrington, the provost, restructured personnel in the Fite Building. They promoted Vickie Butler to vice-president of Advancement and Dr. Tom Huebner to vice-president of Enrollment Management. Dr. David Crutchley was named chair of the Religion Department. There were many challenges to face, but Sloan felt prepared to meet them, in part because of the training he received as a faculty member. C-N has a long tradition of encouraging faculty engagement with student and campus activities, which means everything from presenting original research to running sound equipment if necessary. Professor Sloan would need every skill he possessed to help put C-N back on firm footing. As he put it, "My role is to do everything I can to put Carson-Newman in the best position possible . . . God is in control. I just want to serve Him in my work here and now."

A Firm Foundation

Thanks to the work of the faculty, the interim president, and the Board of Trustees, Carson-Newman began to look toward a brighter future and a firmer financial foundation. Despite the many challenges faced by the college, students still experienced high levels of academic rigor and vibrant campus life. Although the college had many problems, it also had many assets. With that in mind, the Board of Trustees began a search for a new permanent president. During the 2007–2008 academic year, President Sloan worked to raise funds, an endeavor that was quite successful as the campus saw the opening of the new Ted Russell Hall for the School of Business and the completion of the fourth floor of the Henderson Building. Thanks to the tireless work of Ms. Vickie Butler and Dr. Kitty Coffey, the Blye-Poteat Hall for the Division of Family and Consumer Sciences was also built and opened to the public. Student excitement for these new spaces was high, although the work did put a damper on the long-running "Henderson's 4th floor is haunted" tales.

In the summer of 2008, the search committee announced the appointment of a new president, Dr. J. Randall O'Brien. He had big shoes to fill and big challenges to overcome, but he and his wife, Kay, were prepared for whatever came their way. Dr. O'Brien served as provost of Baylor University before coming to Jefferson City. Their decision to leave Texas for Tennessee was a prayerful one, and one they undertook under God's direction. Both O'Briens felt led to make the leap of faith based on Carson-Newman's ethos and community. Dr. O'Brien felt that "our Carson-Newman mission claims that we will be the kind of place where open intellectual inquiry and a deeper spiritual life have a home. And that, it seems to me, is a terribly exciting place to be." Ms. O'Brien emphasized the importance of the college's social ministry in their decision-making process.

Dr. O'Brien spoke to many people across campus throughout September and October in preparation for his inauguration at the end of October 2008. He undertook a process of "right sizing" campus staff, which helped put the college on more sound economic footing. The college also hired a new provost, Dr. Kina Mallard, who had a strong background in faculty development and fundraising at both Gordon College and Union University. At the end of that fall semester, Dr. O'Brien articulated five critical areas to address in order for Carson-Newman to move forward: a clearer mission statement, accountable management, visionary leadership, fundraising, and relationship building. Each of these areas would require the labor of everyone on campus, but the future looked bright for the Eagles. The excitement of a new president had an immediate impact, as Carson-Newman saw some of the highest enrollment numbers in its history that fall.

Randall O'Brien, president 2008–2018.
(Courtesy of Hester Photography.)

The inauguration was an important ceremonial process for the new president and his family, but it also set the tone for the campus moving forward into a new, more hopeful era. As Dr. Kina Mallard said in her speech, "Thank you, Dr. O'Brien, for saying yes to Carson-Newman College. Faculty at Carson-Newman College say yes to you." This was an important vote of trust in a new president, and one that Dr. O'Brien took very seriously. His inaugural speech highlighted the long history of both Christian higher education and the place that Carson-Newman has in that long history. He presented a clarion call to the necessity of academic inquiry within a Christian context:

> Perhaps in our secular age secular colleges and universities will not desire to integrate faith and learning, choosing to go their own way instead. But I would like to join the caravan of sages through the ages, including the company of evangelical confessing scholars today, who hold to the unity of truth, and to the belief that faith and learning, not faith OR learning, is the best way to attain true erudition.

> In our search for knowledge, our quest for truth, why should our learning communities and faith communities remain separate? Let us embrace an open search for truth wherein freedom to think includes permission to ask any question and to analyze every perspective. Open intellectual inquiry may not after all, by self-definition, exclude thinking Christianly across the curriculum.

These words would be the guiding principle throughout Dr. O'Brien's tenure as president of Carson-Newman. The college would remain dedicated to academic excellence within a Christian framework, designed to forge students into servant-scholars prepared to meet the challenges of the world. By 2010, this philosophy was enshrined in a new college mission statement, "to help our students reach their full potential as educated citizens and worldwide servant-leaders by integrating academic excellence and Christian commitment within a caring community." Even today, this mission statement is a guiding principle for the university in its decision-making process and strategic planning.

These priorities can be seen in every part of campus life—from the core curriculum of classes to spring break missionary trips. Each student who earns a bachelor of arts degree from Carson-Newman enrolls in a wide range of classes across multiple departments. They will take history, art, math, science, English, religion, and foreign language just to name a few. The liberal arts tradition is a hallowed one in American higher education; but as other colleges and universities began making cuts into their humanities departments, Carson-Newman remained committed to the well-rounded nature of our system. Educated worldwide servant-leaders needed a strong sense of the world around them, in all its facets, and a strong grounding in their own religious traditions. Faculty and administration remain committed to this idea at Carson Newman.

Women of Vision

At the end of Dr. O'Brien's decade-long tenure as C-N president, he remarked that his wife Kay had been a "co-president." This was an apt description of her role at C-N, as Ms. O'Brien shared in the heavy responsibilities of shepherding the college through the turbulent waters of the post-Netherton years, as well as the hard process of rebuilding campus morale and trust. Her legacy can be seen most clearly in the organization she founded with Vickie Butler, then serving as vice-president for Advancement. Ms. Butler had long desired to build a meaningful organization that would allow alumni to contribute to their alma mater. When she first met Ms. O'Brien, she immediately felt that the "stars had aligned" and knew she would be the perfect partner for this ambitious project. Before Ms. O'Brien settled into her new presidential home, Ms. Butler suggested that they work together to create a new type of organization, one that would build a strong network of female alumni and tap into the long history of women's labor in charitable and religious organizations. Thus, Women of Vision was born, with the goal "to use whatever God has placed in our hands to support the Carson-Newman experience through the pathways of nurturing truth, enhancing beauty, and enriching goodness."

Ms. Butler and Ms. O'Brien suited each other perfectly as partners in goodness. They worked for two years to launch Women of Vision, and by April 2011, the organization had its formal coming-out party in Knoxville, with Ruth Graham presiding over the festivities. The initial leadership council, known as the Oak Table Five, consisted of five women (Betty Catlett, Donna Harmon, Wanda Moore, Kristi Paczkowski, and Sandy Dyer). Very quickly the organization grew to more five hundred members. WOV focuses on matching women with their passions, where they can do the most good, and on small- and medium-scale projects that would make the daily lives of students and faculty better.

Over the past decade, WOV's work has touched almost every building on campus, both academic and residential. One of their first major projects was a renovation of many of the common areas in Sarah Swann Hall, the oldest building on campus. This included the restoration and return of the historic Hypatian stained-glass windows to the building. These windows were commissioned by the Hypatian Literary Society when Sarah Swann Hall was first built in 1904, but the windows were removed in 1965. In 2011, WOV brought the windows out of storage, paid for their restoration thanks to generous donations, and reinstalled them in the grand parlors of Swann Hall. The organization wanted to make the campus more beautiful, but also more livable, evidenced by their project to turn the ironing rooms of Burnett Hall, originally installed in the 1960s, into study rooms. They also worked to update classrooms so that C-N faculty could more easily engage with cutting-edge pedagogical methodologies.

To date, the group has raised more than a million dollars for improvement projects, renovated almost one hundred rooms, and improved every single building on campus. It is not an overstatement to say they have touched the lives and work of almost every student and faculty member of campus. In 2013, the group expanded to include current students in a new branch called Young Women of Promise. These students can provide important information about what projects are most needed on campus, and the hope is that they will one day become fully fledged members of Women of Vision. Although both Ms. Butler and Ms. O'Brien have retired, they both know the organization will continue to go from strength to strength. The group continues to accept project proposals every year, and it has a strong donor base that allows it to focus on plans that fit with the university's motto of Truth, Beauty, and Goodness.

A New Name, A Familiar Mission

Carson-Newman has come a long way since its original iteration as the Mossy Creek Missionary Baptist Seminary. Throughout its long journey, the institution's name has changed multiple times, reflecting both its own broadening mission and the signs of the times. In each chapter of this book, we can see how the wider world impacts Carson-Newman, and how Carson-Newman impacts the wider world. Originally Mossy Creek Seminary taught local students, but by the twentieth century the campus welcomed students from all over the world to experience Truth, Beauty, and Goodness firsthand. Unfortunately, the name was no longer an accurate reflection of that reality, thus a name change was required. In order to honor this moment, as one of its last acts as a college, students and faculty buried a time capsule, to be opened in 2113.

On February 11, 2013, Carson-Newman College became Carson-Newman University, in part to reflect the realities of its academic offerings, but also to ensure that international students understood the academic training they could receive here. International students have become an important part of campus life, both athletically and academically. The current roster of soccer players hosts students from seven different countries, and over the past two decades Carson-Newman has enrolled students from over thirty countries.[817] In the past, these students would have been confused by the designation as a college, which is frequently used in the sense of a high school in their home countries. By changing the designation to university, faculty and staff are better able to meet student need and help ensure the legacy of our mission statement to be "educated citizens and worldwide servant-leaders."

A Simple Justice

For the 2015–2016 academic year, Carson-Newman commemorated the Voting Rights Act with a special program, "A Simple Justice: The Celebration of the 50th Anniversary of the Voting Rights Act." This year-long event impacted multiple courses and departments across campus, saw several important speakers come from all over the nation, and featured a special exhibit created by students in the History Department. Led by Dr. Beth Vanlandingham, this exhibit explained to students just how difficult it was for African Americans in the South to vote before the passage of the Voting Rights Act. It highlighted the violence that civil rights activists faced in their attempts to achieve equality, as well as the historic march from Selma to Montgomery. With Dr. Vanlandingham's capable oversight, students created every single item within the exhibit. One student, Darius Childs, described what he wanted visitors to understand when they visited: "'I hope that . . . they see the sacrifices that not black people made, but that Americans made. Because when you really start studying American history, you can't separate African Americans from the United States." Students also heard from Dr. O'Brien, who had been active in the Civil Rights Movement in his native Mississippi. As part of the celebration, theater students performed *Walk, Don't Ride! A Celebration of the Fight for Equality*. Dr. Kyle Biery said that the play "is an incredibly compelling work, a demonstration of the power theatre has to encourage positive change."

During the spring semester, the college asked Dr. Michael Eric Dyson, alumnus and renowned scholar of race, religion, and contemporary culture, to speak on campus. While a student in the early 1980s, Dr. Dyson challenged the administration on several issues related to black life on campus, including the lack of black speakers invited to speak every year.

Eventually, these confrontations led to his being ejected from the school, although he did earn his diploma in 1985. After receiving his BA degree, Dyson went on to Princeton to get his PhD and is now a Distinguished Professor at Vanderbilt University. His visit in 2016 was the first time Dr. Dyson had been formally welcomed back to campus, and he made the most of his visit, speaking in chapel and later at a public event. It was an important moment of healing for the campus community, and hopefully an important harbinger of things to come.

Campus Life

Students who enrolled at C-N in the fall of 2020 no doubt felt the same strong sense of community that has been a hallmark of the Carson-Newman campus since its founding, but the ways in which they experienced this feeling would be radically different. In the midst of a global pandemic, students met with their new advisors via video chats on the internet and had a special socially distanced orientation. The year was certainly an unusual one, but one that highlighted all the ways that Carson-Newman continues to provide the same sense of home—even as the world outside campus keeps changing.

At the dawn of the new century, students still registered for their classes with sheets of paper in triplicate, and the only way to decide which classes to take was via a printed schedule of classes. Now students and advisors can see all this information online and, critically, they can see which classes are full before they try to register for them! The coming of the digital age changed not only class registrations, but also classes themselves. New online learning systems mean that professors can now assign work to students remotely; they can even grade students' work remotely. It is a rapidly changing world, and changes in campus practices and landscapes reflect that.

In 2000, when students went to the library, they found the main floor full of reference books and a few computers tucked away in the corner. Now the library hosts over a dozen computers for students to use, and the reference books are by and large on those computers. The card catalogue is now available digitally, as are entire books and journals. Professors can now link chapters from books or journal articles directly into the online repository for the class. While the physical space looks quite different, students are using the library more than ever. They might be checking out fewer physical copies of books; but thanks to helpful librarians and digital finding aids, the library's abilities to help students remain top notch.[818] Despite the changes wrought by the digital world, the through line for Carson-Newman remains the student experience. The ways in which professors assign work might change, but the care and attention they feel toward their students have not. This has been the touchstone of every faculty member on campus since the college's founding, even in the midst of turbulent times.

A STUDENT'S LIFE AT C-N

Rose Christa Denor's family came to Tennessee via Haiti. They settled in the Chattanooga area and, when it came time to find a college, Rose Christa wanted a school that would provide lots of student-teacher interaction and a small student-to-teacher ratio. She found all of that in Carson-Newman, where she enrolled in the fall of 2016. In addition to her studies, Rose Christa wanted to change the world. That is one reason she joined the Bonner Scholars. This program provides scholarships for students in exchange for volunteer work related to social justice. Although the requirements for this program are quite rigorous, that did not stop Rose Christa from joining the International Club and becoming president of the history honor's society on campus, Phi Alpha Theta. While a student, Rose Christa majored in history, and she credits several of those classes as her favorites—Literature and Revolution and Imperialism—but she also enjoyed classes from across the curriculum. She credits International Human Rights, Women and Biblical Traditions, and Psychology of Gender with changing her worldview.

When Dr. O'Brien came to campus, one of his most important tasks was to rebuild a sense of campus community and trust, and he proved to be more than up to the task. Students embraced his friendly pastoral nature. In his very first speech to faculty, he promised "to pastor this Carson-Newman family." This was a promise he kept, as evidenced by the outpouring of love and support he received upon the announcement of his retirement. One reason, among many, that students loved him was his dedication to having fun with them, spending time with them, and indeed, pastoring them. One of the best examples of his willingness to do anything for his Eagle family was a promise he made to the soccer teams in the fall of 2013—if one thousand fans came to the home opener, he would go skydiving with Skydive East Tennessee. More than one thousand fans did indeed come to the game, and as promised, Dr. O'Brien went skydiving four days later. Not only did he agree to jump out of a plane for Carson-Newman, but he also agreed to have it filmed, which means his terror and excitement now live forever on the internet.

Sporting Life

Despite the many changes of the twenty-first century, Carson-Newman's dedication to academics, athletics, and campus life remain steadfast. Its most prominent coach was, and still is, football coach Ken Sparks. When Coach Sparks retired on November 14, 2016, he was the winningest active coach in the nation, and the fifth winningest coach in college football history. During his tenure, his teams won five national championships. He coached at Carson-Newman for thirty-seven seasons, had a win-loss record of 338–99, and more accolades than can be listed in a meager book chapter. Despite these formidable achievements, Coach Sparks's main source of pride was his discipleship to his players. He saw football as a way of building a whole person, not just the athlete. The personal relationships developed between players and staff were more important than the wins on the field, and he saw football as an important tool for evangelism. "If football can be used as a tool to bring people to the Lord, then it has done something. If it hasn't, we haven't done a thing, no matter how many games we won." This legacy was important to his successor, Mike Turner, who reiterated the importance of "be(ing) a positive influence on the young men that we work with." Coach Turner was the longtime offensive coordinator under Coach Sparks and felt like a natural replacement for the departing legend.

In March 2017, Coach Sparks passed away, and the tributes came in from all corners of the football world from high-school coaches up the ranks to then-head coach for the University of Tennessee Vols, Butch

A typical campus football game at Burke-Tarr Stadium.

Jones. Even in death, Coach Sparks's priorities were on full display. The president of the Tennessee Baptist Mission Board, Dr. Randy C. Davis, said, "I appreciated his focus on being a witness for Christ, having a strong, crystal-clear, biblical-based conviction, and being a great Tennessee Baptist." This was a fitting tribute to a man whose philosophy remained unchanged from his earliest days of coaching: "It's never about wins on the field, but the victories of the soul."

Coach Turner led the Eagles for three seasons before retiring after the 2019 season. His replacement, Coach Mike Clowney, was announced in January. Coach Clowney, much like Coaches Sparks and Turner, is a C-N alumnus, and he has ably carried on the legacy of spiritual development among his players. Although the global pandemic derailed his first full season as head coach, Coach Clowney looks to carry on the legacy of on-the-field success as well.

The 2017–2018 school year was a special one for many sports on campus. During the 2017–2018 season, the women's basketball team made it all the way to the Elite Eight and won the South Atlantic Conference title. Two players, Haris Price and Mika Wester, were named All-Americans. Although the team is remembered for its high-scoring victories on the court, the most important feeling for the teammates was unity. Near the end of one close game in the regional final, each member of the team locked hands spontaneously as they fought to hold off a hard-charging North Georgia team. They would go on to win that game and eventually make it to the Elite Eight and a SAC championship off the strength of their unity and offensive prowess. They played that game in front of 1,844 fans, a number that included the fanatical subset of student supporters known as the Mossy Creek Maniacs. This intensely devoted set of fans aims to be the rowdiest student section in the South Atlantic Conference, complete with costumes, face paint, and chants.

The women's soccer team also experienced unprecedented success in the 2017 season, as it was unbeaten throughout the regular season and tournament championships. The team made it all the way to the national championship before falling to Central Missouri on penalty kicks. This team achieved this success in Coach Simon Duffy's first season as head coach, and he attributes their success to their "character" and that they "refuse to lose." This winning attitude was on full display in their semifinal win over UC-Colorado Springs, which they won 2–1, thanks to strong play from goalkeeper Jackie Burns and forward Magda Mosengo. Both players also highlight the international appeal of Carson-Newman as a campus and athletic community as they each hail from the United Kingdom.

The End of an Era

After a decade capably leading, pastoring, and mentoring the Carson-Newman family, the O'Briens decided to retire, effective December 2018. This announcement was met with bittersweet feelings by students, faculty, and staff. Both Dr. and Ms. O'Brien had worked hard to rebuild feelings of trust and community on campus, and their absence would be felt keenly by both sides. President O'Brien had overseen many changes to campus, including changing the name of the school itself. But in 2018, the university was on a more solid economic footing, had increasing enrollment, and displayed a renewed sense of identity. Asked to reflect on his tenure, Dr. O'Brien reminded readers that Carson-Newman "is a beautiful, caring, Christ-centered family of faith, called to this place to serve God, our students, each other, church, communities, state, nation, and world. Academic excellence, Christian commitment, and caring community were

A Carson-Newman student enjoys talking with children while on an overseas mission trip.

here before we got here and will remain after we're gone. This is a place where dreams come true, including mine."

Despite all the changes and challenges faced by the Carson-Newman community, this remains true. We remain committed to building strong brains and hearts so that our students can go out into the world and make it better. As our mission statement says, "We help students reach their full potential as educated citizens and worldwide servant-leaders by integrating academic excellence and Christian commitment within a caring community." Carson-Newman's through line has always been academic excellence in a Christian community filled with love.

Epilogue

In 1984, Carson-Newman president Cordell Maddox observed, "One of the things we must do in the future is to tell our story." That's exactly what this book has done—and what a story it is!

One of the major takeaways of reading Carson-Newman's story is understanding how close the school came to closing over and over again. First, very few schools of higher education were financially able to reopen after closing because of the Civil War. Living conditions were desperate for many. Only through Robert Reedy Bryan's persistent advocacy and tireless efforts was Mossy Creek Baptist College able to make a new start in 1868. Bryan, the first such hero in Carson-Newman's story, was an individual who truly made a difference.

Only one year later, Mossy Creek College's debt was so life-threatening that the college's second hero, Jesse Baker, took a year out of his life to travel thirty-five hundred miles on horseback to gather funds to pay the school's debt. Considered "the savior of Carson-Newman" to this day, Baker is one of the few who is still recognized for his tremendous achievement. Of course, the individuals and families who donated sacrificially to eliminate the college's debt over the years are also heroes.

National economic upheavals strongly affected the college's monetary resources as well. Few details have survived about the college during the 1893 financial panic except that the faculty members and president, John T. Henderson, all took pay cuts. In 1895, Henderson publicly thanked two trustees "without whose liberal gifts the College could not have survived the last two years of financial stringency." And the ruinous Great Depression of the 1930s took a devastating toll on the college, degree by degree. President James Warren and his business manager, Roy Myers, were the heroes who forecasted the right long-term solution for Carson-Newman to ride out the economic storm.

In late 1916, the college's beautiful Administration Building burned to the ground. The insurance carried on the building paid the school's debts at that point, but there was no money left for constructing a new classroom and administrative building—a necessity for any college. Nearby cities Morristown and Knoxville wanted Carson-Newman to move there, offering land and civic money for the transfer. But would Carson-Newman be the same college located anywhere other than in Jefferson City? The final answer was no, and once again East Tennessee Baptists and friends of the college donated enough money for Carson-Newman to rebuild on its present site.

In the 1920s, because of an ugly controversy between the president and the dean that spiraled out of control, a lawsuit would have stripped the college's finances and ruined its reputation if an alumnus had not intervened. Dr. J. I. Huggins, a physician who was devoted to Carson-Newman, stepped in as a mediator between the two parties and negotiated a settlement that stopped the lawsuit from going forward. He thus preserved the school's ability to move past the scandal.

Both World Wars devastated Carson-Newman's enrollment and financial health as well, with most male students leaving school to enlist as soldiers. Presidents William Gentry and James Warren brought the school through these severe challenges by a creative means—signing contracts with the government to house young soldiers and provide a conducive environment for their military training.

Carson-Newman's vital accreditation standing must be reconfirmed periodically, a far-reaching procedure requiring detailed examination of every aspect of the college. In the early twenty-first century, certain unfortunate administrative decisions resulted in the school's being put on academic probation—a serious blow. Over time, a majority of concerned faculty members, seeing no emerging strategic planning or resolutions from the administration, cast a vote of no confidence in the president. They foresaw that the college's downturn, left unchecked, would result in its closure. After the president's choice to accept a position elsewhere and the installation of new leadership, Carson-Newman's probation was lifted, with college life again taking an upward turn.

The second main takeaway from Carson-Newman's story is that, in each case when its life was at stake, individuals stepped forward to save the day. The adage that one person can make a huge difference in life is true. Certain qualities are required of individuals who bring about such a difference—commitment, courage, persistence, creativity, and faith. This is a life lesson for everyone.

As Carson-Newman University looks ahead to its 175th anniversary in 2026, readers can appreciate the school's longevity all the more, knowing that its survival was not assured at any point.

Today, Carson-Newman's living alumni number well into the thousands. Many gladly tell their own stories about the university's influence and inspiration at a pivotal point in their life journeys. They have been challenged academically by scholars, nurtured in leadership, and guided by spiritual mentors. Carson-Newman's mission statement has continually encouraged them to "reach their full potential as educated citizens and worldwide servant leaders." Having learned more about the Carson-Newman story after reading this book, they can sing the Alma Mater with a new understanding:

Carson-Newman, how I love you,
Alma Mater, Hail;
Orange and Blue wave high above you
Through the calm and gale!

Sons and Daughters sing your praises
And your name adore,
While each heart your spirit raises,
Carson-Newman evermore!

A Parting Word

There is a spirit about this place known as Appalachia. It is a spirit of natural beauty, colorful history, and precious heritage. The spirit moves. It can be felt by those who take the time to listen to a mountain stream or walk a dusty road or simply gaze at the serenity of the many pastures. One does not have to be a native of the area to experience the sense of appreciation that accompanies communion with the land.

The spirit . . . tells of the one aspect of the land that sets it apart from all others—the people. The land was fierce, but it was fierce, rugged individuals that tamed the land. . . . Many of the values that the people of this area held dear were incorporated into the school. The desire to keep a religious posterity was one of the inducements of the founders of the college to establish Carson-Newman. Values of hard work and service became the foundations upon which the school would grow.

And the physical beauty remains. Located within Jefferson City, the school takes on the qualities of this small town that is distinct in that it retains the rural flavor that is so important to the people. The campus contains that simple yet attractive air, with structures and trees harmonizing in such a way as to reflect the desire on the part of those involved with the college to preserve that which is good in this community.

Such a setting makes this school a special one. In the course of everyday living and experiencing here, the tendency is to forget and take for granted these special aspects. In this age of urbanization, asphalt, and progress, this place remains.

The mountains say it. The trees say it. Through this spirit that comes when we witness the creation, the message comes through. From the scratch of the banjo strings, the silver tones of the dulcimer, from the voices of the mountain people, and from the land itself comes the clear and simple message:

This is good. It must be preserved.[819]

Notes

Chapter One

1. David McCullough, "The Lessons of History," in *The American Spirit: Who We Are and What We Stand For* (New York: Simon & Schuster, 2017), 57.

2. Richard Straw, "Appalachian History," in *A Handbook to Appalachia*, ed. Grace Toney Edwards, Joann Aust Asbury, Ricky L. Cox (Knoxville: The University of Tennessee Press, 2006), 1–2.

3. Michael McCormack, "The Treaty of Holston," in *An Encyclopedia of East Tennessee,* ed. Jim Stokely and Jeff D. Johnson (Oak Ridge, TN: Children's Museum of Oak Ridge, 1981), 475.

4. T. C. Karns, *Tennessee History Stories* (Richmond: B. F. Johnson Publishing Company, 1904), 70–88.

5. McCormack, "Treaty of Holston," 475.

6. Roy G. Lillard, "Rattlesnake Springs," in *Encyclopedia of East Tennessee,* 409.

7. Straw, "Appalachian History," 2.

8. Elizabeth Rodgers Coulter, "Cherokee Education," in *Encyclopedia of Appalachia* (Knoxville: The University of Tennessee Press, 2006), 1529.

9. Straw, "Appalachian History," 3.

10. Albert W. Wardin, Jr., *Tennessee Baptists: A Comprehensive History 1779-1999* (Brentwood, TN: Executive Board of the Tennessee Baptist Convention, 1999), 15.

11. William F. Hall, "The History of Carson-Newman College" (master's thesis, The University of Tennessee, 1936), 7.

12. Isaac Newton Carr, *History of Carson-Newman College* (Jefferson City, TN: Carson-Newman College, 1959), 7.

13. Donna Ray Waggoner, "Samuel Doak," in *Encyclopedia of East Tennessee,* 159–60; "Greene County," in *Encyclopedia of East Tennessee,* 227.

14. Arda S. Walker, "Maryville College," in *Encyclopedia of East Tennessee,* 315.

15. Hall, *History of Carson-Newman College,* 4.

16. Ibid.

17. Evan Philip Comer, Karen Bush Everett, Paul D. Goddard, Sr., Ruth Swann Goddard, and Marguerite Rankin, "Tending the Home Fires," in *Broken Hearts--Broken Lives: Jefferson County, Tennessee, Civilian Life in the Civil War,* ed. Sandra S. Wilson and Dennis L. Snapp (Dandridge, TN: Restore Our

County, 1986), 84; Estle P. Muncy, *People and Places of Jefferson County* (Jefferson County Historical Society, 1994), 109–10.

18. Hall, *History of Carson-Newman College*, ii.

19. Glenn A. Toomey, *The Sesquicentennial History of the Nolachucky Baptist Association and Its Affiliated Churches 1828-1977* (Morristown, TN: Nolachucky Baptist Association, 1977), 7–12.

20. Ibid., 100.

21. John T. Henderson, "Carson-Newman College's Place in the History of Nolachucky Association," *Nolachucky Association of Baptist* [sic], *Minutes, Centennial Session 1927* (Morristown: Triangle Press, 1928), 68.

22. Wardin, *Tennessee Baptists*, 43.

23. Hall, *History of Carson-Newman College*, 4.

24. Ibid., 5.

25. Ibid., 6.

26. Ibid., 8.

27. Ibid., 7.

28. Wardin, *Tennessee Baptists*, 168.

29. Hall, *History of Carson-Newman College*, 7–8.

30. Ibid., 12.

31. "Jefferson County, Tennessee, USA," *History of Tennessee* (Nashville: The Goodspeed Publishing Company, 1887), 15.

32. Muncy, *People and Places*, 65.

33. J. J. Burnett, "Robert Reedy Bryan," in *Sketches of Tennessee's Pioneer Baptist Preachers* (Nashville: Marshall & Bruce Company, 1919), 79.

34. Linda T. Gass and Albert L. Lang, *Carson-Newman College* (Charleston, SC: Arcadia Publishing, 2012), 10.

35. Ibid., 11.

36. Muncy, *People and Places*, 85.

37. John Angus McLeod, *From These Stones: Mars Hill College 1856-1968* (Mars Hill, NC: Mars Hill College, 1968), 92–93, 107.

38. Hall, *History of Carson-Newman College*, 13.

39. Ibid., 14.

40. Toomey, *Sesquicentennial History*, 29.

41. Wardin, *Tennessee Baptists*, 170.

42. Hall, *History of Carson-Newman College*, 14.

43. Muncy, *People and Places*, 81.

44. Hall, *History of Carson-Newman College*, 6.

45. Carr, *History of Carson-Newman College*, 368.

46. Linda T. Gass and Albert L. Lang, *Images of America: Jefferson City* (Charleston, SC: Arcadia Publishing, 2014), 7.

47. "Jefferson County, Tennessee, USA," in *History of Tennessee*, 3.

48. Gass and Lang, *Jefferson City*, 14, 16.

49. Muncy, *People and Places,* 51, 60, 118, 209.
50. Carr, *History of Carson-Newman College,* 10.
51. Hall, *History of Carson-Newman College,* 15.
52. Carr, *History of Carson-Newman College,* 10.
53. Ibid.
54. Ibid., 11.
55. Ibid., 14.
56. Hall, *History of Carson-Newman College,* 15.
57. Carr, *History of Carson-Newman College,* 1.
58. Hall, *History of Carson-Newman College,* 14.

Chapter Two

59. William Shakespeare, *The Tempest,* Act V.i.183.
60. Marcus Tullius Cicero, "In Defense of the Poet Archias," in *Cicero: Nine Orations and the Dream of Scipio,* trans. Palmer Bovie (New York: The New American Library, 1967), 222.
61. Burnett, "John Scruggs," in *Sketches,* 462.
62. Carr, *History of Carson-Newman College,* 10.
63. Ibid., 11.
64. Brenda J. Harnage, *A History of the Speech Activities in the Literary Societies at Carson-Newman College from 1851 to 1945* (Chapel Hill: University of North Carolina, 1972), 16.
65. Carr, *History of Carson-Newman College,* 18.
66. *Carson-Newman College: 150 Years of Faith and Excellence 1851–2001* (Atlanta: Bookhouse Group, 2002), front endpaper, left side.
67. "Samuel Anderson," *The Carson-Newman Baptist* (Jefferson City: Baptist Archives of Carson-Newman College) 2, no. 2 (Spring 2001): 2.
68. *Catalogue, Mossy Creek Baptist College,* 1856-1857, 7–8.
69. Joseph H. Borum, "William T. Russell," in *Biographical Sketches of Tennessee Baptist Ministers* (Memphis: Rogers and Company, 1880), 547.
70. Carr, *History of Carson-Newman College,* 18–19.
71. Borum, "William T. Russell," in *Biographical Sketches,* 547.
72. Ibid., 550.
73. Muncy, *People and Places,* 76.
74. Carr, *History of Carson-Newman College,* 14.
75. *Catalogue, Mossy Creek Baptist College,* 1856–1857, 3–6.
76. Carr, *History of Carson-Newman College,* 18.
77. *Catalogue, Mossy Creek Baptist College,* 1856–1857, 10.
78. Ibid.
79. Ibid., 2.
80. Ibid., 9.

81. "Samuel Anderson," *Carson-Newman Baptist,* 2.
82. Burnett, "Matthew Hillsman," in *Sketches,* 231, 237.
83. Ibid., 237.
84. *Catalogue, Mossy Creek Baptist College,* 1858–1859, 4.
85. Ibid., 10.
86. Ibid., 11.
87. Ibid., 14.
88. Burnett, "Matthew Hillsman," in *Sketches,* 238.
89. Burnett, "N. B. Goforth," in *Sketches,* 180.
90. Ibid., 182.
91. "Samuel Anderson," *Carson-Newman Baptist,* 2.
92. David R. Noonkesser, "War Clouds Ahead," in *Broken Hearts,* 4.
93. Ibid., 5–6.
94. Ibid.
95. William D. Taylor and Darby O'Neil Taylor, *Onward Christian Soldiers! Mossy Creek Baptist College Students in the War Between the States 1861–1865* (Jefferson City: Self-published, 1999), ii.
96. Ibid., iii.
97. David Cleve Smith, "Military History, Part I," in *Broken Hearts,* 14.
98. Ibid., 15.
99. "Jefferson County, Tennessee, USA," in *History of Tennessee,* 40.
100. Taylor and Taylor, *Onward Christian Soldiers,* 152–53.
101. Carr, *History of Carson-Newman College,* 23–24.
102. Gass and Lang, *Jefferson City,* 25.
103. Carr, *History of Carson-Newman College,* 22.
104. Ibid., 24.
105. Ibid.
106. Muncy, *People and Places,* 76.
107. Carr, *History of Carson-Newman College,* 61.
108. Muncy, *People and Places,* 76.
109. Gass, Frances and Thomas Burnett Swann, Jr. *A Burnett Family of the South* (No publication city: Self-published, 1964), 64.
110. "N. B. Goforth," *The Carson-Newman Baptist* 3, no. 2 (Spring 2002): 2.
111. Burnett, "Robert Reedy Bryan," in *Sketches,* 79.
112. Ibid., 80.
113. Ibid.

Chapter Three

114. William James, "Is Life Worth Living?" in *The Will to Believe and Other Essays in Popular Philosophy and Human Immortality* (New York: Dover Publications, n.d., ca. 1956), 47, 59.

115. Burnett, "Jesse Baker," in *Sketches*, 36.
116. "W. T. Russell," *The Carson-Newman Baptist* 4, no. 2 (Spring 2003): 1.
117. Ibid., 1–2.
118. Muncy, *People and Places*, 94.
119. Joseph H. Borum, "Jesse Baker," in *Biographical Sketches*, 101.
120. Burnett, "Jesse Baker," in *Sketches*, 33.
121. Carr, *History of Carson-Newman College*, 26.
122. Burnett, "Jesse Baker," in *Sketches*, 36.
123. Ibid.
124. Ibid.
125. "W. T. Russell," *Carson-Newman Baptist*, 2.
126. *Carson-Newman College: 150 Years of Faith and Excellence*, x.
127. Burnett, "Jesse Baker," in *Sketches*, 36.
128. Ibid.
129. Ibid.
130. *Catalogue, Carson College*, 1882–1883, 3.
131. John T. Henderson, "Carson-Newman College's Place in the History of Nolachucky Association," *Nolachucky Association of Baptist* [sic], *Minutes, Centennial Session*, 71–72.
132. Mark Brown, "Saving the Past for the Future: 192-Year-Old Baker Cabin Saved by Lakins, C-N" and "Gass Helped Fuel Project, in Spirit and with Interest," *Standard Banner* (Jefferson City, TN), November 12, 2020.
133. Burnett, "N. B. Goforth," in *Sketches*, 182.
134. McLeod, *From These Stones*, 34; Burnett, "N. B. Goforth," in *Sketches*, 181.
135. Burnett, "N. B. Goforth," in *Sketches*, 182.
136. Excerpt of an unpublished address delivered at the Dr. Jesse Baker memorial service by Professor W. T. Russell in 1902. A copy of the address was sent to Dr. Isaac N. Carr in 1962 by Mary Russell Barnett of Richmond, Virginia, the daughter of W. T. Russell.
137. Alumnus (no name), "Mossy Creek College Commencement Exercises," *The Morristown Gazette*, June 24, 1874.
138. *Catalogue, Mossy Creek Baptist College*, 1875–1876, 14.
139. Ibid.
140. Ibid.
141. Ibid., 16.
142. Ibid.
143. Ibid., 5.
144. Ibid., 11.
145. Ibid., ii.
146. Gass and Lang, *Jefferson City*, 33.
147. *Catalogue, Mossy Creek Baptist College*, 1875–1876, 15.
148. Carr, *History of Carson-Newman College*, 412.

149. Borum, "I. B. Kimbrough," in *Biographical Sketches,* 405.
150. J. J. Burnett, "I. B. Kimbrough," in *Sketches,* 304–5.
151. Muncy, *People and Places,* 78.
152. *Catalogue, Mossy Creek Baptist College,* 1876–1877, 14.
153. Ibid.
154. *Catalogue, Carson College,* 1879–1880, 21.
155. Carr, *History of Carson-Newman College,* 30.
156. *Catalogue, Mossy Creek Baptist College,* 1876–1877, 15.
157. Ibid., 14.
158. Carr, *History of Carson-Newman College,* 412.
159. "Jefferson County, Tennessee, USA," in *History of Tennessee,* 15.
160. *Catalogue, Carson College,* 1879–1880, 16.
161. J. J. Burnett, "W. A. G. Brown," in *Sketches,* 76.
162. McLeod, *From These Stones,* 35.
163. Ibid., 93–94.
164. Ibid., 35.
165. Muncy, *People and Places,* 67.
166. Burnett, "W. A. G. Brown," 76.
167. Bible, Jean Patterson, *Bent Twigs in Jefferson County* (Rogersville, TN: East Tennessee Printing Company, 1991), 123.
168. Ibid., 121.
169. Ibid., 124–25.
170. Gass and Lang, *Carson-Newman College,* 16.
171. *Catalogue, Carson and Newman College,* 1890–1891, 31.
172. *Catalogue, Mossy Creek Baptist College,* 1877–1878, 20.
173. Burnett, "W. A. G. Brown," 77.
174. *Catalogue, Carson College,* 1879–1880, 21.
175. Ibid., 17–21.
176. Daniel Harley Fite, *Autobiographical Data Concerning Esther and Harley Fite and Genealogical Records of the Fite, Jennings, Robinson, Willard and Related Families in the United States* (Jefferson City, TN: Self-published, n.d.), 107.
177. *Catalogue, Carson College,* 1881–1882, 17.
178. Carr, *History of Carson-Newman College,* 35.
179. *Catalogue, Carson College,* 1881–1882, 6.
180. Borum, "B. G. Manard," in *Biographical Sketches,* 462.
181. "B. G. Manard," *The Carson-Newman Baptist* 5, no. 1 (Fall 2003): 1.
182. Wardin, *Tennessee Baptists,* 241.
183. "B. G. Manard," *Carson-Newman Baptist,* 2.
184. Ibid.
185. *The Carson Index,* published by the literary societies of Carson College, 1, no. 7 (November 15, 1882): 4.
186. *Carson Index* 1, no. 1 (September 15, 1882): 4.

187. *Catalogue, Carson College,* 1881–1882, 6.
188. Gass and Lang, *Jefferson City,* 8, 37.
189. "W. T. Russell," *Carson-Newman Baptist,* 1.
190. From a one-page leaflet attributed to W. T. Russell and S. N. Newman.
191. Carr, *History of Carson-Newman College,* 37.
192. Ibid.
193. William Blevins, "Family Roots," *Standard Banner,* September 24, 1998; *Appalachian* 1951, 12–13.
194. *Catalogue, Newman College,* 1887–1888, 14.
195. *Carson Index,* September 15, 1882, 1.
196. Ibid., 4.
197. Ibid.
198. Ibid., 3.
199. Ibid., 1–2.
200. *Carson Index* 1, no. 6 (October 15, 1882): 5.
201. Ibid., 9–10.
202. *Carson Index,* November 15, 1882, 2.
203. *Carson Index* 1, no. 8 (December 15, 1882): 11.
204. *Carson Index,* November 15, 1882, 5.
205. *Catalogue, Carson College,* 1882-1883, 10–13.
206. *Carson Index,* September 15, 1882, 5.
207. *Carson Index,* November 15, 1882, 5.
208. *Dandridge Republican Banner,* April 26, 1882.
209. *Carson Index,* December 15, 1882, 11.
210. Carr, *History of Carson-Newman College,* 35–36.
211. Ibid., 35.
212. "B. G. Manard," in *Carson-Newman Baptist,* 3.
213. Borum, "B. G. Manard," in *Biographical Sketches,* 463.
214. *Carson Index* 2, no. 4 (June 15, 1883): 4–5.

Chapter Four

215. Wendell Berry, "A Native Hill," in *The Art of the Commonplace: The Agrarian Essays of Wendell Berry* (Berkeley: Counterpoint Press, 2002), 18, 19.
216. "Jefferson County, Tennessee, USA," in *History of Tennessee,* 41.
217. *Catalogue, Carson College,* 1882-1883, 9–10.
218. "Jefferson County, Tennessee, USA," in *History of Tennessee,* 41.
219. *Catalogue, Carson College,* 1882–1883, 21.
220. *Carson Index* 2, no. 3 (April 15, 1883): 4.
221. Ibid.
222. *Catalogue, Carson College,* 1882–1883, 24.
223. *Catalogue, Carson College,* 1883–1884, 15–16.

224. *Catalogue, Carson College,* 1882–1883, 23.

225. Ibid., 20.

226. *Catalogue, Carson College,* 1882–1883, 19.

227. *Catalogue, Carson College,* 1883–1884, 8.

228. Karns, *Tennessee History Stories,* 3, 6.

229. Beth Kinnane, "Thomas C. Karns: How Beaver Ridge Got a New Name," *KnoxTNToday.com,* https://www.knoxtntoday.com/thomas-c-karns-how-beaver-ridge-got-a-new-name/.

230. *Catalogue, Carson College,* 1892–1893, 47–48; *Catalogue, Carson College,* 1893–1894, 44–45.

231. *Catalogue, Carson College,* 1882–1883, 20–21.

232. *Catalogue, Carson College,* 1883–1884, 16, 24.

233. *Carson Index,* June 15, 1883, 1.

234. Ibid.

235. Ibid., 2.

236. Elizabeth Rodgers Coulter, "Cherokee Education," in *Encyclopedia of Appalachia,* 1529.

237. Ibid.

238. *Catalogue, Carson College,* 1883–1884, 12.

239. Letter dated December 1883 from H. Price, Commissioner, Records of the Office of Indian Affairs, Finance Division, vol. 94, to President Samuel Tindell.

240. *Catalogue, Carson College,* 1883–1884, 28.

241. Ibid.

242. *Catalogue, Carson College,* 1884–1885, 12.

243. Carr, *History of Carson-Newman College,* 43–44.

244. Letter dated December 30, 1885, from Eugene E. White of Muskogee, Indian Territory, to the Honorable J. D. C. Atkins, Commissioner of Indian Affairs, Washington, DC.

245. *Catalogue, Carson College,* 1884–1885, 28.

246. *Catalogue, Newman College,* 1887–1888, 12–13.

247. Carr, *History of Carson-Newman College,* 52–53.

248. *Catalogue, Newman College,* 1887–1888, 13.

249. Ibid., 3.

250. Ibid., 13.

251. Ibid., 3.

252. Ibid., 11.

253. Ibid., 13.

254. Ibid., 16.

255. Ibid., 15.

256. *Catalogue, Newman College,* 1886–1887, 3.

257. Carr, *History of Carson-Newman College,* 44.

258. Wardin, *Tennessee Baptists,* 19, 22, 341.
259. *Carson Index,* June 15, 1883, 5–6.
260. Carr, *History of Carson-Newman College,* 331.
261. Burnett, "W. A. Montgomery," in *Sketches,* 371–73.
262. Ibid., 373–75.
263. Ibid., 375.
264. Wardin, *Tennessee Baptists,* 325.
265. Carr, *History of Carson-Newman College,* 51.
266. Ibid., 51–52.
267. Ibid.
268. Ibid., 53.
269. Ibid., 54.
270. Ibid., 53–54.
271. Gass and Lang, *Carson-Newman College,* 22.
272. *Carson-Newman College: 150 Years of Faith and Excellence,* ix.
273. *Catalogue, Carson and Newman College,* 1890–1891, 31–32.
274. Carr, *History of Carson-Newman College,* 52.
275. *Catalogue, Carson and Newman College,* 1889–1890, 5.
276. *Catalogue, Carson and Newman College,* 1891–1892, 21–22.
277. *Catalogue, Carson and Newman College,* 1889–1890, 17.
278. Ibid., 1, 20–21.
279. Carr, *History of Carson-Newman College,* 222.
280. *Catalogue, Carson and Newman College,* 1889–1890, 14–15.
281. Carr, *History of Carson-Newman College,* 248.
282. Ibid., 286.
283. Ibid.
284. Ibid.
285. Ibid.
286. This information is taken from an oral interview by student Jayne Fair conducted with Hypatian member, alumnus, and longtime faculty member Janie Swann Huggins (Class of 1926) on September 17, 1980.
287. *Catalogue, Carson and Newman College,* 1895–1896, 39.
288. Carr, *History of Carson-Newman College,* 56–57.
289. *Catalogue, Carson and Newman College,* 1895–1896, 39.
290. Carr, *History of Carson-Newman College,* 56.
291. Gass and Lang, *Carson-Newman College,* 112.
292. Ibid., 35; Carr, *History of Carson-Newman College,* 58.

Chapter Five

293. J. M. Burnett, "The College and Culture," in *The Carson-Newman Collegian* 1, no. 4 (May 1911): 26.

294. Carr, *History of Carson-Newman College,* 211.

295. John Trotwood Moore, "John Thompson Henderson," in *Tennessee: The Volunteer State 1769–1923* (Chicago: The S. J. Clarke Publishing Company, 1923), 2; 588.

296. Horace L. Jones, "Dr. John T. Henderson," *Bulletin of Carson-Newman College, Alumni Issue.* 2, no. 3 (July 1948): 6.

297. Carr, *History of Carson-Newman College,* 58.

298. J. T. Henderson, *The Carson and Newman Magazine* 1, no. 2 (March 1896): 38.

299. Wardin, *Tennessee Baptists,* 315.

300. Gass and Lang, *Carson-Newman College,* 36.

301. O. L. Hailey, "Red Letter Day For Carson and Newman at Mossy Creek," *Knoxville Journal*, August 31, 1892.

302. Edward Perronet and John Rippon, lyrics to "All Hail the Power of Jesus' Name," *Baptist Hymnal* (Nashville: LifeWay Worship, 2008), 314.

303. Hailey, "Red Letter Day For Carson and Newman at Mossy Creek," *Knoxville Journal.*

304. *Catalogue, Carson and Newman College,* 1893–1894, 34.

305. Carr, *History of Carson-Newman College,* 57.

306. Ibid., 59.

307. *Catalogue, Carson and Newman College,* 1894–1895, 35.

308. Ibid., 51–52.

309. Carr, *History of Carson-Newman College,* 60.

310. Chris Jones, *It Gets Foggy at Mossy Creek* (Jefferson City, TN: Mossy Creek Press, 2012), 24.

311. Ibid., 18, 24–25.

312. *Catalogue, Carson and Newman College,* 1893–1894, 38.

313. Ibid., 46.

314. Carr, *History of Carson-Newman College,* 60.

315. *Catalogue, Carson and Newman College,* 1894–1895, 40.

316. Ibid., 47–49.

317. *Catalogue, Carson and Newman College,* 1895–1896, 13.

318. Carr, *History of Carson-Newman College,* 122.

319. Ibid.

320. Ibid., 261.

321. Ibid., 211; Gass and Lang, *Carson-Newman College,* 52.

322. Carr, *History of Carson-Newman College,* 42–43.

323. Gass and Lang, *Carson-Newman College,* 52.

324. Carr, *History of Carson-Newman College,* 121.

325. Ibid., 121, 292.

326. *Catalogue, Carson and Newman College,* 1897–1898, 58–59.

327. Ibid., 40.

328. *Catalogue, Carson and Newman College,* 1895–1896, 64.
329. *Carson and Newman Magazine* 1, no. 3 (April 1896): 66.
330. *Carson and Newman Magazine* 1, no. 2 (March 1896): 44–45.
331. *Catalogue, Carson and Newman College,* 1897–1898, 38.
332. Ibid.
333. Ibid., 40.
334. Carr, *History of Carson-Newman College,* 124.
335. *Catalogue, Carson and Newman College,* 1897–1898, 45.
336. Carr, *History of Carson-Newman College,* 59–60.
337. Ibid.
338. Ibid., 59.
339. *Catalogue, Carson and Newman College,* 1898–1899, 63–64.
340. Gass and Lang, *Carson-Newman College,* 112.
341. Carr, *History of Carson-Newman College,* 60–61.
342. Ibid., 57.
343. Albert L. Lang, "The Administration Building: Carson-Newman's Lost Jewel, 1890–1916," https://cn.libguides.com/SpecialCollections/University Archives.
344. Harnage, *History of the Speech Activities,* 89–90.
345. Lang, "Administration Building."
346. Ibid.
347. *Catalogue, Carson and Newman College,* 1894–1895, 35.
348. Carr, *History of Carson-Newman College,* 60.
349. Ibid.
350. Ibid.
351. J. T. Henderson, *The Carson and Newman Magazine,* March 1896, 38.
352. Carr, *History of Carson-Newman College,* 224.
353. Gass and Lang, *Jefferson City,* 21.
354. *Dandridge Watchman,* May 15, 1903.
355. Carr, *History of Carson-Newman College,* 62.
356. Ibid., 62–63.
357. *Dandridge Watchman,* September 11, 1903.
358. Carr, *History of Carson-Newman College,* 63.
359. Ibid., 64.
360. *Catalogue, Carson and Newman College,* 1906–1907, 5.
361. Unpublished letter from Rose Jeffries Hart of Johnston, South Carolina, to Glenn "Buster" Jeffries of Knoxville, March 21, 1958.
362. Carr, *History of Carson-Newman College,* 180.
363. Ibid., 64–65.
364. Ibid., 65.
365. Ibid.
366. Ibid., 65, 224.

367. Gass and Lang, *Carson-Newman College,* 111.
368. Carr, *History of Carson-Newman College,* 65.
369. Ibid., 80, 207.
370. Ibid., 65–66.
371. Ibid., 66, 208.
372. Ibid., 66.
373. *Catalogue, Carson and Newman College,* 1905–1906, 47.
374. Carr, *History of Carson-Newman College,* 122.
375. Ibid., 126.
376. Ibid., 123.
377. Ibid., 124.
378. *Catalogue, Carson and Newman College,* 1905–1906, 54.
379. Ibid., 21–23.
380. Carr, *History of Carson-Newman College,* 212.
381. Ibid., 66.
382. Ibid., 66–67.
383. Chris Jones, *It Gets Foggy at Mossy Creek,* 26.
384. Carr, *History of Carson-Newman College,* 68.
385. Ibid., 68.
386. Ibid., 68–69.
387. Ibid., 68.
388. Ibid., 69.
389. *The Carson-Newman Collegian* 2, no. 1 (1911): 30, quoted in Carr, *History of Carson-Newman College,* 309.
390. Carr, *History of Carson-Newman College,* 69.
391. Unpublished letter from Rose Jeffries Hart.

Chapter Six

392. Wilma Dykeman, *The Tall Woman* (Newport, TN: Wakestone Books, 1962), 119.
393. Carr, *History of Carson-Newman College,* 70.
394. Ibid.
395. Ibid., 225.
396. Ibid., 69.
397. Ibid., 70.
398. *Catalogue, Carson and Newman College,* 1892–1893, 50.
399. Gass and Swann, *Burnett Family of the South,* 92, 95.
400. Ibid., 103–07.
401. Carr, *History of Carson-Newman College,* 69.
402. Gass and Swann, *Burnett Family of the South,* 103.
403. Carr, *History of Carson-Newman College,* 69–70.

404. Jesse M. Burnett, "The College and Culture," *The Carson-Newman Collegian*.

405. *Swann* 1912, 8–10.

406. Ibid., 18–19, 21–22.

407. Ibid., 5–6.

408. Carr, *History of Carson-Newman College*, 311.

409. For example, see a journal article of the period: R. R. Abernethy, "A Sane Athletic Program," *The Journal of Health and Physical Education* 7, no. 3 (1936), https://www.tandfonline.com/doi/abs/10.1080/23267240.1936.10627844?journalCode=ujrd16.

410. Chris Jones, *It Gets Foggy*, 26.

411. Ibid., 30.

412. Ibid., 31.

413. Ibid., 30.

414. Ibid., 31.

415. Ibid., 33.

416. Ibid., 35.

417. Ibid., 36.

418. *Knoxville Journal and Tribune*, May 8, 1914, as quoted in Chris Jones, *It Gets Foggy*, 31.

419. Gass and Lang, *Jefferson City*, 38.

420. Jones, *It Gets Foggy*, 27.

421. *Catalogue, Carson and Newman College*, 1913–1914, 38b.

422. Jones, *It Gets Foggy*, 27.

423. Ibid., 29.

424. Ibid., 34.

425. For information on Pryor M. "Humpy" McElveen, see https://peoplepill.com/people/pryor-mcelveen.

426. Jones, *It Gets Foggy*, 30.

427. *Catalogue, Carson and Newman College*, 1913–1914, 38.

428. Carr, *History of Carson-Newman College*, 287.

429. G. J. Meyer, *The World Remade: America in World War I* (New York: Bantam Books, 2016), 80.

430. Carr, *History of Carson-Newman College*, 71.

431. Ibid., 71–72.

432. *Carson-Newman Collegian* 4, no. 9 (May 1914): 20.

433. *Catalogue, Carson and Newman College*, 1915–1916, 28.

434. Maurine Brooks Christopher, *The Artistic World of Zula Pangle Brooks* (New York: Christopher Enterprises, 2000), 1.

435. *Catalogue, Carson and Newman College*, 1916–1917, 39.

436. Joseph Robinson, "The Significance of Commencement," *The Carson-Newman Collegian* 1, no. 4 (May 1911): 9.

437. Unpublished letter from Edmund Cody Burnett to Jesse McGarity Burnett, February 8, 1914.

438. *Catalogue, Carson and Newman College,* 1914–1915, 44.

439. Carr, *History of Carson-Newman College,* 302.

440. Ibid., 72.

441. Ibid.

442. Ibid., 73–74.

443. Wardin, *Tennessee Baptists,* 328–330.

444. Ibid., 327.

445. Carr, *History of Carson-Newman College,* 74.

446. Ibid.

447. Lang, "Administration Building."

448. Carr, *History of Carson-Newman College,* 76.

449. Lang, "Administration Building."

450. *Swann* 1912, 3.

451. Carr, *History of Carson-Newman College,* 76.

452. Ibid.

453. Ibid., 76–77.

454. Ibid., 77.

455. Ibid.

456. Ibid., 76, 78.

457. Wardin, *Tennessee Baptists,* 321–22.

458. Carr, *History of Carson-Newman College,* 78.

459. Ibid., 79.

460. Ibid., 78.

461. Ibid., 79.

462. Ibid., 80.

463. *The Larker* 1917, 3.

464. Ibid., 8.

465. Ibid., 26.

466. Ibid., 128, 134.

467. Ibid., 108–11.

468. Ibid., 21, 26.

469. Carr, *History of Carson-Newman College,* 80.

470. Ibid.

471. Ibid., 81, 83.

472. Ibid., 81.

473. Ibid., 82.

474. *Catalogue, Carson and Newman College,* 1918–1919, 28–29.

475. Carr, *History of Carson-Newman College,* 82.

476. *Grenade* 1920, 2–3.

477. Carr, *History of Carson-Newman College,* 82–83.
478. Ibid., 80.
479. Ibid., 82.
480. Ibid., 83.
481. Ibid.
482. Jones, *It Gets Foggy,* 37.
483. Carr, *History of Carson-Newman College,* 82.
484. Ibid., 85.
485. Ibid., 85–86.
486. Ibid., 83–84.
487. Wardin, *Tennessee Baptists,* 322.
488. Carr, *History of Carson-Newman College,* 84.
489. Ibid., 85.
490. Ibid., 86.
491. *Catalogue, Carson and Newman College,* 1918–1919, 44.
492. Gass and Lang, *Carson-Newman College,* 113.
493. Carr, *History of Carson-Newman College,* 86.
494. Ibid., 87.

Chapter Seven

495. Maltbie D. Babcock, lyrics to "This Is My Father's World," *Baptist Hymnal* (Nashville: LifeWay Worship, 2008), 46.
496. *Grenade* 1920, 138.
497. Carr, *History of Carson-Newman College,* 88.
498. Gass and Lang, *Carson-Newman College,* 40.
499. Carr, *History of Carson-Newman College,* 86, 88.
500. *Catalogue, Carson and Newman College,* 1920–1921, 21.
501. Carr, *History of Carson-Newman College,* 90.
502. Ibid., 85–86.
503. Ibid., 88.
504. Ibid.
505. McLeod, *From These Stones,* 216–217.
506. Carr, *History of Carson-Newman College,* 89.
507. David M. Armbrister, *Lighthouse on the Hill: The Bluefield College Story* (Wytheville, VA: Wordsprint, 2007), 28.
508. *Appalachian* 1923, 25.
509. *Grenade* 1920, 13.
510. Ibid., 136.
511. Ibid., 142.
512. Ibid., 120–21, 126, 128, 129, 132, 134.

513. Ibid., 127.
514. Carr, *History of Carson-Newman College,* 93.
515. Ibid., 89.
516. *Alumni Bulletin, Carson-Newman College,* Centennial Edition 5, no. 2 (January 1951): 6.
517. Ibid.
518. A. Jase Jones, "T. B. Maston: The Man, His Family, and His Ministry," T. B. Maston Foundation, https://tbmaston.org/about/who-was-t-b-maston/.
519. Ibid.
520. For more about T. B. Maston, see https://classic.cn.edu/undergraduate/resources/library/library-resources/special-collections/baptist-archives/t-b-maston.
521. J. I. Reece, "Chaucer's Prologue," *The Karnuargus* 1, no. 3 (February 1908): 97–100.
522. Carr, *History of Carson-Newman College,* 89.
523. Ibid.
524. Ibid.
525. *Wanehi* 1921, 149.
526. Carr, *History of Carson-Newman College,* 89.
527. *Appalachian* 1924, 170.
528. Ibid., 169.
529. Carr, *History of Carson-Newman College,* 209.
530. *Appalachian* 1925, 26, 154.
531. *Appalachian* 1926, 36.
532. Carr, *History of Carson-Newman College,* 94.
533. *Catalogue, Carson and Newman College,* 1920–1921, 53–54.
534. Carr, *History of Carson-Newman College,* 94.
535. *Grenade* 1920, 137.
536. Carr, *History of Carson-Newman College,* 90.
537. Ibid., 89–90.
538. Ibid., 93.
539. Ibid., 94.
540. Ibid.
541. Ibid.
542. *Carson and Newman College Bulletin* (Jefferson City, TN March 1925), 1–8.
543. *Wanehi* 1921, 15.
544. Ibid., 3.
545. Ibid., 5.
546. Ibid., 133–41.
547. Ibid., 21, 93–96.
548. *Appalachian* 1922, 7.

549. Ibid., 8–9.
550. Ibid., 36, 43.
551. Ibid., 124, 128–30.
552. Ibid., 125–27.
553. *Appalachian* 1923, 5.
554. Ibid., 26.
555. *Appalachian* 1924, 16.
556. Carr, *History of Carson-Newman College,* 90.
557. *Appalachian* 1922, 15.
558. *Wanehi* 1921, 13.
559. *Appalachian* 1923, 16.
560. Carr, *History of Carson-Newman College,* 91.
561. Ibid., 89.
562. Ibid.
563. Ibid., 30.
564. Jones, *It Gets Foggy,* 55.
565. *Appalachian* 1923, 147.
566. *Appalachian* 1922, 139.
567. Carr, *History of Carson-Newman College,* 271.
568. *Appalachian* 1922, 139.
569. Carr, *History of Carson-Newman College,* 271.
570. *Appalachian* 1924, 152–53.
571. Carr, *History of Carson-Newman College,* 271–72.
572. President's Report April 5, 1923, *Minutes of Trustees,* as reported in Carr, *History of Carson-Newman College,* 92–93.
573. Conway Sams, unpublished email correspondence with Frieda C. Burts, January 13, 2001.
574. *Appalachian* 1927, 66.
575. *Appalachian* 1922, 134.
576. Carr, *History of Carson-Newman College,* 94.
577. All of the narrative material in this chapter not otherwise documented is taken from an interview with Janie Swann Huggins on September 17, 1980, conducted by student Jayne Fair. Huggins, a longtime and distinguished professor of English at Carson-Newman, was on campus in the early 1920s as a student (Class of 1926) and was a close friend and roommate of Mary Martin, Dean Reece's niece.
578. Carr, *History of Carson-Newman College,* 95.
579. Resolutions written by a committee of trustees, read aloud May 30, 1924, at commencement, as reported in Carr, *History of Carson-Newman College,* 95.
580. Carr, *History of Carson-Newman College,* 94.
581. Ibid., 95.

582. Ibid.

583. Ibid.

584. Ibid.

585. Ibid., 94.

586. *Appalachian* 1925, 20.

587. Ibid., 26, 58.

588. Carr, *History of Carson-Newman College,* 96–97.

589. *Appalachian* 1926, 36.

590. *Catalogue, Carson and Newman College,* 1923–1924, 11.

591. Carr, *History of Carson-Newman College,* 91.

592. Ibid., 92.

593. Ibid.

594. *Appalachian* 1925, 4–5.

595. Edgar M. Cook, *It Happened on a College Campus* (Jefferson City, TN Standard Publishing Company, 1972), 47.

596. Carr, *History of Carson-Newman College,* 92.

597. Conway Sams, unpublished email correspondence with Suzanne Matheny, Director of Alumni Relations, July 24, 2002.

598. Carr, *History of Carson-Newman College,* 224.

599. Ibid., 228.

600. Oscar Sams, "Update," *Bulletin of Carson and Newman College* (Jefferson City, TN: October 1925), 1.

601. The statistics in this sidebar are taken directly from Carson and Newman's official catalogues for the years listed, 1919–1927.

602. President's Report April 5, 1924, *Minutes of Trustees,* as reported in Carr, *History of Carson-Newman College,* 93.

603. For example, this wording is in the *Catalogue, Carson and Newman College,* 1906–1907, 49.

604. Carr, *History of Carson-Newman College,* 93.

605. Ibid.

606. On September 23, 1980, student Jayne Fair interviewed retired coach Sam "Frosty" Holt about his early memories of Carson-Newman when he was a student. This is his comment about the "Ringers."

607. Carr, *History of Carson-Newman College,* 93.

608. Ibid.

609. Ibid., 93, 96.

610. Lake Russell, "Carson-Newman's Athletic Outlook," *The Appalachian* 1925, 140.

611. *Appalachian* 1922, 110.

612. Carr, *History of Carson-Newman College,* 95.

613. Ibid.

614. Ibid.

615. *Civil Minutes,* vol. 12, p. 325 (Office, Circuit Court Clerk, Courthouse, Dandridge, Tennessee), as quoted in Carr, *History of Carson-Newman College,* 95–96.

616. Carr, *History of Carson-Newman College,* 97.

617. Ibid.

618. Ibid., 94.

619. Ibid., 97.

620. Ibid.

621. *Resignation,* as quoted in Carr, *History of Carson-Newman College,* 98.

622. Ibid.

623. *Appalachian* 1927, 3.

624. Cook, *It Happened on a College Campus,* 20.

625. Carr, *History of Carson-Newman College,* 99.

626. Ibid.

627. President Sams's *Report to Trustees* attached to *Minutes of Trustees,* as quoted in Carr, *History of Carson-Newman College,* 99–100.

628. Statement of the Trustees as quoted in Carr, *History of Carson-Newman College,* 98–99.

629. *Appalachian* 1927, 1.

630. *Catalogue, Carson and Newman College,* 1926–1927, 113–14.

631. Carr, *History of Carson-Newman College,* 100.

632. Armbrister, *Lighthouse on the Hill,* 29–32.

633. Carr, *History of Carson-Newman College,* 100.

634. McLeod, *From These Stones,* 75.

635. Conway Sams, unpublished email correspondence with Suzanne Matheny, February 12, 2001.

636. For further information about Dean Reece, search the Find a Grave website for Joseph Isaac Reece (1883-1970) in the Oolenoy Baptist Church Cemetery, Pumpkintown, Pickens County, South Carolina, https://www.findagrave.com/memorial/17726965/joseph-isaac-reece.

637. To read about Josef Reece's military career, see the Veterans History Project, Josef I. Reece Collection, https://memory.loc.gov/diglib/vhp/bib/70167.

638. For more information about Fred and Mary Martin Moffatt, search the Find a Grave website for Fred T. Moffatt Sr. (1898-1970) in Frankfort, Kentucky, https://www.findagrave.com/memorial/206050686/fred-t-moffatt.

639. Carr, *History of Carson-Newman College,* 100.

Chapter Eight

640. Edna St. Vincent Millay, "Renascence," in *Collected Lyrics of Edna St. Vincent Millay* (New York: Harper and Row, 1939), 8. First published in 1917.

641. Carr, *History of Carson-Newman College,* 100.

642. Ibid.

643. Ibid.

644. Ibid.

645. Mark Brown, "The Courage to Stand for 'Righteousness and Justice,'" *Standard Banner* (Jefferson City, TN), January 21, 2021.

646. Carr, *History of Carson-Newman College*, 101.

647. Ibid.

648. Ibid., 103.

649. Ibid.

650. Ibid.

651. Ibid., 104.

652. *Catalogue, Carson-Newman College*, 1930–1931, 31–32.

653. Carr, *History of Carson-Newman College*, 278, 302.

654. These professors' names, starting dates, and longevity have been gleaned from studying the Carson-Newman catalogues of Dr. Warren's tenure and beyond.

655. Carr, *History of Carson-Newman College*, 375–377.

656. Jones, *It Gets Foggy*, 65.

657. *Appalachian* 1931, 139.

658. *Carson-Newman College: 150 Years of Faith and Excellence*, 99.

659. Jones, *It Gets Foggy*, 6.

660. Gass and Lang, *Carson-Newman College*, 78.

661. Carr, *History of Carson-Newman College*, 128; *Catalogue, Carson-Newman College*, 1931–1932, 38.

662. Carr, *History of Carson-Newman College*, 80.

663. Ibid., 299.

664. Ibid., 104.

665. Ibid.

666. Ibid.

667. Ibid., 106.

668. Ibid.

669. Ibid., 104.

670. Ibid., 111.

671. Ibid.

672. Ibid., 104.

673. *Catalogue, Carson-Newman College*, 1939–1940, 77.

674. *Catalogue, Carson-Newman College*, 1946–1947, 42–43.

675. Carr, *History of Carson-Newman College*, 169.

676. Ibid., 193.

677. Jones, *It Gets Foggy*, 69.

678. For more information on the life and work of Carlyle Marney, see https://www.classic.cn.edu/undergrate/resources/library/library-resources/special-collections/baptist-archives/carlyle-marney.

679. Carr, *History of Carson-Newman College*, 106–7.
680. Ibid., 107.
681. Ibid.
682. Ibid., 108.
683. Ibid.
684. Ibid.
685. Ibid., 109, 215–16.
686. Ibid., 109.
687. Ibid.
688. Ibid.
689. Ibid.
690. Ibid., 110.
691. Gass and Lang, *Carson-Newman College*, 113.
692. Cook, *It Happened on a College Campus*, 39.
693. Ibid., 41.
694. Albert L. Lang, "V-12: The Navy Docks at Mossy Creek," in *Journey Magazine* (Fall 2007): 16.
695. Ibid., 19.
696. Ibid., 18.
697. Carr, *History of Carson-Newman College*, 110.
698. Gass and Lang, *Carson-Newman College*, 118.
699. Carr, *History of Carson-Newman College*, 110, 218.
700. Ibid., 112.
701. Ibid., 112–13.
702. Ibid., 114.
703. Wardin, *Tennessee Baptists*, 322.
704. This summary is taken from a comparison of Carson-Newman's statistics by catalogue between 1927 and 1948.
705. Carr, *History of Carson-Newman College*, 139.
706. Cook, *It Happened on a College Campus*, 29.
707. Carr, *History of Carson-Newman College*, 139.
708. *Appalachian* 1949, 16.

Chapter Nine

709. John Newton, lyrics to "Amazing Grace! How Sweet the Sound," *Baptist Hymnal* (Nashville: LifeWay Worship, 2008), 104.
710. Gass and Swann, *Burnett Family of the South*, 107.
711. Daniel Harley Fite's personal recollections as told to student Jayne Fair in a February 2, 1981 interview.
712. Ibid.
713. Ibid.

714. Carr, *History of Carson-Newman College,* 140.

715. Ibid., 141.

716. Daniel Harley Fite, *Reflections* (Jefferson City, TN: Self-published, 1993), 2, 6.

717. Ibid., 5.

718. Ibid., 60.

719. Carr, *History of Carson-Newman College,* 141.

720. Ibid., 141–42.

721. Ibid., 210.

722. Jessie Robinette, "New Providence Demonstration School Led the Way," in *Cumberland Lore* (Clarksville, TN: The Leaf-Chronicle, Nov. 1988), 1.

723. Interview with Imogene Baker Brewer conducted by Melody Marion in Jefferson City, Tennessee, February 11, 2020.

724. Carr, *History of Carson-Newman College,* 214–215.

725. Cook, *It Happened on a College Campus,* 37.

726. Carr, *History of Carson-Newman College,* 214–215.

727. Daniel Harley Fite, *Autobiographical Data Concerning Esther and Harley Fite and Genealogical Records of the Fite, Jennings, Robinson, Willard and Related Families in the United States* (Jefferson City, TN: Self-published, n.d.), 90.

728. The material in this section is summarized from Carson-Newman catalogues of this era.

729. Ibid.

730. Carr, *History of Carson-Newman College,* 53–54.

731. Ibid., 157.

732. Ibid.

733. Cook, *It Happened on a College Campus,* 3.

734. This information was gleaned from the program of the pageant, available in the Carson-Newman Archives.

735. Carr, *History of Carson-Newman College,* 152, 197–98.

736. Ibid., 162–66.

737. "A Brief History of Magnavox in Jefferson City," in *Bicentennial Diamond Jubilee Celebration: U.S.A. 1776–1976; Mossy Creek 1788–1900; Jefferson City 1901–1976* (Jefferson City: Self-published, 1976), 44–45.

738. Carr, *History of Carson-Newman College,* 215–16.

739. Ibid., 217.

740. Ibid.

741. Ibid., 216.

742. Ibid., 255.

743. Ibid., 218.

744. Ibid.

745. Ibid.

746. Ibid., 219.

747. For information on the Bernie Moore Stadium at Louisiana State University, see: https://lsusports.net/facilities/bernie-moore-stadium/.

748. Charles Moffett's statement as related by Chris Jones in *It Gets Foggy at Mossy Creek* (Jefferson City, TN: Mossy Creek Press, 2012), 107–08.

Chapter Ten

749. Excerpt from Abraham Lincoln's Second Annual Address to Congress, December 1, 1962, in Carl Sandburg, *Abraham Lincoln: The Prairie Years and the War Years* (New York: Harcourt, Brace & World, Inc., 1954), 330–31.

750. Excerpts from a February 3, 1995, interview Professor R. R. Turner conducted with Patricia Crippins.

751. Gass and Lang, *Carson-Newman College,* 26.

752. Professor R. R. Turner's 1995 interview with Patricia Crippins.

753. These professors' names, starting dates, and longevity have been gleaned from studying Carson-Newman catalogues of the Fite era and beyond.

754. *Carson-Newman College: 75th Anniversary "Of the Union of Carson and Newman Colleges";* Knoxville, *The Knoxville Journal,* May 16, 1964.

755. Gass and Lang, *Carson-Newman College,* 110.

756. Ibid., 84.

757. Ibid., 97.

758. Cook, *It Happened on a College Campus,* 16.

759. Gass and Swann, *Burnett Family of the South,* 107.

760. Gass and Lang, *Jefferson City,* 50.

761. Cook, *It Happened on a College Campus,* 53.

762. Ibid.

763. Cook, *It Happened on a College Campus,* 43.

764. Ibid., 45.

765. Wardin, *Tennessee Baptists,* 487.

766. Ibid.

767. Gass and Lang, *Carson-Newman College,* 44.

768. *Carson-Newman College: 150 Years of Faith and Excellence,* back endpaper, right page.

769. Wardin, *Tennessee Baptists,* 486.

770. Ibid., 486–87.

771. Gass and Lang, *Carson-Newman College,* 26.

772. This list has been compiled after a study of the 1968–1975 Carson-Newman catalogues.

773. Anthony P. Cavender, "Melungeons," in *An Encyclopedia of East Tennessee,* 316–18.

774. Robert Kollar, "Alex Stewart," in *An Encyclopedia of East Tennessee,* 451–54.

775. Unpublished email correspondence from Alice Pryor to Melody Marion, November 19, 2020.

776. Unpublished email correspondence from Imogene Baker Brewer to Melody Marion, November 6, 2020.

777. Inscribed on the "Penny-a-Day" plaque in the Dougherty Science Center on the Carson-Newman campus.

778. Wardin, *Tennessee Baptists,* 488.

779. Information about the play is in Jefferson City's *Bicentennial Diamond Jubilee Celebration*, inset between pages 23 and 24.

Chapter Eleven

780. *Carson-Newman College: 150 Years of Faith and Excellence*, 80.

781. Ibid., 81.

782. "C-N's Oldest Alumnus Still Writing at 99," *Today Magazine* (Jefferson City: Carson-Newman College) 12, no. 1 (April 1978): 17.

783. Charlotte Young, *Day of Miracles* (Freeman, SD: Pine Hill Press, Poetry Council of North Carolina, Inc., 1978), vi.

784. "C-N's Oldest Alumnus Still Writing at 99," *Today Magazine.*

785. Interview with Jeff Daniel Marion conducted by Melody Marion in New Market, Tennessee, February 3, 2021.

786. *Appalachian* 1984, 58.

787. These details are given in Cordell Maddox's obituary: https://www.farrarfuneralhome.com/obituaries/jesse-cordell-maddox.

788. *Appalachian* 1989, 130.

789. Ibid.

790. Ibid.

791. *Appalachian* 1984, 58.

792. *Appalachian* 1989, 130.

793. *Carson-Newman College: 150 Years of Faith and Excellence*, back endpaper, right side.

794. Gass and Swann, *Burnett Family of the South,* 113.

795. Ibid, 108, 113.

796. For further information on the English Language Institute at Carson-Newman, see https://www.cn.edu/academics/english-language-institute.

797. For more information on the study abroad at Oxford University, see https://classic.cn.edu/undergraduate/undergraduate-studies/religion-undergraduate/departmental-programs/minor-in-oxford-studies.

798. Wardin, *Tennessee Baptists,* 551.

799. For more information on the Ball Institute for Church Music, see: https://classic.cn.edu/undergraduate/undergraduate-studies/music/the-ball-institute-for-church-music.

800. For further information on Vickee Kazee-Hollifield's career, see https://www.cn.edu/university-softball-complex-renamed-for-coach-kazee-hollifield/and https://www.cn.edu/coach-kazee-hollifield-wraps-up-1000th-career-victory/.

801. *Carson-Newman College: 150 Years of Faith and Excellence*, 11.

802. Ibid., 56.

803. Gass and Lang, *Carson-Newman College*, 126.

804. Carr, *History of Carson-Newman College*, 314.

805. Wardin, *Tennessee Baptists*, 556.

806. Ibid., 556–57.

Chapter Twelve

807. April 1998 press release from Carson-Newman College.

808. *Knoxville News Sentinel*, October 24, 1998.

809. Ibid.

810. *Knoxville News Sentinel*, December 10, 1999.

811. *Knoxville News Sentinel*, November 9, 2000.

812. *Citizen Tribune* (Morristown, TN), October 6, 2006; *Knoxville News Sentinel*, October 10, 2006; *Standard Banner* (Jefferson City, TN), October 10, 2006.

813. *Standard Banner*, January 9, 2007.

814. Ibid.

815. *Knoxville News Sentinel*, February 2, 2017.

816. *Citizen Tribune*, January 18, 2017.

817. Information provided by R. Barry Clark, director of Carson-Newman's English Language Institute.

818. Information provided by Bruce Kocour, Dean of Library Services at Carson-Newman.

A Parting Word

819. Anonymous student, *Appalachian* 1977, 2–3, 6–8.

Bibliographic Essay

Resembling the human birth process, some books take a long time to be born. This is one of them. The research and writing began in 1998, and the book was intended to be available for Carson-Newman College's 2001 sesquicentennial celebration. Unfortunately, serious health issues intervened for the original authors and caused the book project to languish for many years. Some twenty-five years after the first word was written, with two completely different authors, the finished book is finally available to peruse!

Previous Books About Carson-Newman University's History

Present histories of Carson-Newman (which became a university in 2013) center on seven books in particular—all of which were used as sources for the writing of this book. An early comprehensive book was researched and written by an alumnus as a master's thesis: William F. Hall, *The History of Carson-Newman College* (Knoxville: The University of Tennessee, 1936). The most comprehensive book of the seven was published just over two decades later: Isaac Newton Carr, *History of Carson-Newman College* (Jefferson City: Carson-Newman College, 1959). Carr's history follows a topical outline; thus "nuggets" are more difficult to find than they are in a chronologically centered book.

Like Dr. Carr, Edgar M. Cook was an alumnus and past academic dean at Carson-Newman; he packed many memories into his less formal sixty-one pages of recollections: Edgar Marion Cook, *It Happened on a College Campus* (Jefferson City: Standard Publishing Company, 1972).

Two books of more recent vintage about Carson-Newman major on pictures, yet present quite a bit of interesting information. For the college's 150th anniversary celebration in 2001, a coffee-table book of just over one hundred pages was published: *Carson-Newman College: 150 Years of Faith and Excellence 1851–2001* (Atlanta: Bookhouse Group, 2002). And in the second, 127 pages of pictures accompanied by informational captions reveal important facts about Carson-Newman's history and the people who have shaped the institution: Linda T. Gass and Albert L. Lang, *Carson-Newman College* (Charleston: Arcadia Publishing, 2012). (Lang and Gass are the excellent staff members in the university's archives.)

Two other books by alumni focus on specific aspects of Carson-Newman's past. The first is a master's thesis that describes the programs of speech involvement within the literary societies: Brenda J. Harnage, *A History of the Speech Activities in the Literary Societies at Carson-Newman College from 1851 to 1945* (Chapel Hill: University of North Carolina, 1972). The second speaks exclusively to the history of sports at Carson-Newman: Chris Jones, *It Gets Foggy at Mossy Creek* (Jefferson City: Mossy Creek Press, 2012).

Naturally, the two master's theses (Hall and Harnage) are available to read in very few locations. *It Happened on a College Campus* (Cook) had a limited publication life and is also hard to find. (All three are available to consult at the Carson-Newman Archives, along with the other major sources.) Thus, three historical resources are quite scarce. For all practical purposes, this list of seven books is largely restricted to four for general readers.

No comprehensive history of Carson-Newman has been written since 1959. While the aforementioned coffee-table book was published in 2001, Carson-Newman's plan was to have a comprehensive history written at the same time. Unfortunately, as noted earlier, that plan was delayed for twenty-five years. This book is, finally, the answer to the void of in-depth material about Carson-Newman since 1959. But this book does not begin in 1960; instead, it is a linear history of Carson-Newman University from its earliest days.

Resources in the Carson-Newman Archives

Located in the Stephens-Burnett Library on the Carson-Newman University campus in Jefferson City, Tennessee, the archives contain an efficiently managed repository of material on several topics of interest to scholars and students. Researchers interested in Baptist church history, education, denominational struggles, or any other aspect of Baptist life, inside or outside of Tennessee, find an absorbing "home" in the Carson-Newman University Archives. Reflective of the university's environment in East Tennessee, studies and books on Appalachia are also part of the archives' holdings. An overview of the relevant archives' material can be found at https://cn.libguides.com/SpecialCollections. There are three main components to the Special Collections: the Appalachian and Rare Book Collection, the Baptist Archives, and the University Archives, all easily accessible on the special collections homepage cited.

Many one-of-a-kind documents and historical treasures are available for scholars to peruse—including artifacts relating to the history of Carson-Newman University itself. Naturally, this aspect of the archives' holdings is the one that undergirds this book.

Unfortunately, primary sources from the first sixty-five years of the university's life are scarce. This sad fact is largely due to a tragic 1916 fire that destroyed the administration building and the historical documents it housed. This huge loss, causing many questions about Carson-Newman's early life to be difficult to answer, is documented in a poignant article: Albert L. Lang, "The Administration Building: Carson-Newman's Lost Jewel, 1890-1916," in the University Archives section of Special Collections. From 1917 on, historical material is much more available within Special Collections as cited earlier.

Each year Carson-Newman University recognizes the life and work of two alumni in particular, Baptist scholars T. B. Maston and Carlyle Marney. To learn more about T. B. Maston, see this article on the Carson-Newman website: Paul Brewer, "T. B. Maston," Carson-Newman University, https://www.classic.cn.edu/undergraduate/resources/library/library-resources/special-collections/baptist-archives/t-b-maston. Information about Carlyle Marney can be found at the same website: "Carlyle Marney," Carson-Newman University, https://www.classic.cn.edu/undergrate/resources/library/library-resources/special-collections/baptist-archives/carlyle-marney.

STUDENT NEWSPAPERS

All available back issues of student newspapers have been used in researching this book: *The Carson Index* (1882–1884), *The Carson-Newman Magazine* (1896), *The Karnuargus* (1908), *The Carson-Newman Collegian* (1910–1916), and *The Orange and Blue* (1916–2010). *The Carson Index*, a most delightful newspaper, was published monthly by the two literary societies of Carson College. The other, later newspapers were published by Carson and Newman College after the merger of the male and female colleges. When quotations from these publications appear, all are referenced in the endnotes except those from *The Orange and Blue.*

Before the mid-twentieth century, data from volume numbers and corresponding issue numbers began showing signs of neglect from the student staff of *The Orange and Blue.* Such numbers are frequently incorrect, repeated, skipped, or nonexistent; indeed, sometimes even the exact issue date is omitted. Therefore, all quotations from *The Orange and Blue* are cited in running copy rather than being gathered in the endnotes, where setting forth the issue numbers was a requirement.

ANNUAL COLLEGE CATALOGUES

Many, but not all, catalogues of Carson-Newman and its predecessors are contained in the university's excellent archives area. The first available catalogue is from the 1856–1857 academic year; it carries the notation "Second Annual Catalogue." From 1851 to 1856 and between 1857 and 1908, apparently, no one thought ahead to preserve a copy of each year's college catalogue. (Of course, the college was closed during the Civil War and its immediate aftermath—1862 to 1868.) The archives has copies of a number of catalogues before 1908; but sadly, there are gaps in available catalogues. Two annual Newman College catalogues are extant from its seven years of existence—1886–1887 and 1887–1888.

From 1908 forward, however, the annual college catalogues have been continuously preserved. The catalogues have served as some of the most valuable historical resources for this book and have been mined extensively for interesting facts about Carson-Newman then and now.

YEARBOOKS

The first Carson and Newman yearbook was *The Swann,* published in 1912. The next was *The Larker* in 1917; then *The Grenade* was published in 1920. *The Wanehi* was the name chosen for the 1921 annual. Beginning in 1922, all yearbooks carried the name *The Appalachian;* only in 1945 was an issue missed (due to World War II). The last *Appalachian* was issued in 2007. The archives holds copies of all yearbooks, which are delightful to examine.

PUBLICATIONS FOR ALUMNI

Ongoing publications for Carson-Newman alumni seem to have begun in the 1920s and occasionally changed titles with subtle variations, but retained the word *Bulletin* for the next several decades. These include the *Carson and Newman College Bulletin, the Bulletin of Carson and Newman College,* and the long-lived *Alumni Bulletin.* The *Alumni Bulletin* has proved to be a wonderful source of information, especially regarding the centennial celebration of the college in 1951 (see Chapter 9).

Beginning in the 1960s, the alumni publications carried the word *Today: Today at Carson-Newman College* (1966–1969) and *Carson-Newman College Today* (1970–1985). The April 1978 issue documents a one-of-a-kind campus visit from a ninety-nine-year-old alumnus, with her irresistible eyewitness comparisons between the Carson-Newman of her day and of 1977. Following brief trials with other titles, the alumni periodical was reissued as *Journey Magazine* (1994–2021). The fall 2007 issue contains a fascinating article by Albert L. Lang about the Navy V-12 program at Carson-Newman during World War II, described in detail in Chapter 8.

VERTICAL FILES

The archives' holdings include a multitude of vertical files, arranged topically. Besides photo vertical files, biographical files have a subset—faculty files—which include available information about each president and many professors. The presidential files contain intriguing unpublished correspondence, such as the memories of Rose Jeffries Hart about her father, president Millard Jeffries, and the letter from historian Edmund Cody Burnett to his brother, president Jesse M. Burnett, recommending a public search for the college's missing catalogues.

Within the file folder for each early Carson-Newman president (William Rogers through Samuel Tindell) is a periodical entitled *The Carson-Newman Baptist* for researchers interested in both early Tennessee Baptist culture and Carson-Newman's history. These newsletters were published by the Carson-Newman

Archives in the early twenty-first century; prohibitive costs eventually forced the cancellation of the publications. Each issue highlighted a biographical sketch of one Carson-Newman president plus other interesting information; several issues have been utilized in research for this book.

The vertical files also contain copies of two handwritten letters related to the experiment of 1884–1885 in which some Cherokee students from North Carolina attended Carson College and the seminary for women in a government-backed educational program. These letters shed a little light on this aspect of nineteenth-century college life in Jefferson City, of which little is known.

RETIRED FACULTY AND STAFF INTERVIEWS

In the early 1980s, Carson-Newman student Jayne Fair conducted a number of interesting oral interviews with retired faculty and staff members, eliciting information about the school, the campus, and notable personalities and events from years in the past. Three of these have been used to enhance this book: interviews with Janie Swann Huggins, English professor; Coach Sam "Frosty" Holt, athletic director and coach of all men's sports; and Harley Fite, twenty-year president.

In 1995, a retired English professor, Robert R. Turner, interviewed former student Patricia Crippins about her experiences as the first four-year black graduate of Carson-Newman. That interview has also been used in this book.

Information from Websites

THE CARSON-NEWMAN UNIVERSITY WEBSITE

Naturally, a wealth of information about Carson-Newman University is available on its website: https://www.cn.edu. Articles about such matters as outstanding alumni, campus buildings, certain past and present faculty members, and current university programs have been utilized as sources for this book, as cited in the endnotes.

MISCELLANEOUS WEBSITES

Within this book are also a few source citations from other websites pertinent to specific topics and cited in the endnotes. These Internet sources often serve as verification for various statements and include such diverse topics as the concept of sane athletics; professional baseball player P. M. "Humpy" McElveen; the Veterans History Project; Find a Grave; and Louisiana State University. Other helpful websites related to Carson-Newman's history are listed within various categories that follow.

EPIGRAPHS

Opening epigraphs give insight into the context of each chapter. Each epigraph was chosen for at least one particular reason.

Chapter 1's epigraph introduces a major historian who set forth a helpful perspective on one role history can play in our lives: David McCullough, "The Lessons of History," in *The American Spirit: Who We Are and What We Stand For* (New York: Simon & Schuster, 2017). McCullough also extols the virtue of recognizing key individuals without whose contributions our lives would be much less meaningful.

Chapter 2's epigraphs represent world-class writers of the past whose material was part of the curriculum at Mossy Creek, then and now. The first reminds the reader that creative, hard-working individuals often populate a new world: William Shakespeare, *The Tempest*, Act V, scene 1, line 183. The Cicero quotation describes the difference a great education can make for the remainder of one's life: Marcus Tullius Cicero, "In Defense of the Poet Archias," in *Cicero: Nine Orations and the Dream of Scipio,* trans. by Palmer Bovie (New York: The New American Library, 1967).

Chapter 3's use of a philosophical exhortation calls upon the reader to exhibit courage and take risks that can make all the difference in life, justifying one's faith in a successful outcome. Such a description epitomizes Jesse Baker's feat on behalf of the fledgling college: William James, "Is Life Worth Living?" in *The Will to Believe and Other Essays in Popular Philosophy and Human Immortality* (New York: Dover Publications, n.d., ca. 1956).

Within Chapter 4's epigraph, nature perfectly describes the process involved in merging two living organisms into one: Wendell Berry, "A Native Hill," in *The Art of the Commonplace: The Agrarian Essays of Wendell Berry* (Berkeley: Counterpoint Press, 2002).

Chapter 5's epigraph was written by a professor of Carson and Newman (later its president) and succinctly describes the means and the worth of an effective education at the turn of the twentieth century—its building blocks, its call, its tools: J. M. Burnett, "The College and Culture," in *The Carson-Newman Collegian* 1, no. 4 (May 1911).

Chapter 6 called for an epigraph that acknowledges the necessity of consistency and hard work even as change after major change roils one's expectations of what life will be like. Such a description applies to the life of an educational institution as well: Wilma Dykeman, *The Tall Woman* (Newport, TN: Wakestone Books, 1962).

Chapter 7's epigraph uses old, familiar hymn lyrics to speak to a disillusioned community that has experienced deceit and wrongdoing at the hand of a leader. The lyrics serve as a valuable reminder that God, rather than any human person, is in charge of this world: Maltbie D. Babcock, lyrics to "This Is My Father's World," in the *Baptist Hymnal* (Nashville: LifeWay Worship, 2008), 46.

Chapter 8's poetic epigraph holds out hope in pointing to the possibility of real healing after a severe disappointment. Sufficient time and the partnership of trustworthy persons can make a great difference. Healing enables new progress in living: Edna St. Vincent Millay, "Renascence," in *Collected Lyrics of Edna St. Vincent Millay* (New York: Harper and Row, 1939 [1917]).

Chapter 9's epigraph returns to the worth of classic hymn lyrics in the ability of God's grace and watchcare to move the reader out of harm's way and back to safety. In these circumstances, gratitude gives one the ability to look back and to look forward at the same time: John Newton, lyrics to "Amazing Grace! How Sweet the Sound," in the *Baptist Hymnal* (Nashville: LifeWay Worship, 2008), 104.

The epigraph for Chapter 10 again compels the reader to act with courage in meeting and resolving difficult situations. The words of a brave leader inspire recognition that a new problem calls for a new solution: Abraham Lincoln, Excerpt from Lincoln's Second Annual Address to Congress, December 1, 1962, in Carl Sandburg, *Abraham Lincoln: The Prairie Years and the War Years* (New York: Harcourt, Brace & World, Inc., 1954).

The two epigraphs introducing Chapter 11 both arise from Carson-Newman's 150th anniversary celebration—a natural time to take stock of all that has been accomplished and all that is yet to be done. The two commentators reflect on the college's seal and a word it bears proudly—*Appalachian*—and its meaning for the days ahead: *Carson-Newman College: 150 Years of Faith and Excellence 1851–2001* (Atlanta: Bookhouse Group, 2002).

BAPTIST RESOURCES

Several resources used for this book are primarily or exclusively Baptist in nature. Second only to the Bible, there is no more accepted traditional worship resource for Baptists than the *Baptist Hymnal* (Nashville: LifeWay Worship, 2008) or its "screen cousins" used in more contemporary worship services. Several hymn lyrics from the *Baptist Hymnal* are used in this book.

Two vintage book resources are about early Baptist ministers in Tennessee: Joseph H. Borum, *Biographical Sketches of Tennessee Baptist Ministers* (Memphis: Rogers and Company, 1880); and J. J. Burnett, *Sketches of Tennessee's Pioneer Baptist Preachers* (Nashville: Marshall & Bruce Company, 1919). A number of ministers who were profiled in these two books were presidents or faculty members of Carson-Newman's early incarnations.

Because Carson-Newman's origins are very much a product of East Tennessee Baptist ties, two books related exclusively to the Nolachucky Baptist Association's history have been valuables resources for this book. The earlier of the two is: *The Nolachucky Association of Baptist* [*sic*], *Minutes, Centennial Session 1927* (Morristown: Triangle Press, 1928). The second, a summary of the first 150 years of the Association, is by Glenn A. Toomey, *The Sesquicentennial History of the Nolachucky Baptist Association and Its Affiliated Churches 1828-1977* (Morristown, TN: Nolachucky Baptist Association, 1977). Both provided essential details of the denominational struggle to launch and maintain a Baptist school in East Tennessee.

A tome that fully lives up to its title is: Albert W. Wardin, Jr., *Tennessee Baptists: A Comprehensive History 1779–1999* (Brentwood, TN: Executive Board of the Tennessee Baptist Convention, 1999). The sections dealing with East Tennessee Baptists in general and Carson-Newman in particular are written with clarity and provide helpful context.

JEFFERSON COUNTY, TENNESSEE, RESOURCES

One of the oldest sources of historical material in Jefferson County, Tennessee, in which Carson-Newman is located, is part of the popular collections known as "Goodspeed," the company that became famous for printing histories of cities and towns all over the United States. The pages on Jefferson County contain information on the area as well as on the early families that settled there: "Jefferson County, Tennessee, USA," *History of Tennessee* (Chicago: The Goodspeed Publishing Company, 1887).

Two particular sources deal with the Civil War period in Jefferson County. One is general in nature and focuses on the life of ordinary people, not soldiers, during the war: Sandra S. Wilson and Dennis L. Snapp, eds. *Broken Hearts—Broken Lives: Jefferson County, Tennessee, Civilian Life in the Civil War* (Dandridge, TN: Restore Our County, Inc., 1986).

On the other hand, the second source has a niche focus—the life of soldiers and other types of military veterans who entered the Civil War as students or faculty members or administrators of Mossy Creek Baptist College: William D. Taylor and Darby O'Neil Taylor, *Onward Christian Soldiers! Mossy Creek Baptist College Students in the War between the States 1861–1865* (Jefferson City: Self-published, 1999), compiled for the sesquicentennial celebration of Carson-Newman College.

Another two resources deal specifically with Jefferson City within Jefferson County. The first has a thorough chapter on the Civil War, but the rest of the book deals well with many other aspects of Jefferson City's history and standout personalities as well: Linda T. Gass and Albert L. Lang, *Images of America: Jefferson City* (Charleston, SC: Arcadia Publishing, 2014). The second contains a lot of local history while also focusing on the two hundredth "birthday" celebrations that took place in 1976 in Jefferson City: *Bicentennial Diamond Jubilee Celebration: U.S.A. 1776–1976; Mossy Creek 1788–1900; Jefferson City 1901–1976* (Jefferson City: Self-published, 1976).

A more recent assessment of the county's history, organized according to town and containing much local color, including stories and historical homes, is: Estle P. Muncy, *People and Places of Jefferson County* (Jefferson County Historical Society). (Rogersville, TN: East Tennessee Printing Company, 1994).

Another source of Jefferson County information almost as recent is: Jean Patterson Bible, *Bent Twigs in Jefferson County* (Rogersville, TN: East Tennessee Printing Company, 1991). Information is imparted, directly or indirectly, in the style of community columns in twentieth-century newspapers. The chapter "Academies and Colleges" provided valuable information for this book.

APPALACHIAN RESOURCES

Two in-depth, excellent encyclopedias on the region of Appalachia provided helpful and succinct information for several parts of this book: Rudy Abramson and Jean Haskell, *Encyclopedia of Appalachia* (Knoxville: The University of Tennessee Press, 2006); and Jim Stokely and Jeff D. Johnson, eds. *An Encyclopedia of East Tennessee* (Oak Ridge, TN: Children's Museum of Oak Ridge, 1981).

A classic book, perhaps little known today, gives beneficial information about many aspects of the settlement of all of Tennessee. Insight is given into several significant personalities who were instrumental to Tennessee's founding and early statehood. For the purposes of this book, details about the State of Franklin and its leaders were particularly helpful: T. C. Karns, *Tennessee History Stories* (Richmond: B. F. Johnson Publishing Company, 1904).

A topical overview of the current Appalachian region gives welcome breadth about aspects such as cultural diversity, history, education, music, religion, and literature. This interesting book is: Grace Toney Edwards, JoAnn Aust Asbury, and Ricky L. Cox, eds., *A Handbook to Appalachia* (Knoxville: The University of Tennessee Press, 2006).

Two informative books about colleges where onetime president Oscar E. Sams played significant roles after leaving Carson-Newman were helpful in detailing Chapter 7. These were: John Angus McLeod, *From These Stones: Mars Hill College 1856-1968* (Mars Hill, NC: Mars Hill College, 1968); and David M. Armbrister, *Lighthouse on the Hill: The Bluefield College Story* (Wytheville, VA: Wordsprint, 2007).

NEWSPAPER ARTICLES INVOLVING CARSON-NEWMAN

Several East Tennessee newspapers, both past and present, have carried articles of interest to the Carson-Newman community that are represented in this book. In Jefferson City, the *Standard Banner* is the primary such source. The *Dandridge Republican Banner* and *The Watchman,* both newspapers from Dandridge's past, are represented. The *Morristown Gazette* and *Citizen Tribune* have also contributed accounts portraying various events at Carson-Newman. The *Knoxville Journal, News-Sentinel,* and *KnoxTNToday.com* have published many articles pertaining to Carson-Newman. Also represented from Middle Tennessee is *Cumberland Lore,* a supplement to Clarksville's *Leaf-Chronicle.*

GENERAL RESOURCES

In retirement, former Carson-Newman president Harley Fite published five books, two of which provided quotations for this book. Both were primarily about his family, with the first a special look back at Fite's childhood: Daniel Harley Fite, *Reflections* (Jefferson City: Self-published, 1993). The second contained more information about his twenty years at the helm of Carson-Newman: Daniel Harley Fite, *Autobiographical Data Concerning Esther and Harley Fite and Genealogical Records of the Fite, Jennings, Robinson, Willard and Related Families in the United States* (Jefferson City: Self-published, n.d.).

Frances Swann Gass, a Burnett descendant and Carson-Newman alumnus, and her cousin also wrote about their joint family members, well represented through many years on campus: Frances Gass and Thomas Burnett Swann, Jr., *A Burnett Family of the South* (No publication city: Self-published, 1964).

Charlotte Young, who learned to love poetry as a student at Carson and Newman at the turn of the twentieth century, published several books of poetry in her last years. She premiered her fourth book on her return to the campus in 1977: Charlotte Young, *Day of Miracles* (Freeman, SD: Pine Hill Press, Poetry Council of North Carolina, Inc., 1978).

Zula Pangle was an early student at Carson and Newman, focusing her studies in art. Her daughter wrote a book detailing her mother's lifelong enjoyment of and skill at creating beautiful artistic pieces: Maurine Brooks Christopher, *The Artistic World of Zula Pangle Brooks* (New York: Christopher Enterprises, 2000).

A state librarian and archivist of Tennessee in the 1920s, John Trotwood Moore was a prolific journalist and writer. He compiled biographical sketches of many Tennesseans of his day in a two-volume massive work: John Trotwood Moore, *Tennessee, The Volunteer State 1769-1923, vols. I and II* (Chicago: The S. J. Clarke Publishing Company, 1923). John T. Henderson, Carson-Newman president 1892–1903, was among those profiled.

An interesting book about World War I covers many Americans' interests in that time period, including two activities Carson-Newman stressed as part of a well-rounded education, debate and public speaking: G. J. Meyer, *The World Remade: America in World War I* (New York: Bantam Books, 2016).

A Note for Future Carson-Newman Researchers

The content of this book formally ends at the close of 2018, with a very few comments from the early 2020s made toward the end. After the events recounted in Dr. Carr's book of the late 1950s, finding important material about latter-day Carson-Newman has become harder because there are fewer sources for research. *The Orange and Blue* (the student newspaper until 2010), *The Appalachian* (the yearbook until 2007), and alumni publications (through 2021) all contributed major information for this book.

With the demise of the student newspaper, the printed yearbook, and printed alumni publications, gathering information for a future history of Carson-Newman will be much more challenging. Other than the more recent books cited earlier, the university catalogues may be the only regular printed sources of information. The school's website will need to be well maintained and complete. Creativity in uncovering source material will be needed!

Index

Page numbers in **boldface** refer to illustrations.